Moreton Morrell Site

An Introduction to Leisure Studies

Pearson Education

We work with leading authors to develop the
strongest educational materials in leisure studies,
bringing cutting-edge thinking and best learning practice
to a global market.

Under a range of well-known imprints, including
Financial Times Prentice Hall, we craft high quality print
and electronic publications which help readers to
understand and apply their content, whether studying
or at work.

To find out more about the complete range of our
publishing, please visit us on the World Wide Web at:
www.pearsoneduc.com

An Introduction to Leisure Studies

Chris Bull

Canterbury Christ Church University College, UK

Jayne Hoose

Freelance writer and lecturer,
formerly at Canterbury Christ Church University College, UK

Mike Weed

Loughborough University, UK

FT Prentice Hall

FINANCIAL TIMES

An imprint of **Pearson Education**

Harlow, England • London • New York • Boston • San Francisco • Toronto • Sydney • Singapore • Hong Kong
Tokyo • Seoul • Taipei • New Delhi • Cape Town • Madrid • Mexico City • Amsterdam • Munich • Paris • Milan

Pearson Education Limited
Edinburgh Gate
Harlow
Essex CM20 2JE
United Kingdom

and Associated Companies throughout the world

Visit us on the World Wide Web at:
www.pearsoneduc.com

_____

First published 2003

ISBN 0 582 32503X

British Library Cataloguing-in-Publication Data
A catalogue record for this book is available from the British Library

10 9 8 7 6 5 4 3 2 1
12 11 10 09 08 07 06 05 04 03

Typeset in 10/13 pt Sabon by 68
Printed and bound in Malaysia

The publisher's policy is to use paper manufactured from sustainable forests.

Contents

Part One
The leisure phenomenon

Part Two

Provision for leisure

List of Figures

List of Tables

List of Boxes

Preface

At the beginning of their seminal work on leisure in the mid 1980s, Clarke and Critcher (1985) speculated on the extent to which Britain had become, or might soon become, a 'leisure society' and considered the various advantages to people's lives and well-being of a future that 'could be more relaxed, more creative [and] more enjoyable...'(p. 1). There was clearly evidence to suppose that leisure was more important in people's everyday existence and new attitudes to the organisation of work and new technologies of production had the potential to deliver this prospect of greater 'emancipation'. While the authors were, quite rightly, sceptical about such a promise being immediately 'around the corner', largely as a result of society's deep-rooted attitudes to work and free time, in many ways the very contemplation of such a prospect was testimony to the important position that leisure had assumed.

Nearly two decades later there is even more evidence to support the importance of leisure. In 1999, for example, the Office of National Statistics reported in its *Family Expenditure Survey* that for the first time households in the United Kingdom were spending more on leisure than on food, housing or transport. While this does not, of course, mean that the 'leisure society' has finally arrived, it is nevertheless a useful indication of the importance of leisure in contemporary Britain. Leisure, for many people, is no longer regarded as simply a marginal, frivolous activity to be pursued only after the essential requirements of work and survival have been satisfied. It is now a much more central component of their lives. Leisure opportunities are being seen as an essential entitlement of modern lifestyles and increased wealth is allowing greater participation in a greater variety of leisure pursuits both in and away from the home. Furthermore leisure industries make a substantial contribution to the national economy and create direct employment for well over two million people.

The expanding importance of leisure in the last few decades has been mirrored by a growing academic interest in the subject. Its development and growth, its significance for individuals, families and society at large, its economic importance and political relevance, and its spatial and environmental consequences have in turn attracted the attention of historians, psychologists, sociologists, economists, political scientists and geographers. As a result, a significant literature has emerged which has examined a variety of problems and issues associated with leisure as well as providing a multidisciplinary basis for its study; and this in turn has led to the growth of leisure studies at both degree and sub-degree level.

It is against this background that this text has been conceived in the hope that its addition to the literature may contribute to a better understanding of leisure, especially by those embarking on undergraduate study. The text will attempt to strike a balance between theory and practice. While recognising the need for a clear theoretical basis and understanding of the various disciplinary contributions to leisure studies, the book will be organised around leisure themes rather than disciplinary ones. Thus, rather than having chapters on leisure economics or the sociology of leisure, economic and sociological theories and concepts will be introduced, where appropriate, in a variety of chapters. Economic concepts, for example, will be introduced in the chapter on leisure demand, in the chapter dealing with the political and economic significance of leisure, in the chapter concerned with leisure places and the availability of land resources for leisure and in the various chapters concerned with leisure providers. In this way it is hoped that a more interdisciplinary approach will prevail.

Leisure, of course, is a contentious term with a variety of meanings. While we all possess some concept of leisure this will clearly differ depending on our particular circumstances and social and cultural backgrounds and one of the key purposes of this text is to explore these different meanings and their consequences. Leisure might be regarded as time free from obligations, as a collection of specific activities (embracing sport, recreation, tourism, arts and entertainment) or simply as a state of mind; it could be defined as whatever people perceive it to be. However, at the outset we make no specific prescriptions as to what we mean by leisure and therefore accept as wide and inclusive a definition as possible.

The text will be conveniently organised into two sections, although these sections will inevitably be interlinked. The first section, the *leisure phenomenon*, will be concerned primarily with the conceptualisation of leisure and the social, economic and political forces and ideas that have shaped both the nature of leisure as well as our understanding of it. It will also examine participation in leisure and the importance of leisure in modern society. The second section, *provision for leisure*, will be concerned essentially with leisure resources and the contextualisation of leisure: with the environments, places and facilities that people use in their leisure time and the various agencies and organisations that are responsible for this provision.

In Part One, the first two chapters are concerned with the nature and development of leisure and it is difficult to know which of these should go first. While it may appear logical to start with a chapter on what leisure is, and various texts follow this pattern, concepts of leisure can only be fully understood in terms of leisure's recent history. Consequently, it has been decided to begin with this historical perspective. Chapter 1, therefore, considers the *historical development of leisure* and examines the way in which political, economic and social forces have shaped its development since the industrial revolution into the patterns we see today. *The nature of leisure* is examined in Chapter 2 and here not only are the various definitions of leisure explored but also the role of leisure in relation to various social circumstances and institutions. Chapters 3, 4 and 5 are designed to examine the ways in which people engage with leisure or may be prevented from doing so. Chapter 3 looks at the *demand for leisure* and examines leisure participation primarily from an economic perspective. Demand is examined in relation to such factors as time, price and income but the psychological determinants of demand such as motivation, needs, wants and desires, and tastes and preferences are also considered. Chapter 4, concerned with *leisure lifestyles, gender and the family*, examines the family unit as a context for leisure and the opportunities and barriers that this may produce. It also looks at the influence of gender on leisure and the extent to which it produces different patterns of leisure activity between men and women, as highlighted by an examination of the family life cycle. Chapter 5 examines *access to leisure and disadvantaged groups* and assesses the various barriers to participation which exist in relation to certain sections of society, especially the elderly, ethnic minority groups and the disabled. Chapter 6 completes the first part of text and is concerned with evaluating the *economic and political significance of leisure*, especially in terms of its income and employment generation and its significance for both local and national economies and the way in which leisure is viewed and used by government to achieve various goals.

Part Two of the text is designed to examine the nature of leisure provision. Chapter 7, *places for leisure*, looks at the great variety of spaces and environments that people use in their leisure activities and examines the various factors involved in their physical and social construction. Chapters 8, 9, 10 and 11 look at the various providers of leisure facilities. Chapter 8 considers the *political framework for leisure provision* and examines the role of central government in setting the framework within which all leisure sectors operate, while Chapter 9 examines the development and range of *local authority leisure*, and especially its changing role in the late twentieth century. Chapter 10 is concerned with *commercial leisure* and assesses the nature and behaviour of the commercial sector and the various leisure forms which attract commercial interest, while Chapter 11 considers *leisure and the voluntary sector* and examines the different roles that voluntary organisations play in leisure provision both individually and in partnership with other groups and sectors. Chapter 12 examines *leisure provision and education* by considering the ways in which schools and other educational facilities provide for a range of leisure opportunities not only in terms of the dual use and joint provision of facilities but also in terms of the specific provision of adult education. The book concludes with Chapter 13, *leisure and the future*, which speculates on future developments in leisure, such as changing work regimes, the development of leisure forms, increasing commercialisation and commodification of leisure, and potential changes in the framework for leisure provision.

Reference

Clark, J. and Critcher, C. (1985) *The Devil Makes Work: Leisure in Capitalist Britain*, London: Methuen.

Author's Acknowledgements

In addition to our respective partners, to whom we owe a large debt of gratitude for their support and patience over a considerable period of time, we would also like to thank various other people for their help and support in the writing of this text: various colleagues in the Department of Geography and Tourism at Canterbury Christ Church University College, including Dr Richard Goodenough for his encouragement and for supplying information on Polo Farm Sports Club; Jim Butcher for various comments on certain chapters; John Hills for producing various maps and diagrams and sorting out computer problems and Arija Crux for various secretarial help; Romano Zavaroni for his infectious enthusiasm and inspirational tutoring and Catherine Green for sharing her experiences as a leisure educator in schools and her excellent home-made wine; and Alan Johnson of the Centre for Tourism and Leisure Studies (CELTS), University of North London, for suggesting the structure for the chapter on leisure and local government.

Lastly, the authors would like to express their appreciation to the various staff at Pearson Education for their continued support for the project and the help they have provided.

Publisher's Acknowledgements

We are grateful to the following for permission to reproduce copyright material:

Figure 1.1 and 3.7 from *Sport and Recreation: An Economic Analysis*, E & FN Spon (Gratton, C. and Taylor, P., 1985); Table 3.1, 3.2 and 4.5 from *Living in Britain: Results from the 1996 General Household Survey*, Office of National Statistics (1996); Figure 3.2 from *An Introduction to Town Planning*, Hutchinson & Co. (Routledge) (Roberts, M., 1974); Figure 3.6 from *The Geography of Tourism and Recreation: Environment, Place and Space*, Routledge (Hall, C.M. and Page, S.J., 1999); Figure 3.8 reprinted by permission of C.A. Metcalf, Canterbury City Council; Table 4.1 and 11.1 from *Leisure and Recreation*

Management, 4th edition, E & FN Spon (Routledge) (Torkildsen, G., 1999); Table 4.2 from *The Leisure Business: The Consumer*, Mintel International Group Ltd (BRMB/Mintel); Table 4.3 from *Women and Finance: Women and Society*, Mintel International Group Ltd (Mintel, 1998); Figure 6.1, 6.2 and Table 6.1 from *Family Spending: A Report on the 1999–2000 Family Expenditure Survey*, Office of National Statistics (2000); Table 6.2 and 6.3 from *The Leisure Business: The Leisure Market*, Mintel International Group Ltd (Mintel, 1999); Figure 6.3 from *Tourism: Principles and Practice*, 2nd edition, Addison Wesley Longman (Cooper, C. et al., 1998); Table 6.4 from *www.staruk.org.uk*, sponsored by the National Tourist Boards and the Department for Culture, Media and Sport; Table 6.5 from *Labour Market Trends*, Office of National Statistics (2001); Figure 6.6 and 6.7 reproduced with the permission of Kent County Council's Tourism Unit; Table 6.6 from *United Kingdom Balance of Payments: The Pink Book 2001*, Office of National Statistics (2001). Crown Copyright material is reproduced with the permission of the Controller of HMSO and the Queen's Printer for Scotland; Figure 7.2 from *Fundamentals of the Physical Environment*, 2nd edition, Routledge (Briggs, D. et al., 1997); Figure 7.3 from *Elements of Human Geography*, George Allen and Unwin (Routledge) (Whynne-Hammond, C., 1979); Figure 7.6 from *The Tourist Historic City*, John Wiley & Sons Limited (Ashworth, G.J. and Tunbridge, V.E., 1990), © John Wiley & Sons Limited. Reproduced with permission. Figure 7.7 from *The Guardian*, 11 November 1990, © The Guardian; Figure 7.8 The Countryside Agency, based on Ordnance Survey mapping with the permission of the Controller of Her Majesty's Stationary Office. Crown Copyright Reserved. CCC14354; Figure 8.1 from 'Towards a model of cross-sectoral policy development in leisure: the case of sport and tourism' in *Leisure Studies*, vol. 20 no. 2, Taylor and Francis Limited (Weed, M., 2001); Figure 9.1 from *Creating Opportunities*, Department of Culture, Media and Sport (DCMS, 1999); Box 9.1 and 9.2 from *Best Value through Sport: Case Studies*, Sport England (1999), reproduced with permission of Sport England; Figure 11.1, 11.2, 11.3, 11.4 reproduced with kind permission of the National Trust (www.nationaltrust.org.uk/learning).

In some instances we have been unable to trace the owners of copyright material, and we would appreciate any information that would enable us to do so.

PART ONE ● ● ● ●

The leisure phenomenon

Chapter 1 ● ● ● ●

The historical development of leisure

The history of leisure is an interesting subject in its own right and forms part of the essential concern of the social historian who attempts to reconstruct and explain the sort of life experienced by people in the past. But its study is also necessary in terms of understanding contemporary leisure, which is the overriding aim of this text. The nature of leisure and the way it is defined, issues that are developed further in the following chapter, can only be fully appreciated from analysing how people have understood leisure in the past and by tracing the development of leisure as an important component of people's lives. Similarly, contemporary patterns of leisure activity can only be understood by examining the way in which they have been shaped over time by social, economic and political forces.

Although people have enjoyed leisure throughout the centuries, it is the changes that have taken place in relatively recent times, largely as a result of industrialisation, that have had the greatest influence on contemporary leisure and thus this chapter will focus roughly on the last two hundred years.

Objectives

To:

- *compare the principal patterns of leisure in pre-industrial times with those of the industrial period*

- *provide an understanding of the Industrial Revolution and the resulting influences and processes that have shaped leisure activity*

- *examine the emergence and growth of mass leisure in the late nineteenth and early twentieth centuries*

- *examine the nature of post-war affluence and the development of leisure in the second half of the twentieth century.*

It should also be highlighted, however, that in achieving these objectives the account will not necessarily cover the leisure patterns of all social groups to the same extent. Although not exclusively so, the emphasis will be largely on mass, popular leisure, partly because this is the emphasis of the book as a whole but also because this more closely reflects what has been researched and published on the history of leisure in recent times. Thus, although there will be some references to the leisure pastimes of the upper classes, much of the coverage will focus on middle- and working-class leisure.

● ● ● ● Leisure in pre-industrial times

The late eighteenth and early nineteenth centuries were a period of profound economic change during which Britain was transformed from an essentially agrarian society into an industrial nation with far-reaching social, economic and political consequences. As will be seen in the following section, this also had a tremendous impact on leisure, such that the pattern of leisure activity that had existed before would be transformed beyond recognition. In fact, such was the magnitude of these changes that some have gone so far as to argue that 'the modern concept of leisure is a product of nineteenth century industrialisation' (Myerscough, 1974).

Although its nature and precise social meaning may have been different to that of today's leisure, there is no doubt that recreation and play figured prominently in people's lives in the pre-industrial period. At times during the sixteenth and seventeenth centuries when Puritan influence had been particularly strong, the extent of popular recreation may have been curtailed; but these periods were short lived and, with the restoration of the monarchy in 1660, this constraint was removed. Certainly throughout much of the eighteenth century there would appear to have been considerable recreational activity (see Malcolmson, 1973). In fact, the period immediately prior to the Industrial Revolution is sometimes referred to as 'Merrie England'.

The leisure that people enjoyed at that time has to be seen in the context of the way in which the economy and society were structured. Most people were directly employed in producing food or servicing agriculture in some way. There was manufacturing industry but this was small scale, often organised on a cottage industry basis with people producing goods in their own homes, sometimes on a part-time basis in conjunction with farm work. Most people lived in small settlements scattered throughout the countryside; there were few towns of any size. Although London had a population of about 600,000 in 1700, the next largest towns of Norwich, York, Bristol, Newcastle and Exeter had populations of no more than about 20,000; what today would be regarded as small towns. Society and economy were, therefore, essentially agrarian and traditional, and leisure and recreation reflected this. Work and play often intermingled, with both being linked to the seasonal cycles and the agricultural and ecclesiastical calendars. Work was not continuous since it varied according to the climate and the seasons and many of the principal festivities in which people indulged were associated with key agricultural events, such as ploughing and harvesting, where hard work would be counterbalanced by drinking and revelry. Recreation was also intermingled with kinship and family obligations such as christenings, weddings and funerals. However, whether this was real leisure is debatable, as often it was obligatory to be involved; there was little choice.

Apart from the more informal leisure activities, there were also some specific leisure resources. One key facility, for example, and one which also reflected the intermingling of work and leisure, was the tavern. Just as the pub is today, the tavern was an important place for leisure but provided the focus for a range of activities. Drinking was a widespread activity but, apart from drink, the tavern also offered a range of comforts absent from men's homes, such as light, heating, cooking facilities, furniture, newspapers and sociability, as well as acting as a brothel and providing opportunities for gambling and blood sports. Animal sports were especially popular in pre-industrial times and taverns were an obvious venue for such activities as dog fighting, bull baiting and cock fighting. But, in addition to providing opportunities for leisure, the tavern was also a place for business transactions. The tavern was a place where business deals were struck, where farm labour was often hired and where weekly wages were paid.

Another popular leisure facility of this period was the travelling fair, which also combined business with pleasure. In addition to the various stalls and amusements with their puppets and sideshows and violent games, fairs were often, like the tavern, places where labour was hired (the hiring fair, as depicted in Thomas Hardy's novel *Far from the Madding Crowd*, provides a useful illustration of this). And fairs would also include animal sports, possibly with bear baiting providing a somewhat more exotic addition to the animals more usually found at the tavern. Fairs were particularly numerous at certain times of the year, with Whitsuntide being particularly important. Malcolmson (1973), for example, cites a number of chroniclers of the eighteenth century, with one recording as many as 314 English and Welsh fairs being held during the fortnight before and after Whit Sunday, 79 of them on Ascension Day and 113 on Whit Monday and Tuesday.

Fairs were often associated with another leisure institution of pre-industrial times – 'wakes'. Wakes originally had a religious origin in that they were celebrations organised to commemorate the feast (birth) day of the saint after whom the local church was named. Just as the distinction between work and leisure was blurred, so too was that between religion and leisure. In fact, the origin of the word 'holiday' derives from 'holy day' and in pre-industrial times such holy days and saints' days were numerous. In fact, according to Myerscough (1974), in the Middles Ages some workers enjoyed one day off in every three as a result of saints'/holy days. Even as late as 1800, the clerks at the Bank of England were enjoying 44 holidays a year. Although originating as a 'holy day', the religious significance of many of the days gradually diminished over time and wakes became an excuse for considerable revelry. They also began to extend beyond a day, often becoming a whole week, and involved a variety of events such as dancing, wrestling, cudgels, racing, animal sports, music and what Malcolmson (1973, p.19) describes as a 'profane and pleasure seeking atmosphere'. They were particularly widespread in the north of England and many towns still retain their traditional annual holiday coinciding with the old wakes week.

The above account has been concerned primarily with popular recreation, that pursued by ordinary people, although much of this would have been largely male dominated; it is unlikely, for example, that many females would have frequented the taverns (other than as prostitutes). However, before concluding this section, it is also worth noting that there were a number of distinctive leisure forms pursued by the upper echelons of society. In the sixteenth, seventeenth and eighteenth centuries the nobility, gentry, merchant and professional classes gradually abandoned popular culture to the lower classes and acquired different tastes and activities (Towner, 1996). Much of this leisure revolved around intellectual and artistic pursuits; entertaining and visiting friends and relations, especially where this involved country retreats and stately homes; country walks and rambles; and a variety of urban leisure pastimes. London, in common with other capital cities in Europe, became an important location of fashionable consumption (Towner, 1996). It was the place where the wealthy and fashionable wanted to be seen and where they could parade their wealth and position. Here they could entertain in their fashionable town houses, stroll and relax in gardens, parades and promenades, and visit the theatre and assembly rooms. Much of this leisure activity was also replicated in the various spa towns, which developed from the seventeenth century onwards (see case study, below), and in fact a series of seasons developed during which people would spend respective periods of time in London, at their country estates and at the spa. A good description of such leisure lifestyles can be found in the various novels of Jane Austen.

Leisure and the Industrial Revolution

The extent to which the economic and social changes occurring in the late eighteenth and early nineteenth centuries might be described as revolutionary is debatable. They clearly did not occur overnight; rather, they developed over a period of about 80 to 100 years. However, while the speed of change might have been gradual, the scale of change was massive, and it is largely on this basis that the term Industrial Revolution is used. Between 1750 and 1830 Britain was transformed from an essentially traditional, agrarian economy and society into a modern industrial, urban nation. The changes and impacts were wide ranging, affecting many aspects of life, and they also had a profound effect on leisure.

In relation to leisure, a number of key changes were of critical importance:

- the nature of work for many people changed, both in terms of what they did for a living and also how work was organised;
- the location of the workplace changed and, correspondingly, so too did the places where people lived;

● the structure of society changed, as seen in particular by the emergence of a large urban industrial working class and a substantial middle class;
● increased wealth and new technologies emerged, which enabled the gradual development of new leisure forms.

The nature of work

As already indicated, prior to the Industrial Revolution most people either worked on the land or in ancillary industries and services, or were employed in small-scale manufacturing industry organised either in small workshops or on a cottage basis scattered throughout the countryside. One of the principal changes of the Industrial Revolution was the large-scale development of manufacturing industry and its centralisation in factories located in a relatively small number of specific towns and cities. As a result of various new technologies, and especially the ability to harness power to drive machines, manufacturing could be pursued on a substantial scale. Large numbers of machines were housed together in factories, which were located at specific sites with access to sources of power – water power in the first instance and then steam power derived from the burning of coal. In addition to power, the factories also required large labour forces, which inevitably led to the growth of associated towns and cities as people had to live close to their place of work. And, as towns grew, the presence of a labour force, together with the various economies derived from having many factories in the one place, led to their continual growth. By 1850 over half Britain's population was living in towns and cities.

Urban, industrial life had a number of consequences for leisure. It separated people from the countryside and thus barred them from a variety of leisure pastimes in which they had traditionally indulged. It created new environments which, although eventually providing new leisure opportunities, were dismal, crowded and polluted. But, above all, it was the factory system which had the most profound effects on leisure. In fact, some would argue that our modern understanding of leisure is largely the result of the work regimes with which it was associated.

Although people worked long hours prior to industrialisation, work was relatively unstructured. If they worked on the land, their labour was governed by the weather and the seasons, which produced periods of intense labour and slack periods of underemployment. If they worked in cottage industry, it was up to the individuals themselves when and how long they worked. The factory system, however, required a rigid system of work. It depended on a large amount of specialisation and thus it was essential that everyone started and finished work at the same time. Also, in the early decades of the Industrial Revolution, factory employers required their employees, including men, women and children, to work excessively long hours – a 12-hour day, 72-hour working week being not uncommon. As a result, leisure became a counter to work. Instead of being intermingled with work, leisure was now very separate. And, because work was so long and hard, the time free from work contrasted even more starkly. Leisure time became a separate and precious commodity.

The nature of factory work in other respects also emphasised the need for a contrasting time for leisure. Factory work was very boring and repetitive, often requiring limited skills. Hitherto a lot of industrial production had been on a craft basis involving skilled craftsmen making complete products. The factory system ushered in a period whereby machines gradually replaced skills (a process that is still ongoing) and where workers were forced to specialise on particular aspects of the process. In his book *The Wealth of Nations*, often regarded as one of the key influential texts of the period, Adam Smith provides the example of a simple pin which involved 16 distinct operations in its manufacture. By allowing people to specialise on one particular operation, overall production and thus wealth was increased substantially. However, most workers derived few benefits from this, at least not in the early years of industrialisation; instead what they did experience was considerable alienation from the workplace. Leisure might therefore be regarded as a means of filling a void – by providing interest, achievement and fulfilment, which were now lacking from work.

Values and social change

In addition to creating a large urban working class, the Industrial Revolution also created a substantial middle class. Traditional society had been characterised primarily by a large agricultural labour force and a small landed upper class. By the end of the eighteenth century there was a growing number of middle-class tenant farmers and merchants, but the growth of manufacturing industry not only created a sizeable number of middle-class factory owners but also a burgeoning number of middle-class professionals – e.g. lawyers, bankers and stockbrokers – who were essential for enabling the wheels of the capitalist economy to run smoothly. These groups possessed a particular set of values as to how work and the urban system should operate, and their views and attitudes impinged both directly and indirectly on the form and development of leisure.

As already mentioned, factory owners were particularly concerned to ensure that their employees worked long hours. They feared that if they were allowed too much leisure time, their work forces would get drunk and absenteeism would prevail. In fact, there is some basis for such fears as a number of contemporary accounts refer to large-scale absenteeism, especially on Mondays. In some regions the term 'Saint Monday' was coined to describe this extra day's holiday that was often taken to extend Sunday's leisure and possibly to allow workers to recover from the excesses of drink. The whole process of industrialisation was strongly influenced by the Protestant work ethic and the belief that work was a virtue and provided its own reward. Hard work and long hours were regarded, at least by employers, as beneficial for both their businesses and for their workers and they campaigned vigorously against idleness, which they regarded as sinful. Saints' days were greatly reduced, as can be seen in the figures quoted by Myerscough (1974) in Table 1.1. Whereas in 1761 the clerks at the Bank of England enjoyed as many as 47 holidays, this had declined to only 4 in 1834.

In many factories, tough rules of attendance and punctuality were enforced with severe fines and punishments, and campaigns were waged against drinking. The

**Table 1.1   Number of days the Bank of England closed
in the eighteenth and early nineteenth centuries**

Date	Number of holidays
1761	47
1808	44
1830	18
1834	4

Source: Figures quoted in Myerscough, 1974; originally listed in the
Departmental Committee on Holidays with Pay, 1938, p. 11.

growth of nonconformist churches, especially Methodism, and the temperance
movement were also especially influential in campaigning against drinking and
many other forms of popular leisure and from the mid 1830s onwards they 'proved
formidable in petitioning the magistracy for the restriction of drink licences' as well
as forming a 'common front with sabbatarians in opposing the Sunday opening of
the pub' (Clark and Critcher, 1985). Factory owners and town councils, on which
such people had much influence, also sought to curtail or ban a wide variety of traditional leisure activities which, it was believed, might encourage opportunities for
drinking, gambling and other revelries. Fairs were gradually abolished and wakes
greatly restricted (Cunningham, 1975).

Apart from an obsession with labour productivity and the associated need to curtail drunkenness and absenteeism, the ruling elite also wanted to ban rowdy leisure
events for fear that they might produce riotous behaviour and ultimately revolution.
Although this may sound somewhat bizarre today, government in the early nineteenth century was not as stable as it might have been. Revolutionary movements
were developing throughout Europe at this time and in 1830 and 1848 there was a
spate of revolutions throughout the continent. Britain was not entirely immune from
such movements. For example, there was much unrest in the countryside, culminat-
ing in the Captain Swing riots of 1830, and for a brief period during the 1830s and
40s, the first nationwide working-class political movement – Chartism – attracted
much support and fuelled considerable fears among the middle classes. It should also
not be forgotten that the French Revolution had occurred not much earlier, in 1789,
and this had begun with the storming of the Bastille by a riotous mob. It is therefore
not difficult to see why some may have feared that large crowds, assembled ostensibly
for a fair or similar leisure activity and plied with drink, might well constitute such
a mob and be manipulated by a clever orator to riot. Certainly the governing classes
used various legislation to restrict public assemblies and thus curtail popular leisure.
Under the provisions of the 1834 Poor Law, various travelling entertainers could be
defined as vagabonds and returned to their parish of origin and the 1835 Highways
Act, designed to clear the streets of nuisances, could be used against football players,
traders and a variety of street entertainers (Clark and Critcher, 1985).

The middle classes also reacted to the popular obsession with animal (blood)
sports, some of which also drew large crowds, such as the annual bull running at
Stamford in Lincolnshire. But opposition to animal sports also stemmed from

another reason, that of a concern for the welfare of animals. The concern was primarily directed at domestic animals in the first instance but, later in the century, this was extended to wildlife. This concern was unique, with no other country expressing such sentiments, certainly not at such an early date. The Society for the Prevention of Cruelty to Animals, for example, was established as early as 1824 (and obtained its royal charter in 1840). Exactly why these values became so important at this time is difficult to say and any explanation must remain speculative. It could be that the concerns were not entirely genuine, as it was only the working-class, popular animal sports that were banned, not the upper-class hunting pursuits, which may suggest that other motives might have been more important. However, it has been suggested that one reason may relate to a possible need by the middle classes to demonstrate human superiority over other animal species (Turner, 1980). By being kind to animals, it is argued, humans could show that they did not behave in a bestial manner and this therefore singled them out as special. Whatever the reasons, animal sports were made illegal in 1835, although some activity continued on a clandestine basis – a lot more than was generally assumed, according to Cunningham (1975) – and the RSPCA continues to bring prosecutions to this day for such activities as dog fighting.

Rational recreation

We have seen how many forms of popular leisure were either severely reduced or even stamped out completely in the early decades of the nineteenth century as a result of various values and attitudes held by the growing and influential middle classes. Another set of values that were also part of this process, but more directly related to leisure, were those associated with what has been described as the rational recreation movement. On one level the movement simply involved replacing those popular leisure forms that were disappearing with something else. It was believed that, if you were going to attract people away from the pub and the fair, it was necessary to provide alternatives and there was a clear need to fill the void where popular pursuits had been stamped out. But rational recreation was much more than this. It was regarded as an instrument of social control and was part of a process aimed at extending middle-class values to the working classes – to replace ephemeral pleasure and entertainment with more enduring virtues such as knowledge, self-improvement, and health and fitness. As Bailey (1987) has remarked, 'improved recreations were an important instrument for educating the working classes in the social values of middle-class orthodoxy'. But such recreations were also linked to genuine concerns about the welfare of the urban masses.

Rational recreation involved a number of specific leisure forms which came to play an important role in the history of leisure development and its legacy is still very much in evidence today. Such activities included those linked to education, outdoor pursuits and countryside recreation, natural history interests and sport. The first of these was clearly concerned with the Victorian middle-class beliefs in both the intrinsic value of knowledge and the importance of self-improvement and involved a range of facilities and institutions. Mechanics' Institutes were established in industrial towns and cities to provide 'useful knowledge' for workers as well as a social venue. While these were quite numerous (Leeds, for example, had 17 in the 1860s) the numbers of people attending were not particularly high and, according to Bailey (1987), they struggled to compete with other forms of leisure, especially in the second half of the century when they were forced to experiment in an attempt to make their activities more entertaining.

While the middle classes were keen to encourage education and self-improvement for the working classes, they were also keen to extend their own knowledge. The nineteenth century witnessed an impressive growth in the number and membership of middle-class learned societies, where members met to listen to lectures on a wide range of subjects. Participation in these organisations, although associated with self-improvement (in terms of acquiring knowledge) was not linked to employment advancement and thus is more easily viewed as leisure activity. The Leicester Literary and Philosophical Society was one such organisation and its socialising and wider leisure relevance is clearly illustrated in an account of an occasion in 1861 when the 70 or 80 members and their guests went on a picnic to Bradgate Park. This involved not only the inspection of a ruin, an open-air lecture on 'The Geology of Leicestershire' and the consumption of lemonade, apple wine and sherry, together with tea taken at a nearby inn, but also a band and dancing (account quoted in Allen, 1976).

The facilities that came to have the greatest significance, however, were libraries and museums. The Museums Act of 1845 and the Libraries Act of 1850 are often regarded as the first significant pieces of legislation specifically linked to leisure. They respectively provided the basis for local councils to levy a small rate to pay for the building and servicing of the facilities (but not for the purchase of books and artefacts, which were intended to be supplied through philanthropy). In the following decades museums and large public libraries were established in towns and cities, usually involving substantial buildings, many of which survive to this day as an enduring legacy of monumental Victorian architecture. It is interesting to note that of the three areas of leisure facilities that local authorities are statutorily obliged to provide today (allotments, libraries and adult education facilities), two clearly trace their origins to this movement.

Another key aspect of rational recreation was its encouragement of activities associated with health and fitness. Just as the pursuit of knowledge was assumed to invigorate the mind, numerous other activities were encouraged to promote healthy bodies. This embraced the development of sport (see below) as well as a variety of activities associated with the outdoors. The growing industrial cities of Britain produced crowded, polluted and unsanitary conditions from which people needed some respite. One response to this was the provision by various philanthropists of large parks, many of which are still in existence. Derby Arboretum was established as early as 1839 and in Liverpool an entire ring of parks was established between 1864 and 1874 which included Stanley, Newsham, Sheil and Sefton Parks (see also Chapter 7, p. 149). As the century developed, however, the need to escape the city environment for recreation, if only briefly, became an important feature of the search for leisure. The countryside became particularly important for the middle classes – offering opportunities for rambling, nature study and, later in the century, cycling; the seaside and its growing resorts, while also popular with the middle classes, eventually became the popular retreat of the working class (see case study).

It was through sport, however, that rational recreation had its greatest impact on the long-term development of leisure. With its rules and order, its emphasis on fitness and physical effort and its reliance on both competition and teamwork, sport was the embodiment of many of the key values espoused by middle-class Victorians and it came to play an important role in social control. A fit and healthy population was also valued both by employers and by those concerned with the quality of recruits to the armed forces. Until the mid nineteenth century most sport was unorganised, with few rules and specialised facilities. Football, for example, had been a game that had been played in the streets but had subsequently been banned from such places. However, it continued to be played in the cloisters of the public schools and it was here that the development of organised sport began as a means of controlling the boys' anarchic behaviour and of redirecting the public school ethos into what came to be defined as 'muscular Christianity' (Clark and Critcher, 1985). The first set of rules was drafted in 1862, the Football Association was founded in 1863 and a Challenge Cup inaugurated in 1872 (for more detailed accounts on this aspect see Mason, 1989; Cross, 1990; and Horne *et al.*, 1999).

● ● ● ● The growth of mass leisure

We have now seen how, in the early decades of the nineteenth century, a variety of economic, political and social developments created conditions that were hostile to the pursuit of leisure on any significant scale, especially as far as most working-class people were concerned. However, we have also seen that, while trying to stamp out many traditional, popular forms of leisure, the governing classes did attempt to encourage certain other leisure pastimes that were purposeful and more in tune with their own values. These various forms of rational recreation became more important as the century wore on but, after the middle of the nineteenth century, leisure expanded in many different ways, so much so that it is possible to discern the beginnings of mass leisure. Apart from the continuing influence of middle-class values, a variety of other factors also played their part, including the growth of free time and real incomes, the spread of commercialisation, the development of new technologies and the role of the local authorities.

The growth of leisure time

While the early decades of the nineteenth century were characterised by long periods at work and a reduction in holidays, the mid century marked a key turning point in this trend. The length of the working week began to decrease for most groups of workers, government signalled its recognition of the importance of leisure time with the Bank Holiday Act in 1871 and increasing numbers of workers began to take annual holidays. However, it should be stressed that, while more leisure time was gradually acquired, the process was an irregular one, with different groups of workers in different parts of the country having very different experiences.

Women and children were the first to benefit from a reduction in the working week with the 1850 Factory Act introducing a 60-hour maximum working week in the textile industry. In 1874 this was reduced to 56 hours and reductions for significant groups of male workers soon followed as the shorter hours for women clearly had an effect on conditions for men in this and other industries (Myerscough, 1974). The building industry generally adopted a 54-hour week in the 1870s, engineering followed in the 1880s and the 1890s saw a wave of 8-hour days in many establishments (Myerscough, 1974). In addition to the gradual reduction in the number of hours worked throughout the week, a further important development was the introduction of the half-day holiday. This originally spread from Lancashire in the 1850s (Clark and Critcher, 1985) and was finally guaranteed to shop assistants in the Shops Act of 1912. For some, and shop workers are a case in point, the half-day was taken during a weekday but, for most workers, it was taken on Saturday and thus established the origin of the weekend. Having Saturday afternoon as well as Sunday free from work provided a significant weekly holiday and, when later in the twentieth century most people acquired the whole of Saturday as a holiday, the weekend became a major period for leisure, a process that was further emphasised with the gradual decline of religious observance and church attendance. The 48-hour week became normal for many male manual workers after 1918, but thereafter there were only modest reductions in the length of the working week over the next 50 years. Even though the official working week eventually fell to 40 hours for many workers in the latter half of the twentieth century, the actual amounts of time worked by many workers remained close to 48 hours as a result of overtime (see also Chapter 4). However, other developments, such as the increase in annual holidays, provided further opportunities for leisure, as will be illustrated below.

The increase in free time resulted from a number of factors, including campaigns by both reformers and the workers themselves, a realisation that any threat to government stability was no longer present and a growing recognition by government and employers alike of the need for leisure (with the possible acceptance that giving workers more free time might even increase their productivity). In describing the gradual process of acquiring more leisure time in the second half of the nineteenth century, most texts highlight the significance of Sir John Lubbock's 1871 Bank Holidays Act. This provided four statutory holidays for bank clerks, and this gradually spread to other groups, but its importance may lie more in its symbolism than its substance. Although the holidays were essentially secular, three coincided with the key religious festivals of Christmas, Easter and Whitsuntide and were probably already enjoyed by many. What was novel, however, was the fourth holiday, which was completely secular. The fact that a secular holiday was recognised, as distinct from a religious holy day, clearly signals an acceptance of the importance of leisure. For the first time, people were entitled to have a day's holiday that had nothing to do with celebrating a saint's day or other event in the religious or agricultural calendar. It was a holiday with no attached obligations and could be used entirely for pleasure and relaxation.

The other significant aspect was the role the secular holiday came to play in shaping the nature of the longer annual holiday. This bank holiday was established as the first Monday in August. With the gradual development of holidays with pay, several other days were added to this particular bank holiday Monday to make a week's holiday, which became established as the principal time when many people would take their annual holiday to the seaside. In fact, so popular was this particular time for annual holidays that in the 1960s the government decided to switch the bank holiday to the last Monday in August in order to stagger holidaymaking.

The gradual development of holidays with pay was the other way in which workers gradually acquired more leisure time. Some groups already enjoyed this facility at a relatively early stage. For example, Myerscough (1974) refers to the clerks of the Royal Exchange Assurance enjoying up to three weeks' annual holiday in the 1880s and Bailey (1987) cites the railwaymen with the Great Northern Railway Company being the first working men to receive regular holidays with pay in 1872. For many groups of workers, however, the acquisition of holidays with pay was a long struggle and its history presents a process that was far from uniform. Many workers simply took unpaid time off work at their own risk and in some instances where workers were absenting themselves in significant numbers at particular times (such as wakes weeks for example), factory owners locked workers out for one or more weeks whether they wanted to work or not. But gradually employers began to change their attitudes. According to Bailey (1987), 'employers in the north increasingly conceded "Wakes Weeks" as legitimate annual holidays which reinvigorated rather than debilitated their workforce', especially where this led to increased efficiency at work. Increasing numbers of workers gradually acquired holidays with pay – it was estimated that 1.5 million manual workers enjoyed them by 1925 and 7.75 million by 1937, with one person in three having a holiday away from home – and the Holidays with Pay Act in 1938 extended this facility still further.

The growth of wealth and real incomes and the commercialisation of leisure

In addition to the great improvements in leisure time, the second half of the nineteenth century also saw increases in real incomes as the wealth produced from industrialisation gradually began to spread, albeit in modest fashion, to the workers themselves. Between 1860 and 1875 working-class real incomes (i.e. incomes that have been adjusted to take account of inflation) rose by 40 per cent, and between 1875 and 1900 by a further 50 per cent. Probably for the first time, significant numbers of working people were beginning to acquire disposable incomes, which could be spent on leisure. As a result, a greater range of leisure activities became affordable to the average family, including some that had hitherto been the exclusive preserve of the elite.

With people's disposable incomes increasing, there was no shortage of enterprise determined to exploit this situation. As the nineteenth century progressed, increasing areas of leisure were commodified, in that they became saleable items, with people being required to pay either as participants or spectators. There were some noticeable exceptions to this, of course, such as access to urban parks and various new facilities provided by local authorities (see below), but gradually more leisure products were manufactured for sale and leisure facilities were created with admission charges. There had always been some level of commercial relationship in earlier times, as people would have bought ale in the tavern or paid for entertainments at the fair. What was different about this 'new' commercialism, according to Clarke and Critcher (1985, p. 66), was 'its heavy capitalisation, the consequent need to control demand to guarantee profit and its ultimate dependence on the State for legal sanction'.

One clear illustration of this sort of development was the changing nature of the pub. Pubs experienced substantial changes during the middle decades of the nineteenth century as they catered for greater numbers of drinkers. New pubs built in the 1830s – the so-called gin palaces – had much more space than the traditional 'domestic' pub, which had often been little more than a parlour or kitchen in a private house, and provided barmaids as well as a range of entertainments, such as billiard rooms, skittle alleys and music in the form of 'free and easies' and 'singing saloons'. The Beershop Act of 1830 had enabled practically anyone to brew and sell beer and thus landlords had to find new ways of competing for trade. By attracting people into their premises with additional entertainments, they were able to sell more drink and food.

It was not long, however, before what had begun as a marginal activity developed into the principal attraction in the form of the music hall. Music halls became one of the most popular forms of leisure in the second half of the nineteenth century and provide one of the best examples of the growing commercialisation of leisure at this time. They were a response to the growing demand for entertainment and a logical development of the 'singing saloons'. Some enterprising publicans gradually expanded the operations of these 'singing saloons' by charging admission and employing performers with substantial salaries. Some music halls involved establishment costs of well over £10,000 and could cater for several thousand people. There were some well-known very large music halls, especially in London, such as the Alhambra in Leicester Square with a capacity of 3,500, but there were also large numbers of smaller halls and it has been estimated that there were between two and three hundred of these in London in the mid 1850s (Bailey, 1987).

As with some of the more traditional forms of popular leisure discussed earlier, the music halls had the ability to attract large crowds and with it the potential for drunkenness, prostitution and unruly behaviour. The authorities were thus keen to control such activities, but so too were the owners of such premises, especially those who had access to the necessary capital that would ensure they could comply with the requirements of the licensing authorities. As a result, between 1860 and 1880 the music halls were transformed into more respectable establishments. As Clark and Critcher (1985, p. 67) point out:

> Gone were drink, food and most of the prostitutes. Tables and chairs had been replaced by fixed rows of seats; and semi-professional and amateur performers had been supplanted by full-time professionals tightly controlled by contract, including guarantees that they would not include in their acts any material 'offensive' to political figures and institutions. In short, what had happened was that magistrates, police and music hall proprietors had worked out an agreement to their mutual advantage. The more 'deviant' potential of the music hall, especially the behaviour of performers and audience, had been eliminated. In return, as it were, drinking saloons were systematically refused licences on the grounds of potential disorder.

Another form of commercial leisure that expanded rapidly in the latter half of the nineteenth century was reading material. According to Cunningham (1975) there was an 'explosion in the sales of literature', especially in the sale of newspapers, and he provides statistics to highlight this growth. At the beginning of the century newspaper sales amounted to about 24 million copies per year. Between 1816 and 1838 sales expanded by 33 per cent, between 1836 and 1856 by 70 per cent and between 1856 and 1882 by a massive 600 per cent. 'Selling cheaply, and exploiting the railway and the telegraph, newspapers and magazines catered to and filled a huge demand for literature' (Cunningham, 1975).

The growth in newspapers is also linked to another example of commercial leisure that serves as a useful illustration of some of the key processes at work and this is the growth of commercialised sport. Cunningham (1975) cites the example of horse racing where the many small courses had given way to a much smaller number of large ones and the Racecourses (Metropolis) Act of 1879 introduced licensing. Good rail communications and fee-paying spectators encouraged considerable investment in courses and grandstands and the demand for tips and news relating to betting played a large part in the development of the popular press. Football was another sport that became increasingly commercialised at this time. Although it was ex-public schoolboys who took the game out of the schools and into the cities, they lost control over it to local businessmen. In 1888 a Football League was established and the amateur ethos gradually gave way to professionalism as working-class players needed to be paid wages. The need to pay wages and to invest in pitches and stadia inevitably led to paying spectators and thus, as Clark and Critcher (1985, p 62) point out, 'what had begun as a moral crusade had become in twenty-five years a form of commercialised mass entertainment'.

Technological change

One of the central features of the Industrial Revolution involved massive improvements in technology. Apart from the general impact of technological development already discussed earlier in the chapter, technological change had a number of more direct effects on leisure itself. One of the most obvious of these involved the substantial improvements in transport, first the spread of the railways and later, in the twentieth century, the development of the motor car. These developments facilitated the expansion of leisure by allowing people to travel considerable distances to new leisure environments and facilities. The railways, for example, had a profound influence on the development of seaside resorts, as the network linked all major towns and cities with the coast and, with the introduction of cheap excursions in the 1870s, the railways transported hundreds of thousands of visitors to the expanding resorts for both day trips and, increasingly, for longer holidays (see case study, p. 22). In addition to carrying people to the seaside, the railways were also important for other forms of leisure, such as horse racing and various sporting events. Horse racing had always been a popular local event but the train was now able to take people to races in other towns as well as to 'hitherto remote country race meetings, such as Goodwood' (Bailey, 1987). And the railways certainly brought large numbers of provincial workers and their families into London for the Great Exhibition of 1851.

Another key development that allowed various new leisure forms to be introduced to tap people's increased income was electricity. Not only did electric lighting transform many existing leisure establishments but it also allowed the development of amusement parks and, later in the twentieth century, the cinema and the radio. According to Clarke and Critcher (1985), moving picture shows had begun to appear in music halls early in the 1900s and by 1926 there were well over 3,000 cinemas in the UK showing 'silent movies', with a cumulative weekly attendance of 20 million.

Role of the local authorities

A further major influence on the growth of leisure in the latter half of nineteenth century, one which still exerts a substantial influence to this day, was the role of the newly established local authorities. From the 1840s onwards, various enabling legislation allowed local authorities to raise money through local rates (taxes) to provide for a variety of leisure facilities. In the first instance this process was an important part of rational recreation (see above) whereby facilities were established to promote educational and healthy pursuits and as 'a direct and deliberate counterweight to the commercialisation of leisure – an attempt to get the working man out of the pub and into the library' (Cunningham, 1975). As mentioned earlier, museums, libraries and public baths were built as a result of various legislation in 1845, 1850 and 1846 respectively. In addition, public money was also made available to provide open spaces and in the third quarter of the century many towns began to acquire public parks. At first many of these were provided by Victorian philanthropists, who had often made fortunes as a result of industrialisation, but after about 1870 they were increasingly provided by local councils.

Although today there would no doubt be substantial public outcry if local authorities stopped providing leisure resources, the original involvement of councils in leisure provision was not due to public demand. Instead it resulted from a range of different motives: some linked to rational recreation and the dissemination of middle-class culture and values; some concerned with regulating, controlling and even prohibiting certain entertainments (drinking, fairs); while others were associated with civic pride, improving the attractiveness of towns and increasing the numbers of visitors, and thus improving wealth creation (especially at seaside resorts). Some parks were even used to segregate social class districts. Nevertheless, while providing for people's leisure needs and wants may not have been the initial concern, local authorities did eventually acquire this role later in the twentieth century (see Chapter 9).

Leisure and the growth of affluence

Throughout much of the first half of the twentieth century the progress of leisure is in some ways a gradual development of what had gone before. In relation to leisure time, the real gains had already been achieved in the latter part of the nineteenth century and the additional improvements during the first 50 years of the twentieth century were modest. Neither did the early decades of the century produce significant rises in real income, at least not for certain groups of industrial workers, many of whom actually experienced long periods of unemployment during the 1920s and 30s. Many forms of leisure that had been popular, such as spectator sport, seaside holidays and gambling, continued to be so, and in fact expanded, and some of the key forces responsible for shaping leisure patterns at the end of the nineteenth century – commercialisation, local authorities and advances in technology – maintained a growing influence.

The 1920s and 30s did however produce some new leisure forms, such as radio, the gramophone and the cinema, and also provided some early indications of the substantial developments in leisure that would occur later in the century. Despite the periods of depression and poverty more normally associated with the inter-war period, there were examples of substantial prosperity and related leisure activity. While manual workers in northern industrial towns suffered hardships, elsewhere there was economic expansion, particularly in the south where new light industries were growing up. There was also a substantial increase in the salaried classes at this time. Significant expenditure was evident on wining, dining and dancing and newly acquired cars were making the trip to the coast or countryside a regular occurrence. It was this leisure activity which characterised the 1920s and which led some contemporaries to pronounce the decade to be 'gay'! (Clarke and Critcher, 1985).

Post-war leisure affluence

The Second World War is generally regarded as a pivotal point in the development of leisure, as it was for many other aspects of life. As with the First World War a generation earlier, many features of everyday life had been interrupted and leisure was no exception. Various trends in leisure patterns that were clearly evident in the inter-war years were disrupted by the war but, following the end of hostilities, these gradually expanded again with football and cinema attendances reaching record levels towards the end of the 1940s. By the mid 1950s the period of post-war austerity was coming to an end and by the close of the decade the then Prime Minister Harold MacMillan could boast that people had 'never had it so good'. Full employment and a booming economy ensured incomes were both secure and rising. Throughout the 1960s real incomes rose steadily, producing a growing disposable income that could be spent on an expanding range of goods and services, many of which were leisure related. In addition, people were also obtaining significant improvements in their leisure time. The normal working week was reduced (see Figure 1.1), although its full impact was offset by many workers choosing to work overtime, and the importance of the weekend was reinforced in 1967 with the closing of banks on Saturdays. In addition, people's holiday entitlement increased substantially. As can be seen in Figure 1.2, whereas in 1960 the vast majority of the population enjoyed only two weeks' annual holiday, by 1980 this had risen to four weeks or more.

Apart from an overall growth in leisure, increased personal wealth also produced some new and specific leisure developments. One was a significant move towards more home-centred leisure as increasing amounts of affordable furnishings and appliances were making homes more comfortable and television ownership was providing an extremely strong counter-attraction to the cinema and the pub. In addition, people were taking more interest in the appearance of their homes with considerable investment in do-it-yourself improvements, although the extent to which this constitutes leisure is somewhat debatable (see Chapter 2). In addition, increased wealth was also producing substantial growth in car ownership

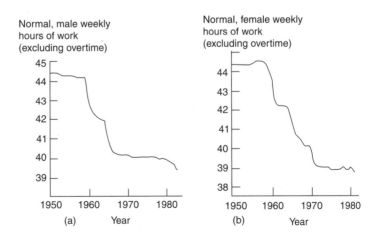

Figure 1.1 Changes in hours of work, 1950–83
Source: Gratton, C. and Taylor, P. (1985) *Sport and Recreation: An Economic Analysis*, London: E & FN Spon.

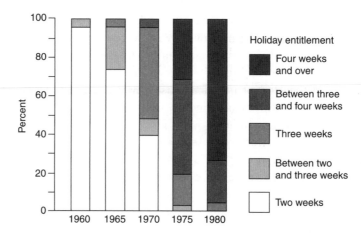

Figure 1.2 Growth in basic holiday entitlement, 1960–80 (full-time adult male manual workers in the UK)

Source: Adapted from data from Central Statistical Office, *Social Trends 9* (HMSO, 1979) and *Employment Gazette* (Department of Employment, April 1981).

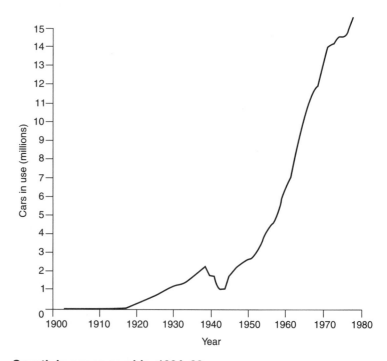

Figure 1.3 Growth in car ownership, 1904–80

Source: Adapted from *Basic Road Statistics* (British Road Federation, annual) and Central Statistical Office, *Monthly Digest of Statistics* (HMSO, monthly).

(Figure 1.3), with widespread implications for leisure, especially the growth of countryside recreation. A survey by the British Travel Association and the University of Keele in 1967, at a time when 45 per cent of all households possessed a car, showed that 89 per cent of car owners used their vehicles for pleasure purposes. People were no longer constrained by a limited transport system and could now travel where they wanted, when they wanted and take with them a considerable amount of equipment, which would also have considerable significance for the growth of many active pursuits. And, of course, increased wealth was a key factor, along with increased holidays and additional transport improvements, influencing the growth of international tourism which started its substantial and inexorable growth in the 1960s.

In addition to the more obvious factors of time and money, other influences played a leading role in the development of leisure in the 1960s. One was a significant change in attitudes and freedoms. The 1960s witnessed a major assault on many of the long-established institutions that had played such a fundamental role in shaping attitudes and mores. Church, government and the family, as well as laws and attitudes relating to moral and acceptable behaviour, were all challenged, with significant consequences for leisure. Nowhere was this more evident than in the development of youth culture, the emergence of 'teenagers' and the growth of sexual freedoms. Before the mid 1950s the transition from school to work to marriage and family obligations had been fairly rapid and young people had been preoccupied with finding and keeping a job that would provide income for their basic needs, with possibly a small amount left over for leisure. Now, for the first time, young people had significant disposable income. As incomes generally were rising, families had less need for their money and young people themselves could also command relatively high wages in the expanding economy. Furthermore, young people had a growing amount of independence that went with their new-found wealth.

New technologies were once again stepping in to exploit this with a range of leisure-related goods such as transistor radios, an ever increasing supply of popular records and the record players to go with them, and substantial quantities of relatively inexpensive, mass-produced, fashionable clothing; there was also an expansion of dance halls and cafes and the appearance of pirate radio stations, which eventually led to the introduction of the BBC's Radio One in 1967. But it was not just the acquisition of leisure goods and services that was important. The newly found independence also produced a widespread questioning of the attitudes and lifestyles of the older generation, and the introduction of the contraceptive pill and easier abortion produced considerable sexual freedom. In the first instance, the liberal lifestyles of the 'swinging sixties' were primarily embraced by the middle-class youth and not widely adopted beyond London, but gradually such attitudes would become more widespread and Bob Dylan's proclamation 'The Times They Are A Changing' was as relevant in Britain as it was on the other side of the Atlantic. Possibly for the first time, people, and especially the young, were identifying leisure and pleasure as central concerns in their lives and, while this was not going to produce the 'leisure society' as some contemporary pundits were suggesting, it would produce a society where leisure would command far greater importance and attention than it had ever done before.

Case study

Seaside resorts

The history of the British seaside resort provides an extremely good illustration of the growth of leisure over the last couple of centuries in that it involves many of the crucial influences and processes that have shaped the development of leisure as a whole. Its origins lie in the search for improved health, fashion and, as Urry (1990) would argue, new places on which to gaze; its growth was enabled by many of the developments of industrialisation (transport, wealth, leisure time); it was encouraged by various values associated with rational recreation and stimulated by the need to escape the polluted urban centres; it provided tremendous opportunities for commercialism as well as involving the local authorities; and, while providing opportunities for all social classes, it displayed vivid illustrations of class division.

It is often argued that the origins of the seaside resort lie in the development of the spas, which became increasingly fashionable after 1660. The upper classes and landed gentry patronised the spas in the first instance because of the health properties associated with the mineral waters found there. However, before too long such places began to provide other attractions to amuse people during their visits and spas acquired a distinctive landscape of pump rooms, baths, assembly rooms, theatres, coffee houses and parades. People would visit spas for several weeks, even months, and, while taking the waters may have provided the original pretext, the importance of spas as fashionable leisure environments gradually became the prime reason for their existence (useful descriptions of the leisure lifestyles associated with spas can be found in several of the novels of Jane Austen). Most spas were inland, the most fashionable at relatively inaccessible places so as to make it costly, and therefore difficult, for anyone other than the very rich to visit. And it was this social exclusivity issue, with the upper classes wanting to distance themselves from the aspiring middle classes, that was one of the key factors in the early development of the seaside resort.

Towards the end of the eighteenth century, increasing numbers of the new middle class also began to patronise the spas and, because the Napoleonic Wars made it difficult to travel to European spas, the upper classes began to visit the seaside in order to avoid these 'persons of inferior quality'. Its fashionability, as with the spas, was aided by the proclaimed health properties of seawater (bathing as well as drinking, although the fashion for the latter was relatively short-lived!) and by royal patronage, with regular visits by George III to Brighton after 1783. After 1800 it became more fashionable to be seen at the seaside than at spas but before too long the middle classes were also visiting resorts, with the result that the upper classes retreated to the more exclusive and less accessible places, such as Bognor, Burton-St-Leonards and Worthing.

According to Lowerson and Myerscough (1977), the English seaside resort in its modern form first became established in the 1840s and many of the classic resorts, such as Brighton and Blackpool, were originally middle-class developments. Although people had been able to travel to some resorts by boat (e.g. from the Wirral and Merseyside to the north Wales coast and from London down the Thames by 'hoys' to Gravesend and Margate) it was not until the development of the railway that a convenient form of transport was available to convey substantial numbers of visitors from towns and cities to the coast. From the 1840s onwards a very dense railway network was established in Britain, such that all urban centres were connected to coastal sites, and the dramatic effect the railways could make is clearly illustrated by the statistics in Table 1.2. These show that the coming of the railway enabled more people to visit Brighton in a single day than had previously visited in a whole year.

Despite such dramatic effects it was not until the railways introduced cheap excursions, mainly from 1870s onwards, that their full impact was felt. The period 1870–1930 is generally regarded as the 'heyday of the resorts' and it was during this time that they became more and more the playground of the working classes. Increased leisure time, better wages and cheap rail fares enabled many millions of people to flock to their nearest seaside resort and, in addition to day trips, increasing numbers of people were also taking annual holidays at the seaside. At the end of the 19th century Great Yarmouth was receiving up to 800,000 visitors a year, Margate 700,000, Scarborough 450,000 and Blackpool possibly about 2 million (Walton, 1983). In order to cater

▶

Case study continued

Table 1.2   Number of visitors to Brighton for selected dates in the nineteenth century

1835	coaches carried 117,000 people per annum
1841	arrival of railway
1853	73,000 visitors in one week
1861	132,000 visitors in one day (Easter Monday)

Source: Figures quoted in Patmore, 1972.

for such large numbers of visitors, the resorts grew from relatively small settlements to quite large towns. For example, whereas in 1871 the population of Blackpool was approximately 6,000, by 1930 it had grown to over 100,000. Resorts that attracted substantial numbers of working-class visitors were those that could provide cheap accommodation. This was certainly true of Blackpool, where landownership was very fragmented and thus, unlike some other resorts, there were no large landowners who could prevent the development of low-quality boarding houses. Brighton was another resort where, even as early as 1870, there were as many as 800 boarding houses (Lowerson and Myerscough, 1977).

Despite the early development of resorts in the south of England, it was the north west that witnessed the first specialised working-class resort development in Britain. The reasons for this have been summarised by Towner (1996) and include a variety of demand, access and supply factors. The Lancashire cotton industry provided opportunities for sizeable family incomes and regular and reliable employment and, in addition, there was a tradition in the region of self-help with saving and mutual insurance schemes, which encouraged saving for holidays. The area also enjoyed blocks of consecutive holiday time way before other regions in Britain, as the local fairs and wakes survived the introduction of the factory system and employers came to accept the tradition of regular holidays. The growing ability to take holidays away was stimulated further by the fact that the textile towns took their holidays at different times, following the pattern of the wakes. This produced a steady flow of visitors throughout the summer months and thus resorts such as Blackpool and Morecambe responded by investing in accommodation and entertainments (Towner, 1996). The railway system allowed the quick and cheap transport of visitors to the resorts, not only from the industrial centres of Lancashire but also from the West Riding of Yorkshire. In fact Morecambe attracted such large numbers of visitors from the latter area that it was sometimes referred to as 'Bradford-by-the-Sea' (for a useful account of this see Urry, 1990).

Following the early development in the north west, other regional links eventually developed between urban-industrial centres and nearby resorts: for example, the West Riding of Yorkshire with Scarborough; the East Midlands with Skegness, Cleethorpes and Hunstanton; Tyneside with Whitley Bay; Glasgow with the resorts of the Ayrshire coast; and links between various parts of London with Southend, Clacton, Margate or Brighton.

The seaside provided a variety of leisure for all social groups. All could enjoy the fresh air, sand and sea bathing and, as the resorts developed, municipal investment provided promenades, piers, parks and swimming pools and increasing commercialisation brought pubs, theatres, dance halls and funfairs. However, the cheap rail links that brought the working classes to the seaside did not produce much social mixing. Just as the upper classes had gone to great lengths to avoid the 'despised middle classes', so too various attempts were made by middle class groups to distance themselves from their perceived inferiors. They too travelled in increasing numbers abroad (100,000 people travelled to the continent per annum in the 1830s, 500,000 by the 1890s and 1,500,000 by 1930) and they patronised more remote resorts and more exclusive resorts. In addition to poor accessibility, often through poor rail links, some resorts, according to Cosgrove and Jackson (1972), also retained an upper- and middle-class clientele by refusing to provide the same amenities that were present in the popular resorts (e.g. St Annes, near Blackpool; Cliftonville, near Margate; Kemp Town, near Brighton and Frinton, near

▶

Case study continued

Clacton). Finally, the different social classes also avoided each other by visiting the resorts at different times of the year. Lowerson and Myerscough (1977) have shown how, in Brighton, a number of distinct seasons operated. Excursionists visited in July and August, family holiday-makers in spring and late summer and the wealthier classes in the autumn, which was regarded as the fashionable season.

The growth of seaside resorts was temporarily halted by the Second World War but thereafter the growth swelled again, 'being driven on by the deferred demand of the war years as Britain returned to peacetime consumption patterns' (Williams and Shaw, 1997). Live entertainment involving big-name artists was now an additional attraction and the 1950s also saw the major expansion of holiday camps, as portrayed in the BBC television series *Hi-de-Hi* (see also Ward and Hardy, 1986). However, this renewed growth was short-lived, for the 1960s witnessed the start of a major decline in the fortunes of British resorts as people began to desert them for sunnier climes. For nearly a century the British seaside resort had been 'the locus of leisure and tourism' as far as popular culture was concerned (Williams and Shaw, 1997) but increased wealth, a decline in the resorts' distinctiveness, cheap and convenient air travel, package holidays and the advantages to be gained in Mediterranean resorts (such as guaranteed sunshine and better-quality accommodation) was to bring this to an end.

● ● ● ● Conclusions

This chapter has attempted to show how leisure has developed over the last couple of centuries and how it has come to play such an important role in modern lifestyles. Such an historical account has been presented, not so much for its own sake, interesting though this may be, but to help explain current and likely future leisure activity. The origins of much contemporary leisure were clearly established in the nineteenth century and many current pursuits are simply extensions of earlier forms. Various factors have played a key role in influencing the patterns and developments that have been described and, of course, many of these factors are still important. Their current relevance will be examined in greater detail in subsequent chapters.

Questions

1 Examine the nature of pre-industrial leisure.

2 Discuss the impact of the Industrial Revolution on leisure patterns.

3 Discuss the factors influencing the expansion of leisure in the latter half of the nineteenth century.

4 To what extent have Victorian attitudes influenced present-day patterns of leisure activity?

5 Examine the factors that influenced the growth of seaside resorts in nineteenth-century Britain.

6 Discuss the principal leisure developments associated with the period of post-war affluence.

7 Examine the changing nature of leisure time during the last 200 years.

References

Allen, D.E. (1976) *The Naturalist in Britain: A Social History*, Harmondsworth: Penguin.

Bailey, P. (1987) *Leisure and Class in Victorian England: Rational Recreation and the Contest for Control, 1830–1885*, London: Methuen.

British Travel Association/University of Keele (1967) *Pilot National Recreation Survey, Report No. 1*.

Clark, J. and Critcher, C. (1985) *The Devil Makes Work: Leisure in Capitalist Britain*, London: Methuen.

Cosgrove, I. and Jackson, R. (1972) *The Geography of Recreation and Leisure*, London: Hutchinson.

Cross, G. (1990) *A Social History of Leisure Since 1600*, State College, PA: Venture Publishing.

Cunningham, H. (1975) *Leisure in the Industrial Revolution, c. 1780–1880*, London: Croom Helm.

Horne, J., Tomlinson, A. and Whannel, G. (1999) *Understanding Sport: An Introduction to the Sociological and Cultural Analysis of Sport*, London: Spon.

Lowerson, J. and Myerscough, J. (1977) *Time to Spare in Victorian England*, Hassocks: Harvester Press.

Malcolmson, R.W. (1973) *Popular Recreations in English Society, 1700–1850*, Cambridge: Cambridge University Press.

Mason, T. (ed.) (1989) *Sport in Britain: A Social History*, Cambridge: Cambridge University Press.

Myerscough, J. (1974) 'The recent history of the use of leisure time', in Appleton, I. (ed.) *Leisure Research and Policy*, Edinburgh: Scottish Academic Press.

Patmore, J.A. (1972) *Land and Leisure*, Harmondsworth: Penguin.

Towner, J. (1996) *An Historical Geography of Recreation and Tourism in the Western World, 1540–1940*, Chichester: Wiley.

Turner, J. (1980) *Reckoning with the Beast: Animals, Pain and Humanity in the Victorian Mind*, Baltimore: Johns Hopkins University Press.

Urry, J. (1990) *The Tourist Gaze*, London: Sage.

Ward, M. and Hardy, D. (1986) *Goodnight Campers! The History of the British Holiday Camp*, London: Mansell.

Walton, J. (1983) *The English Seaside Resort: A Social History, 1750–1914*, Leicester: Leicester University Press.

Williams, A. and Shaw, G. (1997) 'Riding the big dipper: the rise and decline of the British seaside resort in the twentieth century', in Shaw, G. and Williams, A. (eds) *The Rise and Fall of British Coastal Resorts: Cultural and Economic Perspectives*, London: Pinter.

Further reading

Several books provide a detailed coverage of leisure in the period of the Industrial Revolution and the Victorian era including texts by Bailey (1987) *Leisure and Class in Victorian England: Rational Recreation and the Contest for Control, 1830–1885*; Cunningham (1975) *Leisure in the Industrial Revolution, c. 1780–1880*; and Lowerson and Myerscough (1977) *Time to Spare in Victorian England*, while that by Malcolmson (1973) *Popular Recreations in English Society, 1700–1850* also examines the pre-industrial era.

Texts by Cross (1990), *A Social History of Leisure Since 1600*, and Towner (1996) *An Historical Geography of Recreation and Tourism in the Western World, 1540–1940*, provide a slightly longer timescale.

Clark and Critcher (1985) have a chapter in their book, *The Devil Makes Work: Leisure in Capitalist Britain*, which provides an interesting and readable coverage of the nineteenth century and most of the twentieth century.

Detailed histories of sport can be found in the edited collection by Mason (1989) *Sport in Britain: A Social History*, and the text by Polley (1998) *Moving the Goalposts – A History of Sport and Society since 1945*, London: Routledge.

Detailed histories of seaside resorts can be found in Walton (1983) *The English Seaside Resort: A Social History, 1750–1914*; Walton (2000) *The British Seaside: Holidays and Resorts in the Twentieth Century*, Manchester: Manchester University Press; Walvin (1978) *Beside the Seaside*, London: Allen Lane; and Williams and Shaw's edited collection (1997) *The Rise and Fall of British Coastal Resorts: Cultural and Economic Perspectives*.

Chapter 2 ● ● ● ●

The nature of leisure

As history shows, leisure has gained in its significance for both the individual and society. An understanding of the concepts of play, leisure and work is not only a basic requirement for any leisure scholar or professional, but it can also enhance the individual leisure experience.

Objectives

To:

- *explore the concept of play, its benefits and qualities*

- *examine the definition of leisure including time-, activity-, attitude- and quality-based approaches*

- *discuss social theory perspectives on leisure.*

- *achieve a deeper understanding of the nature of leisure and highlight key elements affecting how leisure choices are made and leisure lifestyles are formed.*

●●●● Play

Play at a glance appears to be a fairly straightforward concept recognised by all. The more we explore this concept, however, the more complex it becomes. Play is, nevertheless, a useful starting point for exploring the nature of leisure. It is, after all, childhood play that precedes and to some extent helps determine the adult leisure lifestyle. The benefits of play are not just long-term lifestyle issues but are also more immediate. As highlighted by Bartlett in Graefe and Parker (1987), when denied the opportunity to play, children are denied essential opportunities for physical, cognitive, emotional and social development.

Physical development

The use of muscles and nerves in the act of play assists in their development. This occurs alongside the development of key motor skills through the experience of play. The use of toys, such as building bricks and those that involve the matching of shapes and the feeding of objects through similar-shaped holes, can be seen to encourage motor skill development. More active forms of play, such as chasing, skipping and running games, encourage strong and healthy bone and muscle development.

Cognitive development

Play can fulfil an important role in raising a child's awareness of the world around them. It has the potential to promote intellectual development through the development of an increased ability in the child both to adapt to their environment and to adapt the environment itself. Play allows children to test out how society and the world function and can provide a safe environment for testing out new ideas and new beliefs about the world. In fact, playing with ideas is not only a childhood pursuit but is also an important part of adulthood. A child's understanding of areas such as language, gender roles, moral expectations and standards can all be explored through the medium of play. Play that involves pretend also allows children to explore the boundaries between what is real and what is not real and gives them the opportunity to step back from and suspend reality.

Adventure play is an important area in which children can not only explore the natural world but can test themselves and explore their own limits. This inevitably involves a certain level of risk-taking and allows children to develop risk-assessment skills in a structured and safe environment. This is a development opportunity that has led to increasing levels of debate in recent years. While risk-taking is generally accepted as a necessary element of play, the increasingly litigious nature of society has led to providers being more inclined to steer clear of adventure play (Sutcliffe, 1997; Melville, 1997). The increased awareness of child abuse and abduction has also led to increased limits on the freedom of children to explore without constant adult supervision. This raises questions as to the extent to which this may limit the ability of future generations to assess and understand for themselves their environment and the potential risks and rewards that may arise from engaging with it. It may also limit the opportunities for the development of an individual's personal resourcefulness and problem-solving capacities.

Emotional development

Play can be an important vehicle for developing self-discipline, self-confidence and a sense of self-worth. It has the potential for allowing children to learn not just for themselves but also about themselves. It allows them to suspend the restrictions of the adult world and to explore rules and rule making for themselves. This in turn allows them to engage in conflict resolution and to develop important negotiation skills.

In addition, games provide an area in which children have an opportunity of experiencing competition in a situation of equality; an experience that is rarely available to them in their adult-controlled world. Play can have an important role in allowing self-expression, which is limited in other spheres. The use of play to suspend reality can allow a child to escape from or overcome unpleasant situations. A child may be able to release certain feelings and emotions through play and hence face them and deal with them. It is indeed such outcomes from play that has led to the use of play therapy to deal with behavioural problems and trauma in children.

Social development

A society's dominant cultural values are reflected in the types of play that they develop and participate in. Children's play can therefore be an important enculturation tool. Play can provide information about cultural values and practices, roles within society, societal structures and attitudes towards authority. Children frequently use role-play in their games, allowing them to explore roles like those of mummy, daddy, teacher, nurse or firefighter. Fein (1985, in Graefe and Parker, 1987) showed that children who participate in such games have an enhanced ability to tell what others may be feeling. Such role-play develops a child's ability to empathise with others. Much of children's play incorporates interaction with others and therefore facilitates the development of skills of co-operation and teamwork and an understanding of concepts such as sharing. Hence, play facilitates essential skill development for successful integration into society.

Much of the writing on play, as above, shows a strong concentration on children's play. This may in part be a reflection of the influence of classical play theories and their concentration on children's play as practice and preparation for later life. These theories still rightly form a core part of the contemporary discussions of the biological functions of play. Norbek (1979, as cited in Torkildsen, 1999, p. 23) states that:

> Through infantile play, members of a species acquire motor and other skills needed in adult life for survival. Young human beings with a long period of immaturity are aided in this process by provision of specific opportunities for play experiences.

It is important, however, that a broader examination of play is undertaken. There is much more limited discussion and acceptance of adult play. There is little serious discussion of play as an integral and important element of adult leisure lifestyles. It is perhaps that we find it more acceptable to subsume our discussions of adult play under the wider umbrella of leisure. However, in doing so we are perhaps in danger of losing the importance of applying the capacities of enjoyment, spontaneity and fun developed in childhood. Playfulness is an important element of leisure and we need to explore and value the benefits that arise from its application within adult leisure lifestyles. Not taking leisure activities and ourselves too seriously and having a capacity for enjoyment and pleasure clearly enhance the adult leisure experience. Maintaining play as an element of leisure provides an opportunity to cast off the inhibitions that society places on adults.

Much of the writing on play also concentrates on what can be achieved through it, with more limited discussion of the qualities and intrinsic value of play. This is perhaps due to the fact that play is often characterised by its non-serious nature. It is hence viewed as non-productive and a time-waster. In a culture which is strongly influenced by the Protestant work ethic this has had a limiting effect upon the seriousness with which it has been regarded by providers and by academic institutions, and hence a limiting effect upon the examination of its values and qualities.

There are nonetheless a number of important qualities possessed by play and some of these arise from its non-serious nature. The non-serious nature of play is what leads to its spontaneous, voluntary and enjoyment qualities. If the individual is forced to take part in a specific activity then this removes that activity from the sphere of play. This sense of obligation and compulsion may, however, be seen to be negated if there is a strong sense of enjoyment gained from participation. In such circumstances the individual involved in the activity may still be regarded as being at play.

A focus upon what can be achieved through play can destroy what many regard as one of its important qualities, that of being undertaken for its own sake and not as a means to an end. On the other hand, however, if this quality is used to define play, this results in other complexities. If play is not a means to an end then the consequences of play must stay within the process of play. This makes it difficult to define gambling games as play. How do we, for instance, deal with the fact that the consequence of 'playing' the national lottery may be a multi-million-pound win? For this reason, early writers like Callois (1961) saw play being an end in itself not because it is self-contained but because it is unproductive. This allows the lottery win to fall within the play definition because 'playing' the lottery does not produce money; it merely has the effect of re-distributing it. This approach to defining gambling games as play, however, ignores the value placed on participation by the player. If we take into account the intention and approach of the player then playing the lottery may still fit the criteria of play being self-contained. The player may participate in the lottery simply for the enjoyment of the process. If participation is focused upon a need or wish to win or a compulsion to participate through an addiction then clearly the issues of self-containment, being voluntary and enjoyable are all brought into question.

Gambling games do possess another characteristic often identified as a key element in play, that of unpredictability. This may be experienced as chance, where individuals abandon themselves to luck or to the actions of others, such as the bingo caller or the national lottery machine. Alternatively, the outcome of a game may rely on skill, as in hockey or soccer, but still be difficult to predict. The tension and excitement created by this lack of predictability are qualities that are lost if the result is already known. Playing against an easy opponent quickly loses its interest when the outcome becomes obvious and puzzles become much less attractive when the solution is known.

Another quality of play is its possession of special and specific rules; the respecting of which is integral to the play experience. As Haywood (1995) highlights, even in very informal children's play the rules are of utmost importance; cheats are tolerated but those who refuse to recognise the rules are regarded in a much worse light. This would seem to be no less the case when adults are observed at play. There is, therefore, a certain order to play and a creation of order within the context of play. This can be one of the qualities that attract adults to play as a means of relaxation. Play can be a means of escaping from and suspending everyday chaos.

Some of the rules that are applied during play relate to time and space, both for formal and informal play. Games such as soccer, hockey and basketball have obvious rules of time, with designated lengths for a game, and specific sizes and shapes for the playing area. Rules of time and space are also in evidence in informal play. How many parents have been reprimanded for walking through a river that looks distinctly like a section of the lounge carpet to them? The rules of play in both cases allow the individual to suspend the ordained rules of everyday life. There is, however, an overlap between the two, with the rules of 'fair play' often being called for in other spheres and basic rules of relationships with others often forming the background to the rules of play.

Fantasy is another key quality linked with play. This may involve different levels of secrecy and make-believe and again is a quality not limited to children's play. Much of this secrecy and make-believe is an alternative way of providing rules and boundaries. Certain games and pastimes that fall into this category use different languages and have their own history and culture, which provide boundaries and can alienate those who are not privy to such information. Children will often make up their own languages as part of fantasy play which excludes adults, and 'Trekkies' (for the uninitiated, those avid fans and followers of *Star Trek*) certainly have an ability to 'alienate' the uninitiated when their play involving all things *Star Trek* includes communicating in the language of 'Klingon'.

The creative nature of play is also another quality that attracts its participants. This may be the creation of formal games, such as football, which lead to repeated participation and widespread uptake and ultimately become part of the play tradition, or it may be the creation of fantasy worlds and languages.

In the final analysis both the qualities and the outcomes of play need to be examined, as it is often difficult to differentiate between the qualities of an activity, its value for the individual who partakes in it and the specific function it fulfils. A specific form of play, for example amateur dramatics, may be pursued because it provides a vital outlet for self-expression and role-play as well as the key qualities of fantasy and a time and space for escapism.

● ● ● ● Leisure defined

Any exploration of the concept of leisure will highlight the vast range of different understandings, definitions and theories used within this area of study. It very quickly becomes evident that leisure is most certainly far more easily experienced than defined; defining leisure is fraught with difficulties. There are, however, four major approaches to defining leisure that help clarify the concept. These examine leisure as time, leisure as an activity, leisure in terms of quality and leisure as an attitude of mind.

Time-based approaches

The literature on leisure encompasses a wide range of different perspectives on the relationship of leisure and time. We are often presented with leisure as time left over from work, where work time is that which is spent in gainful employment or quite simply time spent earning money. This is, however, a very broad-brush approach as much of the time that is left over after work, and which therefore remains as part of this leisure definition, is committed to other activities. A large amount of time is, for instance, spent on sleep and personal hygiene. Sociologists have hence tended to prefer a definition that sees leisure as the time remaining after employment and the practical necessities of life have been attended to. Leisure time is then free time and is the time that remains after all obligations have been met and the individual can therefore make a choice as to how that time is spent.

This approach has been taken by numerous research projects that use time budget diaries (see Szalai, 1972 and McInnes and Glyptis, 1986) to identify the way in which individuals divide their day between the specific activities of work, subsistence, existence and leisure. This allows leisure time to be quantified and the point at which it occurs to be identified. This information in turn can be used to identify time trends within society and to inform leisure providers. Such calculations allow leisure professionals to plan current provision and forecast future needs. These calculations also allow comparative analysis over time, between occupations and across different cultures.

There are inherent problems in this approach. It is based on a view of leisure and work that arises from an industrial society, hence the leisure–work opposition. It is therefore relatively straightforward for those in paid employment to calculate the amount of time remaining outside work by comparison with those whose work is private domestic labour. Private domestic labour that has been traditionally most often undertaken by women is generally unpaid and ill defined; work and leisure are therefore not so easily separated. Hence, such definitions fail to take into account the experience of large sections of society.

Another problem with this approach is that it also makes the assumption that life-space and time divide neatly into specific categories. Activities are not, however, discreetly segmented from each other into nice neat time slots. It is not always clear which category an activity falls into. There is often no clear boundary between categories and overlaps are present. The quantification and definition of leisure in terms of time is therefore much more complex than it might at first appear.

These complications become more evident if we explore further the categories used to divide life-space and time. As already implied, in the time-based approach to leisure, work and leisure are usually seen in opposition. They are, however, in reality at opposite ends of a continuum upon which other obligations and practical necessities fall. There are, for instance, activities that are clearly linked to work but do not fall within the normal definition of the working day. These may be regarded as work obligations and include work-related activities such as grooming and commuting. Voluntary overtime may also be regarded as relating to one's main occupation rather than being a part of it. The activities we undertake to meet physiological needs and ensure a healthy existence form another key area on the continuum and include the minimum amount of sleep individuals require and the time they need for personal hygiene, eating and drinking. Another group of activities requiring consideration is those obligations that are generally regarded as being non-work obligations. These arise from a time commitment which, while falling outside the individual's occupation, is required in order to fulfil specific social roles. The servicing of children's leisure by parents would fall into this category; the time, for instance, spent transporting children to after-school clubs, sports and arts activities. This type of obligation may also arise from activities that originally started out as leisure activities. Hobbies such as gardening, which were initially taken up as a leisure activity, may eventually turn into a chore. This can occur because of a fading interest in the activity or because pressures from other obligations mean that there is no longer the time to enjoy the activity in the same way and it turns into a task that has to be fitted in alongside everything else. Another example is walking the family dog. This may start out as a leisure experience but can very quickly become a chore, especially on dark, cold and rainy winter evenings.

Having established what are now five possible categories on the time continuum, that is, those of work, work obligations, physiological needs, non-work obligations and leisure, we can also now explore the difficulties of clearly differentiating between these areas. Time spent playing with children by parents may, for instance, be regarded as an obligation required in fulfilling the role of parent and therefore a non-work obligation, or it may be regarded as a joint leisure experience. Eating out at a restaurant may be time spent fulfilling the physiological needs of eating and drinking but may equally be regarded as leisure, especially where the meal goes beyond fulfilling the basic physiological requirements for food and drink. Categories clearly at times overlap and it is unclear as to which category some activities fall into from a purely time-based approach and without exploring the quality of the time spent and the value it is given by an individual. This makes isolating and hence quantifying leisure time much more difficult.

Despite these problems there is still value in the time-based approach. Time is an important element in the social structure, especially in the Western world. Leisure opportunities and resources occur within the context of that social structure and by necessity, for reasons of effectiveness and efficiency of provision, are usually provided within set time frames. A time-based approach to defining leisure, while limited, does highlight and explore an important element in defining the nature of leisure.

Activity-based approaches

This approach sees leisure as engaging in an activity that is not required as a daily necessity but pursued out of choice and lies outside professional, family and social duties. This is clearly linked to the perception of leisure as time but here the emphasis lies with the nature of the activity pursued. Leisure as activity attempts to deal with the issue of what is done during an individual's free time.

Many of the research projects carried out in the leisure arena take this approach by simply deciding which activities constitute leisure activities and producing a definitive list around which data is collected and analysed. The General Household Survey takes this approach (see Chapter 4, p. 86) and for many such surveys there is clearly a practical need to produce definite lists in order to facilitate efficient data collection and analysis. The difficulty, however, of producing comprehensive lists of leisure activities inevitably limits perceptions and survey responses. The lists used are, by their nature, subjective and formed from what are perceived to be the activities most frequently engaged in during free time. They are usually also limited to activities that are regarded as generally socially acceptable. Lists vary widely from survey to survey but most often have a strong bias towards active and institutionalised leisure at the expense of informal passive forms. Leisure is seen to be taking place when an individual is involved in a specific activity during their free time and usually in a recognised leisure environment. Therefore, the problem of such an approach is that it ignores the element of choice usually assumed to be inherent in leisure, the participant's perception of the activity and any quality of experience as part of leisure. There is an assumption that because an individual is engaged in a listed activity they are engaged in leisure, and activities that fall beyond the list fall outside the leisure remit. This can be particularly problematic where such surveys are used to determine provision and can lead to significant gaps in supply.

Attitude-based approaches

Leisure in this instance is viewed as a state of mind or a state of being. This approach to defining leisure is guided by the motive of the participant. It is the individuals themselves who define what constitutes a leisure experience. They give meaning to chosen activities and places as leisure forms and leisure environments. It is the individual perception and experience that defines what is leisure. Therefore, as the values and perceptions of individuals differ greatly, so too will the experiences that they identify as leisure experiences. Different individuals will feel a sense of control, freedom and pleasure from different contexts and activities. The qualities discussed below, as part of the leisure experience, will be valued to different degrees by different people.

When leisure is defined in such a way it means that the list of activities, the places sought and the time during which leisure takes place are only limited by the perceptions of the individual. Leisure can take place at any time, in any place and in any form. What constitutes leisure will also change as the individual changes and progresses through the leisure life cycle. Skateboarding, once a highly prized leisure pursuit during adolescence, may no longer be defined as such in one's sixties. If leisure is determined in this way, it also means that it can take place during what may for other approaches be regarded as work time. This can be clearly seen if we look at a professional sportsperson. A professional football player may, for instance, experience a match either as a work-based activity or as a leisure experience, depending on their attitude and experience at the time. Perceptions may change from match to match, some matches being approached as a job of work and others being experienced as leisure.

Being at leisure, when approached from this perspective, is intrinsic to people themselves; it is about their attitude and is more internal and spiritual and less about something that is defined by external factors such as time slots or socially defined activities.

Quality-based approaches

Whether or not an individual regards an activity as a leisure pursuit or a particular period of time as leisure is very much dependent upon the quality of their experience. It is not surprising, therefore, that we constantly find qualities linked in with the three approaches discussed above. The quality of freedom is often found in the time-based approaches, that is, leisure being viewed as free time, and activity lists are often drawn up to include leisure forms that have the qualities of being physically active, pleasurable, relaxing or creative.

One of the key qualities claimed for leisure is its re-creative capacity. Indeed, the word recreation is often used interchangeably with leisure and is derived from the Latin *recreare*, which means to re-create, to restore or to renew (Sessoms and Henderson, 1994). This in part arises from the development of the leisure concept from within industrial society. This led to leisure being seen in opposition to work and hence the means by which an individual can recuperate from the effort and stresses of the working day. Leisure is therefore often seen as being earned as a reward for work. Its re-creative quality is seen as supporting work. This has led to problems linked with the rights of the unemployed and those who undertake full-time domestic work to claim leisure or to feel they can make a claim for leisure. For some people the work–leisure opposition in itself is an essential quality in order for an activity to be experienced as leisurely. It is for this reason that 'leisure' activities provided for the unemployed may be experienced simply as mere time-fillers rather than leisure experiences (Kay, 1989).

An examination of the work–leisure relationship can provide insights into a range of qualities that may form part of an individual leisure experience. Parker (1983, cited in Critcher, C., Braham, P. and Tomlinson, A., 1995) identified three types of work and leisure relationships. These are the opposition, extension and neutrality relationships. While his research has its limitations and has been criticised both by Parker himself and other researchers, these three categories are still used to provide structure to academic discussion in this area and serve to highlight key qualities associated with leisure.

The leisure–work opposition relationship builds on the time approaches to leisure, where there is a clear distinction between activities that are viewed as work and those that are viewed as leisure. For individuals exhibiting a work–leisure pattern that shows opposition, there is a deliberate choice of leisure activities that are unlike work. In this case, activities that are markedly different from work are chosen as a means of escape and a way of re-energising oneself. An example of this pattern may be a hotel receptionist who has a people-intensive job and who chooses landscape painting as a leisure activity because of its potential for solitude. In this pattern the re-creative quality of the leisure experience may be seen to be at its most obvious and most valued. Leisure activities that are markedly different from work may also possess compensation qualities. They may provide an outlet for abilities that are not used at work or indeed in other life spheres. A labourer whose work involves intense physical activity may choose leisure pursuits that are mentally challenging, whereas a philosophy lecturer may choose leisure activities that are physically challenging. Leisure activities may also provide compensation in allowing a sense of autonomy, a sense of achievement or a sense of belonging not found elsewhere.

Where the extension relationship between work and leisure is exhibited, the re-creative quality of the leisure experience is not so prominent. For the person exhibiting this pattern, their work is a much more central part of their lifestyle and is something through which they are energised and fulfilled. These people will therefore tend to choose leisure activities that mirror or have a similar content to their work. A sports development officer may choose to coach a football team as a leisure activity. While leisure activities in this context may have the quality of providing energy and may be creative, there may be no sense of re-energising or being re-creative. Here, leisure qualities are intrinsic to the leisure activities as opposed to arising as an antidote to work.

For the person exhibiting the neutrality relationship between work and leisure, the individual is detached from work and therefore does not relate to it when pursuing leisure, that is, leisure is sought neither as an antidote to work nor as an extension of it. It is, as far as possible, unrelated. For this person leisure is more likely to be valued for its entertainment quality as opposed to recuperation. A state of detachment from work means it is less likely to draw on one's energies.

The nature of leisure is undoubtedly influenced by work as, in practice, life experiences form an interconnected web. It would, however, be false today to continue to assume that work is a core factor in the lifestyle decisions of all individuals. There are those in contemporary post-industrial society for whom work is undertaken simply to support their leisure and it is their leisure choices that form their key lifestyle decisions and through which they seek self-fulfilment first. In such cases leisure is defined and sought because of its intrinsic qualities – not by relating it to work. Leisure is no longer simply an offshoot of work but has achieved an independent value.

One of the intrinsic qualities that we have historically found more difficult to pursue is that of the personal pleasure derived from the leisure experience. Leisure as personal pleasure is not so easily sought in a culture with a strong work ethic, where work and productivity are highly prized and have gained strong social approval, and where the activities next in line for social acceptability are those that are seen to be supportive of the family, the community and society at large. The valuing of leisure as personal pleasure has therefore been a long time coming and, even in a post-industrial UK, may still be viewed as a less admirable reason for leisure participation. As with the personal pleasure quality, and for much the same reasons, play is another quality that we have been slow to embrace as an important part of the adult leisure experience. As highlighted earlier, this aspect incorporates the key qualities of leisure being non-serious, non-productive, fun, enjoyable, unpredictable, creative and escapist and may involve both personal and social development.

Freedom is also a quality associated with leisure. We frequently encounter phrases like freedom from obligations, uncommitted time and free time in time-based definitions, but what is actually meant by *free* time? Freedom in this context often relates to freedom of choice – freedom to do as one wishes rather than engaging in activities because others expect or want us to or because we feel they expect or want us to. Freedom in leisure is usually seen as being about a lack of imposition and an escape from obligation. This may not, however, always be the case. A valuing of the social quality of leisure and the relationships developed through this may lead to obligations being welcomed as part of the leisure experience. Obligations, for example, to fellow team members. Obligations are not necessarily unwelcome or burdensome and may be part of the leisure experience rather than detracting from it. In addition, activities that we are initially forced to do may ultimately become leisure activities; for example, being forced to take dance lessons by parents may lead to enjoyment of the activity as a leisure pursuit. Being forced to exercise for health reasons may also lead to activities being taken up as leisure pursuits.

Nevertheless, a degree of freedom, is clearly valued as an important part of the leisure experience, but the extent to which an individual can exercise freedom of choice needs to be explored. Shopping is claimed by some to have arrived as a leisure pursuit because relative affluence has freed us from the need to limit our purchasing power to buying necessities. This does not, however, mean that we exercise complete freedom of choice, especially as others would argue that our leisure shopping is shaped by created needs and advertising. It may indeed be argued that we are simply given permission to choose within boundaries defined by other factors (see Chapter 4, p. 72, for a list of factors affecting leisure lifestyles).

It is important to examine the extent to which individuals are actually able to exercise real freedom in the leisure choices they make. Such an examination involves a consideration of the relationship between individuals and society. Individuals do not act in isolation from society and its institutions – the extent to which freedom of choice is exercised or freedom is controlled by the structures of society is an important debate not just for leisure sociologists, but also for the field of sociology as a whole. Consequently, in addressing freedom as an important issue in the quality of the leisure experience it is important to engage with social theory.

● ● ● ● Leisure and social theory

In examining the perspectives on leisure offered by social theory, many writers present a 'dualistic' or polarised debate that splits social theorists into two distinct and competing camps. The debate is often seen as one between leisure as freedom and leisure as control, or as the extent to which people are able to exercise individual action as opposed to the extent to which they are constrained by societal structures. Aspects of this debate are presented and addressed here; however, an attempt is also made, through the use of areas of subcultural theory, to examine the extent to which a move can be made towards an understanding of leisure behaviour that recognises the influence of both individuals and society in constructing leisure choices.

The early tradition in sociology was to examine the extent to which the structures of society influenced individual behaviour. Such analyses noted the potential for various institutions – such as the state, the workplace and the family – and various broad societal groups – primarily class, but also gender and race – to exert an influence on individual choices in a whole range of areas. Leisure theorists have drawn on this work to discuss and describe the influence of social class, gender, the family and the education system on individual leisure participation choices. However, the field of structural analysis is not as straightforward as this, as there are two very different schools of structural sociology that view society in very different ways.

Functional sociologists focus on consensus within society and use an organic analogy to illustrate the way in which society functions. Society is seen as a system, where a number of parts each contribute to the smooth functioning of society as a whole. Various institutions, such as the family and the education system, are seen as helpful in integrating individuals into society by teaching them the types of behaviours that are appropriate and acceptable in different social situations. There is generally seen to be a broad consensus within society about those behaviours that are appropriate, and so the integration of individuals in this way is seen as important in ensuring society's ongoing functioning.

In contrast, *Marxist* sociologists, drawing on the work of Karl Marx, focus on conflict rather than consensus within society. Such conflict, particularly class conflict, is seen as the major determinant of societal structure. Societal divisions are seen as constructing power relationships within society, where one group is dominant over others. The working classes, or proletariat, were the subordinate group to industrial capitalists in Marx's analysis, but feminist theorists and writers on race and ethnicity have focused on the subordination of women and various ethnic groups in a society that is often seen as being structured for the benefit of white, middle-class males. More recent Marxist writers have discussed the idea of *false needs*, where subordinate groups are led to believe, via slick marketing, commodification and promotion, that they desire goods and services that lead to an illusory state of happiness or, as Marxists describe it, a *false conciousness*.

For both functionalists and Marxists, the norms, values and roles that contribute to the structuring of society are seen as important. Functionalists would see the development of such norms, values and roles in individuals as a positive force that enables society to function effectively, whilst Marxists would see their development as a tool used by dominant groups within society to ensure the continued repression of subordinate groups such as the working class. However, whether norms, roles and values are seen as a positive or negative force, the key issue for an understanding of leisure is that they influence and guide individuals' leisure participation and, in the vast majority of cases, individuals are almost completely unaware of their influence. Structural views of leisure, therefore, see leisure tastes and preferences as being constructed by the family, the education system and, in various guises, the state, and the way in which these factors influence individuals will be further influenced by the class, ethnic or gender group to which they belong.

While there is clearly much value in an analysis that focuses on the influence of societal structure and the way in which, often unknown to the individual, it can constrain the individual exercise of freedom of choice, it is also important to examine those approaches that attempt to put a greater emphasis on the individual. Max Weber, while mostly identified with structuralist analyses, had ambitions, through his social action theory, to focus on the actions of individuals:

> …sociology considers the individual and his action as the basic unit, as its
> 'atom'…Hence it is the task of sociology to reduce concepts to 'understandable'
> action, that is, without exception, to the actions of participating individual men.
>
> (Weber, quoted in Gerth and Mills 1970, p. 55)

However, a criticism of Weber's approach from *interpretive* sociologists (see below) is that he categorises individuals as members of particular types of society or institutions rather than in terms of their individual complexity. Thus, while Weber examined individual social action, he used his typology to define particular types of social order (e.g. bureaucratic, religious, etc.) rather than to analyse the complexities of individual motivation and action. Yet this analysis is useful because it illustrates a key point, often neglected in structural accounts, that, no matter how constrained an individual might be by the structures within which they live, there is always some element of individual choice. Of course, such choices may be limited by the expectations and norms of the social group to which an individual belongs, the type of social order to which Weber refers, but there is almost always some room for the exercise of individual choice. This is something that interpretive sociologists, particularly *interactionists*, influenced by the social psychologist G.H. Mead, have recognised in their greater emphasis on individuals' interaction with society.

Interactionists accept that society constrains and forms individuals, but they believe there is almost always some opportunity for 'creative' action (O'Donnell, 1992). Blumer (1969) emphasised the importance of focusing on how people interpret their social world through the meanings they derive from interaction with others. Institutions (the family, school, etc.) are viewed as the product of the interaction of the people of whom they are composed. Individuals are influenced by such institutions but also wield their own influence in contributing to the social situation in which they are engaged. These accounts allow for greater individual action than Weber's social action theory because they focus on the interactive nature of the relationship between individuals and their social setting. However, a criticism of such approaches has been that, while there is opportunity for individual action in the immediate social setting, individuals are still constrained by the broader macro structures of society as a whole.

Perhaps the central concept to be drawn from this discussion is that leisure choices are exercised, but are done so within constraints imposed by the structure of society. Individuals are integrated into society through learned norms, values and roles appropriate to the social group to which they belong and, consequently, leisure behaviour tends to be that which is seen as appropriate for a member of such social groups. Individual choice takes place within structures, and so it might be said that partial freedom, or freedom within constraint, exists. The ongoing debate, and one that is almost impossible to resolve, is the extent of the constraint that affects individuals.

There are some areas of work that have examined the extent to which individuals can break free from, or rebel against, the norms and values of the society to which they belong. One such area is that of *subcultural theory*, which has largely developed through the study of deviance. Much of subcultural theory is derived from structural analyses, focusing as it does on norms, values and roles, both in society in general and in the subculture in particular. Durkheim (1967), for example, argues that deviance is most likely to occur in circumstances of 'anomie', that is, circumstances where norms are not clear or are not understood, while Merton (1967) argues that deviance is the result of the strain placed on individuals by the pressure to attain defined goals in society, such as economic wealth, by specified means, in this case hard work. Failure to accept either the goals or the means leads to deviance of one form or another. For example, an individual who didn't accept the goal of economic wealth may 'drop out' and become a tramp, while an individual refusing to accept the means may become a robber or a burglar. In developing this work, Cohen (1972) focused on the nature and development of deviant subcultures. He saw a key concept as being that of 'reaction formation' in working-class males against the dominant middle-class norms and values of society. Through anger and frustration, a minority of working-class males adopt values that are the antithesis of middle-class values. Cohen stresses that the most convenient and supportive context in which to pursue such deviant values is to join a group or gang that provides alternative ways of achieving status within that group. Much of Cohen's work focused on what he termed 'folk devil' groups and was illustrated by analyses of Mods and Rockers in the 1960s, groups largely made up of young working-class males who had rejected the roles, norms and values that the society they had grown up in had set out for them. Their 'deviant' subculture was formed with its own norms, values and roles that opposed those of mainstream society.

A useful further illustration of this type of analysis, and one that takes the concept beyond that of deviance, is the body of work on subcultures in sport. Being derived from the types of analyses already discussed, work on sports subcultures has tended to focus on groups 'opposed' to the dominant sports culture of winning and achievement. Such groups have included skateboarders, snowboarders and rollerbladers, groups that are also often seen as 'drop out' groups within society as a whole. The consequence of this intellectual heritage has been that subcultures in the context of sports sociology have largely been seen as outside the mainstream, or even as subversive. Yet some have argued that this need not necessarily be the case. Nixon and Frey (1996, p. 212) have identified subcultures as 'social networks in which participants interact with each other and exchange resources, messages and influence', while McPherson, Curtis and Loy (1989) describe them as mini-societies which can reinforce, negate, or even reverse, hierarchies, statuses and social orders experienced in wider society. Accepting this definition, it would appear that most sports clubs, groups and fraternities could legitimately be described as subcultures, without exhibiting any deviant, oppositional or subversive characteristics. This is confirmed by Albert (1991), who believes that theories that rely on conflict with the dominant culture to explain a sporting subculture will inevitably overlook many of the unique qualities of sport practices. Indeed, the same might be said of many groups in other areas of leisure, be they formal or informal. Such groups, without being deviant or oppositional, allow for the exercise of individual action and choice within an environment that is less constrained by broader societal structures. Of course, such groups have their own 'mini-structures' and these may be similar or deliberately different to those in wider society.

As the earlier discussions on definitions of leisure highlighted, for many people, involvement in leisure is often seen as diversionary, as different from, or even as an escape from, other areas of their lives. While leisure choices are clearly constrained to some degree by societal structures, involvement in formal or informal leisure groups or subcultures can provide a diversion or escape from the broader structures – the norms, roles and values – that may usually constrain individuals. As such, it may be the case that in many areas of leisure the ability to exercise individual freedom is greater than that afforded to many individuals in most other areas of their lives.

● ● ● ● Conclusions

A clear and precise definition of the nature of leisure is clearly difficult to achieve. Our lives do not neatly segment and what is required from a leisure experience is ultimately subjective and individual. Leisure and play are important concepts but ultimately have different meanings for different individuals. Play is an important characteristic associated with leisure and, while it is usually developed during childhood, a capacity for play and playfulness can benefit all individuals at all ages.

An exploration of the four different approaches to leisure highlights the complexity of our behaviour. It is not easily segmented into time slots or activities and, while time and activity approaches give us an insight into certain elements of leisure and allow us to quantify them, they ignore to a large extent the qualitative aspects and the subjective nature of the individual leisure experience. Each of the approaches explored, however, emphasises a different but yet still important aspect of the leisure phenomenon. The true nature of leisure is more about the combination of these parts in a much richer and more integrated experience than any rational analysis can portray. Such an approach inevitably loses something in the dissection of the concept and any rational approach also loses the instinct and intuition that may also be involved in the individual leisure experience.

In addition, in order to be fully appreciated, the already complex leisure phenomenon must be explored not just as an individual leisure experience but within the context of the structures within which it takes place. Leisure is not simply experienced by an individual but occurs in the context of society and its institutions that can be seen to exert shaping influences upon individual leisure choices and lifestyles.

Questions

1   To what extent are individuals' leisure participation patterns entirely of their own choosing?

2   Why do we play?

3   How does an understanding of the relationship between work and leisure impact upon our understanding of leisure?

4   What are the key characteristics of the leisure experience?

References

Albert, E. (1991) *Sociology of Sport Journal*, 8, 341–60.

Blumer, H. (1969) *Symbolic Interactionism*, Englewood Cliffs: Prentice Hall.

Callois, R. (1961) *Man, Play and Games*, New York: Free Press of Glencoe.

Cohen, S. (1972) *Folk Devils and Moral Panics*, London: MacGibbon and Gee.

Critcher, C., Bramham, P. and Tomlinson, A. (eds) (1995) *The Sociology of Leisure: A Reader*, London: Spon.

Durkheim, E. (1967) *The Division of Labor in Society*, Illinois: The Free Press.

Gerth, H. and Mills, C.W. (eds) (1970) *Character and Social Structure*, New York: Harcourt Brace.

Graefe, A. and Parker, S. (eds) (1987) *Recreation and Leisure: An Introductory Handbook*, Pennsylvania: Venture Publishing.

Haywood, L., Kew, F., Bramham, P., Spink, J., Capernerhurst, J. and Henry, I. (1995) *Understanding Leisure* (2nd edition), Cheltenham: Stanley Thornes.

Kay, T. (1989) 'Active unemployment – a leisure pattern for the future?' *Loisir et Société*/Society and Leisure, vol. 12, no. 2.

McInnes, H.A. and Glyptis, S. (1986) *The Use of Leisure Time*, Paper for the Department of Physical Education and Sports Science, Loughborough University of Technology.

McPherson, B., Curtis, J. and Loy, J. (1989) *The Social Significance of Sport*, Illinois: Human Kinetics Publishers.

Melville, S. (1997) 'Will kids be kids?' *The Leisure Manager*, vol. 15, no. 4.

Merton, R.K. (1967) *On Theoretical Sociology*, Illinois: The Free Press.

Nixon, H. and Frey, J. (1996) *A Sociology of Sport*, Belmont: Wadsworth Publishing.

O'Donnell, M. (1992) *An Introduction to Sociology* (3rd edition), Walton on Thames: Thomas Nelson and Sons.

Sessoms, H.D. and Henderson, K.A. (1994) *Introduction to Leisure Services* (7th edition), Pennsylvania: Venture Publishing.

Sutcliffe, R. (1997) 'Risky business?' *The Leisure Manager*, vol. 15, no. 4.

Szalai, A. (1972) 'Concepts and practices of time budget research', *The Use of Time: Daily activity of urban and suburban populations in twelve countries*, European Co-ordination Centre, The Hague.

Torkildsen, G. (1999) *Leisure and Recreation Management* (4th edition), London: Spon.

Further reading

Ellis, M.J. (1973) *Why People Play*, New York: Appleton. A classic and comprehensive text on play.

Torkildsen, G. (1999) *Leisure and Recreation Management* (4th edition), London: Spon. Chapter 2 provides a more detailed discussion of play, including its history and play provision.

Godbey, G. (1994) *Leisure in Your Life: An Exploration*, Pennsylvania: Venture Publishing, and Sessoms, H.D. and Henderson, K.A. (1994) *Introduction to Leisure Services* (7th edition), Pennsylvania: Venture Publishing, pro-vide further reading of a more philosoph-ical nature on approaches to leisure and leisure definitions, work and leisure rela-tionships and play.

Parker, S. (1995) 'Towards a theory of work and leisure', and Roberts, K. (1995) 'Work and its corollaries', in Critcher, C., Bramham, P. and Tomlinson, A. (eds) (1995) *The Sociology of Leisure: A Reader*, London: Spon, provide a more in-depth discussion of the relationships between work and leisure.

Virtually any introductory sociology text – e.g. Macionis and Plummer's (1998)

Sociology: A Global Introduction, London: Prentice Hall – will provide a basic but more detailed introduction of the various schools of social thought outlined in the social theory section. Jarvie and Maguire's (1994) *Sport and Leisure in Social Thought* (London: Routledge) discusses the contribution of a range of sociological perspectives to the study of sport and leisure, while *The Sociology of Leisure: A Reader*, edited by Critcher *et al.* (1995), London: Spon, also provides a fairly comprehensive coverage of the area.

Chapter 3 ● ● ● ●

The demand for leisure

One of the principal features of the social history of the last 150 years has been the continuing growth in leisure activity and, while we may not have achieved the 'leisure society' as some commentators were predicting, there is, nevertheless, little doubt about the prominent role leisure plays in modern lifestyles. People are involved in a great variety of different forms of leisure and why these attract the numbers they do and why patterns of activity change are clearly crucial concerns of this text. In attempting to describe and explain these phenomena, many writers have used the term 'demand' but, unfortunately, the use of the concept in relation to leisure raises a number of problems. First, demand is basically an economic concept but is often used in a broader sense as a term to describe participation. Second, where the economic concept of demand is applied to leisure, the particular attributes of leisure make its application problematical. It is the intention of this chapter to examine these and other aspects of participation.

Objectives

To:

- *discuss the different definitions and terminology associated with leisure demand*

- *consider the use of 'demand' as an economic concept and evaluate its application to an understanding of leisure patterns*

- *consider the influence of non-economic influences on leisure participation*

- *identify and describe the demand patterns of certain types of leisure activity.*

Definitions of demand and participation

The term demand is essentially an economic concept used to describe a relationship between the quantities of a product that people will purchase and the prices they will pay; in other words it refers to a desire which is backed up by ability and willingness to pay for the product that is desired. The amount of demand at some given price indicates the amount of consumption of the product which will occur at that price. While this is an idea that can also be applied to leisure (see section below), the term has often been used in the leisure literature simply to describe levels of participation. In many respects it would be simpler to restrict the term demand to its narrower economic meaning and, instead, use the word participation to describe levels of activity. However, the widespread adoption of the term in its broader sense now makes this impossible, and it could also be argued that using the term in this way may also be beneficial in that it allows a wider range of influences to be examined, rather than just the narrow economic factors. For example, in attempting to explain demand/participation, demographic, social, psychological and environmental factors can be considered in addition to price and income.

In addition to describing the number of those participating in leisure, many of the definitions of demand also identify the idea of some people's desire to participate being unfulfilled. Thus, a number of different elements or components of demand might be identified as follows:

1 *Effective, expressed or actual demand* is the actual number of participants. For example, it might be the number of people involved in countryside recreation or the level of cinema attendance and the numbers might be expressed for a particular time or over a particular time period (i.e. number per day, number per year). Effective demand may also refer to change – for example, the graph in Figure 3.1 shows the way in which cinema attendance has changed throughout the latter half of the twentieth century, involving gradual decline until the mid 1980s and then a steady increase thereafter to the end of the century. Effective demand is the component that is most commonly and easily measured and most leisure demand statistics refer to this.

2 *Latent or suppressed demand* is unfulfilled demand. It refers to a desire to participate which, for one reason or other, remains unsatisfied, although such a desire may become effective demand in the future if circumstances change. This is clearly more difficult to measure as it depends on establishing people's wishes and desires. Nevertheless, although it may be difficult to establish, it is something upon which planning for future leisure depends and it is clearly an important part of leisure forecasting (see Chapter 13). The precise reasons for latent demand also give rise to two additional elements – *deferred demand* and *potential demand*.

3 *Deferred demand* is demand that is unfulfilled because of a lack of facilities. For example, if, in a particular town, a substantial number of people wish to go

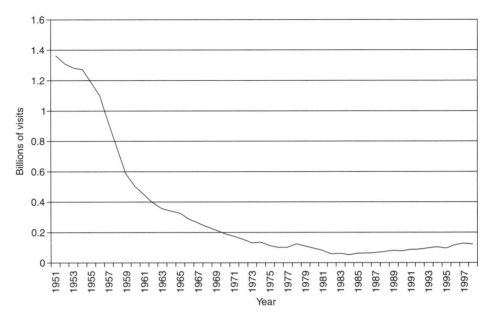

Figure 3.1   Cinema attendance, 1951–98

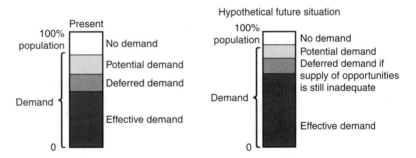

Figure 3.2   Components of demand for two points in time

Source: Roberts, M. (1974) *An Introduction to Town Planning Techniques*, Hutchinson & Co., (Routledge).

swimming but there is no swimming pool then this desire will remain unfulfilled and demand will be deferred until such time that a swimming pool is provided.

4 *Potential demand* is demand that is unfulfilled due to a lack of personal resources such as income or mobility. As with deferred demand, this potential could be realised at some future date if personal circumstances improve.

5 Finally, it should also be realised that there will be some who do not desire leisure and thus it is necessary to identify a further category of *no demand*. Although it might be difficult to think of this category if we consider leisure as a whole, it is certainly appropriate to have this category when considering the demand for individual leisure activities.

These particular components are illustrated by Figure 3.2. This shows the demand situation for two hypothetical points in time during which a certain amount of latent demand (both deferred and potential) is transformed into effective demand due to the provision of new or additional facilities and the improved personal circumstances of the population. These particular graphs could well describe a pattern no doubt experienced in many towns in recent years, where the building of new leisure facilities (e.g. sports and leisure centres, swimming pools, multiplex cinemas and bowling alleys) has transformed substantial deferred demand and the general rise in living standards has also reduced potential demand. There may also be a reduction in 'no demand' as increased knowledge may change people's attitudes about wanting to pursue particular forms of leisure; also the establishment of a new facility may well generate new demand where before no demand existed at all.

The economic basis of demand

As mentioned at the beginning of this chapter, demand is essentially an economic concept and describes a relationship between price and quantity. This is illustrated by the graph in Figure 3.3. As can be seen, the higher the price, the less people will be willing to consume and vice versa. At price P1 people are willing to consume Q1, but if the price is raised to P2 then the amount people are willing to purchase will drop to Q2. The trend line depicted on the graph is known as the demand curve and can be used in conjunction with the supply curve to identify the market or equilibrium price (Figure 3.4). The behaviour of suppliers is opposite to that of consumers in that suppliers wish to sell as much as possible at the highest possible price and thus the supply curve moves upwards from left to right. In theory, where the two curves cross is the equilibrium situation, where both buyers and sellers can agree a price. Although we rarely haggle over prices today, in traditional markets this is exactly what people would have done in order to arrive at a price. Of course, when economists produce supply and demand curves they are not describing a particular individual but rather illustrating average trends based on the aggregate behaviour of large numbers of people.

In applying the economic concept of demand to leisure, one common approach would be to use consumer choice theory in an attempt to establish how various

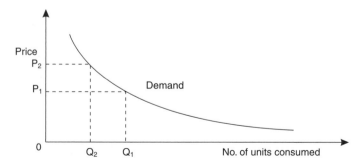

Figure 3.3   Simple demand curve

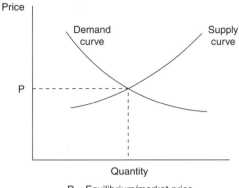

Figure 3.4   Supply and demand and equilibrium/market price

factors might influence the consumer decision. Such factors would include the price of leisure, people's incomes, the prices of other goods and services on which people could spend their income, and tastes and preferences. The latter is not an economic factor and, as Gratton and Taylor (1985) point out, some economists choose to ignore it, arguing that it is the province of the psychologist. However, in order to obtain a full understanding of why people consume leisure it is vital that these aspects are also included in the analysis.

Price

From an economist's perspective, the key factor in the consumer decision is that of price but, unlike many other goods, the price of leisure is more complicated. Whereas in the case of normal goods there is a single price, the price of most leisure activities involves a number of separate components. Depending on the precise nature of the leisure, one or more of the following prices/charges may be involved: entrance charge, transport costs, parking charge, charge for clothing and equipment, and cost of accommodation. In addition, economists would also argue that, as leisure involves time, the opportunity cost of that time in terms of its potential earning power should also be included in the list (see section below on the leisure–income trade-off). These different prices can be illustrated by considering a number of different leisure activities. For example, skiing would involve most of them. Given that most people do not live immediately adjacent to ski slopes, they would be involved in travel and accommodation costs, they would have to purchase (or hire) specialist clothing and equipment, and they would have to pay some form of entrance charge in order to gain access to the slopes. Clearly, not all forms of leisure involve the full range of costs in this way, but even a simple trip to the cinema will possibly involve travel costs in addition to the entrance charge and the optional costs of refreshments.

   In addition to the idea of leisure involving a composite cost, leisure demand is further exacerbated by the fact that a number of leisure pursuits do not involve any direct cost at all, with consumers being provided with resources free of charge, at least at the point of consumption. People do not pay directly to use urban parks, to go on the beach or for access to significant parts of the countryside. They may pay indirectly through taxation for the provision and maintenance of some of these resources and they may well incur substantial travel costs in order to reach them but, unlike the cost of a theatre ticket or a round of drinks in the pub, such costs are not easily identified.

It is clear, therefore, that identifying a price that might be included in any demand function is problematical, as most leisure activities involve a composite price and some components of this composite price may be difficult to estimate. Furthermore, although it may be possible to estimate some of these costs, it is not always clear how they are perceived by consumers. Travel costs, for example, now figure in many leisure activities, as most people who own cars will even use them to travel relatively short distances for leisure purposes as well as for the more obvious journeys to countryside and coast. In terms of the latter, as mentioned above, this may be the only obvious cost involved, but how obvious it is to the consumer is unclear. The extent to which someone planning a trip to the countryside will undertake a detailed assessment of the full transport costs involved could well be quite small. Although there is some evidence to suggest that substantial increases in fuel prices (e.g. in the 1970s) have been accompanied by decreases in visits to the countryside, it is also clear that the numbers of visitors have recovered quite quickly, suggesting that such price rises are either easily absorbed or their full effects are perceived inaccurately.

The price factor affects demand in two different ways. The first is the *average cost* of participation, which takes account of all types of cost (equipment, entrance charges, travel and time costs), and this, according to Gratton and Taylor (1985), is the major influence on the decision to participate. The higher the average cost, the lower the participation rate. The *marginal cost* refers to those costs that determine the frequency of participation. For example, with some leisure activities there may be a large element of fixed costs, such as the purchase of equipment and membership fee of a golf club. But, once this expenditure has occurred, the actual costs of playing each time (the marginal costs) may be quite small, involving only the travel cost, golf balls and possibly some drinks in the clubhouse. In general, all other things being equal, the lower the marginal costs, the greater the frequency of participation. Thus, whereas a golfer living relatively close to a golf course may well play very frequently because the travel and time costs would be very low, a camping enthusiast, who may have similar fixed costs, may go camping less frequently because the travel and time costs would be considerably greater in that camping would probably involve travelling far greater distances and would involve more than a few hours.

One of the key reasons for wanting to understand the effect of price on demand is to facilitate future planning. If it is known how people behave in relation to price changes then it might be possible to estimate, given certain assumptions about future price rises, how many people will be participating in various types of leisure.

In this regard, another important economic concept is relevant, that of price elasticity. *Price elasticity of demand* may be defined as the percentage change in quantity consumed divided by the percentage change in price. If modest price changes produce substantial changes in consumption levels then demand is described as *elastic*, whereas if changes in consumption levels are relatively small then demand is said to be *inelastic*. This can in fact be stated numerically and illustrated graphically, as in Figure 3.5. Elastic demand is where the percentage change in quantity consumed is greater than the percentage change in price and therefore the value of elasticity exceeds 1. Inelastic demand is where the percentage change in quantity

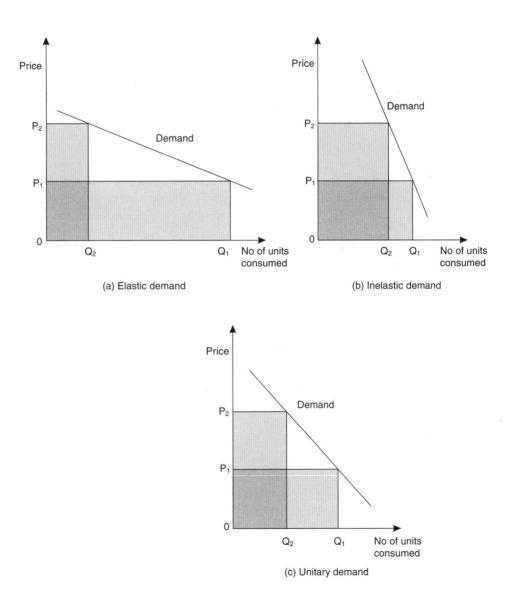

Figure 3.5   Elastic, inelastic and unitary demand

consumed is less than the percentage change in price and thus the elasticity value is less than 1. Unitary demand is where change in one is equal to a change in the other and the resulting value is exactly 1. The three graphs in Figure 3.5 describe these three situations and show that elastic demand has a very shallow sloping curve while inelastic demand has a very steep curve. Goods normally associated with elastic demand curves are those that are non-essential, where people are prepared to do without if the price is too high, whereas inelastic situations are associated with essential, staple items (e.g. televison). With essential items people might grumble if the price rises, but they will still pay that price and thus consumption will not be changed much as a result.

Traditionally leisure was regarded as a non-essential, even luxury item, which therefore should be associated with elastic demand. However, because it now plays such a significant role in people's lives there is evidence that in certain instances it has come to be regarded as an essential item and behaves in an inelastic manner.

Prices of other goods

In addition to the price of the particular good (leisure activity) in question, a full economic analysis of demand also needs to consider the prices of other goods and services that people will have to spend their money on. If the cost of other commodities is high, this may limit the amount of money available for leisure and vice versa. The cost of essential items such as food, fuel, transport and housing will clearly have an important influence on the amount of disposable income available in household budgets and thus the amount available for leisure.

One of the key issues associated with the price of other goods, and also one of the factors affecting price elasticities, is the extent to which products are associated with complements and/or substitutes. Complements are additional goods that have to be bought along with a particular good, whereas substitute goods are those that people can switch to if the price of one becomes too expensive. Thus, if the price of the complement rises then demand for the good will fall because the price of one inevitably raises the price of the whole package. A good example of a complementary good is petrol in relation to cars. If the price of petrol increases then the demand for cars will fall, as the overall price of motoring will increase. However, a substitute good will have the opposite effect. For example, in the case of substitute goods tea and coffee, if the price of one rises then the demand for the other will also rise as people switch to the relatively cheaper good. In terms of a leisure example, if the price of skiing equipment (the complementary good) rises, the demand for skiing holidays will fall, but the demand for other types of holiday might increase as they may be seen as substitutes.

Income

The final economic aspect relating to the ability of people to purchase leisure is that of income. As outlined in Chapter 1, it was only when real incomes began to grow significantly in the second half of the nineteenth century that the development of mass leisure began, and the steady rise of incomes since then has clearly had a substantial influence on its continued growth. Although it is obvious that a positive relationship exists between income and leisure – after all, the wealthy have always enjoyed leisure in substantial quantities – the exact nature of this relationship is not so clear. As with price, economists also use the concept of elasticity in relation to income and, while there is substantial evidence to suggest that demand increases with increases in income, the opposite behaviour is not necessarily discerned if incomes fall. While the income elasticity of demand for leisure appears to operate elastically in one direction, it would appear to operate inelastically in the other (Ryan, 1991).

Another issue concerning income and leisure involves the extent to which people may switch from certain forms of leisure to others as their incomes rise. If this is so then, although it could be established that in the case of certain activities participation would rise in relation to income rises, a different pattern would be experienced for those activities that were being abandoned. For example, the decline in visits to British seaside resorts in the 1960s and 70s occurred when incomes were rising substantially; but, of course, people were not abandoning their holidays – instead, rising incomes and other factors were allowing people to switch to foreign holidays in the Mediterranean.

Leisure–income trade-off

A further issue linked to income is that concerning the extent to which leisure is taken at the expense of income. In some ways it might be more appropriate to consider this issue under price, as it essentially involves the opportunity cost of leisure. Put simply the issue refers to the fact that if someone spends time on leisure, this time could otherwise have been used to earn income; in other words, there is an opportunity foregone. It can be argued that an individual will gain utility or satisfaction from both work and leisure; so how will a rational person behave when faced with this problem? Should he/she work longer hours for more money or fewer hours for more leisure time? An economist might argue that people will continue to work as long as the benefits from income outweigh the benefits from leisure time. As Gratton and Taylor (1992) point out, there will come a point when enough time is spent in work and enough money is earned. At this point the person reaches an optimum trade-off between time spent at work and time spent in leisure. As wage rates increase, however, the cost of not working (and thus the cost of leisure) increases, making it economically more tempting to opt for more work (the substitution effect). However, it could also be argued that higher wage rates will produce the same level of income for less hours worked and thus, assuming higher wage rates do not produce excessive inflation, this may make it easier to have more time for leisure (the income effect).

In practice, of course, it is difficult to replicate exactly this theoretical scenario. To begin with, many people do not have a choice as to whether they can work fewer or more hours – the work contract usually stipulates what the hours will be. For many professional workers additional hours worked are not necessarily financially rewarded anyway, and other people may only work extra hours if over-time is available. In addition, non-work time is not all devoted to leisure, with various obligatory chores being involved, and thus the idea of a simple trade-off is somewhat unrealistic. Also, work itself does not simply involve disutility (which is compensated by income) but may provide various additional social and psychological benefits. And, finally, the concept also assumes that consumers are economically rational and interested in maximising utility in this way.

Nevertheless, it is interesting to examine what has actually occurred over the last few decades at a time of increasing wage rates. According to Gratton and Taylor (1992), who examined the period 1971 to 1991, the evidence is not altogether clear. While hours of work in a typical week had fallen, the overall decline was small and in the late 1980s the average working week had actually risen. These trends, together with a further fall in the early 1990s, were almost certainly linked to the fluctuations in the overall economy. But, while they might suggest that where overtime is available people are choosing to work longer hours (substitution effect), there are some jobs, such as those in the construction industry, where overtime may be required by the employer at times of economic expansion. Thus some of this activity may not be optional. The evidence relating to labour force activity rates (the percentage of the population of working age actually in the labour force) is also unclear. The figures for males shows a steady decline during this period, whereas for females it was steadily increasing. While this may suggest that the income effect was influencing men and the substitution effect influencing women, in reality it is more complex. The sharp decline in the male rate was largely due to early retirement, which may be linked to leisure but may also be linked to greater opportunities to retire as a result of ill health and to pressure/inducements by employers who may see early retirement as a means of achieving voluntary redundancy. For women, the apparent rise in activity rates may not be at the expense of leisure but rather to a reduction in unpaid household work (see Chapter 5 for a more detailed discussion of women's leisure).

Tastes and preferences

The final element influencing demand is that of tastes and preferences. The import-ant influence of tastes and fashion in the history of leisure development has already been noted in Chapter 1 and it is clear that it exerts just as great an impact today (e.g. foreign holidays, clubbing). However, while there may well be a psychological basis to some of this explanation, tastes and preferences are also affected by a range of social influences and these will be considered in the following section.

● ● ● ● Psychological and social influences on demand

The factors of price and income that have been discussed so far are basically con-straining influences, but what causes people to desire leisure in the first instance?

Some would argue that individuals' personal tastes and preferences are due to differences in attitudes, values and motivations.

An attitude may be defined as a learned predisposition to respond in a consistent manner with respect to a given situation (after Fishbein and Aajzen, 1975). It contains three basic features: the notion that an attitude is learned, that it predisposes to action, and that it is relatively consistent over time. Attitudes are therefore enduring and clearly influence motivation in that where they are strongly held they tend to influence a person to react in a certain way (Gold, 1980). Values are similar to attitudes, although attitudes are broader and, at times, less personal than values. A value may be defined as 'an enduring belief that a specific mode of conduct or end-state of existence is personally or socially preferable to an opposite or converse mode of conduct or end-state of existence' (Rokeach, 1973, quoted in Hayes, 2000, p. 538). Values act as underlying standards and motives and have a direct influence on the attitudes people hold towards specific ideas or objects (Hayes, 2000). Values and attitudes will have an important influence on how people see leisure; for example, whether leisure is viewed as pleasure and an end in itself or whether it is seen in more instrumental terms, as a means of achieving something else such as improved health or knowledge. The influence of values and attitudes has already been encountered in Chapter 1 in relation to the conflicts between popular leisure and the attempts of the Victorian middle class to replace such activities with so-called rational recreation forms. In more recent times others have suggested that leisure is now being affected by 'postmaterialist' values. For example, Crum (cited in Standevan and De Knop, 1999) relates this to sport and describes a shift from work ethic values to values emphasising pleasure, hedonism and self-realisation. The values of achievement and competition, while still important to some, are less desirable to others, who see sport as an activity to be enjoyed for its own sake or as a fashionable lifestyle activity. One result of this is that such value change has lowered barriers to sports participation and thus widened participation.

However, while attitudes and values can clearly be seen to have an important bearing on people's leisure preferences, they may not explain the basic reasons why people desire leisure in the first place, and thus the deeper aspects of motivation need to be examined. Motivation may be defined as the force that leads people to seek certain goals in relation to their needs. In relation to leisure motivation, several writers refer to the work of Maslow (1954) and his hierarchy of needs. This suggests that people are motivated by various needs ranging from basic physiological needs to high-order ones such as those of personal self-fulfilment (self-actualisation); as lower-order needs are satisfied, people are then motivated by those of the next level (see Figure 3.6). As leisure is a complex phenomenon, it is likely that it satisfies a number of different types of need within the hierarchy. Despite Maslow's influence on research into leisure demand, according to Cooper *et al.* (1998) it is not clear from his work how and why he selected five basic needs or why he never tried to expand the original set of motives. Cooper *et al.* (1998) conclude that the model's attractiveness is based partly on its convenience, in that it provides a comprehensive coverage of human needs that can be organised into an understandable

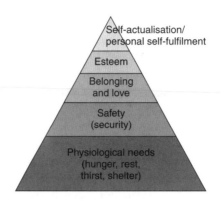

Figure 3.6 Maslow's hierarchy of needs

Source: Hall, C.M. and Page, S.J. (1999) *The Geography of Tourism and Recreation: Environment, Place and Space*, London: Routledge.

hierarchical framework, and also on its moral overtones, in that it suggests people can become less concerned with materialistic aspects of life and more interested in 'higher', more spiritual needs.

The whole area of motivation relates to an important debate within leisure studies concerning the extent to which people are free to choose the amount and nature of leisure they consume and the extent to which they are constrained by various social and economic factors. In some respects this lies at the very heart of the debate about what is leisure (see Chapter 2). Although people do clearly differ in terms of their individual tastes and preferences, which are influenced by individual attitudes, values and motivations, all of these will be influenced by people's particular circumstances, as will the extent to which people's leisure wants can actually be fulfilled.

Not surprisingly, therefore, all studies of leisure participation acknowledge the significance of various factors that describe the personal or social circumstances of individuals and family groups. Such factors will influence the overall amount of leisure as well as participation in individual forms. Income apart, age, gender, social class, family circumstances, education, ethnicity, residential location and personal mobility all exert some influence on the nature and extent of leisure activity. Although the importance of such factors is generally agreed, their precise effect is less certain and some of this complexity will be examined more fully in Chapters 4 and 5. It is almost impossible to isolate the effects of individual factors on leisure, as the factors themselves are often interrelated and their effect on leisure is usually a combined one. For example, even the simple factor of age is complex. Although it is clear that there is a relationship between age and leisure, particularly in relation to active leisure pursuits, the way in which age operates is also affected by gender, family circumstances, education, work and personal mobility. In fact, the social dimensions of age are possibly far more important in influencing leisure than simple chronology and related biological processes (Haywood *et al.*, 1995). For example, when it is established that substantial numbers of people in their late teens stop playing sport, is this due to age *per se*, or is it due to leaving school or changing family circumstances or the social conditioning of peer group pressure?

Some writers refer to these social factors as constraining people's choice. According to Haywood *et al.* (1995), people might choose their own leisure but they do not do so in circumstances of their own choosing. Their general upbringing, family background, residential location, social class and level of education, for example, will all have combined to influence such circumstances and make it more or less probable that certain leisure activities will be pursued rather than others. While it may be possible for a factory worker to play polo or attend the opera at Glyndbourne, the probability of this happening is very low, not merely because of cost and other access constraints, but also because the person's particular social circumstances would probably not have allowed such choices to be considered in the first place. The work of Pierre Bourdieu, which is summarised in Haywood *et al.* (1995, pp. 239–41), is also relevant in this context. Bourdieu is concerned with examining how tastes and preferences are acquired for different leisure activities and on what basis choices are made. He suggests that tastes and preferences are learned and developed in early childhood within the family and its surroundings. According to Haywood *et al.* (p. 240):

> Bourdieu's 'Theory of Practice', is that childhood practices and experiences give rise to a 'habitus'. This habitus is a 'system of transposable dispositions' which function as a collection of perceptions, tastes, preferences, appreciations and actions; forming a way of perceiving the world and distinguishing between appropriate and inappropriate activities. By transposable, Bourdieu means that an individual's leisure tastes and preferences in any one leisure activity are inter-related with or interdependent on the taste and preferences manifested in all other leisure activities.

The habitus is the basis upon which all leisure choices are made and through this individuals acquire a range of 'cultural competences', or 'cultural capital', which makes particular leisure activities more or less accessible or possible for them (ibid).

A final illustration of these ideas is provided by Rodgers (1977, cited in Gratton and Taylor, 1985), who refers to the concept of probability filters in relation to sport. As can be seen in Figure 3.7, the various factors of age, gender, social class, mobility, education and income all combine to reduce the potential market as various people are filtered out. Further examination of how these various factors influence participation can be found in Chapters 4 and 5.

● ● ● ● Temporal and spatial patterns of demand

While much of the focus of leisure demand is concerned with overall numbers, the ways in which these numbers vary though time and space is also important. The analysis of rates of growth through time has already been mentioned (see Figure 3.1) and forms a major aspect of demand studies. Change in demand over time may be affected by economic change, such as a recession, changing technologies and changing fashions and trends. In addition to analysing such long-term trends, temporal patterns over relatively small time periods are also important. For example,

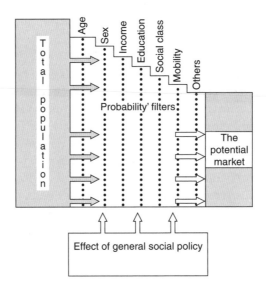

Figure 3.7 Participation – the social filters

Source: Rogers (1977), in Gratton, C. and Taylor, P. (1985) *Sport and Recreation: An Economic Analysis*, London: E & FN Spon.

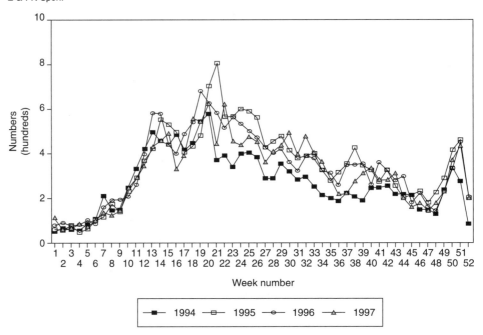

Figure 3.8 Coach parking in Canterbury, 1994–8

Source: Canterbury City Council.

many leisure activities display distinct seasonal patterns, especially in countries like the UK where this is linked to major seasonal variations in climate, with obvious variations occurring in relation to outdoor sport, countryside recreation and tourism. But seasonal variations are not just linked to climate. The graphs in Figure 3.8 show the annual pattern of coach visits to Canterbury and the well-established peak period here is explained primarily by the arrival of large numbers of French schoolchildren on educational day trips during the summer term, with the minor peak in December being due to continental visitors coming to do Christmas shopping.

In addition to seasonal patterns, variations may also occur on a weekly and diurnal basis, with leisure activity being related to work regimes. Not surprisingly, most leisure activity occurs at weekends and evenings, although more flexible working conditions, the emergence of the 24-hour society (see page 280) and early retirement are having a slight reducing effect on such patterns. However, the nature of diurnal patterns is not just related to work. For example, studies of countryside recreation over several decades have shown a recurring pattern of peak activity occurring at mid afternoon on Sundays and the daily pattern of tourists to Canterbury also shows a distinct peak, this time occurring at midday (Figure 3.9), with most visitors staying for only a few hours before leaving.

To a certain extent the spatial patterns of demand are determined by the location of resources and facilities and the factors that are responsible for this supply are examined in Chapter 7. However, the extent to which pre-existing resources are utilised for leisure and the precise location of new facilities are both linked to the ability and willingness of people to travel to such locations. As indicated earlier in this chapter, this clearly involves a cost in terms of both money and time and is thus a crucial aspect of the economic concept of demand. The distances people are prepared to travel for leisure have received considerable attention, especially by geographers, and various relationships have been established between distance, time and quality of resource. Various studies have shown the average distances people are prepared to travel for half-day and day trips and

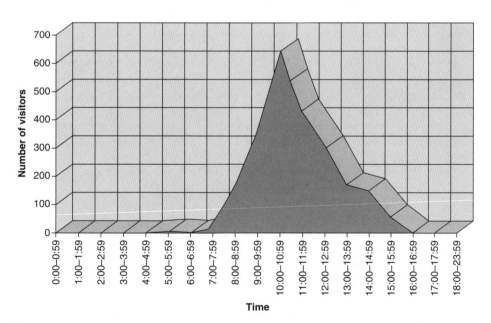

Figure 3.9   Diurnal pattern of visitors to Canterbury in terms of arrival time

the different distances people are prepared to travel for different types of leisure. For example, if the leisure activity involves a relatively small amount of time then people will not be prepared to invest in a lengthy period of travel, whereas if the leisure activity is quite time-consuming, investment in travel time is more acceptable. In addition, it is argued that people will also be more willing to travel greater distances to visit resources they regard as more attractive or more valuable and, in fact, such ideas form the basis of certain methods used to evaluate leisure resources (see, for example, references to cost benefit analysis and travel distance methods in Clawson and Knetsch, 1966; Smith, 1983; Stephens and Wallace, 1993).

Case study

Leisure activities

Leisure is often divided into a number of separate categories, such as indoor and outdoor leisure, sport, countryside recreation, arts and entertainment and tourism. These are not clearly demarcated, discrete categories and in some cases the amount of overlap is substantial. For example, what is the difference between countryside recreation, rural tourism and rural sport? A gentle stroll in the countryside would not qualify as sport but many other countryside recreations, such as cycling, angling, orienteering and climbing, no doubt would. However, a gentle countryside stroll might involve tourism, as it could well be undertaken as part of a rural holiday or, depending on how tourism is defined, by someone who had travelled to the countryside from further afield for a day trip. Despite these problems, many texts do attempt to distinguish between different groups of activities as, given the massive variety of leisure activities, some classification system is needed in order to allow any discussion to be manageable. By way of providing some case study examples of the changing nature of demand and participation within leisure, three such areas will be examined here: home-centred leisure, countryside recreation and sport.

Home-centred leisure

The home has always played some role in leisure provision, if for no other reason than that most people have always spent a good part of their lives there and have needed some amusements to occupy themselves. However, its relative importance has changed through time and it has possessed different significance for different age, gender and social groups. In earlier times the cramped, uncomfortable conditions of working-class homes may have persuaded men, at least, to spend much of their spare time at the tavern, although the middle-class Georgian and Victorian parlour was certainly the venue for considerable leisure activity, such as reading, music, painting and social entertaining. The home has also been the centre for much leisure associated with the family, an aspect that is covered in Chapter 4. In the twentieth century, and especially in the later decades, as homes became more comfortable to live in, home-centred leisure flourished (see Chapter 1). Table 3.1 highlights the growth of some of this activity for the period 1977 to 1996; with the exception of dressmaking/needlework/knitting, all the forms listed have experienced growth. Furthermore, a recent report by Leisure Industries Research Centre (1998) forecast home-centred leisure to increase by 20 per cent between 1997 and 2002 (see also Chapter 6). Such leisure includes both traditional forms – e.g. children's play and many hobbies and crafts – and various activities linked to new technologies.

Although some hobbies can be pursued elsewhere, many occur in the home. They include long-established, traditional activities, such as gardening, painting and various forms of collecting, together with various crafts, such as modelling activities, tapestry and knitting, furniture making and upholstery, dressmaking, cookery and flower arranging (a more detailed discussion of hobbies and crafts can be found in Haywood *et al.* (1995)). According

▶

Case study continued

Table 3.1   Participation in various forms of home-centred leisure, 1977–96

Persons aged 16 and over	Percentage participating in the 4 weeks before interview							
Leisure activities	1977	1980	1983	1986	1987	1990	1993	1996
Watching TV	97	98	98	98	99	99	99	99
Visiting/entertaining friends or relations	91	91	91	94	95	96	96	96
Listening to radio	87	88	87	86	88	89	89	88
Listening to records/tapes	62	64	63	67	73	76	77	78
Reading books	54	57	56	59	60	62	65	65
Gardening	42	43	44	43	46	48	48	48
DIY	35	37	36	39	43	43	42	42
Dressmaking/needlework/ knitting	29	28	27	27	27	23	22	22

Source: Office for National Statistics (1996) *Living in Britain: Results from the 1996 General Household Survey.*

to the General Household Survey (Table 3.1), in 1996 22 per cent of adults participated in dressmaking, needlework or knitting and as many as 42 per cent in DIY and 48 per cent in gardening.

Many hobbies, such as gardening, DIY and various crafts, possess some interesting aspects when viewed in a leisure context. Many were no doubt born of necessity, especially in working-class households where such activities provided many products that otherwise could not have been purchased. Today, the extent to which the utility element is of paramount importance or whether such activities are pursued for their intrinsic value is often unclear and, thus, how far they can be defined truly as leisure is debatable (see Chapter 2). Many hobbies have often been associated with children's leisure, no doubt because they can be pursued on an individual basis in the home, as children will not necessarily have the freedom to spend as much time elsewhere. And it is generally accepted that many such hobbies will be abandoned once children become adults and embrace other opportunities.

While many of these home-based activities have been pursued for generations, what is relatively new is the huge demand for associated artefacts and literature and an equally massive industry and related retail business that is ever eager to supply such demand. The modest hardware store and ironmongers have given way to garden centres and large-scale DIY retail outlets which can now supply anything, no matter how large or small, that the enthusiastic gardener or house-improver might require. Furthermore, a huge market for hobby-related books and magazines has also developed to cater for such interests, as an observation at any bookshop will readily demonstrate. Children's leisure is another example of this. Various toys were already being manufactured for middle-class children in Victorian times but today the demand for toys is huge and is no longer capable of being catered for by the traditional high-street toy shop. Department stores and mail order firms all have substantial toy departments, while the most recent development is the establishment of large-scale toy outlets such as Toys Я Us, often located in suburban retail parks (see Chapter 8). Of course, a lot of this demand could be supply-led, especially given the enormous advertising that is pursued, and it could also be part of a very different form of leisure activity, that of leisure shopping. Nevertheless, whatever the reason, the opportunities provided by such widespread commercialisation have certainly transformed the nature and quality of much of this home-centred leisure, even though the underlying interests may not have changed dramatically.

The other major development in home-centred leisure is also linked to substantial commercialisation but involves those activities associated with new technology. As

Case study continued

indicated in Chapter 1, the expansion of television owner-ship in the 1950s and 60s radically changed home-centred leisure and at the end of the twentieth century, 95 per cent of all households owned at least one television (ONS, 2001). Since then a succession of technological developments – colour television, stereo systems, video recorders, electronic games systems, compact disc play-ers, home computers and DVDs, the Internet, satellite and digital television and interactive television – have brought into the home a whole array of leisure-related, electronic gadgetry that has totally revolutionised home leisure. At the end of the 1990s, 38 per cent of house-holds possessed a personal computer compared with 18 per cent a decade earlier and the ratio of households possessing a video recorder had increased from 1 in 5 in 1983 to 4 in 5 in 1999. Not only is it possible to see a whole range of films on television at scheduled times (over 50 per week on terrestrial channels and an add-itional several hundred per week via satellite), video recorders also allow still more films to be seen at times that are convenient to the viewer. And this is just fea-ture films. Satellite and, more recently, the revolution in digital television mean that well over 100 channels can be available to viewers. Home computers and electronic games' consoles allow arcade games, as well as many others, to be played at home and the Internet provides access to yet more games and amusements, as well as opportunities for social intercourse throughout the globe from the confines of the living room. Using a personal computer and modem link it is also possible to play computer games with friends, without friends having to leave their respective homes.

This expansion in the amount and quality of home-centred leisure contains what appears to be a paradox, for it has often been assumed that high levels of home leisure were in some way related to a lack of other oppor-tunities due to limited wealth, freedom or personal mobil-ity. In the same way that children may be restricted to home leisure because they will lack such facilities, so certain adults may be similarly restricted. Groups such as the disabled and women with young children, especially if they also lack income, are obvious examples (see Chapters 4 and 5 for a fuller account of the constraints on leisure for such groups). But, apart from the plight of such obvious groups, the last few decades have witnessed a growth in home leisure at a time when people have become more wealthy and acquired greater freedoms and substantial mobility. However, the paradox is not all it seems because home-centred leisure has not necessar-ily expanded at the expense of other forms. It is true that television did initially reduce cinema attendance but, despite the even greater availability of television and video today, cinema attendance is expanding (see Figure 3.1), with 56 per cent of the adult population attending in 1999/2000 compared to 34 per cent in the late 1980s (ONS, 2001). While some forms of outdoor leisure have declined, for example certain spectator sports, overall there has been a noticeable expansion in the demand for many forms of leisure that are enjoyed away from the home. In addition to increased cinema attendance, visits to various attractions, especially those concerned with heritage, have also expanded (see ONS, 2001) and the 1998 UK Day Visits Survey showed that between 1994 and 1998 the number of day visits grew by almost 15 per cent, from 5.2 to over 5.9 billion.

Countryside recreation

One form of outdoor leisure that is enjoyed away from the home is countryside recreation, which embraces many different forms. As with home-centred leisure, the cate-gorisation is based on place rather than activity and, because the countryside contains many different types of environment as well as substantial areas of space (see Chapter 7), it caters for a wide array of pursuits. As a result, countryside recreation is often subdivided into various groups on the basis of whether it is *formal* or *informal*, *passive* or *active* and *market* or *non-market*.

Formal activities incorporate organised activities, which may be centred on a private club. They often involve essential equipment and an element of organi-sation and cannot, therefore, always take place spontan-eously. Golf, water skiing and organised team games all fall into this category. Informal activities tend to be less organised and more spontaneous. They often involve little or no planning or equipment and include such pursuits as sitting, strolling or picnicking. There is no fine distinction between these two broad categories and activities such as casual sailing and fishing do not obviously fall into either group. The Venn diagram (Figure 3.10) illustrates these problems of classification in relation to activities that may take place on or near a stretch of water.

►

Case study continued

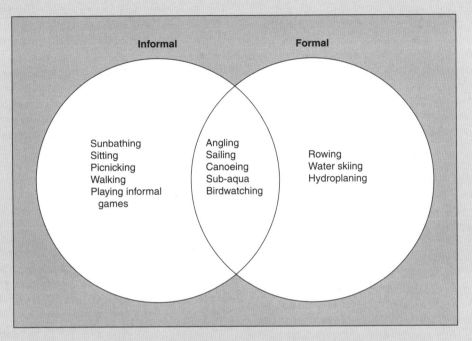

Figure 3.10 Venn diagram classifying examples of formal and informal leisure activities

The distinction between *active* and *passive* pursuits is self-explanatory but here also there is similar potential for overlap between the two categories. When, for example, does a passive stroll become an active walk? As for *market* and *non-market* activities, here the distinction is simply whether or not the participants are required to pay (market) or whether facilities are 'free' (non-market). Much countryside recreation has been traditionally free, as people are normally not charged when they walk along rural footpaths, visit country parks and picnic sites or even, in many cases, when they park their car. The extent to which visitors should be charged has attracted much debate in recent times (see, for example, McCallum and Adams, 1980; Bovaird *et al.*, 1984; Curry, 1994) and in some instances there are examples of charging being introduced for car parking and private landowners charging visitors for the recreational use of their land. However, it is difficult to see how the non-market nature of most countryside recreation will change in the foreseeable future and, as already highlighted earlier in this chapter, this makes it difficult to demonstrate the true economic nature of demand.

Various forms of countryside recreation have existed for centuries, with areas established for hunting by the aristocracy dating back to Saxon times. The urban middle classes were also attracted to the countryside in the latter half of the nineteenth century for rambling, cycling and nature study. However, as indicated in Chapter 1, it was during the 1960s that countryside recreation began to grow substantially and, although various active countryside pursuits displayed substantial rates of growth, it was the growth of informal, passive recreation that was most spectacular on account of the numbers involved. Increases in wealth, leisure time and education were all key factors in this growth but it was the improvements in personal mobility resulting from increased car ownership that is generally regarded as the most important factor. The flexibility and convenience of car ownership in a recreational context was aptly illustrated at the time by Wager (1964) – 'the motor car has become an extension of the Sunday parlour; it is a picnic hamper, carrycot and rucksack all in one'.

Various studies since the 1960s have attempted to highlight the growth and significance of countryside

Case study continued

recreation and describe its principal characteristics. Despite substantial growth in the 1960s and 70s, the overall level of countryside recreation activity has probably levelled off in more recent times. Nevertheless, while it may not be expanding, it still involves substantial numbers of people. For example, the Countryside Agency reported that in 1998 1,253 million day visits were made to the English countryside involving 66 per cent of the English population. Of these visits:

- 35% were to go walking;
- 14% were to eat and drink;
- 50% were within five miles of home;
- 69% were made regularly;
- 38% were made on foot.

Other studies have also shown that a substantial proportion of the population visits the countryside. For example, according to a frequently quoted Countryside Commission (1985) study, over 80 per cent of the population was making at least one trip to the countryside during the year and about 30 per cent were visiting on a frequent basis (at least five times per month). Of course, such statistics need to be treated with caution, as percentage figures couched in this way may give a false impression of importance. While 80 per cent of the population may have made at least one visit to the countryside during the year, a greater proportion would no doubt be watching television every day! Such figures do not really tell us much about the total level of involvement (either in terms of time or money invested).

Various surveys of countryside recreation have shown that it has more appeal for certain social groups than others (Countryside Commission, 1985; Glyptis, 1991; Harrison, 1991). While this will vary to some extent across specific forms, the profile of the typical countryside recreation-seeker would be someone who was middle-class, with a higher than average income, well educated, with access to a car, aged between 25 and 45, married with children, and possibly belonging to one or more voluntary organisations connected with the countryside. These characteristics can be explained partly as a result of certain groups lacking the necessary resources. For example, relatively poor inner-city families without their own transport would find it both expensive and physically difficult to reach the countryside, as opportunities presented by public transport are limited. However, some authorities have suggested it is connected to the intrinsic interests of various groups; that non-participation among some of those who are less well off may be due simply to lack of interest (Blunden and Curry, 1988) but that the countryside would seem to be a particularly important component of middle-class lifestyles. Work by Harrison (1991) has also shown clear differences in attitudes towards the countryside. She found that working-class people were more interested in particular countryside facilities, such as villages, pubs and 'pick-your-own' farms, whereas middle-class people tended to prefer wilderness areas, solitary activities and so on (see also Chapter 7).

Sport

With all these categories there is a problem of definition and sport is no exception; in fact, deciding exactly how it should be dealt with under this heading involves considerable complexity. Although initially sport might be regarded as active recreation, Haywood *et al.* (1995) point out that it can also be included within other categories. People engage in sport not just as participants but also as spectators and thus sport may be viewed as entertainment; and such entertainment can be enjoyed both in and away from the home. It is also the focus of a massive gambling industry, another distinct form of leisure. As has already been seen, many countryside activities can be regarded as sport and sport is also linked with tourism, with people travelling both to participate (e.g. skiing and golfing holidays) and to spectate (e.g. travelling to see the Olympics or the World Cup). Finally, sportswear is also very fashionable and has given rise to substantial retail activity, with people buying such clothing for a range of different reasons. Despite these different possibilities, however, this case study will concentrate primarily on the demand for active participation. However, even here the complexity does not end. If we take a currently accepted definition of sport, such as that suggested by the Council of Europe (1992), it is clear that many diverse forms fall under this umbrella. The Council defined sport as:

all forms of physical activity, which through casual or organised participation, aim at improving physical fitness and mental well being, forming social relationships, or obtaining results in competition at all levels. (p. 1)

▶

Case study continued

It includes both team games and solitary activity; activities with highly organised rules and those pursued informally; competitive and non-competitive pursuits; activities that require large spaces or special facilities and those with limited resource needs; indoor and outdoor pursuits; and it includes a range of activities that appeal to different age, gender and social class groups.

According to the 1996 General Household Survey (GHS), 64 per cent of those aged over 16 years had taken part in some sport or physical activity during the four weeks before interview, 46 per cent if walks (defined

as being over 2 miles) are excluded. As can be seen in Table 3.2 walking is by far the most popular physical activity, involving 44 per cent of the adult population, followed by swimming (15 per cent) and keep fit/yoga/aerobics (12 per cent).

In the last few decades, most sports have experienced significant growth rates in participation. Gratton (1996) analysed participation rates during the period 1977 to 1986 and showed that not only did participation levels increase, especially in relation to indoor sports, but that the frequency of participation also increased significantly.

Table 3.2   Participation in various forms of sports, games and physical activities (*Persons aged 16 and over*; Great Britain 1996*)

Active sports, games and physical activities	(a)	(b)	(c)	(d)
Walking+	44.5	68.2		
Any swimming	14.8	39.6	4	8.2
Swimming: indoor	12.8	35.1	4	5.9
Swimming: outdoor	2.9	14.9	6	2.3
Keep fit/yoga	12.3	20.7	7	10.8
Snooker/pool/billiards	11.3	19.2	4	6.6
Cycling	11.0	21.4	8	11.6
Weight training	5.6	9.8	7	5.3
Any soccer	4.8	8.5	5	3.3
Soccer: outdoor	3.8	6.9	5	2.3
Soccer: indoor	2.1	4.8	4	1.0
Golf	4.7	11.0	4	2.5
Running (jogging, etc)	4.5	8.0	6	3.5
Darts ++		8.6		
Tenpin bowls/skittles	3.4	15.5	2	0.7
Badminton	2.4	7.0	3	1.0
Tennis	2.0	7.1	4	1.0
Any bowls	1.9	4.6	6	1.4
Carpet bowls	1.1	3.0	5	0.8
Lawn bowls	0.9	2.8	6	0.7
Fishing	1.7	5.3	3	0.7
Table tennis	1.5	5.3	3	0.6
Squash	1.3	4.1	4	0.6
Weight lifting	1.3	2.6	8	1.3
Horse riding	1.0	3.0	8	1.0
Cricket	0.9	3.3	3	0.4
Shooting	0.8	2.8	4	0.4
Self defence	0.7	1.7	6	0.6

Case study continued

Table 3.2   (continued)

Active sports, games and physical activities	(a)	(b)	(c)	(d)
Climbing	0.7	2.5	2	0.2
Basketball	0.7	2.0	3	0.3
Rugby	0.6	1.3	4	0.3
Ice skating	0.6	3.2	1	0.1
Netball	0.5	1.4	3	0.2
Sailing	0.4	2.3	4	0.3
Motor sports	0.4	1.6	3	0.2
Canoeing	0.4	1.6	2	0.1
Hockey	0.3	1.1	4	0.2
Skiing	0.3	2.6	4	0.2
Athletics – track and field	0.2	1.2	5	0.2
Gymnastics	0.2	0.7	6	0.2
Windsurfing, boardsailing	0.2	1.1	2	0.1
At least one activity (exc. walking) ††	45.6	65.9		
At least one activity ††	63.6	81.4		
Base = 100%	15696	15696		

a) Percentage participating in the 4 weeks before interview
b) Percentage participating in the 12 months before interview
c) Average frequency of participation per participant in 4 weeks before the interview
d) Average frequency of participation per adult per year
* Includes only activities in which more than 0.5% of men or women participated in the 12 months before interview
+ In 1996 respondents were not asked how often they went walking
++ In 1996 respondents were asked about darts only in relation to the last twelve months and not the last four weeks
†† Total includes those activities not separately listed

Source: Office for National Statistics (1996) *Living in Britain: Results from the 1996 General Household Survey.*

GHS (1996) data show that this growth had levelled off and that between 1987 and 1996 there had been no significant change in overall participation. The growth of sport can be linked to a range of factors. As with many other forms of leisure, increases in leisure time, wealth and personal mobility have clearly been influential. However, there are a number of other factors that have played an important role and these include education, health promotion, fashion and the provision of facilities.

The role of education in sport is a long-established one. As outlined in Chapter 1, some of the key features of modern sport originated in the public schools of the mid nineteenth century. Throughout the twentieth century sport has been an important part of the curriculum (see Chapter 12) and for many people their only contact with sport has been through school. Apart from making sport compulsory for certain age groups, schools have also provided various facilities for sport that are not so readily available outside school. Thus, for many people, once they leave school, contact with sport is lost. In recent decades more children have remained at school for longer, partly as a result of the raising of the school-leaving age in 1974 and partly to gain extra qualifications to gain entry to the expanded higher education sector. Thus, more people are likely to have continued playing sport as a result of this but also, with student numbers in higher education having increased from 416,000 in 1970 to 1,107,000 at the end of the 1990s (ONS, 2001), the continuation will have been further extended.

Education is also linked to the promotion of certain perceived benefits associated with sport, especially those of health and fitness. Such benefits are clearly emphasised in schools but they are more widely advertised as well, such as 'Sport for All' campaigns. Not only

Case study continued

is regular physical activity promoted as being good for health, both physical and mental, it is also seen as a means of making the body more attractive. And, with Western civilisation becoming increasingly obsessed with health and personal appearance, sport has been identified by many as a means of achieving these desired goals and adopted as an integral part of their lifestyles. Such developments have clearly helped to make sport fashionable, even glamorous, and this is further reinforced through leading sports players becoming important role models and fashion icons.

Sport also attracts considerable media coverage, with satellite television devoting four separate channels exclusively to sport and the different television companies offering substantial sums of money to secure the right to broadcast an ever-increasing number of sporting events. While this in itself is only evidence of a growth in the demand to watch sport, it is hard to think that it will not have some influence in encouraging active participation as well.

Finally, sport has also been promoted through the provision of facilities. In addition to provision at educational establishments (see Chapter 12 for a fuller account of their use) and provision for some sports in the private sector (see Chapter 10), local authorities, often with grant aid from the Sports Council, have also provided substantial facilities, such as swimming pools and sports centres, in the last three decades. For example, Gratton and Taylor (1991) concluded that the large increase in participation in indoor sport was due to the massive public investment in indoor swimming pools and sports centres during the 1970s and 1980s (see Chapter 9).

While many more people are now engaging in sport, there are various constraints that limit participation for some. Apart from the problem of *deferred demand* in some places arising from lack of facilities, there are also various social constraints (see Figure 3.7). Age and physical disability, for example, may prevent some from pursuing certain sports and traditionally much sport has also been male oriented (although this is now changing) or related to certain social class groups. All these factors are examined in more detail in the following chapters.

● ● ● ● Conclusions

This chapter has attempted to examine various aspects of leisure demand in terms of both its general usage and its more specific economic meaning. It has considered key definitions, the various economic, social and motivational factors affecting demand, and its temporal and spatial aspects. In addition, it has also examined a number of leisure forms – home-centred leisure, countryside recreation and sport – in order to illustrate some of the key themes. Given its focus on 'demand', the chapter has emphasised economic considerations and has only briefly considered the various social aspects that also affect participation. These will now be considered in more detail in the following chapters.

Questions

1 Identify the various costs involved in participating in a range of different forms of leisure and discuss the problems of this for an economic analysis of demand.

2 What factors might influence people in their decision to work longer hours or have more leisure time?

3 Discuss the problems associated with the use of the term 'demand' when it is applied to the study of leisure.

4 To what extent do economic factors influence the demand for leisure?

5 Examine the influence of non-economic factors on the demand for leisure.

6 With reference to the graph in Figure 3.1, suggest reasons for the changing nature of cinema attendance during the second half of the twentieth century. You might also wish to refer to Chapter 1.

References

Blunden, J. and Curry, N. (1988) *A Future for Our Countryside*, Oxford: Blackwell.

Bovaird, T., Tricker, M. and Stoakes, R. (1984) *Recreation Management and Pricing*, Aldershot: Gower.

Clawson, M. and Knestch, J. (1966) *Economics of Outdoor Recreation*, Baltimore: Johns Hopkins University Press.

Cooper, C. *et al.* (1998) *Tourism: Principles and Practice* (2nd edition), Harlow: Longman.

Council of Europe (1992) *European Sports Charter*, Strasbourg, France: Council of Europe.

Countryside Commission (1985) *National Countryside Recreation Survey, 1984*, CCP 201, Cheltenham: The Commission.

Curry, N. (1994) *Countryside Recreation, Access and Land Use Planning*, London: Spon.

Fishbein, M. and Ajzen, I. (1975) *Belief, Attitude and Behaviour*, Reading, Mass: Addison-Wesley.

Glyptis, S. (1991) *Countryside recreation*, Harlow: Longman.

Gold, J.R. (1980) *An Introduction to Behavioural Geography*, Oxford: Oxford University Press.

Gratton, C. (1996) 'Great Britain', in Cushman, G. *et al.* (ed.) *World Leisure Participation: Free Time in the Global Village*, Wallingford: CAB International.

Gratton, C. and Taylor, P. (1985) *Sport and Recreation: An Economic Analysis*, London: Spon.

Gratton, C. and Taylor, P. (1991) *Government and the Economics of Sport*, Harlow: Longman.

Gratton, C. and Taylor, P. (1992) *Economics of Leisure Services Management* (2nd edition), Harlow: Longman.

Harrison, C. (1991) *Countryside Recreation in a Changing Society*, London: TMS Partnership.

Hayes, N. (2000) *Foundations of Psychology*, London: Thomson Learning.

Haywood, L., Kew, F., Bramham, P., Spink, J., Capernerhurst, J. and Henry, I. (1995) *Understanding Leisure*, Cheltenham: Stanley Thornes.

Leisure Industries Research Centre/Leisure Consultants (1998) *Leisure Forecasts 1998–2002*, Sheffield: Leisure Industries Research Centre.

McCallum, J.D. and Adams, J.G.L. (1980) 'Charging for countryside recreation', *Transactions of the Institute of British Geographers*, vol. 5, 350–68.

Maslow, A. (1954) *Motivation and Personality*, New York: Harper and Row.

Office of National Statistics (2001) *Social Trends, No. 31*, London: The Stationary Office.

Ryan, C. (1991) *Recreational Tourism: A Social Science Perspective*, London: Routledge.

Smith, S. L. J. (1983) *Recreation Geography*, Harlow: Longman.

Standevan, J. and De Knop, P. (1999) *Sport Tourism*, Champaign, Ill: Human Kinetics.

Stephens, B. and Wallace, C. (1993) 'Recreation, Tourism and Leisure through the Lens of Economics', in Perkins, H.C. and Cushman, G. (eds) *Leisure, Recreation and Tourism*, Auckland: Longman Paul.

Wager, J. (1964) 'How Common is the Land?' *New Society*, 30 July.

Further reading

The economic nature of demand can be found in two texts by Gratton and Taylor (1985) *Sport and Recreation: An Economic Analysis* and (1992) *Economics of Leisure Services Management*, as well as the text by Tribe (1999) *The Economics of Leisure and Tourism*, Oxford: Butterworth-Heinemann.

Cooper *et al.* (1998) *Tourism: Principles and Practice* provides a good coverage of tourism demand.

The text by Haywood *et al.* (1995) *Understanding Leisure*, provides detailed coverage of the demand for various leisure forms.

Useful websites

www.statistics.gov.uk/
www.english.sports.gov.uk/
www.staruk.org.uk/

Chapter 4 ● ● ● ●

Leisure lifestyles, gender and the family

The range of different individual factors that affect our leisure lifestyles, and the interplay between those different factors at different times, mean that not surprisingly our leisure lifestyles are highly dynamic. Torkildsen (1999) divides the factors influencing our participation and leisure choices into three distinct groups (Table 4.1):

1 Personal factors – those that are specific to the individual and include 'his or her stage in life, needs, interests, attitudes, abilities, upbringing and personality'.
2 Social and circumstantial factors – those relating 'to the circumstances and situations in which individuals find themselves, the social setting of which they are a part, the time at their disposal, their job and their income'.
3 Opportunity factors – these include the 'resources, facilities, programmes, activities and their quality and attractiveness, and the management of them'.

While each of these factors in turn are deserving of in-depth analysis, it is both difficult and false to isolate them from each other. This leaves the problem of which starting point or angle to take in any exploration of leisure lifestyles, and it is indeed difficult to justify one approach over another. The remainder of this chapter, however, starts this process by concentrating on the influence of the family on the individual and visa versa. This inevitably draws in personal, social and opportunity factors, and highlights the complex nature of their interplay. The different influential factors interact to produce differing effects on the individual at different points in the family life cycle. In the traditional family life cycle this results, in particular, in marked differences between men and women's leisure.

Objectives

To:
● *outline the traditional family life cycle and understand its impact on both family and individual leisure lifestyles*

- *understand the effect of the needs and preoccupations of individuals on family leisure*

- *explore the effect of contemporary lifestyle changes on the family life cycle and leisure lifestyles*

- *understand the particular and changing impact of gender/gender roles on family and individual leisure lifestyles.*

Table 4.1   Influences on leisure participation and choices

Personal factors	Social and circumstantial factors	Opportunity factors
Age	Occupation	Resources available
Stage in life cycle	Income	Facilities – type and quality
Gender	Disposable income	Awareness
Marital status	Material wealth and goods	Perception of opportunities
Dependants and ages	Car ownership and mobility	Recreation services
Will and purpose of life	Time available	Distribution of facilities
Personal obligations	Duties and obligations	Access and location
Resourcefulness	Home and social environment	Choice of activity
Leisure perception	Friends and peer groups	Transport
Attitudes and motivation	Social roles and contacts	Costs: before, during, after
Interests and preoccupation	Environment factors	Management: policy and support
Skills and ability – physical, social and intellectual	Mass leisure factors	Marketing
	Education and attainment	Programming
Personality and confidence	Population factors	Organization and leadership
Culture born into	Cultural factors	Social accessibility
Upbringing and background		Political policies

Source: Torkildsen, G. (1999) *Leisure and Recreation Management*, 4th Edn., Table 5.1, p. 114, London: E & FN Spon (Routledge).

● ● ● ● Leisure defined and the family

Torkildsen (1999) identifies duties and obligations as one of the social and circumstantial factors affecting our leisure patterns. This is an area of particular importance when leisure is explored within the context of the family. It, in fact, raises a number of key questions regarding the very nature of leisure. How can leisure, for instance, which has freedom as a defining part of its nature, take place within the social context of the family unit, which by definition involves constraints, duties and obligations arising from specific role requirements. Dumazedier explored this issue as early as 1967 and indeed regarded all leisure within the context of family at best to be 'semi-leisure' because of the attachment of such duties and obligations.

Nevertheless, many individuals place great value upon family leisure, giving it preference over alternative leisure forms and contexts. According to Kelly (1982, cited in Critcher, Bramham and Tomlinson, 1995), this is due to a number of key factors:

- It may be that individuals do not value freedom as highly as we might at first think and instead prefer the relative comfort of constraint and familiarity.
- Role comfort within the context of the family unit brings with it the ease of acceptance and trust, and hence the relaxation gained from participation in a context where one is comfortable, familiar and can predict the behaviour of others, which is conducive to a positive leisure experience.
- The types of leisure which complement individual roles within the family may provide us with more satisfaction because of the relationships involved and therefore be valued more than freedom.
- Family members are convenient companions, they may also most often be the most available at a given time, therefore affecting the decision of the leisure context and companionship, that is, they live in the same place and may be more likely to have complementary timetables.
- Leisure can be used as an important vehicle to develop and strengthen key relationships. Leisure forms an important focus for sharing and communication within the nuclear family. It can provide an area of shared interest and a space for more spontaneous interaction, as well as a legitimate reason for independence. The family is not only an important resource for leisure but, conversely, leisure can be an important tool for family development.

An individual's role within the family unit undoubtedly profoundly affects their leisure participation, resources and opportunities. An individual's leisure lifestyle is heavily dependent on the expectations, duties and obligations placed on them by the family and on the way in which the family unit allocates its resources, including material, financial and time resource allocation (see Chapter 4 case study for further detail of family expenditure on leisure). The family unit, on the other hand, may provide the necessary companionship, safety, finance and freedom to facilitate a fulfilling leisure experience. It is also instrumental in forming the individual and their attitude towards leisure because of the type of leisure opportunities it provides, and through the sanctioning or disapproval of specific leisure pursuits.

●●●● Leisure in the context of family

Rhona and Robert Rapoport (1975) produced one of the most influential accounts of the family and leisure. Alongside writers such as Kelly (1970, cited in Critcher, Bramham and Tomlinson, 1995), Roberts (1970) and Sillitoe (1969), they saw the family as the basis for an individual's leisure lifestyle. This perception is supported in recent work by Godbey (1994), who clearly identifies the family as the key social unit within which an individual learns about the world. The family plays a key role in the whole socialisation process including, as indicated above, the development of an individual's leisure values and behaviour.

The Rapoports proposed a family life cycle model, which charted the interplay of the family lifestage, work and leisure. An individual's leisure needs, wants and attitudes are shown to be profoundly affected by the preoccupations of career and family. These preoccupations constantly change focus throughout the family life cycle, which results in leisure lifestyles undergoing constant revision and adjustment. Changing preoccupations bring about conflict because of competing pressures within the spheres of family, occupation and leisure. Examples of such conflicts include the competing pressures of children's leisure needs and wants and those of their parents, and the pressure on young couples to continue to partake in peer group activities competing with the opportunity for leisure participation as a couple. These preoccupations and conflicts are expressed differently by different individuals and different family members in relation to their leisure lifestyles and the different interests and activities that they encompass. The individual choices made, needless to say, will often require trade-off and sacrifice within certain spheres to restore a life pattern that incorporates re-creation and harmony.

The resultant changes in leisure patterns that may arise are explored by the Rapoports within four key stages of the family life cycle.

1 Youth/young people

This first stage in the family life cycle concentrates on adolescence and is sometimes stated as the school years between 15 and 19. Chronological age is, however, misleading in that leisure lifestyles and life preoccupations are more dependent on psychological and physical maturity. This is a stage of immense change and unpredictability due to the experimentation and exploration that arises as a result of the preoccupation of establishing an individual personal identity.

During this stage, leisure preferences can change almost by the minute and are strongly affected by fads and fashions. There is a constant generation, up-take and then lapsing of new and different activities. Leisure choice at this stage is strongly influenced by peers and often a need to rebel against authority, including the family. Rebellion against and difference from those in authority are emphasised through youth culture in leisure and are expressed not just by activities but also by clothing and language. Music is a key leisure pursuit that has been used by youth in this way; for example, Beatlemania and flower power in the 1960s, glam rock and punk in the 1970s, New Romantics, indie and rap in the 1980s and, more recently, the rave scene and house music, hip-hop and garage in the 1990s. Leisure provides an avenue for independence and a key means of developing self-confidence and self-knowledge. It can be a vital tool for self-expression and exploration, including sexual and social identity.

It is the characteristically rebellious and exploratory nature of leisure at this stage that has led to public concern about anti-social forms of leisure arising within this group. This has historically created a feeling that society needs to provide for and to channel youth into productive, socially acceptable pursuits. The wider public ironically has often seen leisure as a potential means of control for youth/young people. It has attempted to channel self-expression, exploration and rebellion through the provision of acceptable social and leisure spaces, and activities 'policed' but not overtly adult-controlled and constrained. Not surprisingly, this has often proved unsuccessful, as highlighted by Cohen (1997) in a case study where leisure facilities were provided to counteract vandalism and subsequently resulted in the vandalism of those very facilities.

Despite this rebellion, the types of leisure pursuits engaged in at this stage are in reality controlled by a number of different influences including family, school and the wider community. Ability to pursue key leisure forms is often limited by financial resources, which certainly in the early part of this stage are usually provided by parents and perhaps later supplemented by part-time work. The school attended by the young person can also play an important role in providing them with the resources to develop and explore meaningful and fulfilling interests. It may equally stifle creativity and personal development if all the goals set are vocational or academic. This is an important phase for a more holistic educational approach. However, it could be argued that the type of leisure education received within the formal education system will largely depend on family background including class and hence the type of schooling available (see Chapter 12 for further exploration of the impact of education on leisure lifestyles).

An adolescent in a working-class family is not only less likely to have choice in respect of the type of schooling received but is also more likely to be an early school leaver. Early leavers are likely to be low paid and often in less fulfilling employment and, although financial independence may be achieved, this may not be supported by resourcefulness and a supportive work environment for developing a satisfactory, challenging and fulfilling leisure lifestyle. This combined with the sudden absence of facilities provided by the education system can be problematic. Club membership is less likely in working-class families, leading to an absence of knowledge, for instance, of the skill levels, vocabulary and dress code required in order to easily integrate into the relevant club scene. Such exclusion during adolescence is more likely to promote the uptake of anti-social leisure activities.

Community influences may also be dependent on family characteristics, for example, children of less affluent families are likely to have less experience of the wider community and are more likely to have a knowledge that is restricted to local opportunities and influences. Individuals of influence on the leisure lifestyle may be quite remote. Role models may be found in, for example, the music industry and the national and international sports arena.

The resultant leisure lifestyles at the end of this stage will reflect the individual's ability to successfully use their changing preoccupations to develop a personal identity and meaningful leisure interests. Those who channel preoccupations into meaningful interests at this stage are often more successful in maintaining and developing a meaningful leisure lifestyle in later years.

2 Young adults

The Rapoports took this next phase to start with school leaving and to extend to approximately the first few months of marriage, at which point a young couple would move from the young adult stage into the early establishment phase. While the search for personal identity continues in this stage, and probably throughout life, this is no longer the preoccupation at the forefront for most individuals. The pursuit of goals that relate to social identity are now of greater importance. This leads to the use of leisure to pursue four key areas of interest: occupation, intimate and committed relationships, parental and family interests (including siblings and the extended family), and friendships.

The social institutions identified with, and the extent of this identification, differs. Work is a key area of identification and traditionally more so for men than women. Although individuals differ in the extent to which they are committed to work and take their social and personal identities from their occupation, unemployment in this stage can be particularly difficult given the social identity preoccupation and the use of work in many cases to define social status. When the young adult does enter the workplace, this marks a period in which there is usually considerable disposable income with few financial and family (social) responsibilities. Hence, this phase is characterised by financial independence, allowing greater exploration of the commercial entertainment and leisure sectors (see Table 4.2).

Financial independence provides the freedom to pursue leisure activities that may be categorised as relationship-seeking, such as nightclubs, bars and commercial sports facilities. Leisure activities and the leisure environment play a key role at this stage in providing the context within which intimate relationships and friendships can be developed. Individual relationships and intimate relationships become key foci as opposed to peer groups. This was particularly regarded as the case for women when traditionally marriage was seen as the key institution from which they gained their social identity.

New friendships are formed in this stage, moving away from school and peer groups to couples relating to each other, and to association with work colleagues. Friendships are still important but are focused on developing a social rather than

Table 4.2   Penetration of leisure activities by lifestage, April/May 1999 (Base: 1000 adults)

Lifestage	Cinema	Nightclub/ discotheque	Health and fitness club	Tenpin bowling
	%	%	%	%
Pre-family	85	73	43	43
Family	69	35	32	34
Empty nesters/ no family	50	19	23	21
Post-family	29	5	8	6

Source: BMRB/Mintel, *The Leisure Business: The Consumer*, Figure 104.

individual (personal) identity. Friends provide routes for introductions to new social contexts – organisations, interests and new networks. It is difficult without this for young adults to break into more established social groups, due to many clubs and associations treating new (young adult) members as outsiders and with suspicion.

This second phase is also marked by a more general reintegration into the family, a rebuilding of relationships with parents and siblings. There is a need following the rebelliousness of the previous stage to reintegrate within the family on new terms that recognise the individual as an independent adult, and usually, eventually, as part of a couple. Leisure again may play a key role in this reintegration and in building relationships between the individual's partner and their family. Potential in-laws are often tested out in leisure contexts, such as visits to restaurants and pubs and the sharing of interests and hobbies.

3 Establishment

The most extensive stage of the life cycle is the establishment stage, characterised by investment in long-term relationships through marriage and children, and investments in work, friends and the community. As the key intimate relationship develops there is a move away from the leisure environments used for meeting a partner to those supporting the building of a longer-term relationship. Activities shift from being group based to those shared as a couple. Leisure at this point may often again become home and family based, with a developing focus on saving to support the formation of a new family unit.

The most dramatic change in amount and quality of leisure time for a couple, however, comes with the birth of children. The commitment of parenting ensures that leisure becomes concentrated around the needs of the children. Traditionally for most couples, the arrival of children leads to a concentration by the man on financial productivity, in order to support the increasing needs of the family, and a concentration by the woman on home-making, in order to produce a stable home environment.

During this period the husband may still maintain leisure activities outside the home and family that relate to his occupational social network. Leisure pursuits are often used during this stage to assist in career development – for example, the classic case of the business deal clinched on the golf course or tennis court. Being a member of the correct leisure club can provide the most appropriate social group and contact for career advancement. Leisure is also valued at this stage for its re-creative capacity. Productivity is a key part of this phase and leisure is used in opposition to work and to restore productive efficiency.

This can be a time when there is the danger of a serious problem within family development and relationships. There is a danger of the man resenting his partner for having the opportunity to spend leisure time and gain enjoyment from participating with the children. He may feel trapped into a specific form of 'leisure' linked with work and financial productivity. For women within the traditional family structure, they may feel they are losing out in not having access to any leisure time outside the home and in spending all of their available time servicing the leisure needs of their children.

Towards the middle of the establishment stage, when work and parenting patterns become more established, career choices have been made and individual parenting roles and styles have been developed, there often comes a period of increased stability. This period may even be characterised by a certain level of routine, built around a long period of supporting children through school and 'growing-up'. Leisure continues to be family centred, often with consumption forming an important part of those shared leisure experiences. This can be seen from the growth in the number of pubs with excellent family facilities and the focus on leisure shopping as a family day out at out-of-town shopping centres such as Bluewater in Kent and Meadowhall in Sheffield. This is usually fuelled by optimism about future ability to meet financial commitments, which is supported by an established career with retirement at this stage not being in view.

In this period leisure pursuits may have some focus on meeting needs ignored in the early establishment phase due to the intense concentration on career progression for the man and on child-rearing for the woman. Mobility and travel is often limited in the early part of this phase and may be pursued as increased day trips and family holidays. There may be greater experimentation with food as a leisure pursuit as it becomes easier to eat out as a family. There is, however, a continuing strong emphasis on home-centred pursuits, especially given the new leisure technologies available to the modern family.

For the woman in the traditional family this part of the establishment phase sees a reduction in the time needed for parenting, as schooling takes up a large part of the day for the children. This can be problematic as there is a sudden lack of focus for leisure, but equally it can be an opportunity to take on new challenges and interests, and to further develop existing hobbies (see Chapter 3, Home-centred leisure, for further details).

For the man of a traditional family, work may now be more stable and secure, allowing greater involvement in family leisure. On the other hand, where promotion and increased responsibility continues to be sought and gained, this may create the difficulty of constantly feeling torn between family and work. It has been argued that where career advancement continues in this stage there is an inevitable sacrificing of both personal and family leisure involvements.

Mid-establishment deals with the adolescent phase of offspring, a phase involving a great deal of negotiation and boundary establishment. This can be a time of great difficulty that may be aided by effective negotiation in the family leisure arena, with particular regard to identifying and respecting the time needed for both joint and independent leisure by all family members.

The end of the establishment stage brings new challenges, with children becoming more independent, leaving school and home. Leisure, particularly for women, can at this point provide the essential new source of self-esteem and psychological investment previously attached to child-rearing. Children no longer place the same limits upon a couple's leisure lifestyles and there is a need to refocus leisure pursuits, given the 'empty nest'. This provides an important opportunity to refocus leisure away from the home and to explore and take up new activities. In addition, this is a time when there is an opportunity to pursue leisure as a couple again, through new interests or drawing each other into previously individual interests. It can be an exciting time in which leisure can play a major role in rediscovering each other and the rediscovery of identity as a couple. Grandchildren may also provide a potential new focus for leisure at this time.

4 Later years

The later years' stage is dominated by retirement, with the core preoccupations of 'social and personal integration'. There is a need to achieve a sense of meaning and harmony with the world. The Rapoports identified this as a particularly difficult stage for those in a society where youth and productivity are held to be of great importance. This integration is more readily achievable in a society where the wisdom and experience of those in this stage are highly valued and they are seen as important role models. While those societies such as the UK, which are relatively highly productive, provide the best support for this group, individuals within this group are often valued less. This value system is reflected in the leisure environment, which becomes goal directed and competitive and can alienate those in the later years' phase. Partly because of this emphasis, and hence a need for continued productivity, voluntary work may form a strong focus for leisure in later years. This may be reinforced by a preoccupation with the auditing of the meaningfulness of an individual's life and, as a result, the need to pursue areas yet unfulfilled through the voluntary sector (see also Chapter 11). For others, rather than a positive refocusing, such auditing results in passive acceptance of ambitions not fulfilled, resentment and even depression.

The engagement in less physically active pursuits, often seen as characteristic of the elderly, such as reading and television, only becomes prominent in the later phases of this stage. Activities pursued in this stage will often reflect a continuation of earlier leisure patterns. Those with previously active and busy leisure lifestyles are more likely to continue with these; those holding off until retirement to pursue certain activities find it more difficult to engage with the social and cultural context for many leisure interests. Continuation of previous leisure patterns may, however, prove difficult for some individuals. For men, where leisure has been tied up with work and particularly with career progression, the absence of the work environment may psychologically, if not actually, provided a barrier to continued participation.

Financial restriction may make continuity of some activities difficult at this stage, especially for those reliant on a state pension. Those with a substantial private income are more likely to have been in the type of occupation that allows continued involvement, for example, professions where those beyond retirement may continue to write or be a board member or to do consultancy work. This in turn allows continuity for leisure patterns through contacts, in addition to adequate financial resources (see Chapter 5 for a more detailed discussion of leisure and ageing).

●●●● The family life cycle: a contemporary analysis

As highlighted above, Rhona and Robert Rapoport identified a number of key periods of transition for individuals and key turning points within a person's lifetime that inevitably impact upon their leisure lifestyle. Their four-stage family life cycle, however, begins with adolescence as the first key period of transition, without first exploring childhood leisure. While it might be argued that leisure is very much prescribed by adults prior to adolescence, it cannot be denied that the family has a profound effect at this stage. Not only does the family to a large degree control the types of activities pursued, when, where and with whom, but in doing so it forms attitudes and builds leisure skills that will also affect an individual's leisure lifestyle during the later stages of the life cycle. It is important in the light of this that this stage is therefore acknowledged as it will determine the physical and psychological resources an individual brings to the later stages.

In addition, the Rapoports' model is formed on the basis that lifestyle decisions give priority to work and family, which then impact on leisure. There is, however, evidence that for an increasing group in contemporary society the primary motivation is leisure, which then impacts on work and family. There are those who clearly choose their social network, occupation and relationships to fit in with their primary commitment to specific leisure pursuits. One example of such a group is the surfers on the west coast of England. For this group their priority is to build their lifestyle around the activity of surfing and the social networks linked with it. Their choice of where to live is determined by the surf, not by their work. Their jobs are chosen to fit around their need to be on the west coast and the freedom required in order to allow them to pursue their love of surfing.

Given the wider picture and the acknowledgements of some changes of emphasis, it can, however, be seen that the key issues identified within the life cycle by the Rapoports are still of relevance today. These must, nevertheless, be considered within the context of the generally busier modern life cycle with the increased number and impact of the turning points experienced. We must, therefore, encompass the following additional aspects within a modern analysis of the family life cycle and leisure lifestyles:

(a) An increase in divorce and remarriage in recent decades compared with the 50s, 60s and early 70s (see Table 4.3), which preceded the work of the Rapoports, means that individuals may return to and re-enter the establishment phase more than once.

Table 4.3 Marriage trends for women in England and Wales

	1961	1996
First marriages	312,300	192,800
Remarriages of divorced women	18,000	79,000

Source: Mintel (1998) *Women and Finance: Women and Society*, ONS/Mintel.

This may result in individuals having ties with more than one family. For men in particular, it is a situation that may mean, for instance, responsibilities at weekends to children from previous relationships, which provide a different dimension to family leisure. This can widen the range of pursuits for each party, but it can also place constraints on participation with those outside the family. For those who remain primary carers for the children (currently, in the main, the mother), as a single head of the household the parenting commitment required can severely restrict leisure time and resources (see also (d)). This can restrict the use of leisure for building further intimate and committed relationships. The phases of being married, single, separated and a parent are now much less predictable. While this may restrict leisure participation, leisure can provide a much needed area of continuity during these periods of change and can also assist in adapting to change and building new relationships.

(b) As more women have entered the workplace (Table 4.4) and developed careers there is less of a concentration on men being the ones identifying with the social institution of work during the young adult stage. Young women increasingly identify with the workplace.

There is a change from mainly men giving priority to occupational identity to more women also seeing this as primary or at least equal to marriage and family. This has led to increasing numbers of women in the workplace and returning to work after pregnancy, or after children start playschool, nursery or full-time schooling. This again adds to the number of turning points in the family life cycle.

The increase in full-time employment for women affects the available resources for servicing family leisure. While two-worker families may have greater financial resources and hence greater buying power in terms of leisure space and equipment, the time resource may be limited. This time resource for children may be provided by others, for example, nannies, childminders and grandparents, but may severely limit the leisure lifestyles of the parents, as well as their involvement and influence upon their children's leisure. For grandparents who take a more active role as carers in these circumstances, this may be both restrictive and/or provide a much needed focus for leisure in the later stage of the life cycle.

(c) There is a general and continuing increase in single households. In 1981, 22 per cent of households in Great Britain were single-person households and by 1996 this had increased to 27 per cent. In addition, there is a tendency towards later marriages, although some of the increase in the average age of marriage for both men and women can be countered by an increase in the number of couples

Table 4.4   Economically active women in the UK

	1961	1971	1992	1998
Economically Active Women (%)	37.5	43.6	49.2	51.1

Source: Rapoport, R. and Rapoport, R.N., with Strelitz, Z. (1975) *Leisure and the Family Life-Cycle*, Routledge & Kegan Paul, London, p. 189; Mintel (1998) *Women and Finance: Women, Income and Employment*, ONS/Mintel.

entering into a committed relationship in the form of cohabitation before marriage. Both these trends provide a longer period where the individual has fewer resource constraints on their leisure. They have the freedom to pursue their own leisure lifestyle and the finances to support it. This is also the case because of an increased tendency to put off having children until later. The average age for women giving birth rose from 26.4 in 1976 to 28.6 by 1996 (Mintel, 1999, *Childcare Facilities*, p. 2). On the other hand, these individuals may experience an absence of the key leisure resources provided by the nuclear family. There is evidence, however, of these being replaced for many people by a strengthening of the role of the wider community in developing their leisure lifestyles.

(d) A general increase in single parents, through parenting before marriage, divorce or bereavement, means that many go through the establishment stage with minimal support and resources, and highly constrained leisure lifestyles. *The General Household Survey 1996* found there to be 7 per cent of households with a lone parent and dependent children, an increase from 4 per cent in 1979 and 5 per cent in 1989 (Mintel, 1999, *Childcare Facilities*, p. 8).

(e) During the later stages of the youth/young people phase it is now much more likely that the additional turning point of higher education will be entered into, prolonging the onset of the establishment phase. According to HESA (cited on *The Times Higher Education Supplement* website, 2001), there were only a little over 400,000 British students in the 1965/66 academic year compared with a little under 1.8 million in the 1999/2000 academic year.

While this may mean that the individual is late in addressing the responsibilities of adulthood, leaving the education system later may lead to an increase in the skills and resources required for developing a fulfilling leisure lifestyle. The importance of the developmental experiences of students relating to a number of life spheres is increasingly recognised. There is, for instance, some acceptance that part of student life is about reaching out, experiencing and developing further/different interests and skills for meaningful leisure lifestyles and leisure interests.

College and university provide opportunities to expand networks of friends and interests and provide a much wider community influence. On the other hand, many students traditionally spend most of their time in the exclusive and false community of the college or university campus, deferring participation in the 'real' world. This all-consuming adjustment may then mean that difficulties arise on leaving.

(f) During the establishment phase the tradition of the male provider being secure in one job where promotion is gradually achieved has changed. In part this is due to individual life expectancy being increased and, therefore, with a greater amount of active time available, men are more likely to have one or more changes of jobs, occupations and careers. This, in turn, means that work patterns are less likely to become routine in the mid-establishment phase. In addition, this is less likely to be the case because of increased geographical mobility linked to job promotion and career changes, which can limit family leisure resources in terms of the involvement and support of the extended family in servicing leisure needs. Increased mobility has led to a much larger number of nuclear families living at a distance from the extended family. This can have a particularly significant impact on the servicing of the leisure needs for children of dual-worker families who may have previously relied upon grandparents, aunts and uncles and cousins.

(g) The visibility, self-confidence and acceptance of same sex couples have increased significantly in recent years. While like heterosexuals, there is no typical homosexual leisure lifestyle, there is clearly a gay leisure scene, for example, Manchester's gay festival and gay village, and the gay scene in Brighton. Leisure lifestyles are also affected by the degree of gay-friendly or gay-indifferent attitudes found at venues and facilities. A number of London businesses concentrate on providing for only this market, for example, shops such as Clone Zone, restaurants such as Balans and clubs such as Heaven. The London Tourist Board also operates a 'pink' phone line that provides information on gay interest exhibitions, clubs and restaurants. This leisure market tends to have a higher level of 'leisure poundage', that is, income not otherwise committed. Same sex couples are most often DINKs (double income, no kids) and in the establishment phase will therefore have fewer turning points and fewer constraints placed on their leisure resources, particularly those of time and mobility (Wood, 1999). This as a significant trend, however, may change in the future as increasing numbers of gay couples pursue adoption, surrogacy and donor IVF.

Gender and the family

It becomes apparent as we work through the family life cycle that the leisure lifestyles of individual members of the family are affected differently as we progress through the different stages. It is particularly evident in the traditional life cycle that women and men are affected differently during the course of changing family circumstances. The traditional life cycle, it can be argued, affords women only 'leisure' of a highly regulated nature that tends to be family centred and home based. The constraints faced by women led them to be regarded in 1977, by the Department of the Environment, as a recreationally disadvantaged group and to be a target group in the Sports Council's campaigns to promote 'Sport for All'. It is important, therefore, to explore the different constraints placed on individuals by the traditional family life cycle in relation to gender and to examine the changes that have taken place in contemporary society. It is also important in this context to recognise that a discussion of gender differences is not simply a discussion of the biological differences of males and females more usually defined as sex roles. Gender differences relate to social traits and characteristics associated with maleness and femaleness including issues of status, power and inequality. In practice, however, as the biological and social aspects interact and at times are indistinguishable, the examination of leisure and gender needs to incorporate both (Golombok and Fivush, 1994; Kimmel, 2000).

Differences in leisure lifestyle and education for leisure with respect to gender start very early and serve to reinforce the need to explore the impact of family prior to adolescence. The toys traditionally given to children would often reinforce gender difference, the playtime of girls being centred on so-called 'female' toys, for example, dolls and cooking and cleaning implements, with boys being provided with soldiers, guns and cars. This would reinforce the socially perceived masculinity and femininity of certain leisure pursuits and occupations. Gender expectations would also often be further reinforced by girls spending more time inside the home while boys spent time on rough-and-tumble outdoor activities.

Upon starting school, role expectations were further defined. Books used in schools often reinforced gender roles with specific leisure activities and professions again being identified as male or female. It was certainly rare in the 1960s to see male ballet dancers and female football and rugby players being portrayed. Girls and boys, even pre-adolescents, would usually be segregated for certain leisure activities such as soccer, rugby, netball and hockey. This is an approach that, certainly at primary level, has been shown to be unnecessary on the grounds of physical ability. The emphasis on the different types of sports taught to the different sexes also continued, with perhaps the more necessary segregation, at secondary level, and was extended into subject areas other than physical education. Handicraft subjects, for example, would often be segregated, with boys being offered woodwork and metalwork and girls being offered needlework and home economics (or more traditionally referred to as domestic science). Such approaches disadvantage both sexes in limiting freedom of choice for leisure lifestyles through lack of exposure and training in the skills required for a range of different leisure pursuits, simply because they are traditionally regarded to be the forte of one gender.

As compulsory education draws to an end, we have already seen that society traditionally places stronger pressure on women to accept marriage as 'career' and hence to be less career oriented in the workplace. These social pressures of fulfilling the role of wife and mother profoundly affect the leisure participation of young women, their leisure activities often being strongly focused towards meeting a partner. The types of leisure opportunities available to young women have also been restricted because of parental concerns regarding the moral and physical safety of female offspring. This has resulted in young women being more strongly restricted in the times and places they can pursue leisure by comparison with their male peers. In addition, because leisure pursuits tend to be used more by young women than men for meeting a suitable marriage partner, this often means that, having achieved their aim, women give up leisure activities previously participated in.

Marriage brings different changes for men including the societal pressure of being responsible for providing for their wife and eventually children. This may mean a change in leisure pursuits not brought about through choice but by the need to achieve in the work sphere, a need to fit in and be noticed in the work environment. This, in turn, may affect their partner, who may also need to adjust their leisure patterns in order to be seen to fulfil the expected social role. This may mean playing a servicing role for their husband's leisure, for example, serving tea at cricket matches and spectating at football matches. While men are clearly affected by the social pressures and expectations upon them as husbands and fathers they do, however, more often continue their leisure pursuits after marriage and find it easier to negotiate free time for leisure as recuperation from work. This is more difficult for women who have traditionally been home based, where there is a less clear differentiation between work and leisure and where negotiating leisure time can be more difficult. In addition, loss of income for women when they stop work to raise a family can provide yet another restriction on leisure opportunities. The family reduction in income at this stage, plus the additional cost of rearing children, will inevitably restrict the leisure poundage available for all family members. However, there is less likely to be a loss of economic independence for the man.

As the children grow up the couple must start to adjust to the later years' stage and the onset of retirement. For men, particularly those whose leisure activities have been strongly focused on the workplace or have taken place outside the home with work colleagues, retirement can be a difficult period. For the couple as a unit, re-adjusting to being at home together and perhaps again having the opportunity to share a great deal of leisure time can be difficult. The women may already have adjusted when the children left home, taking on new hobbies and voluntary work with a different circle of friends, and may find it difficult or may resent the need to adjust once again. This will also most often be followed at some point by adjust-ment for the woman to being widowed and in a position where she has to once again develop a leisure lifestyle without a partner.

In this brief exploration of gender and the family life cycle it is evident that gender issues are influential in leisure participation in terms of time, space and activity. It is perhaps surprising, then, that it was not really until the 1980s that there was a serious attempt to examine the relationship between leisure lifestyles and gender. This concern developed in part through the feminist movement, supported by legislation such as the Equal Opportunities Act in 1972 and the Sex Discrimination Act in 1979. This led to a heightening of awareness of the lifestyle differences and opportunities for men and women and highlighted discrepancies in participation levels that were found to be generally higher for men, especially in the areas of indoor and outdoor sports. This was not exclusively the case for all pursuits, however, participation in the arts being higher for women.

Since that early research there is no doubt that the participation levels of women have increased; for example, *The General Household Survey* reported an increase of 2.5 million in women's weekly participation in sports activities between 1987 and 1990 (Horne, J., Tomlinson, A. and Whannel, G., 1999). Effective sports provision for women has improved with the continued recognition of the need for basic support services such as the crèche. This has also partly been created by the changes in family circumstances: there are now more families where the woman is working and is financially independent, and there has been an increase in two-car families and the number of women qualified to drive, as well as a more general trend towards shared responsibility for childcare and the running of the family home. Nevertheless, there is still a significant gap in participation levels in leisure between men and women to be bridged (Table 4.5).

Table 4.5   Leisure participation for men and women in the UK

	Percentage participation in the following activities in the four weeks before interview	
	Men	Women
Indoor		
Snooker/pool/billiards	20	4
Keep fit/yoga/aerobics	7	17
Swimming	13	17
Weight training	9	3
Badminton	3	2
Squash	2	–
Tenpin bowling/skittles	4	3
Outdoor		
Horse riding	–	1
Running/jogging	7	2
Cycling	15	8
Golf	8	2
Tennis	2	2
Soccer	10	–
Fishing	3	–

Source: Adapted from Office for National Statistics (1996) *Living in Britain: Results from the 1996 General Household Survey*, p. 221, Table 13.8.

To understand these changes we must examine what lies behind the increases that have occurred. Hargreaves in 1994, for example, pointed out that, although there had been an increase of one million women participating in sports in the previous five years, this had involved a relatively narrow group of women. There continues to be under-representation of young women, single mothers, black and ethnic women and those who are unemployed or who have disabilities. Increased participation has tended to be among the white, affluent, middle class and able-bodied women (Hargreaves, 1995). Additionally, there is evidence that increased participation may largely be due to the participation of women in new sports such as windsurfing and fitness activities rather than there being any significant inroads made into sports that have traditionally been male dominated (Horne, J., Tomlinson, A. and Whannel, G., 1999).

There is clearly still a need to review and address the barriers to leisure, which prevent a more equal participation both between genders and within gender-specific groups. As identified by Clarke and Critcher cited in Haywood (1985), women are still in the position of having less leisure time, of participating less in most leisure activities and of drawing from a more limited range of options for leisure than men. Women also still spend most of their leisure time in and around the home.

While there has been a significant increase in dual-income families with both parents working, where one parent remains at home to care for children it is still, in the majority of cases, the woman. In addition, where both parents are working it is still more likely to be the case that the woman is working part time and is the primary carer for children. Even where both parents work full time it is usual for the woman to take most of the responsibility for the home and organising childcare.

Domestic responsibilities and primary responsibility for childcare make it much more difficult to structure time in a way that provides leisure time that is clearly differentiated from work. Where there is a primary role of childcare, this area of work cannot be neatly sectioned into a particular time frame in the same way as paid work outside the home. Leisure time is more often incorporated within the work time and space, which makes the primary definition of leisure as free time difficult for most women. Participation in sports activities such as, for instance, swimming may take place alongside the children, so there is therefore also a responsibility for the enjoyment and safety of the children. Even where sports facilities provide a crèche and childcare programmes there is still the need to ensure that the children are prepared and cared for first.

The apparent, if not real, difficulty of organising leisure pursuits outside the home often leads to most women caring for children concentrating their leisure lifestyle around home-based leisure. This limits the type of leisure space available and hence the number of leisure activities and opportunities. Leisure activities are, therefore, more likely to be arts and craft, reading and the watching of television. This is also borne out by the fact that men are much more likely to be members of leisure/sports clubs than women are. This is particularly the case where many of the leisure opportunities available are based on the outskirts of towns and villages and require private transport or the use of public transport to reach them. Although there has been an increase in two-car families and the number of women holding driving licences, women who are not working or who are working part-time are still likely, where there is only one family car, to have restricted access to it. The car is often needed for the occupation of the husband, especially given the increased need for commuting to the workplace.

Where women choose to remain at home and take prime responsibility for the home and children, this usually means that they are financially dependent and rely on their husband for disposable income available for leisure. This provides a psychological difficulty in relation to buying leisure. Where money is provided by the husband and has not been earned by the woman, this money is often regarded as having been provided for the running of the home and not seen as available for personal use. Money can be more easily seen as available to be spent on leisure by the person who earns it. Leisure pursuits can also be seen as more expensive for women given the addition of childcare or a crèche to the basic cost of the activity. In addition, leisure is often seen as earned as compensation for work. Domestic and family responsibilities are usually not regarded in the same light as an occupation outside the home; therefore, many women will feel they have not earned leisure in the same way as if they were working outside the home. Where women work either full or part time and have a degree of financial independence there is, however, the cost of the reduction in time and energy for personal leisure in addition to work, domestic and childcare responsibilities. It is also still the case that women are generally lower paid than men, which restricts their disposable income and hence leisure opportunities even when working.

There are still yet other factors that have an impact on women in couples, women in couples with children, and single women with and without children. One of these is access alone to leisure spaces. A number of leisure spaces have traditionally been more intimidating for women to visit alone, either from a perceived or real fear of physical danger or social stigma. Nightclubs and bars, in particular, fall into this category, as well as some sports facilities. There are also specific images historically linked to many sports. Key perceptions, characteristics and attitudes that are associated with both men and women in sport, while now being actively challenged, have left a legacy of expectations in relation to the level of participation and the types of leisure activities chosen. This was certainly traditionally true of sports activities where the active, powerful, competitive, aggressive and skilful characteristics associated with masculinity were aligned with being good on the sports field. The perceived feminine characteristics of gentleness, weakness, submissiveness, grace and agility were seen as being more conducive to the arts. While these assumptions may not directly prevent either men or women participating in specific leisure activities, they do affect individual choice and steer individuals towards specific areas of leisure. Such perceptions and control are at times achieved through the consent of women and men reinforcing a specific view of masculinity or femininity that men or women then guard.

Media images are known to be particularly influential in developing the personal and social identities of young women. Although we have moved a long way from the prejudice apparent during the 1970s, when Teresa Bennett took the Football Association to court to allow her to play (Ted Croker, the Secretary of the Football Association at the time, stating, 'We just don't like males and females playing together. I like feminine girls. Anyway it's not natural.'), we still have a long way to go in providing effective role models within sport. Women's sport is still by far the poor relation in terms of media coverage on television, radio and in newspapers. Sport journalism, broadcasting, commentating and producing is still very much male dominated. Greater kudos and financial reward are also gained through sports participation for men.

In general, leisure provision and image creation is still very much male dominated, with leisure participation for women taking place within structures that were created for men and by men. While great strides have been made within the last two to three decades, at the dawn of the twenty-first century we are still in a position where women's involvement in leisure, particularly sport, at all levels of participation and provision, is relatively new. While there are difficulties in discussing women as an amorphous group, because of the impact of class, ethnicity, age, financial independence and motherhood on individual women, it is still the case that gender has an impact upon leisure lifestyles to the disadvantage of women. There are still socially prescribed patterns that relate to gender and affect leisure opportunities, choices and participation levels.

● ● ● ● Conclusions

The dynamic nature of our individual leisure lifestyles is evident when we explore the effect of the complex interplay of a wide range of personal, social, circumstantial and opportunity factors. These factors combine to produce the ever-increasing number of lifestyle – and hence leisure lifestyle – changes that occur over the course of the family life cycle. The key lifestyle changes identified by the Rapoports in the four stages of the life cycle of the traditional family can clearly be seen as still exerting major influences on individual lifestyles. The commitments and social institutions identified with now, however, change more frequently, with greater movement between being single, separated, married and divorced and a greater diversity in the make-up and structure of the family unit. The changing nature of the family unit and the number and speed of changes within the family life cycle are likely to continue to change and adapt.

Questions

1 To what extent is the integration of family and leisure a social fact?

2 What changes might you expect in an individual's leisure participation during the course of the four stages of the Rapoports' family life cycle?

3 What changes in contemporary society pose problems for the application of the Rapoports' model of the family life cycle?

4 What differences might become apparent in a gender-based analysis of leisure participation in the UK?

References

Cohen, P. (1997) *Re-thinking the Youth Question: Education, Labour and Cultural Studies*, London: Macmillan.

Critcher, C., Bramham, P. and Tomlinson, A. (1995) *Sociology of Leisure*, London: Spon.

Dumazedier, J. (1967) *Towards a Society of Leisure*, New York: Free Press.

Godbey, G. (1994) *Leisure in your Life: An Exploration* (4th edition), State College, Pennsylvania: Venture Publishing.

Golombok, S. and Fivush, R. (1994) *Gender Development*, New York: Cambridge University Press.

Hargreaves, J. (1995) *Sporting Females: Critical Issues in the History and Sociology of Women's Sports*, London: Routledge.

Haywood, L., Kew, F., Bramham, P., Spink, J., Capenerhurst, J. and Henry, I. (1995) *Understanding Leisure* (2nd edition), Cheltenham: Stanley Thornes.

Horne, J., Tomlinson, A. and Whannel, G. (1999) *Understanding Sport: An Introduction to the Sociological and Cultural Analysis of Sport*, London: Spon.

Kimmel, M. S. (2000) *The Gendered Society*, Oxford: Oxford University Press.

Mintel (1999) *Changing Work Patterns*, 11/01/99, ONS/Mintel.

Mintel (1999) *Childcare Facilities*, 01/05/99, ONS/Mintel.

Mintel (1999) *The Leisure Business: The Consumer*, 07/09/99, BMRB/Mintel.

Mintel (1998) *Women and Finance: Women and Society*, 27/10/98, ONS/Mintel.

Mintel (1998) *Women and Finance: Women, Income and Employment*, 27/10/98, ONS/Mintel.

Rapoport, R. and Rapoport, R.N., with Strelitz, Z. (1975) *Leisure and the Family Life Cycle*, London: Routledge & Kegan Paul.

Roberts, K. (1970) *Leisure*, London: Longman.

Sillitoe, K.K. (1969) *Planning for Leisure*, London: HMSO.

Sports Council and Women's Sports Foundation *Women and Sport*, information pack.

Torkildsen, G. (1999) *Leisure and Recreation Management* (4th edition), London: Spon.

Wood, L. (1999) 'Think pink! – attracting the pink pound', *Insights*, English Tourism Council, A107–A110.

Further reading

Craven, L. (2000) 'Case study: Bluewater: retail tourism in the south east', *Insights*, English Tourism Council, C37–C46, provides a detailed case study on family leisure trends and consumption.

Critcher, C., Bramham, P. and Tomlinson, A. (1995) *Sociology of Leisure*, London: Spon. Chapters 4–8 provide further discussion on the family life cycle, home-based leisure, youth cultures and leisure and leisure and the elderly. Chapters 11 and 12 also examine further aspects of gender and leisure.

Fornas, J. and Bolin, G. (eds.) (1995) *Youth Culture in Late Modernity*, London: Sage. This provides a more detailed study of the nature of youth culture and further insights into its impact on leisure participation.

Godbey, G. (1994) *Leisure in your Life: An Exploration* (4th edition), State College, Pennsylvania: Venture Publishing, presents a more philosophical examination of the leisure life cycle.

Hargreaves, J. (1995) *Sporting Females: Critical Issues in the History and Sociology of Women's Sports*, London: Routledge, provides a comprehensive examination of the historical development and the contemporary issues affecting women's participation in sport.

Office of Population Censuses and Surveys, Social Survey Division (1996) *General Household Survey 1996*, London: HMSO, is an important and regularly updated source of a wide range of statistical data on the family, gender, leisure and more general social themes.

Pritchard, A., Sedley, D. and Morgan, N.J., 'Exploring issues of space and sexuality in Manchester's gay village', in Robinson, M., Sharpley, R., Evans, N., Long, P. and Swarbrooke, J. (eds) (2000) *Developments in Urban and Rural Tourism*, Sunderland: Business Education Publishers Limited, is one of only a limited number of detailed case studies on leisure participation and sexuality.

Useful website

www.thes.co.uk/higher_education

Chapter 5 ● ● ● ●

Access to leisure and disadvantaged groups

In order to participate in leisure there is a need to overcome certain barriers first. This is a point of fact for all potential participants. We all experience intrinsic barriers, that is, barriers that arise from our own physical or psychological make-up, and in addition we are limited by conditions imposed by our environment and communication barriers that limit our interaction with our social environment (Smith, 1985). For some groups, however, there are more extensive barriers to overcome than for others. Factors such as economic and social disadvantage (including homelessness), racial, ethnic, age (in particular youth and elderly) and gender prejudice, and mental and physical disabilities mean that some sections of the community experience discrimination and greater difficulty in accessing leisure programmes. There are many barriers that prevent equality of opportunity for participation in leisure.

Objectives

To:

- *explore the increased number of barriers imposed on three particular groups in the UK:*

  - *ethnic minorities*

  - *disabled persons*

  - *50+ age group*

- *highlight the barriers that need to be addressed by society at large, and leisure providers and decision makers, in order to facilitate social inclusion.*

● ● ● ● Ethnicity and leisure

Haywood *et al.* (1995, p. 143) define ethnicity as referring to 'a cluster of beliefs, attitudes and behaviour which distinguishes one social, racial or cultural group from another'. Ethnic groups are groups of people with a common culture and although ethnicity is often associated with race this need not be the case. Ethnicity encompasses a wide range of different associations including those of language and religion.

Everyone belongs to an ethnic group and belonging to a particular ethnic group affects our leisure participation. Leisure, like all others aspects of our lives, is thoroughly ethnic. It is *in* and *of* particular cultures (Jackson and Burton, 1989). Leisure is part of what we are socially and culturally and it plays a role in how we learn to be who and what we are. We learn and form our leisure lifestyles with reference to the groups in which we form our social and cultural identity. The symbols and language used in the leisure context, for example, arise from within particular cultures. The value of specific leisure forms is also assessed through the value systems of particular social institutions and cultures. Leisure opportunities are therefore provided in forms that are acceptable within such contexts.

Different cultural heritage, value systems and expectations about personal interactions have a profound effect upon leisure participation. Some religious communities, for instance, have social customs and values regarding the public social interactions, particularly of women, and hence the public recreational behaviour of women is impacted upon by these expectations. Belonging to a particular ethnic group can profoundly affect our access to certain leisure forms, especially where that ethnic group forms a minority. Leisure facilities tend to reflect the needs of the majority participants and decision makers, which in the UK are white and male.

Inequality of experience by ethnic groups is not, however, homogeneous; it very much depends on how they were initially established in the UK and the length of time they have been established. The longer groups have been established, the greater the chance of them having overcome economic, social and cultural barriers. The extent of the inequality experienced by an ethic group may also be a reflection of its history in relation to the majority ethnic group. The effect of previous trading and colonial relationships can still impact on some ethnic groups, as can current global perceptions of different ethnic groups.

Structures, institutions and individuals can all have a profound effect on the ability of particular ethnic groups to achieve their leisure potential. Structures that constrain ethnic minority groups to low levels of education, low-status occupations and hence low income levels restrict them to certain areas of residence and experience (Haywood *et al.*, 1995). As well as immigration resulting from the need for asylum, Britain has in the past used immigration to recruit cheap labour in times of labour shortage. As a result of this, whole groups of migrants have suffered from low incomes, poor housing and low levels of education. This has led to a 'cycle of deprivation' from which it can be difficult to break free, as successive generations are limited by their levels of awareness, employment opportunities and access to education (Veal, 1994).

The generally poorer areas of residence of ethnic minority groups are usually also the poorest in terms of leisure facility provision. Leisure participation is restricted through a lack of good-quality local provision and a low income that prevents participation in activities that would require the use of expensive public or private transport. In addition, individuals within such groups are often limited in the amount of private space available for leisure through, for instance, lack of gardens and space within the home. These factors can severely restrict access to leisure opportunities for members of ethnic minority groups when compared with other members of the community.

The key institutions associated with leisure may also either consciously or unconsciously erect barriers to participation for certain ethnic groups. The subcultures that are built up around leisure forms and leisure institutions can encompass values and practices that alienate the ethnic minorities. Access to some aspects of leisure education may be limited within ethnic groups because their own social networks do not provide opportunities for exposure to some leisure forms and the formal education system does not effectively address leisure education needs (see Chapter 12 for further details on education and leisure). We must also be vigilant not just about the structural and institutional problems. There is clear evidence of individuals who, either as fellow participants or as those affecting policy and provision, bring with them unacceptable prejudice towards members of ethnic minorities.

Structural, institutional and individual impacts are reflected in a number of ways when we examine the participation of ethnic minority groups in leisure. Certain key leisure forms, for instance, show both under- and over-representation of ethnic minority groups. Where sport is concerned there is an over-representation of black athletes in track and field, basketball, combat sports (particularly boxing) and football. What may be regarded as traditional white middle-class sports, however, show an under-representation of black players including sports like tennis and golf. These sports tend to be club based, which is another area of under-representation for ethnic minorities. Ethnic minority groups tend, on the other hand, to be over-represented in less expensive leisure activities and activities that are taught in school. This supports the presence of, in particular, the structural and institutional barriers highlighted above and the argument that participation rates, particularly in sport, do not arise because of levels of ability but because of unequal access to the necessary facilities, instruction and structures (Graefe and Parker, 1987; Haywood *et al.*, 1995).

Over- and under-representation can arise through barriers created at all levels of influence. Stereotyping is one barrier that can arise and impact at structural, institutional and individual levels. Carrington and Wood (1995) highlighted complaints by parents of West Indian children in the UK that their children are channelled by teachers into physical education as opposed to more academic pursuits. They complain of a perception by teachers that their children will be more capable physically than academically and they hence encourage them to concentrate on sports activities at the expense of their academic achievements. This perception promoted Carrington and Wood's research in the early 1980s, which did indeed find that for pupils in a multi-ethnic schools those with West Indian backgrounds were 3.7 times more likely to participate in extra-curricular sport than white pupils were. In addition, they found that most white male participants were likely to be in the upper academic band while most West Indian male participants were likely to be from lower academic bands. While there was no evidence of overt or intentional racism from staff, there was evidence that they had lower expectations academically of West Indian pupils and more readily accepted a lower academic standard from them. Some staff also clearly expected their West Indian pupils to have greater physical abilities arising from biology and saw sport for them as an acceptable compensation for a lack of academic achievement. Such racial stereotypes do affect pupil behaviour and choices. Carrington and Wood's research showed that some pupils had taken on board these stereotypes and expectations. Stereotypes are built in a number of ways including through the media, where the language used by commentators can often be seen to be affected by perceived stereotypes relating to the ethnicity of the participants (see McCarthy and Jones, 1997, for further details).

Such stereotyping adds to the problem of achieving equal opportunities both professionally and in the leisure sphere. It can, alongside other barriers, close down professional opportunities through lack of academic achievement and skills recognition that focuses individuals further towards fields that appear to be more accessible, such as sport and entertainment. Over-representation in the sports and entertainment fields can highlight them as possible means of escape from deprivation and a way of achieving acceptance for ethnic minorities. These avenues, however, only provide such opportunities for a limited number of individuals and leave many more disenfranchised and disempowered. The prominence of members of ethnic minorities who are successful in these fields, linked with the relative abundance of role models, can lead to a skewed perception of the extent to which these areas provide the perceived equality and opportunities. In addition, it leads to the loss of talent and personal fulfilment through a lack of opportunity in other areas of leisure and work. The absence of role models in other leisure activities aids in the continued under-representation in these areas and may affect not just participation but also spectator representation.

The level of representation of ethnic minority groups within a particular area of leisure has an important influence on how those groups in general interact with that leisure environment and activity. Those who participate in activities where the minority group to which they belong is already established, or where they form part of the majority group, do not face the same role performance, visibility and informal interaction barriers as those who originally gained the established presence. The first person(s) from a minority who participate in a given activity are usually very visible and their behaviour is seen to be of additional symbolic importance. This is especially seen to be the case for professional sports persons who would tend to be subjected to heavy media coverage and constant scrutiny around fulfilling the expected stereotype of their group within that sporting context. The minority individual is expected to be, for example, the 'model black' player. They are expected to perform exceptionally both within and outside the sports arena.

The introduction of team and club members from minority groups can lead to others becoming guarded in informal interactions and social contexts in order to avoid causing offence. This can, however, result in the minority group member being unintentionally marginalised at social events and excluded from more relaxed club interaction and humour. It can also lead to individuals from minority groups becoming subdued and striving to display what may be regarded as conventional behaviour in order to conform to expectations and 'fit in'. This, in turn, denies any real chance of an integrated and shared leisure experience. Where there is a more equal representation or a minority group has an established presence in the particular leisure arena, individuals are freer to take on different roles, freely express aspects of their own subculture and generally be much more of an individual in their own right (Snyder and Spreitzer, 1989).

In order to avoid the difficulties that might be experienced in pursuing what may be regarded as majority ethnic group leisure pursuits, some minority groups have turned to developing their own leisure lifestyles with their own subcultures of, for example, language, dress and music. Discrimination and lack of access to key public facilities and programmes has been met with innovative approaches to developing different leisure lifestyles and forms. Support for ethnic leisure forms can, however, be difficult to obtain. In the arts, theatre and music, they are often the poor relation to what may be regarded as more classical and traditional art forms. Arts sponsorship, for instance, tends to favour mainstream established art forms, as exemplified by the vast majority of the Arts Council budget being spent on major national companies. Only a tiny portion of their grants is given to planning and development projects, which includes the area of ethnic minority arts. In addition, where both national and local grants are available they are often not taken up because of a lack of awareness of their existence and a lack of access to information about the required application process.

On the other hand, membership of an ethnic minority group exposes an individual to a range of leisure forms and experiences usually not available to outsiders. There are shared traditions that form part of their joint cultural heritage. Key social and cultural events will often include special foods, handicrafts, art, literature, music, dance and sports. Leisure forms that centre on the family and the community are often of great importance, particularly for first-generation immigrants. These leisure patterns form part of their cultural heritage and are an extension of those found in their country of origin. Such activities can provide a source of familiarity and security in what may be a very alien and unfamiliar environment (Ishwaran, 1983; Mindel and Habenstein, 1976, cited in Graefe and Parker, 1987).

Later on, shared leisure lifestyles may become an attractive means of maintaining group boundaries and an important means of expressing dual identity. There is a strong argument for a model of racial equality that emphasises ethnic differences and retains ethnic cultures and identities. This argument runs counter to some of the initial approaches to immigrant cultures in the UK, where the assumption was that assimilation would take place and the culture of immigrants would quickly be more or less indistinguishable from that of the indigenous population. Surely, however, the challenge of contemporary society is neither to 'ghettoise' nor seek assimilation but to achieve equality while gaining the cultural benefits that ethnic diversity can offer. Leisure forms from all cultures have a strong tradition of gaining and undergoing positive development through responding to new influences, as well as being an important means of preserving and sharing parts of our cultural heritage with each other. The arts and sport can provide an important tool for bridging cultural gaps through shared experiences that, unlike other areas, do not rely on linguistic skills for a shared understanding (Waters, 1989).

Disabled persons and leisure

It is commonly estimated that in the UK there are around 6 million people who have a disability. McGinnis (1994) points out that this is, however, a conservative estimate based around a narrow medical definition and that one in every four people (approximately 15 million) is a more realistic estimate. The problem of the type of definition used to estimate the number of disabled people is compounded in leisure by the fact that providers often narrow the definition by equating provision for disabled persons with provision for wheelchair users. Wheelchairs users, however, form only 2 per cent of the 6 million estimate and, hence, provision based on this approach can largely ignore 98 per cent of disabled people.

Addressing the issue of disabilities therefore means raising awareness that this involves a diverse group of people. There are whole areas of disability involved that will have a wide range of different implications for access to leisure opportunities. These can be broadly categorised into five different areas (European Community, 1996, p. 5):

- Physical disabilities that will most commonly involve impaired mobility, with disabled persons using, for example, wheelchairs, crutches or sticks.
- Sensory disabilities that will include those who are blind or visually impaired and/or hard of hearing or deaf.
- Learning disabilities, where a person's level of understanding is less than that expected for a person of their age.
- Mental health problems, which include depression, anxiety, irrational fears and phobias, obsessions and dementia.
- Other disabilities that are in the main invisible disabilities, such as asthma, heart conditions, diabetes, epilepsy, kidney failure and allergies.

If we are to explore the reasons for limited access to leisure opportunities for disabled persons we must however move beyond simply defining and categorising disabilities to identifying the barriers to leisure participation that arise for disabled persons. In considering these barriers we must remember that if a leisure opportunity is not accessible to a disabled person then, because of the social element of many leisure forms, in excluding that person you will in turn exclude their family and friends. We must also be clear about the difference between the therapeutic use of leisure activities to achieve medical and social aims and access to leisure opportunities. The potential therapeutic value of leisure activities is reflected in the increased use of play, art and sports therapists in, for example, hospitals, clinics and special needs schools. Such programmes are, however, by their nature, prescriptive, therapeutic and rehabilitative – not leisure based. It is important, therefore, that these are not confused with leisure provision for disabled persons, which is centred around ensuring access to leisure opportunities in the same way as for the general population but taking into consideration the removal of any additional barriers that may arise if not addressed.

There are three key groups of barriers that need to be prevented from affecting access to leisure opportunities. These are physical, social and perceptual barriers. Physical barriers are direct in their influence on access and, hence, are more easily recognisable than social barriers. Common physical barriers are architectural and include stairs, auditorium seats, curbs, steep slopes, pathways, pavements, and corridor obstructions and lighting (particularly important for the visually impaired), in addition to a general lack of space in elevators, at entrances to buildings, in car parks and in toilets. These barriers prevent both effective use of the leisure environment and access to it, including restricted access to necessary public transport. They occur because environmental design is usually based on the needs of an average-sized 30-year-old male in relation to mobility, size, strength and capabilities. Such physical barriers have the problem of an innate resistance to change, in that leisure facilities and infrastructure projects are generally built as long-term projects because of the level of capital investment needed for their construction.

Social barriers are more difficult to change for other reasons. By their nature social barriers are subtler and certainly less instantly recognisable. To change a social barrier requires a change in attitudes and levels of awareness, as they arise as a result of social expectations and cultural norms. As argued by Rebecca McGinnis (1994), these are very significant influences on the integration of disabled persons:

> The biggest barrier to access for disabled persons is not a set of steps or a label
> in small print but shortsightedness about disabilities. Lack of awareness and
> knowledge mars communication, creating a gap that no ramp can bridge.

Social structures also pose significant barriers. For instance, structures that limit employment opportunities for disabled persons in turn limit available disposable income and hence access to leisure opportunities. It is still a fact that the incomes of the majority of disabled families fall below the national average. As with all low-income groups, a sensitive pricing policy is therefore essential in order to remove this barrier. This policy will also need to take into account that a disabled person will often need to be accompanied, which leads to an additional cost for participation. This can be dealt with by providing free or reduced cost access for companions and carers.

Haywood *et al.* (1995, p. 146) highlighted the problem of perceptual barriers; that is, barriers that relate to 'people's awareness of the existence of facilities, organisations, and also to an assessment of their own capabilities in relation to different recreation activities'. Lack of experience of leisure activities and leisure environments and/or previously negative access experiences can lead to a lack of confidence and a tendency to underestimate individual abilities. Care needs to be taken in communicating the facilities and support available at leisure venues. Information needs to be disseminated within the context of an inclusive and well-researched communications strategy. Consultation with disabled persons and support groups is a key way of avoiding some of the pitfalls. Lack of effective communications, planning and research become obvious when we find advertisements for wheelchair basketball in public buildings without wheelchair access. This means that information can clearly only be passed on to the target audience through a third party, which hardly inspires confidence in a potential participant that facilities will be welcoming and appropriate. Perceptual barriers can also be addressed through the employment of people with disabilities at recreation facilities and the effective use of role models for outreach work and promotion. This may be as simple as using disabled athletes or artists appropriately on publicity material. Perceptions of others, not just those of disabled persons themselves, can also act as barriers and public education needs to deal with the fear and lack of awareness of other participants and staff. Effective staff training and consultation can quickly dispel fears of doing or saying the wrong thing.

Disabilities are conditions imposed by the barriers that arise within society; they are not the inevitable consequence of impairment. Such barriers are external to the disabled person that they affect and not only can they be created by society, but they can also be changed and removed by society. In order for such progress to be made there is a need for consultation and the involvement of disabled persons, as barriers can often be transparent to those who are not affected by them. A well-intentioned US museum put on a series of events supported by sign language interpreters and were disappointed when no one attended. It was only when they evaluated their lack of success that they realised the events had been timetabled on the one evening in the week when there were a number of key television programmes with sign language interpretation. This problem could easily have been avoided with one brief conversation with an informed member of the deaf community or by seeking advice from the press officers of organisations representing the deaf community. Press officers of organisations representing disabled persons are excellent points of contact for advice on appropriate provision and effective communication to disabled persons.

We should not, however, assume that there is unanimity of attitude towards such barriers to participation in leisure. There is, for instance, one school of thought that argues in favour of the environment being designed to serve the majority, with minority groups being supported in learning to cope with that environment through increased education, training and medical aids. This approach is presented as positive action in providing an additional motivation for the provision of education and training for disabled persons and for them to seek education and training.

It seems, however, insulting to assume that disabled persons are any more or less motivated than any other individual. The level of motivation of disabled persons is the same as within every other group; differing levels of motivation are exhibited by different individuals. It seems arrogant for others in society to assume the role of motivator by asking disabled persons to overcome difficulties that are, after all, in place because the environment is geared to suit them. It is also true that no amount of motivation, training or education will overcome barriers such as large flights of stairs for wheelchair users.

The many barriers that form part of the environment for disabled persons often go unnoticed by those unaffected by them, and hence their removal also goes unnoticed. The presence or absence, for instance, of lowered sections of curbs (curb cuts) often go unnoticed by those unaffected by curb heights. There is no real need for the environment to be designed to suit only the majority user when simple design changes and raised levels of awareness can extend and provide ease of access for minority users. Many of the design features required by disabled persons are also appreciated by other members of the public; clear large print and well-lit signs benefit most of us and the use of wide doorways, lift spaces and ramps make access with a pushchair or pram much more straightforward. More importantly, there is a need to recognise the equal rights of disabled persons to the same level of access to public services, buildings and transport (Coles, 1995).

The 1995 Disability Discrimination Act was a move to reinforce such rights by law and can be seen to act in support of Article 27 of the Universal Declaration of Human Rights, which states:

> Everyone has a right to participate in the cultural life of the community, to enjoy the arts and to share in scientific advancement and its benefits. (Cited in McGinnis, 1994)

The 1995 Act means that those providing goods, facilities and services have a duty to end and prevent discrimination. Leisure providers can no longer refuse disabled persons services or provide them with services that are of a lower standard or are provided under less favorable terms than those offered to others. Restauranteurs can no longer ask disabled persons to sit at out-of-the-way tables and leisure centres can no longer ask for larger deposits from disabled persons because they regard them as being a greater risk in terms of cancellation of bookings through ill health (Phillips, 1996). It is also no longer acceptable for the only seats that can be accessed in a threatre to be the ones that are more expensively priced.

This legislation required that by 1998 reasonable steps should have been taken to change procedures, policies and practices that either make it impossible or unreasonably difficult for a disabled person to use a leisure service. It also required that by the year 2000 reasonable steps should have been taken to provide any aids that make access to a facility possible or easier; for example, the introduction of audio tapes in museums. In addition, by 2005 the requirement is that reasonable steps have been taken so that physical barriers that make facilities difficult to use or inaccessible have been removed or circumvented or that the service is offered in an alternative manner. The reasonable measures requested mean that the cost falls below a cap set by government; it does not require a change in the nature of the service and it does not disadvantage or pose a risk to other users (Stuart-Smith, 1996). Legislation is, however, only a starting point and there is a strong argument for a more comprehensive and targeted approach to leisure education that addresses attitudinal and perceptual barriers and prevents an approach that is based upon the minimum required to stay within the law.

There is a popular misconception that providing access for a disabled person is much more expensive than for other groups. The reality is that this is only true where such provision is an add-on. When considerations are made during the planning and building phases, the cost of making most activities accessible is negligible. According to Sessoms and Henderson (1994) there is less than 1 per cent of additional expenditure required to include ramps and accessible changing areas in the construction of a new building. Positive proactive approaches to include the necessary changes for disabled access when renovation occurs can help to limit unnecessary spending. Support towards costs is also available through grant applications to national sports and arts bodies for facility adaptation, specialist equipment and staff training. The inclusion of disabled persons in many leisure programmes requires no specialist modifications. Disabled persons can often easily be integrated into current programmes using effective promotion techniques that include them as part of the target community. Effective provision can often be achieved by simple changes in promotional strategies and approaches to information dissemination that fill information gaps, help overcome perceptual barriers and fall within the mainstream promotion budget for current programmes.

There are strong arguments for the development of organisational philosophies that concentrate on ensuring that all leisure opportunities available are made as accessible to as wide a population as possible. Disabled persons do not wish to be unnecessarily singled out as different at leisure facilities. The provision, for example, of separate interpretative trails at informal sites such as country parks may not be as welcome as one might expect, as this can be seen to be drawing attention to disabilities rather than treating disabled persons the same as other groups. It is preferable that, where possible, the same trail is used by all groups and that Braille or large print is added to the general information boards. It is also possible to use audiotapes for the dissemination of information generally, rather than only for those who are visually impaired.

Care needs to be taken, however, that effective inclusion is not seen simply as disabled and non-disabled persons participating together. Inclusion requires equality of opportunity. Segregated activities with specially adapted programmes and equipment will be required by some individuals and should be developed when appropriate. An effective leisure programme will usually include both integrated and separate provision. Generally the approach within the arts has been to open up existing provision to disabled persons rather than providing separate or different activities. However, sometimes there is a need for special provision, for example, libraries stocking Braille books, large-print books and books, magazines and newspapers on tape. Many disabled sports organisations also now provide information and access to adapted leisure forms, specialist learning strategies and specialist equipment where necessary. This allows a refocusing on the abilities of the individual rather than their disabilities.

● ● ● ● Leisure and ageing

One of the most significant demographic changes in recent decades has been the ageing of the UK population. This has led to an increased need for leisure provision for those who are now often defined as being part of the 'third age', that is, those who are 'in late middle age and no longer gainfully employed'. This usually refers to those who have retired but also includes the unemployed in late middle age (Carnegie Inquiry cited in Richards, 1993). This group is often targeted as the 50+ group by providers and was the target of the '50+ and All to Play For' campaign by the Sports Council in the early 1990s.

In the UK, where youth and productivity are highly prized, those who have retired, or are older and unemployed, are traditionally assigned a role that focuses on passive dependence. Behaviour norms and expectations arise from this assigned role, which impacts on all areas of the individual's lifestyle including leisure and leisure choices. This can lead to leisure provision that tends to be centred on activities that support this negative image of the third age. Western capitalism, which so highly values youthfulness and productivity as markers for measuring success, serves to marginalise this group and their leisure choices. The leisure industry, the media and the cosmetic surgery industry can be seen to reinforce this negative image with its concentration on fitness and appearance and stigmatisation of ageing. As our sense of self is strongly influenced by the way in which society perceives us there is a tendency for us to take on the role expectations laid down by others. Although there are clearly exceptions, it is difficult to form a self-image and take on a role that counters that of society in general, and the tendency is towards conforming.

Conforming to the passive dependence image can have a profound impact on self-confidence and social expectations. This can lead to isolation and disengagement. Such disengagement is evident in this group's leisure lifestyles. Despite this group having the largest amount of time available for leisure there is a significant fall in participation, which cannot be explained simply by the effects of biological changes and the ageing process. It may therefore be accounted for by the tendency for individuals to avoid situations that produce negative feedback and feelings of being unwelcome or 'out of place'. In the absence of concessions being made for others, the domination of leisure environments by young people and images of youth does not promote wider access and can lead to disengagement. This is not confined, as may be expected, to sports and fitness facilities but extends across a whole range of leisure forms. Cinema audiences, for example, do not reflect population demographics and the time richness of the third age. They provide a clear example of a participation gap not accounted for by the restrictions that may come later in the third age. They are more a reflection of the target audience of films and the provision of a leisure environment that is youth focused. Programmes, décor and promotional strategies for cinemas, as with most clubs, pubs and bowling alleys, all show a strong bias towards young people.

It can be argued, however, that this does not indicate a forced disengagement in order to avoid negative experiences but rather a mutual withdrawal that frees the retired from the societal pressures of productivity and engagement. This group may be seen to willingly disengage and seek an identity away from mainstream society. It is difficult to see, though, why this interpretation applies to leisure, which by its nature is non-productive, and, more specifically, how such an interpretation would be of relevance to a visit to somewhere such as the cinema. It may, however, be the case that some individuals still view leisure as a reward for work or productivity and hence something that they have not earned. If this is so, it highlights a need to promote leisure and its qualities much more positively in their own right, rather than with reference to work, in order to promote successful life-long leisure participation (see Chapter 2 for further discussions on the leisure–work opposition).

Health and mobility are also cited as reasons for a decline in participation levels in the third age. However, while health may be accepted as having some impact later it is not so significant early in this stage. It was also highlighted by Comfort as early as 1977 that 75 per cent of the disabilities of old age could be attributed to institutional approaches and attitudes rather than biology. As argued earlier, at whatever age an individual experiences disabilities, it is society than allows barriers to arise that prevent their participation; it is not an inevitable consequence of impairment but a lack of effective provision. It is the lack of supportive social networks and social approval that allows these barriers to arise.

Active participation in leisure is in fact proven to help delay if not prevent the onset of a whole range of health and mobility problems. It can be highly beneficial in maintaining strength, flexibility and endurance, as well as preventing the psychological problems that can arise through isolation and loneliness (Dinan 1994; McCormick and McGuire, 1996). This helps individuals live healthy and independent lives for longer. Such benefits led the Health Education Authority to launch the Active for Life scheme in 1996, which promoted the benefits of life-long active leisure and concentrated in its second year on older people. Alongside this, Age Concern has promoted the PALS (Promoting Active Leisure for Seniors) scheme. This helped support the increased call through the 1990s to challenge the segregation and marginalisation of this group and to promote a more 'active' lifestyle, encompassing not just physical but also mental and social activity. There is some evidence of change in the increased coverage by the media of older participants in a whole range of leisure pursuits including more active and even extreme sports. This may at times be presented as a novelty item but it does assist in challenging role expectations, providing role models and countering the consistent image of leisure participation as being the perogative of the young. There has also been increasing support available through the growth of veteran sports and leisure clubs.

If progress in providing equal access for this group is to continue, it is important that providers move away from perceptions of a homogeneous group limited by biology to recognise the wide range of needs and abilities present within the

50+ age group. The tendency to treat this target audience as one large homogeneous group is supported by the state treatment of this group as being broadly uniform through the provision of standard state pensions and benefits. This is an important problem because society assigns specific roles to particular groups that strongly influence provision for the whole group. This age group spans more than 30 years and at no other point in the life cycle would we expect to provide in the same way for individuals separated by such a time frame. Policy and provision decisions need to move away from mass definitions of the third age. Ageing occurs at different rates for different individuals and occurs in different spheres at different rates, that is, ageing is not just biological but is also sociological and psychological. Some individuals are comparatively 'old' at 50, while others stay young into their 80s. This applies both physically and psychologically. Being older is not about chronological age but about attitude and health. Being elderly is certainly not synonymous with being retired, especially given the current trend towards early retirement. Providers and decision makers also need to take into account the different life experiences of different generational groups and the difference in exposure to world events, education and information systems. Providers need to recognise and respond to this diversity. There is a great degree of diversity between individuals in this group in terms of health, wealth, status, experiences, values, education and interests.

Although there is an increasing number of people who retire with private pensions and no mortgage, those in rented accommodation and on state pensions, which have not been index linked, will be much more financially restricted. The commercial sector tends to concentrate on the former group, with the latter less well provided for. Also, while those who retire are now generally increasingly well educated, there are still significant differences in the levels of education between individuals, particularly with reference to leisure education. While some may have clear ideas about the types of leisure they want to pursue, others may be ill equipped to make such decisions. The vast majority of older people in the UK, however, do belong to some sort of organisation, such as church and community groups. These provide excellent outlets for information dissemination and taster sessions. They provide the opportunity for leisure education in a non-threatening and familiar environment (McKeever, 1992). Other differences arise from the social support networks available to different individuals. Some will be actively involved with a wide range of different groups and part of a number of social networks, and some will also have the support of the extended family. Others may live away from relatives and, particularly when faced with the loss of a partner, may find these factors to be substantial hurdles to participation. Participation on one's own when leisure patterns have previously been formed as couples can take a great deal of courage and self-confidence. Easy access to information on participation profiles for leisure activities can be vital. Will they be the only person who attends on their own? Segregated provision through singles' activities may be important for the latter person but not so for the former.

The later stage of the third age can see decreasing economic and social resources, especially where the family are increasingly mobile and living away. Physical limitations become more of an issue at this stage and make the tasks necessary for personal care and domestic independence more difficult and hence less energy and resources are available for leisure, particularly outside the home. This again requires a flexible approach by providers and the recognition of the need to take leisure provision closer if not to the individual's home, for example, with the provision of mobile services such as libraries (Haywood *et al.*, 1995). Packages that include transport, meals and social arrangements become increasingly important as health and other means of support decline.

As with disabled groups and for women from some ethnic groups, segregated provision can be beneficial and appropriate for some members of this group. It may be provided for this group particularly in sport and leisure, to avoid negative comparison with younger athletes. Where segregated sports and fitness programmes are provided, however, they should still be designed around the abilities of the participants and not in relation to some preconceived idea of the capabilities of a stereotypical member of this group; a stereotypical individual who inevitably will not be present. The programme should be flexible enough to deal with a range of abilities. Clearer communication of the fitness levels required for general programmes would also allow for more effective integration. While some older individuals may prefer segregated programmes, many will seek a positive integration in mainstream activities (Buchanan, 1995; McKeever, 1992). Access to appropriate leisure opportunities and leisure choices is no less important for this group than any other (Richards, 1993). It requires the same commitment to providing resources and information, to consultation and negotiation as provision for any other group in society and needs to be supported in the same way by education leading to attitude changes and effective staff training (Age Concern, n.d.).

Effective provision can support successful ageing, lifestyle maintenance and the development of new leisure interests (Godbey, 1997). Leisure can play an important role in the transition between work and retirement. While retirement affects different individuals in different ways, a large number of people are not prepared for the changes brought by this phase in the life cycle. There is a real need for effective pre-retirement training of which leisure education could play a vital part. Where an individual's identity has been strongly tied in with their work role, leisure activities can replace the work sphere as a focus for social status and positive self-esteem. Leisure can provide a replacement structure to the day or week that is lost through retirement and can provide the focus for a new timetable. It can also be an important means whereby the social contacts lost through retirement can be replaced. There is a lot of evidence of a strong positive association between leisure participation and life satisfaction in retirement.

● ● ● ● Conclusions

This chapter has examined a number of disadvantaged groups and the various barriers that impede their access to leisure and has highlighted the fact that many of the barriers are similar for the different groups, or at least have a large degree of overlap. The existence of these barriers raises a number of key issues for those responsible for leisure provision and, although provision is the concern of Part Two of this text, it would seem remiss not to comment on the policy implications of such barriers.

The extent to which effective leisure provision for the local community has been achieved is reflected in the balance of the levels of participation of all community groups. At its best, leisure can be a tool that supports social integration and builds confidence and self-esteem and, at its worst, it can be a means of social exclusion and can serve to emphasise difference.

However effective leisure provision that supports social integration needs to be fostered by the development of strong leisure policies that are clearly communicated in writing to ensure that the policy is implemented and does not just remain a good idea. Without the effective dissemination of such policies, policy makers will tend to produce systems that reflect their own cultural values, leisure needs and lifestyles. It is essential that action plans are then developed which ensure that employment policies, consultations, training and outreach counter such tendencies. Libraries and museums, for example, have been seen to provide an improved and more diverse service that benefits all the community when they employ specialist staff and/or seek advice from appropriate community groups. Sports and entertainment facilities also provide an improved service for the whole community when the sensitivity to customer needs is raised through training that includes developing a knowledge of the needs of minority groups. Consultation with groups should be regularly carried out as part of the planning process and accessibility should be regularly audited, including the organisation's communications and marketing policies. Long-term development of links with relevant community groups and support networks are the most effect way of ensuring well-informed action and progress. Equal access should not be about complying with legislation but should be an integral part of an organisation's culture and philosophy. It needs to be developed in an atmosphere where there is a strong sense of ownership, partnership and social responsibility at all levels (Foley and Pirk, 1991, cited in Sessoms and Henderson, 1994).

Leisure policies that seek to move towards greater equality must, however, be handled sensitively in the broader context of social and economic equality. While leisure service providers may be genuinely pursuing equality of provision, if this is not supported by provision in areas such as education, housing and employment then it may be seen as a cynical exercise in placating disadvantaged groups.

In most instances, however, increasing accessibility and equality of leisure opportunity is not about making extensive changes to facilities or delivery but is more often an issue of developing an increased level of sensitivity and knowledge. Most barriers to leisure participation arise because of a lack of a clearly developed philosophy of inclusion, which allows professional insensitivity, that brings about exclusion. Most barriers are put in place by structures, institutions and/or individuals in society and, hence, can equally be removed by those structures, institutions and/or individuals.

Questions

1 What are the structural, institutional and individual factors that prevent equal access to leisure opportunities for ethnic minorities?

2 What is required to achieve successful integrated leisure provision for disabled persons?

3 Can the leisure needs of the 50+ age group be effectively provided for through a homogeneous group approach?

4 What common steps can be taken in order to achieve more effective inclusion for all disadvantaged groups?

References

Age Concern England, Centre for Policy on Ageing, Chief Leisure Officers Association and Help the Aged (n.d.) *Leisure Life: A Local Authority Code of Practice for Effective Provision of Leisure for Older People*.

Buchanan, C. (1995) 'Gaining in maturity', *Fitness*, July.

Carrington, B. and Wood, E. (1995) 'Body talk: images of sport in a multi-racial school', in Critcher, C., Bramham, P. and Tomlinson, P., *Sociology of Sport*, London: Spon.

Coles, A. (1995) 'Access all areas', *The Leisure Manager*, April/May.

Comfort, A. (1977) *A Good Age*, London: Mitchell Beazley.

Dinan, S. (1994) 'Fitness for older people', *British Medical Journal*, vol. 309, 30 July.

European Community (1996) *Making Europe Accessible for Tourists with Disabilities*, Luxembourg: EC.

Godbey, G. (1997) *Leisure and Leisure Services in the 21st Century*, State College, Pennsylvania: Venture Publishing.

Graefe, A. and Parker, S. (1987) *Recreation and Leisure: An Introductory Handbook*, London: Spon.

Haywood, L., Kew, F., Bramham, P., Spink, J., Capenerhurst, J. and Henry, I. (1995) *Understanding Leisure* (2nd edition), Cheltenham: Stanley Thornes.

Jackson, E.L. and Burton, T.L. (1989) *Understanding Leisure and Recreation*, London: Venture.

McCormick, B.P. and McGuire, F. (1996) 'Leisure in community life of older rural residents', *Leisure Sciences*, vol. 18, pp. 77–93.

McGinnis, R. (1994) 'The disabling society', *Museums Journal*, June.

McKeever, E. (1992) '"What's age got to do with it?" Leisure for the over 50s – an unfulfilled market', *WLRA Journal*, Spring.

Phillips, D. (1996) 'In on the act', *Leisure Opportunities*, 28 Oct–10 Nov.

Richards, J. (1993) 'A good few years yet', *Leisure Manager*, November.

Smith, R.W. (1985) 'Barriers are more than architectural', *Parks and Recreation*, October.

Sessoms, H.D. and Henderson, K.A. (1994) *Introduction to Leisure Services* (7th edition), State College, Pennsylvania: Venture Publishing.

Stuart-Smith, J. (1996) 'Right of entry', *Museums Journal*, August.

Synder, E.E. and Spreitzer, E.A. (1989) *Social Aspects of Sport* (3rd edition), London: Prentice Hall.

Veal, A.J. (1994) *Leisure, Policy and Planning*, London: Longman.

Waters, I. (1989) *Entertainment, Arts and Cultural Services*, London: Longman/ILAM.

Further reading

Baines, J. (1996) 'Missing in action', *When Saturday Comes*, April, vol. 110, pp. 6–7, discusses the reasons for the low participation rate of Asians in football.

English Sports Council (1998) *Sports and Ethnic Minorities*, Bibliography 15. This bibliography provides a good basic list of publications that relate to sport and ethnic minorities.

Holmes, S. (1997) 'Sporting chance', *The Leisure Manager*, vol. 15, no. 4, examines the ASPIRE project, which was set up to encourage greater participation of disabled people in sport through raising awareness and training sports coaches who could provide integrated opportunities for participation.

Kelly, J.R. (1997) 'Activity and ageing: challenge in retirement', in Haworth, J.T., *Work, Leisure and Well-being*, London: Routledge, gives a more detailed account of leisure in the 50+ age group. Alongside this Age Concern England, Centre for Policy on Ageing, Chief Leisure Officers Association and Help the Aged, *Leisure Life: A Local Authority Code of Practice for Effective Provision of Leisure for Older People* provides a very practical overview of key issues and approaches to provision for the 50+ age group.

McCarthy, K. and Jones, R.L. (1997) 'Speed, aggression, strength and tactical naivete: the portrayal of the black soccer player on television', *Journal of Sport and Social Issues*, vol. 21, no. 4, pp. 348–62, examines the language used by commentators in relation to the ethnicity of the player.

McGinnis, R. (1994) 'The disabling society', *Museums Journal*, June, an excellent article that highlights the approaches required for effective provision for disabled persons by a proactive leisure facility.

Parmar, P. (1995) 'Gender, race and power: the challenge to youth work practice', in Critcher, C., Bramham, P. and Tomlinson, P., *Sociology of Sport*, London: Spon, examines the approaches to youth work and the needs of young Asian women.

Chapter 6 ● ● ● ●

The economic and political significance of leisure

Previous chapters have considered the way in which leisure might be defined and understood as well as a range of factors and situations that influence the extent to which people have access to it. Much of the emphasis, therefore, has been on leisure and the individual, but the importance of leisure involves broader strategic concerns in terms of its national economic significance and its role in achieving various social goals. As such, leisure has become an important area for policy makers. It is the intention of this chapter, therefore, to consider both its economic and political significance.

Objectives

To:

- *examine the nature of consumer spending on leisure and its significance for the national economy*

- *recognise the importance of leisure for employment*

- *discuss international trade in leisure and globalisation*

- *analyse the significance of leisure in the informal economy*

- *examine leisure and regeneration*

- *discuss political ideologies and leisure*

- *analyse the state as promoter of leisure*

- *discuss leisure and control.*

●●●● The economic significance of leisure

Leisure has been acquiring increasing economic importance since its commercialisation first became significant in the nineteenth century; but for the greater part of the last 150 years this development has been a gradual one. During the twentieth century the service sector, of which leisure is a part, has replaced the manufacturing sector as the dominant mode within the economy and in the last couple of decades leisure industries have become particularly prominent within this sector. Leisure now accounts for a substantial proportion of people's disposable incomes, many people are employed in a variety of leisure industries and some of the largest firms are those specialising in leisure goods and/or services. Leisure is now big business and both local and national economies may depend on its continual success. Furthermore, leisure in its various forms, but especially tourism, may play a crucial role in developing local economies or as a means of regenerating certain areas whose economies have declined.

Consumer spending and leisure

Consumer spending on leisure goods and services in the UK has been rising steadily for a number of years. The long-term growth of expenditure on leisure goods and services can be seen quite clearly in Figure 6.1, taken from the report on the 1999–2000 *Family Expenditure Survey* (ONS, 2000). This shows the relative trends in expenditure for a variety of categories over the last 30 years of the twentieth century and highlights the fact that at the turn of the millennium households were for the first time spending more on leisure than on food, housing or transport. In 1999/2000 an average household in the United Kingdom was spending a total of £351.40 a

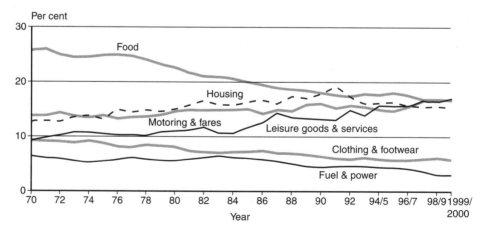

Figure 6.1   Percentage of total expenditure on selcted categories, 1970–1999/2000
Source: Office of National Statistics (2000) *Family Spending: A Report on the 1999–2000 Family Expenditure Survey.*

Table 6.1   Household expenditure on holidays, 1969 to 1998/99

Year	Expenditure*
1969	3.95
1974	5.15
1979	5.99
1984	7.14
1989	11.04
1994/95†	14.55
1998/99	18.30

* £ per week at 1998/99 prices.
† From 1994 onwards, data are for financial years.

Source: Office of National Statistics (2000) *Family Spending: A Report on the 1999–2000 Family Expenditure Survey.*

week, £60.30 of which was on leisure goods and services, followed by £58.90 on food (17.2% and 16.8% respectively). This contrasts markedly with earlier times. In 1956, for example, 35 per cent of spending was on food and only 4 per cent was on leisure, and in 1968 the relative figures were 26 per cent and 9 per cent.

In the leisure sector it is the growth of expenditure on leisure services that has been most significant. Since 1970 the proportion of household income spent on leisure goods has remained fairly constant at around 4 or 5 per cent but that spent on leisure services has trebled from 4 per cent in 1970 to 12 per cent in 1999–2000 (ONS, 2000). One illustration of this can be seen in Table 6.1, which shows the amount households have spent on holidays for selected years over a 30-year period. Whereas in 1969 the average household would spend £3.95 a week, at the end of the 1990s this had risen to over £18.

In addition to the expenditure classified by the *Family Expenditure Survey* under the headings of leisure goods and services, there is also expenditure under other headings that is inevitably linked to leisure. A significant proportion of the expenditure on transport must be associated with leisure, as must that on eating out and take-away meals, which is listed under the food category. Figure 6.2 shows that expenditure on take-away, restaurant and café meals has continued to rise during the latter half of the 1990s (see also Table 6.2) and, while this could be due to people leading busier lives with less time to prepare their own food, it is also likely that at least some of it is due to lifestyle changes linked to leisure. On the one hand, there is the social aspect of eating out, and this may also be part of a package of leisure activities (e.g. eating out in association with going to the cinema or theatre, attending a sports event or leisure shopping). On the other hand, there is the simple aspect of saving time for leisure activities. Consequently, leisure is producing substantial consumer spending in its own right and may also be influencing significant indirect expenditure.

One key aspect that is particularly clear in the trends outlined in Figure 6.1 is that, while the long-term trend in family expenditure on leisure was one of overall

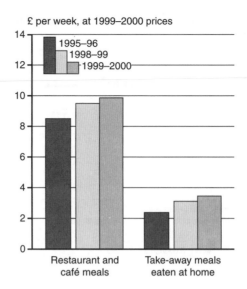

Figure 6.2   Expenditure on take-away meals and eating out

Source: Office of National Statistics (2000) *Family Spending: A Report on the 1999–2000 Family Expenditure Survey*.

Table 6.2   UK leisure business market size trends, 1994–98

	£bn	% change	Index	£bn at 1994 prices	% change	Index
1994	49.1	–	100	49.1	–	100
1995	52.6	+7.3	107	51.4	+4.8	105
1996	54.4	+3.4	111	51.3	−0.2	105
1997	57.5	+5.6	117	52.6	+2.4	107
1998	59.0	+2.7	120	52.5	−0.2	107
1999 (est)	60.3	+2.1	123	52.4	–	107

Source: Mintel (1999) *The Leisure Business: The Leisure Market*, 07/09/99, BMRB/Mintel

growth, the rate of growth did differ at various times. There is clearly a link between economic growth and leisure expenditure. Leisure has traditionally involved discretionary expenditure, in contrast to what is spent on essential items (e.g. food, clothing, accommodation, energy, transport). As such, it is often the first to be cut back in times of recession, as Gratton and Taylor (1992) have illustrated. The slowdown in growth, even slight decline, during the recessions of the early 80s and early 90s is very apparent, as is the relative fall in leisure spending at times when other key items (such as housing, transport, fuel and power) have increased in price.

Leisure spending and the national economy

Given the relative importance of leisure expenditure within household budgets, it is clear that overall expenditure on leisure is going to be substantial. At the end of the twentieth century, consumers were spending approximately £113 billion on various forms of leisure, £36 billion in the home and £77 billion away from home and both these segments were expanding (LIRC/Leisure Consultants, 1998). Not all of this expenditure was spent in the UK, of course, as some of the goods and services will have been produced overseas, such as that spent while on holidays abroad. However, there will also be various leisure goods and services that will be exported from the UK, such as overseas visitors to the UK, and thus, to get a full picture of the contribution of leisure to the national income, various adjustments would need to be made. For example, the value of overseas tourists to the UK at the end of the twentieth century was estimated to be approximately £12.5 billion. Whatever the exact value, however, it is clear that a substantial amount is spent on leisure and that this supports many businesses and involves significant employment (see below).

A recent report by Mintel (1999) has estimated that the UK leisure market (in terms of leisure services) was worth over £60 billion in 1999 (see Table 6.2). Not only is this a major contribution to the economy as a whole, but it is also a contribution that is expanding. In terms of actual expenditure, the leisure market has grown by 23 per cent in the five-year period from 1994, although if the figures are adjusted for inflation then the growth is more modest.

Table 6.3 provides a more detailed analysis of this UK leisure market and highlights the size and changing value of its various sectors. Leisure catering is by far the largest sector, especially in terms of pubs and bars. However, although the consumption of beverages is the largest component, its growth is somewhat static and it is the other aspects of catering that are displaying substantial growth. In terms of leisure activities, gambling, health and fitness and cinema have all experienced substantial growth, the first no doubt influenced greatly by the introduction of the national lottery. Finally, all the leisure accommodation/tourism sectors have grown substantially during this period. In fact, of the 19 separate components listed for the 3 key sectors that Mintel identify, only the leisure activity of theatregoing has experienced any decline and the level of spending here was relatively small anyway.

It has already been established that producing exact figures for the total contribution of leisure to the economy is difficult because some aspects of expenditure can be difficult to disaggregate and some may involve double counting as is suggested in Table 6.3. However, even if all the necessary statistics could be included, the figures would still not portray the full economic significance because they relate to what economists call 'static analysis' in that they discuss expenditure figures relating to a particular point in time. Expenditure on leisure, as with other things, also has dynamic effects due to the circular flow of income and expenditure in the economy (Tribe, 1995). Expenditure on leisure is not simply consumed by the business providing the leisure good or service with that being the end of the matter. Part of the income is paid out as wages to employees of the leisure business, who will then spend some of this in other businesses, which in turn will be paid to its employees and so on. Furthermore, the leisure business may also need to buy in goods and services and therefore more of the initial expenditure will be circulating in the economy in this way. A dynamic process is thus established and the total

Table 6.3 The UK leisure business, by sector, 1994–99

	1994 £m	1995 £m	1996 £m	1997 £m	1998 £m	1999 (est) £m	% change 1994–99
Leisure catering	*32,031*	*32,844*	*33,756*	*34,922*	*35,786*	*36,488*	*+13.9*
Fast food/take-aways	4,065	4,263	4,461	4,684	4,962	5,060	+24.5
Restaurants	3,674	3,757	3,970	4,238	4,445	4,505	+22.6
Pubs and bars (catering)	3,570	3,752	3,932	4,143	4,414	4,590	+28.6
Pubs and bars (beverages)	15,245	15,450	15,397	15,421	15,332	15,428	+1.2
Pubs and bars (other)	2,811	2,869	3,147	3,452	3,484	3,680	+30.9
Wine bars	415	430	450	460	465	470	+13.3
Roadside catering	361	372	389	418	449	460	+27.4
In-store catering	790	830	870	935	985	1,035	+31.0
Other catering	1,100	1,120	1,140	1,170	1,250	1,260	+14.5
Leisure activities	*7,294*	*9,572*	*9,869*	*10,659*	*11,080*	*11,394*	*+56.2*
Cinema	518	505	586	702	717	798	54.1
Theatre	339	343	324	319	314	310	−8.6
Tenpin bowling	176	180	187	193	201	210	+19.3
Nightclubs and discotheques	1,759	1,883	2,005	2,074	2,156	2,101	+19.4
Gambling	3,810	5,892	5,914	6,399	6,600	6,750	+77.2
Health and fitness	692	769	853	972	1,092	1,225	77.0
Leisure accommodation/ tourism	*9,750*	*10,218*	*10,777*	*11,871*	*12,153*	*12,370*	*+26.9*
Other holidays at home	3,764	4,080	4,207	4,457	4,525	4,650	+23.5
Hotels (leisure only)*	2,116	2,300	2,513	2,788	2,975	3,100	+46.5
Short breaks*	2,635	2,540	2,640	3,110	3,000	2,900	+10.1
Days out	1,235	1,298	1,417	1,516	1,653	1,720	+39.3
Total	*49,075*	*52,634*	*54,401*	*57,452*	*59,019*	*60,262*	*+22.8*

* likely to have some double counting.

Source: Mintel (1999) *The Leisure Business: The Leisure Market*, 07/09/99, BMRB/Mintel

income that will be spent in the economy will therefore exceed the initial expenditure on leisure. This process is known as the *multiplier effect*.

The multiplier process is illustrated in Figure 6.3, where it can be seen how initial tourist expenditure, possibly that spent at a hotel, might circulate. Some money would be paid in wages and would provide income for various households; some would flow to other local businesses that might supply the hotel with various goods and services (e.g. food, drink, maintenance); some would be paid to government in the form of taxes; and some would be spent on imported goods and services that the local area was not able to supply. As can be seen from the diagram, some of this money will be spent again as secondary or indirect expenditure, but the overall

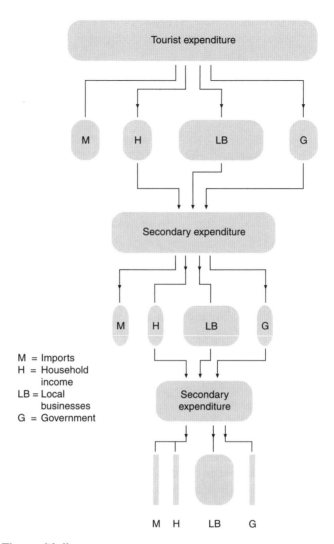

Figure 6.3   The multiplier process

Source: Cooper *et al.* (1998) *Tourism: Principles and Practice* (2nd Edn.), Harlow: Addison Wesley Longman.

amount is smaller. The amount initially spent on imports is clearly no longer available as this has now leaked out of the economy. Further *leakages* will involve household income, as some of this will be saved, and some of the money going to government may also leak from the local economy, although government may also 'return' some of this in the form of state services. Thus, as Cooper *et al.* (1998, p. 133) explain:

> during each round of expenditure, some proportion of money accrues to local residents in the form of income (wages, salaries and profits). Some of this money will be saved (by either households or businesses) and will cease to circulate in the economy: that is, there will be a leakage. The income which accrues to local households and is not saved will be respent. Some of it will leak out of the system as imports and some of it will go to the government as tax. The remainder will be

respent as household consumption. This spending of income accrued as a result of initial tourist expenditure will generate further rounds of economic activity.

With each round of expenditure the amount gets smaller as a result of leakage and this process continues until there is no longer any of the initial money left to circulate.

The multiplier concept was originally used to provide a rationale for government intervention in the economy in order to reduce unemployment. The overall economic benefit was therefore shown to be significantly greater than the initial expenditure and thus a worthwhile investment of taxpayers' money. Since the 1980s governments have been reluctant to solve unemployment in this way but have, nevertheless, promoted the idea of job creation through tourism and leisure developments, especially at the local level, on the basis of the very same multiplier process (see section below on leisure and regeneration).

Employment in leisure industries

Britain, along with other developed nations, has experienced major change in its employment structure, with the service sector having grown substantially in recent times with a corresponding decline in manufacturing industries (see Figure 6.4). The decline in manufacturing employment has resulted in part from technological progress replacing labour by machines and also from intense competition from overseas, where firms can exploit low labour costs. In some parts of Britain, entire industries have disappeared as part of this process, sometimes referred to as 'de-industrialisation'. In contrast to this decline, service industries have experienced substantial growth with the service/public sector now accounting for almost 80 per cent of total employment.

Leisure has played an important part in this process and Table 6.4 shows recent employment trends in the main leisure services industries. Leisure and tourism services collectively account for over 2 million jobs, representing about 9 per cent of total British employment. This has risen substantially over the last few decades – in 1971 leisure services accounted for only 6 per cent of the total. In fact, leisure and tourism service industries accounted for approximately one-quarter of the net increase in employment during the 1990s.

Although not as important as leisure services, there are also significant numbers of people employed in the manufacture of leisure goods. Not all the employment associated with these activities is easily identified in official statistical sources as it is often linked with the manufacture of non-leisure items. For example, the manufacture of leisure clothing and footwear is not easily separated from the manufacture of clothing and footwear as a whole. Some categories, however, are more readily identifiable and three of these are listed in Table 6.5. As already mentioned, manufacturing industry has been declining in the UK for a number of decades and those concerned with leisure goods are no exception to this.

While the above statistics have provided clear evidence of the substantial contribution of leisure to overall employment and, certainly in the case of leisure services, to employment growth, the figures do not describe the full significance. Just as multipliers operate in relation to income generation, they also operate in similar

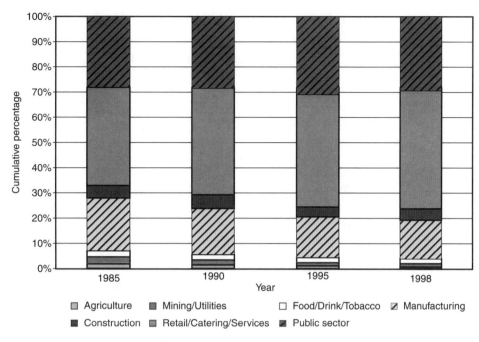

(a) Overall employment structure for selected years

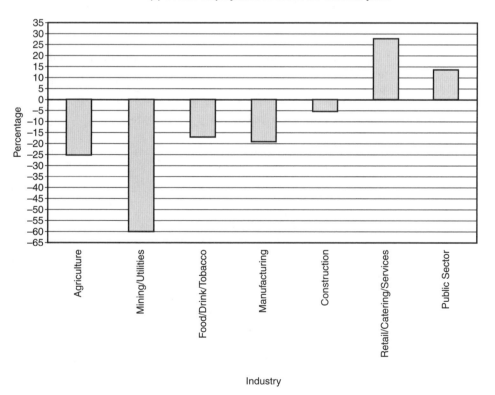

(b) Percentage change in each sector, 1985–98

Figure 6.4   Employment change in key economic sectors, 1985–98

Table 6.4 **Employment in leisure and tourism service industries in Great Britain, 1996–2000**

	1996 (000)	1997 (000)	1998 (000)	1999 (000)	2000 (000)	% change
Hotels and other tourist accommodation	421.7	400.8	427.3	403.5	405.9	−3.7
Restaurants, cafés and snack bars	462.9	479.2	489.2	536.6	547.9	+18.4
Public houses, bars, nightclubs and licensed clubs	515.8	577.2	563.0	559.0	567.5	+10.0
Travel agencies/tour operators	93.8	105.1	107.5	136.9	144.5	+54.5
Libraries, museums and other cultural activities	80.4	83.8	80.6	81.7	87.1	+8.3
Sports and other recreational activities	379.3	377.1	365.9	377.2	388.3	+2.4
Self-employed	231.8	228.1	178.6	148.9	167.0	−27.8
Total	1953.9	2022.7	2033.5	2094.9	2141.2	+9.6

Source: www. staruk.org.uk, sponsored by the National Tourist Boards and the Department for Culture, Media and Sport.

Table 6.5 **Employment in selected leisure goods industries in the UK, 2000–2001**

	2000-(000)	2001 (000)	% change
Beverages and tobacco	54.4	55.8	+2.6
Publishing, printing and reproduction of recorded media	364.3	358.6	−1.6
Radio, TV and telephone apparatus; sound and video recorders, etc.	71.8	66.4	−7.5

Source: Office of National Statistics (2001) *Labour Market Trends*, vol. 109, no. 10, October 2001.

fashion in relation to employment (see previous section). Consequently, additional jobs are created in other sectors of the economy as a result of leisure spending and by the spending of people working in leisure industries. These jobs are sometimes referred to as *indirect employment*. For example, it is estimated that in Kent, whereas there are 29,069 people directly employed in tourism, a further 11,607 jobs (indirect jobs) are created in other sectors as a result of this (see case study, below).

International trade in leisure and globalisation

As indicated earlier, leisure goods and services are traded between countries just as other goods and services are and, thus, leisure can be an important factor in a country's *balance of payments*. The balance of payments is an account of inflows and outflows of currency and thus shows a country's financial transactions with the rest of the world. Ideally these flows must balance, but deficits in the *current account* (the record of payments for trade in goods and services) can be offset by borrowing or selling assets (such as gold reserves). The current account is divided into two parts – visible and invisible trade. The former would involve such items as sportswear, sports equipment, alcoholic beverages, books, magazines and newspapers, and a wide array of electrical goods such as televisions, audio equipment and computers. Invisibles would include trade in services and, in terms of leisure services, this is virtually all accounted for by tourism. Britain is a net importer of both leisure goods and services. Since the mid twentieth century there has been a long-term decline in the share of the British consumer goods market that is supplied by home producers, and imports of manufactured goods has steadily increased, a trend that is also true of leisure goods (Gratton and Taylor, 1992). In relation to leisure services, although there has been a substantial growth in receipts from foreign tourists to Britain throughout the last few decades, there has also been even greater growth in the expenditure by British tourists travelling abroad. Thus, tourism also is in deficit on the current account, as is clearly shown in Table 6.6.

Table 6.6   Overseas travel: UK earnings and expenditure, 1990–2000 (£m)

	1990	1991	1992	1993	1994	1995	1996	1997	1998	1999	2000
Exports (visitors to UK)											
Business travel	2190	2142	2211	2489	2633	3292	3306	3586	3989	4112	4230
Personal travel	6469	6188	6630	8020	8249	9698	10,385	10,219	10,313	9948	10,176
Total	8659	8330	8841	10,509	10,882	12,990	13,691	13,805	14,302	14,060	14,406
Imports (UK visits abroad)											
Business travel	1907	1885	2000	2364	2657	3115	3490	3507	4349	4549	4970
Personal travel	8317	8370	9557	10,955	12,071	12,678	13,152	13,936	15,852	18,381	20,362
Total	10,224	10,255	11,557	13,319	14,728	15,793	16,642	17,443	20,201	22,930	25,332
Balance											
Business travel	283	257	211	125	−24	177	−184	79	−360	−437	−740
Personal travel	−1848	−2182	−2927	−2935	−3822	−2980	−2767	−3717	−5539	−8433	−10,186
Total	−1565	−1925	−2716	−2810	−3846	−2803	−2951	−3638	−5899	−8870	−10,926

Source: Office of National Statistics (2001), *United Kingdom Balance of Payments: The Pink Book 2001*, London: The Stationery Office.

The growth in tourism is part of the process of globalisation, which involves markets, trade, labour relations and culture itself attaining global dimensions, in that the forms of organisation that connect them have a global character (Horne *et al.*, 1999). As a result, the influence of nation states has declined and multinational companies and international organisations have come to acquire increasing power and influence. International tourism is an obvious example of this, with a few major companies controlling substantial amounts of the tourist market and owning hotels throughout the world, as well as integrating airlines and travel agencies into their overall business. Furthermore, no matter where in the world tourists may visit, they will be able to stay in the same style of hotel, be served the same food, and enjoy the same range of hotel attractions. In most major resort complexes and major cities throughout the world people will also be able to find familiar stores and facilities, such as McDonald's or Pizza Hut. Disneyworld in California is replicated in Florida (Disneyland), France and Tokyo.

The globalisation of leisure, however, is not just about tourism but involves other forms of leisure. Sport, for example, is now a global phenomenon affected by the emergence of a world media system, especially television, the ease with which goods, services and people can move around the world, and corporate capitalism. Horne *et al.* (1999) highlight the fact that, whereas in 1950 there were 5 million TV sets worldwide, with television only available in Great Britain, the USA and the USSR, by 1970 there were 250 million sets in 130 countries and since the early 1970s television has spread rapidly to most of the developing world. Television is a major global business and sport is one of many phenomena that can be commodified and sold to an ever-growing audience. Now sport can be watched round the clock on several different television channels. Television has popularised a great many sports and highlighted their benefits and spectacle to a mass audience and this, in turn, has encouraged international exchange in sport and the expansion of international sporting competitions (Tomlinson, 1996; Whannel, 1985), as well as encouraging the growing international travel of spectators. Television companies pay huge sums for the rights to screen key international competitions, such as the Olympic Games, Commonwealth Games, World Cup and continental cup football competitions, test matches, golf competitions, Wimbledon, and Grand Prix motor racing meetings, which attract massive audiences and provide substantial opportunities for obtaining advertising revenues. However, there is also a significant growth in the screening of national league sport events to other countries, especially soccer. For example, Italian football has been regularly screened on terrestrial channels in the UK for a number of years and various Sky channels, Eurosport being an obvious one, now screen a variety of national events. British football is also keenly followed in other countries, with premier league teams like Manchester United and Liverpool having a huge international following. Football, of course, is particularly globalised in terms of the number of foreign players who now play for British club teams, where, in some cases, foreign players are in the majority.

While corporate capital can make money through television advertising to a global market, capital can also be invested in more tangible items, such as the global merchandising of sports products and sportswear. Mega international sports events, such as the Olympics and venues such as Wimbledon, promote a variety of products bearing their brand name and logo. Wimbledon, for example, markets clothes, shoes, wallets, belts, luggage, bone china, preserves, sheets, towels, stationery and calendars (Wilson, 1988). In addition, sports clubs, especially football clubs, sell a wide range of products associated with their team. This has become somewhat controversial in recent years as the team strip has often been changed on an almost yearly basis, requiring the fans to make repeated purchases if they wish to keep up to date. For the big clubs such items are marketed worldwide and international 'pre-season' tours are as much about marketing the merchandising opportunities of the club as they are about football training. For example, in 2001 the signing by Arsenal of a Japanese player was seen by some as a useful means of extending the marketing operation in the Far East.

Leisure and the informal economy

Although it has been shown that expenditure on leisure is extremely important in the national economy, it must be realised that such statistics are based on information that is formally recorded. It is very apparent, however, that a lot of leisure involving some sort of expenditure or cost goes unrecorded and thus the overall economic significance of leisure is likely to be considerably higher than the official statistics suggest. These unrecorded costs and expenditures are part of what economists sometimes refer to as the *informal economy*. This involves a number of different activities, such as:

- the non-money production of services within households, which substitutes for the production of services within the formal economy;
- the black (or underground) economy, where goods and services are provided for 'cash-in-hand' payments to avoid paying taxes; and
- 'the communal production system' (see Gratton and Taylor, 1992, and Gershuny, 1979).

A good example of the household production of leisure services is where people hold dinner parties or invite friends and relatives to stay. Both these activities are, in effect, providing the services that would otherwise be provided by restaurants or hotels. But, whereas in the latter money transactions are involved and are recorded, in the household they are not. While this may seem a fairly obvious point, given the scale of such activity it is important to highlight the fact. For example, various surveys have shown just how widespread visiting friends and relatives (VFR) can be. Bull and Church (1998) in their study of London's tourism suggested that of the 23.7 million tourist visits to London in 1995, 6.8 million (29%) were VFR and VFR was the dominant domestic motivation for an overnight stay in London.

An example of the black economy operating in the leisure sphere would include the many street traders who operate wherever large crowds are gathered. Such traders are often to be found at sports events, fairs or popular tourist attractions and, given that all transactions are strictly in cash, the likelihood of many transactions going unrecorded is high. The city of Canterbury, for example, which receives over 2 million visitors a year, has many street traders who sell a range of goods, especially souvenirs, to such visitors.

The third aspect of the informal economy, that of the communal production system, involves members of communities helping each other out by providing services for each other. One obvious leisure example of this would involve babysitting circles where people often provide such a service in order to allow each other to indulge in leisure activities. As Gratton and Taylor (1992, p. 14) point out:

> No money changes hands but there is a kind of token system. A household is in credit if it does more than its fair share of communal production (ie it provides babysitters more often than other households in the circle). However for the communal production system to survive there must be a balancing out within a reasonably short period of time such that no household remains in net credit or net debit.

Another example of communal production involves the voluntary sector, where people organise themselves into groups or organisations to provide services for themselves that either the market (or the state) fails to provide (see Chapter 11 for more details). A lot of leisure is provided by such organisations; the voluntary sector plays a prominent role in countryside recreation and in sport the voluntary sports club is the most common form of provision. In these areas volunteers will provide substantial amounts of their time and expertise free of charge, and thus no income details are recorded. However, as highlighted in Chapter 11, the value of such involvement, if market rates were involved, would run into billions of pounds (see page 242).

Leisure and regeneration

The overall economic importance of leisure is such that in recent times it has been seen as a significant vehicle for regenerating local economies. As mentioned above, the last few decades of the twentieth century saw the economies of many towns and cities experience considerable upheaval as traditional manufacturing industries (steel, engineering, chemicals, textiles) declined and other industries migrated to peri-urban or ex-urban locations. Not only did such change result in massive job losses, with consequent impacts on other businesses, but it also produced derelict sites, leading to unattractive, rundown environments. Rural areas also witnessed decline in their traditional industry, farming, with substantial reductions in the agricultural labour force, as well as a fall in demand for food, leading to a lowering of farm incomes. In both locations leisure, especially tourism, has been promoted to help reduce the impact of such decline and redevelop the economy. The idea of using tourism to regenerate urban economies was initially encountered in North America in the late 1970s, with the city of Baltimore often being cited as a classic example. Not only was tourism seen as a growth industry and generator of jobs, but its development was also capable of providing environmental improvements (Shaw and Williams, 1994). Figure 6.5 illustrates the way in which tourism can help regenerate urban areas. The basic strategy is that tourists will generate income and jobs and that, as tourism develops further, new facilities will help create a better urban environment, which will not only attract more tourists, but also create benefits for local residents through improved facilities and an improved image of the city to potential investors (Law, 1992).

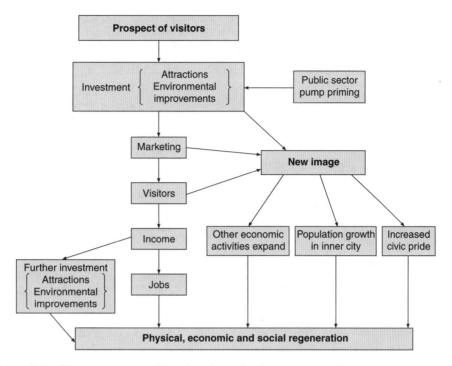

Figure 6.5   The processes of tourism-based urban regeneration

Source: Law, C.M. (1992) 'Urban tourism and contribution to economic regeneration', *Urban Studies*, vol. 29.

In the early 1980s several cities in Britain specifically marketed tourism as a means of regenerating their declining economies, a process further encouraged by a number of reports that appeared in the mid 1980s which highlighted tourism's economic role (Banks, 1985; CBI, 1985; Young, 1985). These stressed three key elements of tourism: its labour-intensive nature, its strong local economic multiplier effects and the low capital cost of job creation (Shaw and Williams, 1994). In addition, grants were available from the English Tourist Board. Manchester, for example, created the Castlefield Urban Heritage Park, using an old warehouse as a new museum of science, and other visitor attractions, such as the Granada TV studios. Since the mid 1980s many new projects have emerged, such as the former Central Station being converted into a large exhibition centre (GMEX), a new concert hall (Bridgewater Hall), the Imperial War Museum in the north (costing £235 million) and the NYMEX arena (Europe's biggest indoor entertainment complex). In addition, sport, and related sports tourism, has been a major factor in Manchester's strategy and approach to regeneration and has been at the heart of a central marketing initiative focused on football, cricket, the Commonwealth Stadium, the new swimming and diving complex at the university and the world-class velodrome, a benefit of its failed Olympic bid. While many cities have obtained substantial benefits from hosting the Olympic Games, Manchester is a good example of a city benefiting from a failed bid, as the project created investment and development opportunities and allowed linkages and partnerships to flourish.

Economic impact of tourism in Kent

The Kent tourism industry is a major industry within Kent, with total direct expenditure estimated at £1.2 billion in 1998. Further estimates for that year put the number of staying trips at 5.48 million involving 18.53 million nights spent by visitors in the county. In addition, Kent received 32.8 million day visitors, of which 1.4 million were from overseas. Staying visitors injected about £554 million of direct tourism expenditure into the local Kent economy and day visitors spent a further £625 million (£50 million by overseas day visitors), bringing the total direct tourism expenditure to £1.2 billion. This tourism expenditure supported a total of 40,676 jobs, 29,069 in establishments directly receiving tourist expenditure and 11,607 indirect jobs. This makes tourism the fourth-largest sector of

employment in the county after public administration, education and health (144,707 employees in 1998), banking, finance and insurance (85,440) and manufacturing (83,563).

Figures 6.6 and 6.7 highlight the main beneficiaries of this tourist impact. In terms of expenditure, the catering and retail sectors received almost two-thirds of the total, with catering accounting for 32 per cent and retail 26 per cent. Other key beneficiaries of the estimated £1.2 billion direct tourist spend were the accommodation (15%) and attractions/entertainment (10%) sectors, along with transport-related industries. Figure 6.7 shows that the most important sectors for tourist employment are pubs/restaurants (with 12,000 direct jobs) followed by accommodation and retail.

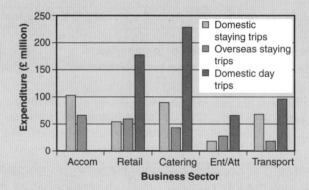

Figure 6.6   Tourist expenditure in Kent in relation to key economic sectors

Source: KCC (2001) *The Economic Impact of Tourism in Kent Factsheet*, Maidstone: Kent County Council.

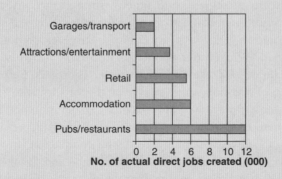

Figure 6.7   Tourism employment in Kent in relation to key economic sectors

Source: KCC (2001) *The Economic Impact of Tourism in Kent Factsheet*, Maidstone: Kent County Council.

Political significance of leisure

The first half of this chapter has established that over the last few decades leisure, in its various forms, has become an increasingly important sector in the British economy, as it is in many other economies throughout the world. It would not be surprising, therefore, to see government taking an interest in leisure and developing policies accordingly. However, it would be wrong to think that government interest in leisure was simply linked to economic concerns or was entirely a recent phenomenon. A wide range of government policies concerned with various aspects of social life (e.g. culture, education, health, social control, and social deprivation) have also involved leisure, and governments have been pursuing such policies for at least the last couple of centuries, if not longer. In addition to using leisure to achieve various economic and social goals, however, there are also important debates about the role of the state in providing for people's leisure needs *per se*. In other words, should the state be involved in providing for people's enjoyment and pleasure? It would thus appear that there is a clear political dimension in relation to the study of leisure and it is the intention of this section to explore its various facets.

Politics is essentially about the ways in which people organise themselves in order to gain access to the resources they need or desire. It therefore concerns the ways in which various institutions (such as the state) operate to facilitate this process and the various ideas and ideologies that relate to this. Linked to this is the concept of power, the ways in which the state exercises such power and the extent to which individuals, or groups of people, have access to power, especially in terms of controlling their own lives. In order to pursue or acquire leisure, people will need time and possibly other resources such as land, facilities, equipment and money. In addition, they may also require certain freedoms. And the availability of all of these 'resources' may well be influenced, or even determined, by the state or other institutions that exercise various forms of power or control.

In addition to the state controlling and banning certain forms of leisure through various forms of legislation, some people have also identified a 'micro-politics' of leisure, such as the power exercised by family relations, especially in relation to gender where women's leisure may be subjected to male domination and control (Deem, 1986). It is the intention of this chapter to concentrate on the macro aspects of leisure politics, rather than these micro aspects which to some extent were covered in Chapter 4, although it is still important that students are aware of these interrelations.

Political ideologies

As outlined above, there are significant questions about the extent to which government should promote social policies, let alone policies specifically concerning people's enjoyment and pleasure. The answers to these questions are inextricably linked to political ideologies. According to Hall (1982), ideology can be defined as 'a framework or network of values, concepts, images and propositions which we employ in interpreting and understanding how society works'. In addition, ideologies may be prescriptive in that they define how society should work, and it is frequently this meaning that is at the heart of policy-making debates. In simple terms, the key ideologies affecting political thinking revolve around the extent to which government should or should not intervene in the economic and social affairs of its citizens.

At one extreme is the ideology of 'liberalism', which is reflected in Adam Smith's *The Wealth of Nations*, published in 1776. This liberal economic theory provided a rationale for a non-interventionist approach by the state and argued that the free market would be the most efficient generator of public goods. As a result, social policies would be minimal and restricted to easing any obstruction to market forces (Haywood *et al.*, 1995). As has already been shown in Chapter 1, it was this thinking that underpinned the *Industrial Revolution* and it still remains a potent influence on contemporary political thought, having had a significant influence on Thatcherism and related policies (see Chapter 8).

At the other end of the political spectrum is the ideology of 'socialism', where state intervention is all-embracing. This position draws its thinking from the ideas of Karl Marx and is based on the view that collective action by the state is necessary to correct the inequalities generated and perpetuated by liberal capitalism. Of course, as will be apparent, there are many variants of these positions for, as Henry (1993, p. 27) points out, 'the relationships between political ideologies are multi-faceted, and cannot be accommodated on a single, simple, unidimensional continuum'. In fact, much of the history of British politics throughout the last two centuries has concerned the way in which the various ideological variants have developed and been replaced or accommodated by others.

Market intervention

The free market liberal ideology has more recently and more succinctly been expressed as 'the market knows best', a philosophy that underpinned much Thatcherite thinking in the 1980s. Advocates of free markets would argue that they have the potential to deliver economic efficiency, allocative efficiency, consumer sovereignty, and economic growth (Tribe, 1995). Economic efficiency involves maximising output for minimum input; allocative efficiency relates to the efficient distribution of limited resources; consumer sovereignty means that consumers exercise power in the market place, with production being driven by consumer demand; and economic growth, so it is argued, will be encouraged under conditions of free competition, as firms will strive to increase productivity and resources will be transferred from unprofitable and inefficient firms to those which are profitable and efficient. In essence, according to Tribe (1995, p. 90), 'under a competitive free market system consumers will get the goods and services they want at the lowest possible prices'.

Despite its apparent advantages, the ability of the free market to deliver has attracted much criticism and, as suggested in the previous section, it is this debate between the proponents of the free market and those who argue its limitations and harmful effects that lies at the heart of ideological differences. One key area of criticism involves the failure of the market to cater adequately for the welfare of society and, in relation to leisure, two broad categories of market failure might be identified: efficiency-related and equity-related (Gratton and Taylor, 1991). It is generally argued that leisure produces various social (collective) benefits over and above the benefits that individual participants (consumers) obtain from their purchase of leisure. While an efficient free market may well take account of the value to the participant and the cost of supply, it fails to take account of any additional social benefits and is thus likely to underprovide the necessary resources (Gratton and Taylor, 1991). Various forms of leisure, especially sport and recreation, are capable of providing wider social benefits such as improved health and possibly reduced crime rates (Gratton and Taylor, 1991) and, thus, government may well wish to encourage greater provision and participation by subsidising consumers, subsidising suppliers or directly supplying the product at a lower price. However, governments may also wish to make similar subsidies in order to provide a more equitable distribution of leisure resources and opportunities for its population if, as discussed in the previous section, society accepts that access to leisure is an 'entitlement' and the free market fails to deliver.

Other arguments against the free market revolve round its underlying assumptions, its inability to provide for public goods and the external costs (externalities) that the operation of the free market may produce. The benefits of free markets are based on a number of assumptions that may not always be met in reality. These include the existence of perfect markets involving many buyers and sellers, homogeneous products, perfect knowledge, and freedom of entry and exit. However, in practice this is clearly not the case, as many markets are dominated by a few suppliers, considerable product differentiation occurs and consumers may possess limited information. Another assumption is that of consumer sovereignty, but this does not exist for those with insufficient purchasing power to influence a market.

Many forms of leisure, especially much outdoor recreation and sport, may be viewed as 'public or collective goods'. These are goods that are both non-rival and non-excludable. Non-rival means that a person can consume the good without preventing someone else enjoying exactly the same product at the same time. Non-excludable means that no consumer can be prevented from enjoying the product (Gratton and Taylor, 1991). Clearly, under these conditions, supply is not going to be provided by the free market because returns are dependent on selling to private individuals, who can be excluded if they are unwilling to pay the price. If there are no mechanisms for excluding users then people can still consume but pay nothing; in other words, they can take a 'free ride'. Examples of such public goods include many countryside and coastal resources, such as forests, mountains and moorlands, lakes, rivers and beaches, but many urban public spaces would also come under this heading. While there are examples of such resources where it is possible to control access and thus exclude people, in many cases this is not possible or to do so would be very expensive. Given that the private sector will therefore be unlikely to provide such resources, provision thus falls to the public or voluntary sectors (see Chapters 9 and 11). Therefore, government, through the Countryside Agency, provides funding to develop and manage access to a range of countryside resources, such as national parks, country parks, picnic sites, and long-distance footpaths.

The final problem with free markets and leisure concerns the argument that they do not always consider all the costs or negative 'externalities' that leisure activity may produce. As Tribe (1995, p. 91) points out, 'the selling of alcohol is associated with the private benefit of feeling happy but has the unwanted public costs of fighting and accidents', and this raises the question of who 'picks up the pieces' and foots the bill. Similarly, tourism produces a variety of environmental impacts – e.g. noise, congestion, water and atmospheric pollution, erosion of vegetation – which neither tourist nor tourist provider normally pays for. Usually it is the state that pays and, to reduce such costs, it may wish to control certain activities (see section below on control).

The state as promoter of leisure

The history of government involvement in leisure has clearly been influenced by a variety of political ideologies. As has already been demonstrated in Chapter 1, the nineteenth century witnessed various attempts by government to influence the nature of leisure, but such policies were not part of an interventionist ideology as such, but pursued as part of a liberal philosophy concerned with helping free market capitalism to develop. Much of this involvement concerned control or suppression of leisure (see section below) and even where policy might appear to have had more positive aims, such as the 1871 Bank Holiday Act or the Acts concerning Public Baths and Washhouses (1846), Museums (1849) and Libraries (1850), there were often other motives at work, such as health or self-improvement or a refreshed workforce, again with advantages for the smooth running of the capitalist system. More recently, in the twentieth century, policies to promote sport and physical recreation have often been motivated more by a need to provide a healthier population rather than to provide for public enjoyment. A healthier population not only means fewer days absent from work, and thus better productivity, but it also reduces the call on the health service and, in earlier times, also meant fitter recruits for the armed forces. In addition, it has also been argued that leisure activity, and especially sport and physical recreation, is likely to reduce crime and, thus, support for leisure may be pursued as part of a wider policy of social control. As Gratton and Taylor (1991, p. 66) point out:

> one of the target groups often chosen by sports providers is that of young people, and both implicitly and explicitly it is often recognised that provision of sporting opportunities for this group will help promote constructive leisure pursuits, at the expense of more negative activities such as crime and vandalism.

If leisure were to produce such effects, and it must be highlighted that as yet there is limited evidence to support the thesis, then clearly there would be wider external or social benefits being provided, beyond those that relate to the individual participant, which might merit state support. Thus, even those who are driven primarily by a 'free market' or 'conservative' (liberal) ideology may not necessarily deny the need for government intervention in these areas.

Another factor that has influenced government support for leisure concerns its support for sport and the political and economic gains that may accrue from this. This may provide governments with international sporting contact and high-profile opportunities for publicising their policy on international issues or towards specific states, or as a vehicle for manipulating the state's international image and projecting its political ideology (Houlihan, 1994). A number of famous examples might be cited to illustrate this, such as the Nazi government's attempts to enhance the prestige of the Third Reich through the 1936 Olympic Games (Mandell, 1971 as quoted in Houlihan, 1994; Hart-Davis, 1986, quoted in Houlihan, 1994), and the USA sending table tennis and basketball teams to China in the early 1970s as part of a broader process of improving relations between the two countries.

A further way in which sport is used by the state is as an agency of political socialisation (Houlihan, 1994; Horne *et al.*, 1999). As indicated in Chapter 1, sport and other forms of leisure (or rational recreation) have been encouraged in order to promote desirable attributes and values, such as obedience, fitness, loyalty and leadership skills. Furthermore, the competitive nature of sport was also regarded as a useful means of reinforcing the virtues of capitalism. Socialist countries have also used sport as a means of promoting the ideals of revolution and the development of communist and socialist vales (Sugden *et al.*, 1990 as quoted in Houlihan, 1994), as clearly seen in high-profile involvement of the former USSR and East Germany in events such as the Olympic Games. Sport has also been used as an aid to nation building, for example, the importance of sport, particularly cricket, in the emergence of an Australian national identity, and cricket has also acted as an important focus for West Indian identity (Houlihan, 1994). Finally, sport may also be funded by governments in order to foster morale through national success. When the national team does well, people feel better about themselves, and the incumbent government may well benefit from such a 'feel-good factor'.

It was not until the second half of the twentieth century, with the growth of the welfare state, that political thinking broadly acknowledged government obligations to provide for people's leisure wants. As with healthcare, education, and old age security, leisure came to be seen as an entitlement or social right. According to Marshall (1950, p. 11, quoted in J. Wilson, 1988, p. 101) social rights refer to 'the whole range from the right to a modicum of economic welfare and security to the right to share to the full in the social heritage and to live the life of a civilized being according to the standards prevailing in society'. Social rights thus include an equal claim to a 'style of life', as well as money/income; furthermore, leisure came to be seen as an important element of such lifestyles and, hence, a basic individual right. Of course, the acceptance of such thinking runs counter to the free market principle of capitalism (J. Wilson, 1988) and thus it raises fundamental ideological debate. To what extent should the state raise taxes to provide or subsidise various forms of leisure to enable access for everyone? How far should the provision of leisure services be left to the private sector?

For most of the latter half of the twentieth century there was a generally accepted consensus that the state should make a substantial provision. However, with the growth of the New Right thinking in the 1980s, the debate has been rekindled and the state's importance somewhat reduced (for a detailed coverage of these issues and the growth and nature of state provision, see Chapters 8 and 9).

Control

As discussed in Chapter 2, one condition that is usually required for leisure is freedom; that leisure involves 'activities undertaken voluntarily, without constraint or sense of obligation' (J. Wilson, 1988, p. 11). However, the Latin root of the word 'leisure', *licere*, suggests two very different meanings – the freedom to choose (licentiousness) and permission to choose (licence), a positive and a negative component. In fact, much of the history of leisure, as shown in Chapter 1, has involved a struggle between 'liberation and control' and 'freedom and constraint', what Coalter (1989) refers to as 'an unresolvable dualism'; and the state, as well as other powerful institutions such as the Church, has played a major role in exerting this control.

The basis of the state's involvement in the control of leisure revolves round concepts of what is considered appropriate and inappropriate behaviour. This might involve the time when people can indulge in certain types of leisure, the space that they might wish to use or the impact their leisure activity might have on other people or things, as well as various religious or moral grounds (which have often been invoked to legitimise the introduction of regulations and controls introduced to further the interests or values of one particular influential group or class over another).

A substantial amount of the state's engagement with leisure has involved regulative policies of one sort or another, and this began in a comprehensive way in the period 1780–1820, when the landed gentry and the emerging industrial middle class, represented in Parliament and in the local magistracy, attempted to suppress popular recreations (Henry, 1993). As outlined in Chapter 1, this was due to two main reasons – the need to instil a work discipline and concerns about public order. An essential feature of the Industrial Revolution was the way in which work time and leisure time became demarcated and highly structured, with work being seen as the priority. Middle-class factory owners required workers to work long, regimented hours and to be available for labour at the appointed hour. Absenteeism and drunkenness were not to be tolerated and thus steps were taken to control and curtail recreation in an attempt to get rid of such practices, very much part of the liberal philosophy of government intervention designed to ease the operation of capitalism. Many holidays, fairs and wakes were abolished and the licensing of 'beer houses' was introduced in 1820. The various licensing laws that have been introduced since then provide a good example of the way in which government controls leisure time, even to this day. The sale of alcohol on licensed premises is only permissible during certain hours of the day; until relatively recently this was restricted to a few hours at lunchtime and during the evening. Similarly, the hours of opening for other leisure facilities, such as various clubs and sporting venues, are also restricted and the Sunday trading laws, although relaxed to some extent in the 1990s, also curtail the extent to which people may shop on Sundays.

In addition to time, the state has also controlled the spaces that are available for leisure. Just as the early part of the Industrial Revolution was a period when leisure time was regulated, so too government attempted to control and restrict the use of leisure space. Hitherto the streets had been public places, where various unregulated forms of leisure had occurred. The streets were venues for fairs, carnivals, animal sports (e.g. bull running) and football matches. But in the early years of the nineteenth century, government began to ban them from the streets because, along with alcohol, they were viewed as a threat both to industrial production and to public order (see Chapter 1). While some of these activities disappeared entirely, others, such as various animal sports, went 'underground', and sports, such as football, became regulated and confined to specifically designated spaces that were deemed more appropriate. Wilson (1988, p. 25) argues that:

> this effort to privatise the use of space was, and continues to be, inevitably class biased, given the inequality of access to private space, much more available to the wealthy than the poor and hard to find for the young, who routinely have been forced to resort to public space for their leisure.

He cites the 1906 Street Betting Act as further evidence of this class bias, as it prohibited only off-course, cash, street betting, while permitting betting in private clubs or at racecourses. This prohibition continued until the 1960s, when betting shops and working-class gambling activities such as bingo were legalised.

Such developments, however, were not purely confined to towns and cities. In rural areas the enclosure movement of the late eighteenth and early nineteenth centuries removed many public spaces, as certain areas of 'common' land, previously available to villagers for communal use, were privatised. Also, in the uplands, landowners successfully restricted public access. Strong landowning interests and sympathies in Parliament have meant that, despite various campaigns over the last century to secure public access to unenclosed land, legislation to allow such access has not occurred until quite recently (Countryside and Rights of Way Act, November 2000). In addition, a prevailing consensus about what the countryside should be used for (that is, passive, quiet, contemplative, non-gregarious forms of leisure) has had a major influence on town and country planning and thus ensures that certain other forms of leisure, especially those that involve noise, are severely restricted (see Chapter 7).

While contemporary governments may not resort to such draconian policies as exercised in the early nineteenth century, the need to ensure public order through the control of leisure activities is still evident. Fear of riot leading to the overthrow of government may no longer be present (although riot in itself is still an issue), but the need to control public space is still important in terms of keeping the streets safe for decent people. While this would appear at face value to be a laudable aim, the policing of public spaces in this respect, and its impact on the leisure activities of certain groups, has attracted much controversy in recent times. According to Clark and Critcher (1985, p. 126), commenting on the 1970s and 80s:

> While robbery on the streets grabs the headlines, the mundane reality of public policing concerns offences against public order – the playing of games prohibited by local bye-laws; trespass; loitering with intent; being drunk and disorderly; causing a breach of the peace; and being a suspected person. Unlike robbery and theft, these offences against public order depend heavily upon police discretion, and their interpretation of social behaviour. By the early 1980s, the policing of public space in Britain's inner cities had become one of the most explosive 'leisure' conflicts.

As Clark and Critcher further argue, 'given the inequality of access to *private* space in our society (available more to the wealthy than the poor, to older rather than younger), those groups who have to resort to public space for their leisure time are automatically more vulnerable to policing'. And the most vulnerable have tended to be primarily working-class (particularly black) youth and confrontations between the police and such groups has been a frequent occurrence. Although the 'sus' laws were abolished and the stop and search powers have subsequently been curtailed, many of the fundamental issues remain. In addition, the 1990s and new millennium have witnessed new public order concerns, as urban centres have attracted large numbers of relatively affluent young people spilling out on to the streets from pubs and clubs, somewhat inebriated and behaving in an 'anti-social' manner. Some local authorities have banned the drinking of alcohol in the streets and alcohol has also been banned at various sports venues.

While much control and regulation has been about creating a disciplined work-force and ensuring public order, other factors have also been influential. In the nineteenth century the attempts to ban popular recreations, such as drinking and blood sports, were also about the middle and upper classes trying to impose their values about appropriate leisure forms and modes of behaviour on the working classes (see Chapter 1). But debates about what are appropriate leisure forms are still ongoing. For example, drug-taking and pornography are either illegal or seriously curtailed, and banning the ownership of handguns in 1998 has also made certain forms of recreational shooting difficult to pursue. Similarly, certain so-called 'extreme sports' are banned in certain countries (e.g. BASE jumping – parachuting from a fixed object rather than a plane). The ongoing debate about hunting with dogs will, if legislation to ban it is forthcoming, result in another example, although this would be an interesting contrast to much previous regulation, as it would involve popular sentiments prevailing against what many would regard as upper-class interests.

These particular leisure forms raise a number of ethical and ideological questions, as they are leisure activities that involve a risk of injury, even death, to the individual or other people or, in the case of hunting, to animals. In some areas it would be argued that the leisure pursuits of some would clearly harm others, especially where children or other vulnerable groups of people are concerned (e.g. the licensing of films, the sale of alcohol and child pornography). However, not only is there considerable debate as to the level of risk and potential injury but, irrespective of how much injury may be involved, libertarians would argue that it is up to the individual, not the state, to decide, certainly in the case of personal risk.

Leisure developments also come within the realm of town and country planning legislation, which is concerned with the efficient use of land resources as well as ensuring that different land uses are relatively harmonious. Leisure facilities that attract large crowds and produce lots of noise should not ideally be located in residential areas where they might cause a nuisance but, nevertheless, should be located at sites that are accessible. Planners therefore need to consider these sorts of implications when drafting plans and making decisions on planning permission (see Chapter 7 for a more detailed account of planning).

It should also be highlighted that, although much regulation concerns reducing or controlling certain perceived problems that may result from leisure, the state also regulates in order to improve leisure experiences. In licensing various premises, and insisting that the goods and services that people purchase meet certain standards, the state ensures that people can enjoy their leisure in safer and more comfortable circumstances and that certain leisure activities do not conflict with others. Leisure consumers want to know that the premises they use are free from fire risks and other hazards and that restaurants are hygienic. Country walkers will not wish to be confronted by horse riders, and so the latter are restricted to specific bridleways. Furthermore, it should not be forgotten that, while maintaining public order and controlling crowds may be inhibiting some people's leisure, it may also be enhancing that of others. Urban centres attract many leisure seekers, other than those frequenting pubs and clubs, many of whom may not wish to feel threatened by groups of drunken youths. In addition, while much regulation is designed to protect the leisure consumer, it is also there to ensure that legitimate commercial interests are also protected from 'cowboys' and 'pirates' (Clarke and Critcher, 1985).

● ● ● ● Conclusions

This chapter has examined both the economic and the political significance of leisure. It is clear from the various sections in the first half of this chapter that leisure, in its various forms, has wide-ranging and substantial economic importance. Consumers spend an ever-increasing proportion of their income on leisure goods and services and leisure makes a major contribution to the national economy, employment and international trade. It is therefore not surprising that leisure also has an important political dimension and is often seen by policy makers as a major vehicle for economic development, and especially economic regeneration. The political significance of leisure is, however, much wider than this and the chapter has also examined fundamental questions about the role of the state in influencing and facilitating people's access to leisure, the extent to which people are free to pursue leisure as they wish and the extent to which the state has promoted leisure to achieve various social goals.

Questions

1 Examine the economic importance of leisure for the national economy.

2 In what ways can leisure help to stimulate local economies?

3 What is meant by the 'informal economy' and what is its relationship with leisure?

4 Examine the concept of globalisation in the context of leisure.

5 Examine the extent to which leisure has been used as a vehicle for achieving social goals.

6 Discuss the various arguments for greater or fewer controls on leisure.

References

Banks, R. (1985) *New Jobs from Pleasure – A Strategy for Creating New Jobs in the Tourist Industry*, London: HMSO.

Bull, P. and Church, A. (1998) 'Urban tourism in the 1990s: understanding the figures for London', *Geography Review*, vol. 12, no. 2, November, pp. 37–40.

Clark, J. and Critcher, C. (1985) *The Devil Makes Work: Leisure in Capitalist Britain*, Basingstoke: Macmillan Education.

Confederation of British Industry (1985) *The Paying Guest*, London: CBI.

Coalter, F. (1989) 'Leisure Politics: An Unresolvable Dualism?' in Rojek, C. (ed.) *Leisure for Leisure: Critical Essays*, Basingstoke: The Macmillan Press Ltd.

Cooper, C., Fletcher, J., Gilbert, D., Shepherd, R. and Wanhill, S. (1998) *Tourism: Principles and Practice* (2nd edition), Harlow: Longman.

Deem, R. (1986) 'The politics of women's leisure', in F. Coalter (ed.) *The Politics of Leisure*, London: Leisure Studies Association.

Gershuny, J.I. (1979) 'The Informal Economy: Its Role in Post-Industrial Society', *Futures*, 12, no. 1, pp. 3–15.

Gratton, C. and Taylor, P. (1991) *Government and the Economics of Sport*, Harlow: Longman.

Gratton, C. and Taylor, P. (1992) *Economics of Leisure Services Management*, Harlow: Longman.

Hall, S. (1982) *Conformity, Consensus and Conflict*, Open University Units 21 and 22 of Social Sciences Foundation Course, Milton Keynes: Open University.

Haywood, L., Kew, F., Bramham, P., Spink, J., Capenerhurst, J. and Henry, I. (1995) *Understanding Leisure*, Cheltenham: Stanley Thornes.

Henry, I.P. (1993) *The Politics of Leisure Policy*, Basingstoke: Macmillan Press.

Horne, J., Tomlinson, A. and Whannel, G. (1999) *Understanding Sport: An Introduction to the Sociological and Cultural Analysis of Sport*, London: Spon.

Houlihan, B. (1994) *Sport and International Politics*, Hemel Hempstead: Harvester Wheatsheaf.

Law, C.M. (1992) 'Urban tourism and its contribution to economic regeneration', *Urban Studies*, vol. 29, pp. 597–616.

Leisure Industries Research Centre/ Leisure Consultants (1998) *Leisure Forecasts 1998–2002: Leisure Away from Home*, Sheffield: LIRC.

Mandell, R. (1971) *The Nazi Olympics*, New York: Macmillan

Mintel (1999) *The Leisure Business: The Leisure Market*, 07/09/99, BMRB/Mintel.

Office of National Statistics (2000) *Family Spending: A Report on the 1999–2000 Family Expenditure Survey*, London: The Stationery Office.

Shaw, G. and Williams, A. (1994) *Critical Issues in Tourism: A Geographical Perspective*, Oxford: Blackwell.

Sugden, J., Tomlinson, A. and McCartner, E. (1990) 'The making of white lightning in Cuba: politics, sport and physical education 30 years after the revolution', *Arena Review*, vol. 14, no.1, pp. 101–9.

Tomlinson, A. (1996) 'Olympic spectacles: opening ceremonies, and some paradoxes of globalisation', *Media, Culture and Society*, vol. 18, pp. 583–602.

Tribe, J. (1995) *The Economics of Leisure and Tourism*, Oxford: Butterworth-Heinemann.

Whannel, G. (1985) 'Television spectacle and the internationalisation of sport', *Journal of Communication Enquiry*, vol. 2, pp. 54–74.

Wilson, J. (1988) *Politics and Leisure*, London: Unwin Hyman.

Wilson, N. (1988) *The Sports Business*, London: Piatkus.

Young, Lord (1985) *Pleasure, Leisure and Jobs – the Business of Tourism*, London: HMSO.

Further reading

There are a number of general texts dealing with the economics of leisure that contain chapters on various aspects of the economic importance of leisure. These include texts by Tribe (1995) *The Economics of Leisure and Tourism*, and Gratton and Taylor (1992) *Economics of Leisure Services Management*.

Several texts cover the politics of leisure including those by Henry (1993) *The Politics of Leisure Policy*, and Wilson (1988) *Politics and Leisure*.

A number of texts provide a useful coverage of the politics of sport: Houlihan (1994) *Sport and International Politics*; Horne et al. (1999) *Understanding Sport: An Introduction to the Sociological and Cultural Analysis of Sport*; and Gratton and Taylor (1991) *Government and the Economics of Sport*.

Useful websites

www.statistics.gov.uk/
www.staruk.org.uk/

PART TWO ●●●●

Provision for leisure

Chapter 7 ● ● ● ●

Places for leisure

Practically anywhere can be a place for leisure. Given the variety of leisure forms and the many different circumstances in which leisure can occur, virtually any space, place or environment can be utilised. Such places can include natural, semi-natural and 'man-made' environments; they can be small (e.g. a garden) or large (e.g. a national park); they can be informal (e.g. a back street where children play football) or facilities provided for formal activities (e.g. theatre, cinema or sports stadium); they can be rare (e.g. an Olympic-quality swimming pool) or located at specific sites due to the precise environmental requirements of certain activities (e.g. ski slopes) or they can be common, almost ubiquitous, such as the home itself. In fact, the home is probably the most utilised leisure environment for the simple reason that most people spend most of their leisure time there (see Chapter 3). However, despite its undoubted importance and interest, especially in the way in which the home environment has changed through time (for example in terms of utilisation of space and the size of gardens), this chapter will be primarily concerned with land and water resources beyond the home environment. This is for two key reasons. First, it is assumed that most people are reasonably familiar with the places in which they spend most of their time and thus will already possess a good understanding of how these environments function and, second, the way in which homes are adapted and utilised for leisure is primarily due to individual action and is not influenced to quite the same extent by broader ecological, economic, political and social forces that shape the development of other leisure resources.

It is, therefore, the intention of this chapter to examine the nature and supply of leisure places, not so much in terms of cataloguing the many different types, but rather in terms of the key influences that have produced them in order to highlight the variety, complexity and spatial components of leisure environments.

Objectives

To:

- *understand the ecological basis of leisure environments*

- *recognise the economic forces influencing the availability of land and water resources for leisure*

- *explore the social and cultural construction of leisure places and the ways in which different places are perceived as leisure environments*

- *examine the influence of town and country planning on the provision and nature of leisure places.*

The ecological basis

This chapter begins by examining the ecological basis, not because this is regarded as more important, for in fact it is not important in many urban situations, but rather because it could be argued that the ecological base provides the original canvas on which all other developments subsequently occurred. If we were to take a region such as Britain and trace the evolution of the landscape through time, we would begin with the natural ecosystem and see how this has been destroyed and transformed to make way for agriculture, industry and urban development, as well as providing places and environments for leisure. While approximately 10 per cent of the original landscape might now be covered by stone, bricks and concrete, the remainder still comprises some form of ecological community (even though very little could be regarded as 'natural') and much of this has some relevance for leisure.

Although in certain parts of the world it is possible to find natural environments where plant and animal communities have been largely unaffected by human activity (e.g. equatorial rainforests, deserts and tundra regions), over large areas of the globe this is not the case. In fact, in some countries there is very little so-called natural environment remaining, and this is certainly the case in Britain. Over the last couple of millennia the natural vegetation of Britain, primarily woodland, has been removed or modified for a variety of human activities. Even certain landscapes that might appear 'natural' – such as woodlands and moorlands – are often heavily managed. The countryside is just as much an artificial environment as is the town or city.

Although these environments may not be natural in the strict sense of the word, they are often perceived as such and are valued for the particular ecological communities that are found there. Many of these places are important in leisure terms because they either provide the basis for particular leisure interests, such as birdwatching or orienteering, or they provide an important landscape or backdrop for a wide range of passive and active pursuits. Many might be described as having

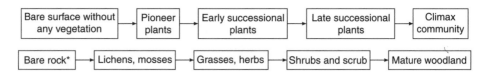

* The example listed here describes the likely sequence that might occur on a bare rock surface.
Different types of succession will occur on different unvegetated surfaces such as sand or water
or bare earth (where there has been vegetation in the past).

Figure 7.1   The process of plant succession

important scenic qualities and thus provide an essential resource for sightseeing and tourism, as in the national parks of England and Wales. Given their importance for leisure, many ecological resources are managed specifically for this purpose.

If left to the forces of nature, natural vegetation will change through time as one plant community is replaced by more dominant species, a process referred to as *ecological succession*. This is illustrated in Figure 7.1, which shows how an area of bare ground will initially be invaded by lichens and mosses (early pioneering plants), which will gradually be replaced by grasses, then shrubs and scrub and eventually woodland. When there are no more dominant species to invade, a *climax community* is said to exist and, for most areas, such a community would be some form of woodland. For example, the natural vegetation over much of southern Britain was originally oak woodland.

In many areas the natural process of succession is interrupted or arrested and this can result from either natural phenomena or human action (either accidental or intentional) and can be permanent or temporary. One of the most significant disruptions of natural ecosystems is due to agricultural development where climax communities have been cleared to be replaced by sub-climax, managed plant communities. Were farming to be abandoned, however, these communities would soon be transformed, as the natural processes would once again take hold and eventually the original climax community would be restored. It should not be forgotten that it is the farmed landscapes with which people are familiar that are often valued as a scenic resource (see section below).

Although various climax communities provide opportunities for leisure, sub-climax, arrested communities also play an important role. Heather moors, chalk grasslands and sand dunes, for example, which are all attractive environments for various leisure activities, are maintained in that state due to various forms of management. It is now generally accepted that most moorland or upland heath communities that provide the core resource for most national park areas in Britain are not true climax communities. In other words, the key resource that attracts millions of tourists each year, and which provides an open landscape for ramblers, is not natural but rather the result of a particular management regime. The true climax community of much of the uplands is probably that of scrub birch and this woodland has been cleared over the centuries for fuel, sheep farming and grouse shooting (another leisure pursuit). The short, springy heather that is characteristic of these environments is maintained by periodic burning and sheep grazing. Burning kills off the older, woody heather and allows new plants to grow, providing young shoots for the grouse to eat. Were the heather allowed to grow naturally it would either grow quite tall (up to about 10 feet in sheltered spots) or, more likely in the windy uplands, fall over and grow in a more prostrate form, eventually to be replaced by the more dominant birch.

Similarly, the chalk grassland, so characteristic of downland areas of southern England, is also a sub-climax environment resulting from pastoral farming. The grazing of the slopes by sheep and cattle prevents more dominant species invading, as their shoots are either trampled or eaten. However, if this activity ceases, the more dominant species quickly establish themselves. In cases such as this, landscapes resulting from particular farming practices may have to be managed in different ways if the particular form of farming ceases. Hawthorn may have to be cleared by axe and chainsaw or, if the invading scrub is not too advanced, animals may have to be reintroduced to keep the invading species at bay. For example, goats have been used in some places and the White Cliffs Countryside Project near Dover employs a herd of Dexter cattle to do this job.

The two previous examples illustrate how particular environments, which have considerable significance for leisure and appear to most people as natural, are in fact the result of farming or a related activity. It has also been demonstrated that, where such activity ceases, the fortuitous benefits for leisure can disappear unless specific management takes over. This could involve some public body but more likely it will involve some scheme whereby the original farmer or landowner is paid to manage the resource for leisure and amenity benefits. For example, the Environmentally Sensitive Areas scheme, dating from the 1986 Agriculture Act, pays farmers so much per hectare to continue to farm in traditional ways and thus preserve such ecosystems. Furthermore, the Countryside Stewardship scheme, introduced in 1991, pays farmers to re-establish certain habitats that were destroyed to make way for different forms of agriculture. For example, in southern England many downland and lowland heath areas were ploughed up during and after the Second World War in order to expand arable production and the Stewardship Scheme is allowing some farmers to restore the original landscapes.

Another example where ecological succession is arrested to maintain particular communities can be seen in many nature reserves. Despite the implication of 'naturalness', most nature reserves are far from natural and, instead, are highly managed resources. Although in one sense they are managed to protect and conserve wildlife, they are also important leisure resources, as many afford opportunities for people to watch the wildlife as well. For example, there are now over one million members of the Royal Society for the Protection of Birds (RSPB) and the Society would not be very successful if it did not allow its members, and non-members for that matter, to visit its reserves and watch the birds (see also Chapter 11). In order to attract particular bird species it may be necessary to maintain certain sub-climax communities. Although once quite extensive in parts

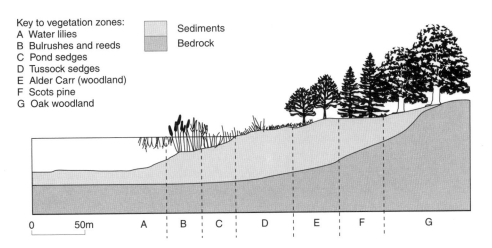

Key to vegetation zones:
A Water lilies
B Bulrushes and reeds
C Pond sedges
D Tussock sedges
E Alder Carr (woodland)
F Scots pine
G Oak woodland

Sediments
Bedrock

0   50m   A   B   C   D   E   F   G

Figure 7.2   Plant succession from open water to oak woodland

Source: Briggs, D. *et al.* (1997) *Fundamentals of the physical environment*, 2nd edn, London: Routledge.

of eastern England and the West Country, reed marsh is now a rare community in Britain and a number of reserves have been established to maintain this ecosystem. Once again, if not managed, reed marsh will be quickly invaded by willows and will gradually be transformed into carr woodland and eventually oak woodland. In fact, the early champions of nature reserves did not appreciate the process of ecological succession and the Society for the Promotion of Nature Reserves, having acquired the reed marsh reserve of Wicken Fen, soon discovered that it was becoming an impenetrable thicket through the invasion of sallows and had to sell one of its other properties in order to raise sufficient money to pay for the necessary remedial action.

In fact, in many reserves it is not just the reed marsh that has to be protected against invading tree species, but also open water areas, which have to be protected from invading reed marsh. Figure 7.2 provides a useful illustration of this process, showing how an area of water will be invaded by water plants, which will then give way to reed marsh and ultimately woodland. The Norfolk Broads, which caters for a wide range of leisure pursuits and which attracts 5.4 million visitors every year, provides a useful illustration of this. The series of Broads or shallow lakes, once thought to be natural features, are in fact the product of old peat workings that had been flooded as a result of rising sea levels in the Middle Ages. The water areas were much more extensive earlier this century, as the surrounding reeds were regularly harvested for a wide range of products such as thatched roofs and baskets. However, the demand for such products has fallen substantially in recent times and, consequently, the harvesting of the reeds has been vastly reduced, with the result that the reed marsh has advanced at the expense of the water areas. As it is the water areas rather than the reed marsh that are the principal attraction here then, once again, management is required to protect the key leisure resource.

Leisure impacts

The previous pages have shown how various ecosystems have developed and how a knowledge of ecological succession is vital if such resources are to continue to be managed for leisure. Some of these ecosystems are the result of other activities and their significance for leisure is serendipitous; others are managed specifically for leisure. Another ecological issue that is important in the leisure context, however, is how leisure activities impact on the ecosystem and the extent to which such activity produces ecological change. While particular environments attract visitors, what impacts do visitors have on these places?

Over the last few decades various studies have highlighted the environmental impact of leisure (e.g. Mathieson and Wall, 1983; Siddaway, 1988; Croall, 1995). A particular problem is that some of the most attractive leisure environments are often those with the most fragile ecosystems. Two examples of such communities in Britain are highland communities and dune systems. The problem with the former is that, because the unfavourable cold climate allows only very slow plant growth, once damaged, plants take a long time to recover; and if there is little respite in visitor numbers then the damage will be permanent, with a total loss of vegetation cover. This can be seen along many of the long-distance footpaths such as the Pennine Way or the Lyke Wake Walk in the North Yorks Moors where vegetation has been completely eroded and, as people have walked to the side to avoid the resulting muddy path, the eroded routeway has become ever wider. At times sections of the footpaths have been closed and walkers have been re-routed in order to allow the original path to recover.

With dune systems, the marram grass, which helps to stabilise the dune, is easily damaged by visitor pressure, with the result that the sand can blow away. As dunes are popular for various forms of leisure, damage may arise from a number of sources: parked vehicles and caravans at the landward edge; use of motorcycles and four-wheel drive vehicles to cross the dunes; trampling; camping; and fires, especially with the popularity of barbecues. (For a more detailed account of dune systems see Selman, 1992.)

Various management techniques are employed to cope with these sorts of problems. With sand dunes, groynes and fencing can be used to trap sand and prevent it blowing away and revegetation can help to stabilise the dunes. Fencing can also be used to control the movement of people and boardwalks can encourage people to cross the dunes along particular routes. At many sites various types of barrier can be used to channel visitor movement in particular directions and keep people away from sensitive parts of a site – for example, bushes, grass, gorse, stinging nettles, fences, moats, ditches, gates, stiles (see texts by Seabrooke and Miles, 1993, and Bromley, 1990, for detailed coverage of these issues).

In considering the planning and management of sites in relation to visitor impacts, the concept of *recreation carrying capacity* is often employed. This describes the level of recreation use an area can sustain without an unacceptable degree of deterioration of the character and quality of the resource or of the recreation experience (see Patmore, 1983, and Curry, 1994, for fuller discussions of the concept). Many authorities identify a number of different components of recreation carrying capacity – physical capacity, ecological capacity and perceptual capacity. Physical capacity involves the absolute number of people a site or facility can accommodate. Whereas this idea is very appropriate for many leisure facilities (e.g. the number of seats at a sports facility or a theatre), it is not very useful for the management of much of the countryside, although at countryside sites it can be employed in terms of car parking space. Perceptual capacity refers to the maximum number of people a site can tolerate before the leisure experience of visitors deteriorates. This is essentially concerned with levels of crowding and how people relate to this. It is a relatively subjective concept as different people will react to crowds in different ways and there is some evidence that some people actually prefer to be with crowds (Burton, 1974). There is certainly plenty of evidence to show that many people are not deterred by the impact of large crowds *per se*, as witnessed by the many crowded beaches. Nevertheless, whereas the visitor to Brighton on a sunny bank holiday may find crowds to be part of the leisure experience, this is unlikely to be the case for those walking the hills, where for some even the appearance of a single extra person may spoil the moment!

In the context of this section, however, it is ecological capacity that is the more relevant. This is defined as the number of visitors a site can tolerate before unacceptable ecological impact is sustained. However, the precise impacts are particularly difficult to measure and capacity levels difficult to predict. Also, while appearing objective, the concept is in reality subjective, as it relies on the attitudes of those who establish the capacity levels. Vegetation communities can be affected in many different ways – for example, a chalk grassland community, popular with walkers, sightseers and picnickers, might experience several different types of change, depending on the level of impact. Some impact might result in certain species, such as orchids, declining or disappearing; further impact might result in greater loss of vegetation and reduction in butterfly species; but it would probably require substantial impact before the vegetation cover disappeared entirely. It is likely that it is only at this point that the majority of visitors would be concerned, but those interested in orchids or butterflies are likely to see the capacity being reached well before this. So at what point is ecological capacity established?

It is clear, therefore, that the appearance and availability of many places for leisure will be affected not just by the ecology itself, but also by the attitudes and interests of those who exercise power in the management of leisure resources.

● ● ● ● The economic basis

The previous section has examined the basis of a number of leisure resources that many people no doubt would regard as free. Although a select few may pay enormous sums to shoot grouse in moorland areas, the vast majority of people who visit such places do not pay anything, and this would also be the case for those walking along chalk grassland, using dune systems or walking along the public right of way system that traverses the British countryside. In reality, of course, there are costs involved in maintaining such environments. Either they are managed specifically for leisure, and thus the cost is likely to be paid directly out of the public purse, or they are being managed by farmers and landowners, who initially bear the cost. However, even here it can be argued that, given the massive subsidies farmers receive, sometimes specifically to provide for recreation and amenity (see page 142), then the public is still paying through taxation. While the costs of resource management are easy to appreciate, even though it might be more difficult to identify who is bearing such costs, there are also various other economic influences affecting the location and nature of leisure resources that are less visible, such as land markets and the values placed on land resources, and these are the issues on which this section will concentrate.

Although land can be valued in various different ways, and from a leisure perspective its value might be conceived in terms of its scenic quality or its wildlife resources, in practice most land is valued in strict economic terms. Land is bought and sold and its market value is based on its ability to produce financial returns. In this respect its value is related to its inherent qualities, such as morphology, soil fertility and location. Grade 1 agricultural land, capable of allowing a wide variety of different agricultural enterprises to be pursued, is going to be far more valuable than Grade 5 land, typical of large parts of upland Britain, where soils are thin and relatively infertile and where the only possible farming is the extensive rearing of sheep and hill cattle and, more recently in the Highlands, deer for venison. It is partly because of this essentially economic fact that the uplands are farmed in this way and have the appearance they do; and why they have relevance for leisure, as outlined in the previous section. It is also why much of the uplands remains unenclosed common land. Due to its relatively low level of economic return, it would not be worthwhile investing in the establishment and maintenance of fences or walls and, thus, landowners and farmers agree to graze their livestock communally. However, just because it is common land does not mean that it necessarily allows public access. Most common land is still privately owned, although in some cases landowners do tolerate *de facto* access and in some national park areas the National Trust has acquired substantial tracts of land, such as Kinder Scout in the Peak District, and opened such land to the public (see Chapter 11). In much of the farmed lowlands farmers and landowners are less tolerant of visitors using their land, as farming is more intensive and the potential for visitor damage is greater. However, the long campaign to establish access to unenclosed land has recently achieved success with the 2000 Countryside and Rights of Way Act, which will eventually ensure greater access to at least 4,000 square miles of England's open countryside.

Apart from the public rights of way network that traverses farmland, many farmers in recent years have also developed recreation and tourist enterprises. In many cases these have been used to provide small amounts of supplementary income and have included farmhouse accommodation such as bed and breakfast and small caravan sites (involving up to 30 per cent of farms in some parts of the south west and the Lake District), horse riding or stabling facilities, often utilising old cowsheds, and shooting and fishing enterprises. More recently, some farmers have diversified in a major way, with golf courses and even pleasure parks (e.g. Lightwater Valley near Ripon) being developed.

One important aspect of leisure is that it does not command a strong position in competing for land. As has already been shown, a lot of countryside leisure is free, or at least relatively cheap, and many potential leisure providers would face problems in demanding high charges against this long-established tradition and thus would be incapable of making sufficient return to offset the purchase cost of land. A lot of countryside recreation also involves large amounts of land that would be difficult to acquire if leisure was to be the sole use of such land. Land for leisure in towns and cities also faces similar difficulties, a point to which this account will return below. One of the consequences of this situation is that much leisure, both in town and countryside but especially in relation to the latter, shares land with other uses. In other words, leisure involves multiple land use and shares the same piece of land with agriculture (as already demonstrated), forestry and water supply operations in the countryside, as well as with educational establishments in urban areas.

Leisure is also often seen as an alternative afteruse for much derelict land, such as old mineral workings, power stations and factory sites. Where public bodies have been involved in land purchase, for example the Forestry Commission and the original water authorities (the latter are now private companies), it was established practice that the resource would also be used for leisure. The 1968 Countryside Act gave the Forestry Commission statutory powers to provide facilities for recreation and, similarly, the 1973 Water Act required Regional Water Authorities to do the same (note: water authorities were reorganised and privatised following the 1989 Water Act). In fact, all the large reservoirs established in the 1960s and 1970s, such as Grafham Water, Rutland Water and Kielder, had the value of recreational use as part of the cost benefit analysis. In other words, recreation was included as part of the justification for the substantial financial outlay in their construction and a variety of facilities for both passive and active recreation was subsequently established at all these sites. Similarly, the Forestry Commission has developed a large variety of specific recreational facilities on its properties, which by the late 1980s, according to Travis (1990), included 14 forest drives, 732 car parks, 621 picnic sites, 540 forest walks, 126 forest trails, 54 bridle tracks, 40 wayfaring courses and 21 visitor centres.

Urban land markets

Much of the emphasis so far in this chapter has been on countryside resources but, of course, most leisure occurs within towns and cities, and the distribution of places for leisure within urban areas is also partly determined by the land market that operates there. It should be pointed out that the urban land market is a totally separate one to that operating in the countryside. Whereas the average price for good agricultural land may be £5,000 per hectare, in the town or city the average price of land with planning permission for development could be 10 or even 100 times higher. Once again, leisure fares badly in this market and certainly any leisure development that requires a large area of land will be unable to compete and will be relegated to poorer locations. The essential competition for land in urban areas revolves round the need to obtain the most accessible locations. At one time such locations were always at the centre of the urban area, although modern communications have complicated this pattern in more recent times and alternative locations of high accessibility may now be found elsewhere, sometimes in suburban areas at the points where radial and arterial routeways converge (see below).

Throughout the twentieth century, geographers and other social scientists have produced various models in an attempt to explain how the form of towns and cities are structured in relation to this land market, and a number of these are illustrated in Figure 7.3. Although the precise patterns vary, depending on the different models, they are all based on the simple idea of different land uses outbidding each other to obtain the most accessible land. This is illustrated by means of bid–rent curves, as shown in Figure 7.4. The activity that can best afford to acquire the land (or which can least afford not to) will outbid the others. Commercial and retail businesses that need a central location in order to be accessible to the greatest number of customers will always win this competition, and other land uses will be pushed further out. A similar competition for land will also occur in the next zone and so on.

Unfortunately, many leisure uses cannot compete with retail, financial, industrial and residential land uses and are therefore pushed out to the periphery of the urban area. Parks, sports facilities, playing fields and golf courses, for example, are usually found,

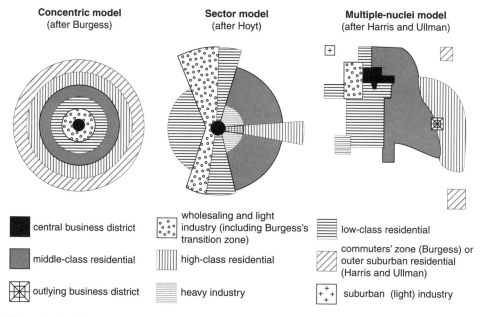

Figure 7.3 Models of urban structure

Source: Whynne-Hammond, C. (1997) *Elements of Human Geography*, London: George Allen and Unwin (Routledge).

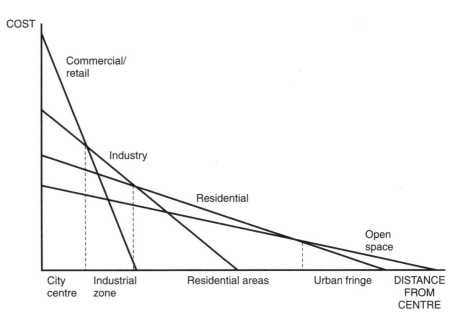

Figure 7.4   Generalised bid–rent curves

at least when they are initially established, just beyond the built-up area in peri-urban or rural-urban fringe locations. If they are now found within the city it is because they reflect an historical pattern where certain leisure spaces have been protected by local authorities or other non-commercial institutions (see Chapter 9). For example, the map in Figure 7.5 shows the distribution of open space in Bedford in 1901. Most of this open space was established during the latter part of the nineteenth century and is located where one might expect, at the edge of the town. Although today the town has extended well beyond this point, most of this open space remains but is therefore no longer at the edge. A similar historical development of parks and gardens has been studied by Strachan and Bowler (1976) in relation to the city of Leicester and a useful summary of this work can be found in Hall and Page (1999). Despite the fact that in many urban areas such spaces often remain, there are great economic pressures to sell such sites for urban development. Some inner-city football stadia have been sold and new facilities built on the outskirts, often involving substantial financial surpluses as a result of selling the high-priced inner-city site. For example, Middlesbrough FC has recently moved from its old ground at Ayresome Park to the new Riverside Stadium. Similarly, during the 1980s and 1990s about 10,000 sports fields were sold off for development, roughly half of which had been school grounds and most of the rest of which had been in local authority ownership (Fyson, 1998).

Not all urban leisure, however, requires large amounts of land and some leisure activity is commercially oriented. The centres of towns and cities are therefore not entirely devoid of leisure; in fact, many central areas have become the focus of substantial leisure activity. Apart from their significance for leisure shopping (see below), urban centres also contain cinemas, theatres, restaurants, clubs and

Build-up area
Open space

Figure 7.5   Open space on the outskirts of Bedford in 1901

pubs – as service industries they require central locations to attract a large clientele. In addition, they are also concentrated in such locations due to the economics of clustering (all these businesses are serving the same population and no one wants to be located elsewhere and thus be at a disadvantage). Furthermore, many visitors to the city centre will not simply use one of these facilities but may take in several during their visit. An evening at the theatre or cinema may also involve a restaurant meal and a visit to the pub. It would certainly appear that the growth of clubbing involving young people has also produced a corresponding growth of restaurants and pubs alongside that of the clubs themselves. Although the numbers of pubs overall has been declining in recent times, especially in rural areas, inner-city pubs have been increasing, with many becoming themed. It would appear that many are taking over vacant properties at the edge of the central business district (CBD), especially in areas where certain businesses have become locationally marginalised due to the development of new shopping centre complexes.

   Not only do cities provide leisure facilities for their own populations but many also provide such facilities for tourists. According to Law (1993), the principal cities of the world are the most important tourist destinations but most cities attract some visitors from further afield. The principal attractions are the historic/heritage resources and cultural facilities and events, and most of these are located near the city centre because they were usually the original urban focus and the city has subsequently grown up around them. Some have no doubt been destroyed by more recent commercial development but where the preservation of such facilities has been paramount,

Original city containing CBD and residential and tourist functions

Growth in the city
Separation of CBD and tourist functions remaining in original city
Residential/industrial expansion outside original city

Part-relocation of some CBD functions
Redevelopment of part of original city
Growth of conservation of remaining parts of original city

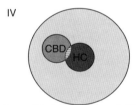

Establishment/consolidation of relocated CBD functions
Consolidation of conserved original city as "tourist-historic" city
Establishment of transition zone facilities used by both tourists/
residents/commercial visitors.

Figure 7.6 Evolutionary model of the historic city
Source: Ashworth, G.J. and Tunbridge, J.E. (1990) *The Tourist Historic City*, Chichester: Wiley.

especially where it provides the basis for a tourism industry, a newer commercial centre has sometimes developed adjacent to the historic centre (see Figure 7.6).

In some areas, derelict sites have been developed for leisure and tourism, aided by government grants and commercial sponsorship. The idea of using tourism as a spur to urban economic and environmental regeneration originally came from North America but has now been adopted in many towns and cities throughout the developed world (Law, 1992; Swarbrooke, 2000). Various dockland areas, such as Liverpool and London, are classic examples of this, influenced to a large extent by the success of similar developments in the city of Baltimore (see Shaw and Williams, 1994). London now contains the Docklands Sailing Centre, Surrey Docks Water Sports Centre, and the London Wetbike Club and has become an important tourist destination (a useful case study of tourism in London docklands can be found in Hall and Page, 1999). The area was also the site for the Millennium Dome. Liverpool's Albert Dock development provides the award-winning Maritime Museum and attracts several million visitors per year and Hartlepool in north-east England has seen its abandoned port facilities transformed into a marina. Also, the naval dockyards at Chatham, abandoned by the Royal Navy in 1984, have been developed into the World Naval Base heritage attraction. Elsewhere, areas of old heavy manufacturing industry have also been transformed, with leisure facilities playing a major role in such developments, such as the steelmaking area of the Don Valley in Sheffield. And old industrial premises have become tourist facilities in their own right as industrial heritage attractions (see section below).

It is also necessary to remember that leisure, sport and tourism are big business and, as outlined in Chapter 6, there are some large leisure companies that are able to purchase substantial land resources where the market returns promise to be worthwhile. Center Parcs, for example, has developed leisure parks/holiday villages in Elveden, Longleat and Sherwood Forests. These sites occupy approximately 400 acres of relatively poor-quality land that has been transformed into attractive environments with indoor heated ('subtropical') water areas and provision for a wide range of indoor and outdoor sports, as well as more leisurely activities.

Before concluding this section on economic aspects it is also necessary to consider provision of space for a relatively new area of leisure that has emerged in recent years, namely leisure shopping. Although traditionally shopping would have been regarded as a non-leisure activity, concerned with obtaining necessary items to satisfy essential human needs, it is clear that much shopping today is undertaken primarily for pleasure and, as such, it has created new retail centres, both within and out of town, which cater for a vast array of consumer demands. The growth in leisure shopping has transformed the centres of many towns, not simply as a result of the shops themselves selling a vast array of consumer-durable goods, but also because of the additional developments linked to this leisure activity. Leisure shopping involves substantial amounts of time and often involves the whole family and, as a result, town centres have attempted to cater for this with fast food outlets, pedestrian precincts, covered walkways and a more attractive environment generally. Also, given the importance of the car, many towns have established retail parks at the edges of towns adjacent to urban ring roads, often at the point where the ring road intersects with an arterial road leading out of the town. Such developments often provide a supermarket, a DIY store and a variety of shops selling electrical goods, household furnishings, toys, clothes and footware, together with fast food outlets and substantial free car parking space (for a detailed discussion of leisure developments on the urban periphery, see Evans, 1998).

In addition to the sorts of developments on the edges of most towns and cities, there are also some extremely large shopping developments that have been established at a small number of strategic locations in Britain, such as the Metro Centre at Gateshead, Lakeside at Thurrock in Essex and Bluewater near Dartford in Kent. Bluewater, which was opened in March 1999, is the largest complex in Europe and covers an area of

240 acres. It cost £1.2 billion to build and has over 300 shops, as well as 40 restaurants, cafés and bars, a 12-screen cinema and extensive facilities for children's activities. It has been planned to cater for 80,000 visitors per day (30 million a year) and includes 12,000 car parking spaces, together with good public transport links (bus and train) to key urban centres in the south east. It is also surrounded by 50 acres of parkland, contains walkways and cycle routes, and the whole complex has been landscaped with lakes and trees and designed to provide an attractive leisure experience.

The social construction of leisure places

Various facilities have been constructed or developed specifically for different leisure activities and their function and significance is no doubt generally recognised, even though their particular importance for individuals will vary greatly. There are many other resources that are used for leisure, however, where this may not be true and, while it may be possible to measure the physical extent of such places and describe their key characteristics, it cannot be assumed that everyone will perceive such places in the same way or that their significance for leisure will remain the same for all time. For example, until the nineteenth century the uplands were generally regarded as dark and dangerous places to be avoided wherever possible, whereas today upland areas are viewed by many as some of the most attractive landscapes, with some areas designated as national parks and attracting millions of visitors every year. Similarly, as has been shown in Chapter 1, the leisure significance of coastal areas is a relatively recent phenomenon.

Resources are generally regarded as cultural appraisals and those for leisure are no exception. Different cultures may view the same resources differently and, as societies change through time, their perceptions of resources may change or new technologies may be developed that allow resources to be exploited, which hitherto had not been possible. For example, one reason why the perception of upland and coastal areas changed was because improvements in transport technology made them easily accessible, and the way people now perceive the home as an important leisure environment is also the result of substantial technological change.

In many ways, the idea of places being socially constructed relates to the opening comment of this chapter about anywhere having potential for leisure use. Some of the most unlikely of places might be regarded as leisure resources for some people. For example, sewage farms are clearly not everybody's favourite place but their ability to attract particular bird species may provide interest for birdwatchers. Similarly, old abandoned factories, having been transformed into industrial heritage attractions, now attract increasing numbers of visitors.

But this section is not so much concerned with the varying perceptions of individuals, interesting though this might be, but rather the way in which substantial groups within society have constructed particular perceptions about places and the way in which some places are often falsified specifically for the purposes of leisure.

Two key areas will be considered: the countryside and themed environments.

The countryside as a leisure resource

As outlined in Chapter 3, the countryside attracts large numbers of visitors for various forms of recreation, sport and tourism. In part, this is because it provides specific resources for particular activities – woodland, water, rock faces and so on. However, whereas increasing numbers of people are indulging in active countryside pursuits, much of the interest concerns passive recreation, whereby people visit in order to walk, cycle, picnic, look at the landscape or simply drive through it. Of course it does not necessarily attract everyone and some authorities have suggested that it is mainly the middle class for whom it exerts such an influence. But why is the countryside so important? Part of the explanation would appear to involve a particular perception of countryside often referred to as *idyllic*. This views the countryside in an extremely attractive and positive way, involving such ideas as Constable-type landscapes, healthy lifestyles, close-knit, friendly communities, tranquillity, stability, simplicity, naturalness, unspoilt, and greenness. All these aspects can, of course, be challenged; the countryside has undergone profound change in recent times, often quite rapid change, and the landscapes of many rural areas have been totally transformed by modern farming; many rural communities contain diverse groups that do not necessarily get on well with one another; traditional rural dwellers are some of the poorest people in Britain; modern farming is complex and, as has been demonstrated earlier in this chapter, the countryside is certainly not 'natural'. There is also a counter-view that the countryside is boring and backward. Nevertheless, the idyllic image is a very powerful one which, in addition to attracting large numbers of visitors, has also persuaded many people to move from towns and cities to live there (commuters, retired people, and second homeowners) and is used to sell products ranging from chocolate bars to motor cars.

The explanation for the emergence of this widely held image may involve several factors that would most likely include various aspects of culture, such as art and literature, the influence of key image makers and 'educators', and the various psychological needs of people. Throughout the centuries literature has always painted an attractive view of the countryside; in fact, Williams (1973) has traced this tradition back to the Greeks. In the past those who wrote about the countryside either belonged to the upper classes, who derived their wealth from country estates, or were patronised by them. In either event, writers and poets were therefore most unlikely to write unattractive accounts of such places and the communities that lived there and, as a result, critical, negative writings of countryside are very rare indeed. However, even in more recent times the tradition of idyllic writing has not changed and, if anything, has become even stronger, as a survey of any bookshop will testify. During the last couple of centuries there has also emerged a strong tradition of landscape painting, which has further reinforced the attractive image. Such ideas have thus become ingrained in people's consciousness and they are continually being reinforced by the publicity of organisations such as the Tourist Boards. In fact, some would go much further and argue that, for many, the countryside, or at least the imagined idyllic view, is an important aspect of Englishness, another reason why it is so important (see, for example, Matless, 1990, and Paxman, 1998). Finally, it has also been suggested that many people are happy to maintain such images because they act as a means of escapism, as a counter to the seemingly harsher reality of urban living. It is convenient to ignore the reality of the countryside and comforting to think that there is this idyllic environment to hand; that if life really did get too much for us, we could always escape there.

However, apart from its importance for individual people and the middle classes in particular, the idyllic image also has considerable significance for countryside protection and thus leisure opportunities. As will be outlined in the following section, Britain possesses strong town and country planning legislation that is based, above all, on a policy of urban containment and protecting the countryside from development; and it is clear that idyllic notions of countryside have played an important role in establishing such policies. In addition to idyllic notions of countryside and associated preservationist values, there is also a related consensus among those with power and influence about the nature of rural areas and what activities are permissible. The countryside is seen as a place for those leisure activities that are quiet and contemplative, such as walking, cycling and various pursuits connected with the study and watching of wildlife, or those traditional rural pastimes such as horse riding and fishing. There is also a presumption against gregarious activities such that, ideally, only individuals or small groups of people should be involved. There has long been a fear of the countryside becoming overrun with visitors, a belief that caused Wordsworth to campaign against the Kendall to Windermere railway in 1844, and later, in the 1960s, with the growing level of car ownership, provoked Michael Dower's famous analogy of the countryside being inundated by a great wave (Dower, 1965). In fact, it was primarily this fear that led to the establishment of *country parks* in an attempt to attract and contain large numbers of visitors at specific sites (see following section). And finally, it is no surprise that noisy sports, such as motorcycle scrambling or water skiing, are regarded as totally inappropriate. As a result, a further social construction is placed on the countryside with important implications for leisure in terms of what is allowed and encouraged and what is not.

Themed environments

The previous section examined an important leisure environment that has acquired a particular falsified image. Although in certain circumstances this image has been overtly influenced by propaganda, as for example in the publicity of the Tourist Boards, in the main the image is one that has developed gradually and unintentionally over a substantial period of time. More recently, however, various explicit attempts have been made to construct false environments or develop particular false perceptions of places based on the idea of theming, and such themed environments include particular regions, shopping complexes and various tourist attractions, in particular theme parks themselves.

Although the development of regional images linked to tourism can be seen in the county Shell guides and texts such as *The Shell Guide to Britain*, with its idiosyncratic

Figure 7.7   A tourist image of England and Wales

Source: *The Guardian*, 11 November 1990.

artistic impressions of individual counties, a more recent development of falsified regional images can be seen in those that are labelled and sold to tourists on the basis of themes acquired through history, novels or television (Pocock, 1992). Such themed regions can be seen in Figure 7.7.

As indicated earlier in this chapter, shopping has become a major leisure activity and many new shopping centres have been developed to cater for this, or possibly to encourage it, both in terms of transformed town centres and as new out-of-town retail complexes. But, given that the shopping trip is now much more family oriented and of longer duration, some shopping centres have been developed with the expressed intent of providing a broader leisure experience. The most famous of such developments, certainly the one that has received most attention in academic literature, is the West Edmonton Mall in Canada. This development contains over 800 shops and 10 per cent of its floorspace is given over to leisure facilities. In addition, the environment is themed in order to sell 'an ambience of foreignness' such that the visitor can be in France, England, Asia or West Coast America (Shaw and Williams, 1994). In Britain also, similar developments, although smaller in scale, can be found at the Metro Centre in Gateshead, Meadowhall in Sheffield, Lakeside in Essex, and the new Bluewater complex near Dartford in Kent.

The ultimate development of a falsified, socially constructed environment is the theme park itself, where the main aim is to create a wonderland in which the visitor is immersed in fantasy. The various Disney theme parks in America, Europe and Japan are the most vivid expressions of this development, where the environment is planned to provide entertainment, excitement, clean and attractive surroundings, a variety of geographical environments, numerous funfair rides, and safety. According to Eco (1986, cited in Urry, 1990), 'Disneyland tells us that faked nature corresponds much more to our daydream demands'; and Urry (1990) comments that the 'scenes are . . . more real than the original, hyper-real in other words'. While there is, as yet, nothing in Britain to compare with Disney, the Disney Worlds in both Florida and France are popular destinations for British visitors. But, while Britain may lack large theme parks, there are many other smaller-scale themed attractions, many involving heritage, which falsify both time and place.

One such example is the Beamish Open Air Museum in north-east England, where an old coal mine site has been transformed into a replica mining village and town of the early twentieth century. As the publicity material illustrates, 'the word "museum", is not really appropriate . . . At Beamish, visitors find themselves on another planet, and in another age . . . Here, they can experience the industrial, social and rural history of the region.' Other examples of themed attractions include the Jorvik Centre in York, the Chessington World of Adventures, the White Cliffs Experience in Dover and the Canterbury Tales in Canterbury.

Urry (1990, p. 105) also highlights the fact that 'some of the most unlikely of places have become centres of a heritage-based tourist development'. He goes on to cite Bradford as such a place. Until quite recently Bradford was perceived as a northern industrial town whose woollen industry had experienced serious decline. However, the intact industrial heritage of buildings, railways and canals has been used as part of a package of attractions, alongside proximity to Haworth and the dales and moors, designed to appeal to the short-break holidaymaker. Another aspect of this package has included the large Asian community, with over 50 'Asian' restaurants and the largest Asian store in Europe which, Urry (1990) points out, has been used to promote an Asian experience for visitors. Thus Bradford's environment was socially and deliberately reconstructed in a number of different ways to provide a particular type of leisure space.

While Britain may not possess Disney-style theme parks, one commentator has remarked that Britain as a whole may be viewed as 'one big open air museum'. This comment is quoted in Hewison (1987, p. 24), whose book on the heritage industry is very critical about the history that is being presented in such places and the falsification of time and place that is involved. In fact, the idea forms part of the plot in the recent Julian Barnes (1998) novel *England, England*, in which the Isle of Wight is transformed into a vast heritage centre containing replicas of everything 'English', from 'Buck House' to Stonehenge and Manchester United to the White Cliffs of Dover, based on the premise that most tourists are as satisfied with a replica as they are with the real thing.

Planning and leisure space

Another key factor affecting the provision and nature of places for leisure is that of the role of government. This has already been acknowledged in Chapter 6 and earlier in this chapter, in the case of local authorities providing urban open space and also where various leisure resources in the countryside are influenced through public subsidy to farmers. Although the role of government will be examined further in Chapter 9, its particular influence on the location and character of leisure spaces through the establishment and application of town and country planning legislation will be considered in this chapter.

A major concern of town and country planning involves the efficient and harmonious ordering of land use. Given the importance of leisure in contemporary society, the appropriate location of land for that purpose and the way in which leisure space is integrated into the wider environment are becoming ever more important issues within planning. Town and country planning is the ultimate responsibility of the Department for Transport, Local Government and the Regions but is exercised through the local authorities. County councils produce structure plans, requiring the official approval of the Secretary of State, which provide broad guidelines for the development of land within their regions and district councils produce more detailed plans at the local level, guided by the relevant structure plan. Where land is proposed for development, the developer must apply to the local authority for planning permission and the planning decision will be based, to a large extent, on the provisions within the particular plans. It is important to recognise that development involves the 'carrying out of building, mining and other operations in, on, over or under land, or the making of any material change in the use of any building or other land', and thus development control is all-embracing.

This particular system influences places for leisure in a number of ways. The establishment of leisure facilities certainly constitutes development but, because they are generally regarded as adding to the quality of life, leisure developments may be considered more favourably by planners than other developments. In fact, new housing estates may well have to provide opportunities for leisure, such as open spaces and play areas, in order to win planning approval. As mentioned in the previous section, the containment of the urban area has been an important feature of modern British planning and one consequence of this has been the establishment of housing estates containing houses with ever smaller gardens but with a greater area of communal parks and open space. Planners have also been keen to support the conversion of many derelict sites into leisure spaces and, in granting planning permission for mineral extraction, often impose afteruse conditions that involve leisure development – for example old sandpits may be filled and turned into playing fields and wet mineral workings become sites for various water activities; in fact, many country parks owe their origins to old gravel workings. Sometimes the concept of *planning gain* is invoked, whereby developers agree to provide a facility for the local community in exchange for planning permission. For example, in Bedford a supermarket chain provided a beach pool in order to obtain planning permission to build its store and, in a nearby village, a housing developer provided a village hall and sports field to persuade villagers to agree to its proposal to add a substantial number of new houses to the existing settlement.

However, it would be wrong to think that all leisure development proposals will automatically obtain planning permission. Although those involving open space and the 'cleaning up' of derelict sites undoubtedly improve the physical environment, others will bring environmental problems. Leisure developments may well require land that might be more appropriately used for other purposes and they may involve physically intrusive buildings. They will inevitably attract people and noise and may attract considerable objections from those who live in the area. Large-scale developments such as theme parks and sports stadia are obvious examples of this but new cinemas, nightclubs and public houses may attract similar concerns. Floodlit sports pitches may also cause considerable light pollution. Even those developments that do ostensibly produce environmental improvements may not be totally benign. The establishment of country parks may involve the rehabilitation of derelict sites and the establishment of trees and shrubs to provide attractive settings for a variety of passive recreational activities. However, in that such sites will attract people, most of whom, according to surveys, will visit in their cars, there may well be problems of car parking and potential congestion on approach roads.

Another good example of a leisure development that at first sight appears to be environmentally beneficial but can indeed produce environmental impacts is the golf course. There has been considerable attention paid to golf course development in recent years, partly because of substantial deferred demand and also because golf course development would appear to be a suitable enterprise for farm diversification. A number of new courses have thus been developed and even more proposed. Many people have argued that golf courses improve the environment and there is certainly evidence to show that the amenity value of such facilities increases property values in the immediate vicinity (Bowen, 1974). However, there have been considerable objections to such developments by various environmental groups. Some argue that in order to produce the ideal grass for greens and fairways, non-native grass species are used, to the detriment of local wildlife. Others argue that the golf course provides an artificial, manicured environment that is alien to the British rural landscape. They make excessive demands on water resources in relation to the regular watering of greens. And further objections relate to other intrusive developments that are inevitably associated with golf course development, such as club house, practice range and car parking space.

While the previous paragraphs have looked primarily at specific sites, the influence of planning on leisure places can also be seen to be operating at a more strategic level. One concern of planning involves the efficient allocation of resources, and this would involve ensuring that resources are located so as to make them accessible to the greatest number of people. In certain situations market forces resolve this problem, although market conditions do not relate to all leisure resources. In the case of public open space, for example, local authorities might wish to ensure that there is an equitable distribution of such space across their urban areas. They can do this by ensuring that land is allocated for parks and play areas and that developers provide sufficient open space in their plans. Usually planning permission for housing developments will only be granted if certain open space standards are included. Some of the best examples of urban land use planning affecting the provision of open space can be seen in the various new towns, such as Milton Keynes, Crawley and Cumbernauld. Here virtually all land uses could be planned from the outset, and thus not only could sufficient open space be provided for each community, but also housing and amenity land could be separated from industrial land.

On a broader strategic level, planning can also be seen to be operating in terms of the distribution of such resources as national parks, areas of outstanding natural beauty, heritage coasts, national trails, community forests and country parks (see Figure 7.8). National parks were created as a result of the National Parks and Access to the Countryside Act of 1949, primarily as a means of preventing urban development encroaching on what were regarded as some of the most attractive and unspoilt areas of England and Wales. Scotland was left out of the original legislation, as it was felt at the time that similar areas in this region were not under any threat, although more recently it has been agreed that national parks should also be designated in Scotland. Although part of the original campaign had been to provide for countryside recreation, by the time the parks were established this had become a secondary consideration, with conservation and landscape protection being the principal goals. This was in fact reiterated in 1974 by the Sandford Commission, which stated that, where conservation and recreation came into conflict, the former should always take precedence. Despite this, however, the parks, which collectively cover approximately 9 per cent of the total land area of England and Wales, provide for a wealth of recreational opportunities and attract many millions of visitors each year.

Despite the label 'national park', they are neither national nor park in the strict sense of the words. Only a small proportion of the land is actually owned by government, and most of this is either in the hands of the Forestry Commission, primarily for growing timber, or the Ministry of Defence, for military training. Most of the land is privately owned, with about 70 per cent overall in some form of farming. The national park authorities possess only about 1 per cent of the land, although the National Trust, a voluntary organisation, owns about 10 per cent (about 30 per cent in the Lake District) and much of this land is available for

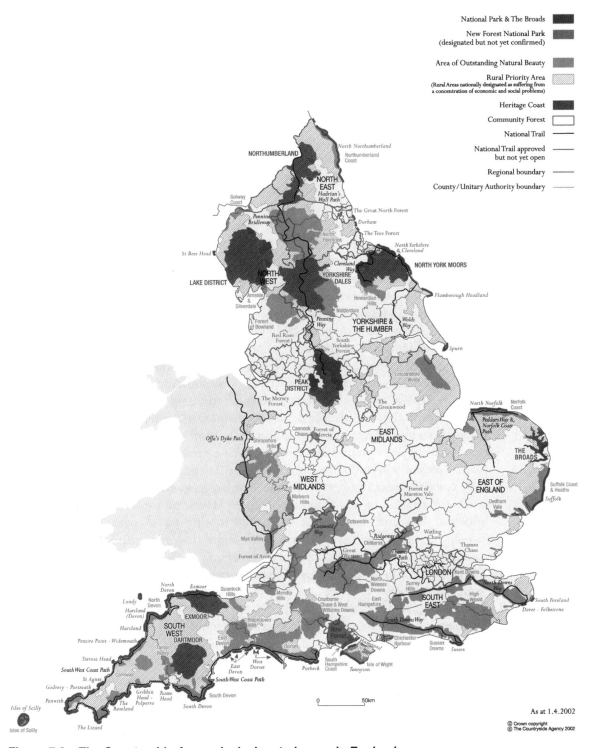

Figure 7.8   The Countryside Agency's designated areas in England

Source: Countryside Agency, based on Ordnance Survey mapping with the permission of the Controller of Her Majesty's Stationary Office. Crown Copyright reserved. CCC14354.

public access (see Chapter 11). Thus national parks in Britain are not the same as those in most other parts of the world, as they are primarily working landscapes, with public access to large areas of land denied (as discussed earlier in the chapter). Leisure is restricted primarily to various passive forms (walking, sightseeing, nature study), with some active pursuits undertaken on a modest scale and restricted to particular routes and sites. Tourists tend to congregate in particular 'honey pot' locations, such as Ambleside in the Lake District and Hutton-le-Hole in the North Yorks Moors, and only the more active minority tend to venture into the higher, wilder heartland areas of most of the parks. Nevertheless, despite the various restrictions on leisure, their designation and the strict planning regime that is applied has meant that these landscapes have remained relatively unscathed by development and they have continued to provide an important resource and backdrop for particular leisure forms.

Country parks were established following the 1968 Countryside Act, which provided grant aid for the purpose. Located primarily in rural-urban fringe zones, they were promoted as places affording relatively easy access to countryside sites for people living in urban areas. However, an alternative view is that they were established as a strategic response to the concerns being expressed in the 1960s about the impact of visitors on the countryside. By locating a ring of countryside sites, providing a variety of recreational opportunities, around towns and cities, it was hoped that people might visit these instead of venturing into the deeper countryside where it was thought they would cause substantial conflict. In order to be recognised as a country park and be eligible for grant aid, sites had to satisfy the following conditions: be easily accessible to large numbers of people; have the capacity to absorb large numbers; be able to offer a variety of recreational activities; and enable town dwellers to enjoy open air recreation without travelling long distances and without congesting the roads (Glyptis, 1991). There are now over 200 country parks throughout Britain ranging from large parks such as Clumber Park (1273.5 ha.) and Cannock Chase (1088 ha.) to Hartshill Hayes in Warwickshire and Clare Castle in Suffolk (both 9 ha. in size). Most are in the 25–75 ha. range and many provide little more than opportunities for a narrow range of passive recreation. Some, however, such as Ferry Meadows near Peterborough, provide for a wide range of different pursuits including various water resources, a bird reserve, golf courses, children's play area, camping and caravanning and a trimtrack.

Community forests are a more recent planning initiative launched in the late 1980s by the Countryside and Forestry Commissions. They are located within rural-urban fringe areas with substantial areas of derelict and degraded land and designed to promote the concept of multi-purpose forestry by providing extensive opportunities for a thriving farming and forestry industry, with increased scope for diversification, as well as for recreation, education and new wildlife habitats (Countryside Commission, 1989). Following the initial designation in 1989 of three projects in north-east England, south Staffordshire and east London, nine further areas were designated in February 1991, giving a total area for the whole programme of more than 470,000 ha, approximately 3.6 per cent of all land in England and equivalent to about half the combined size of all the national parks (see Figure 7.8). They are long-term projects, possibly taking 30 to 40 years to achieve, and designed to expand the overall woodland area, in some cases from as little as 3 per cent to over 30 per cent. But one of their principal aims is to increase opportunities 'for all kinds of sports and recreations' (Countryside Commission, 1989). Like national parks, most land within the forest areas is privately owned and, therefore, the key process is to persuade farmers and landowners, with the help of grant aid, to plant trees and possibly extend public access opportunities on their land. One of the principal mechanisms operating, however, is that of planning, for, while it cannot compel landowners to undertake developments, it can certainly ensure that certain developments are prevented and thus, once established, particular landscapes can enjoy some level of protection.

Conclusions

This chapter has considered a number of key factors that are responsible for both the nature and location of the environments and facilities that are utilised for leisure activities. It has highlighted the great variety of leisure places and shown how ecological, economic, social and cultural forces, together with the implementation of planning policies, have shaped their characteristics and development. However, while this chapter may have outlined some of the key underlying influences, the availability of leisure resources and facilities is also about how such influences operate within, and are perceived by, the public, commercial and voluntary sectors. The following chapters will therefore examine each of these in turn to provide a more complete picture of leisure provision.

Questions

1   Illustrating your answer with appropriate examples, explain why a knowledge of *ecological succession* is important in understanding the nature of particular leisure environments.

2   Analyse the reasons why urban tourism and leisure facilities have distinctive and diverse spatial distributions.

3   Discuss the factors that influence the availability of land resources for tourism and leisure in **either** rural **or** urban areas.

4   Discuss what is meant by the 'social construction' of leisure places.

5   Examine the view that a substantial amount of modern tourism is concerned with artificial environments and 'imagined' places.

6   How is the location and availability of leisure places influenced by land use planning policies?

References

Barnes, J. (1998) *England, England,* London: Jonathon Cape.

Bowen, M.J. (1974) 'Outdoor Recreation Around Large Cities', in Johnston, J.H. (ed.) *Suburban Growth: Geographical Processes at the Edge of the Western City,* London: Wiley.

Bromley, P. (1990) *Countryside Management,* London: Spon.

Burton, R.J.C. (1974) *The Recreational Carrying Capacity of the Countryside,* Keele University Library Occasional Publication No. 11.

Countryside Commission (1989) *Forests for the Community,* Cheltenham: The Commission.

Croall, J. (1995) *Preserve or Destroy: Tourism and the Environment,* London: Calouste Gulbenkian Foundation.

Curry, N. (1994) *Countryside Recreation, Access and Land Use Planning,* London: Spon.

Dower, M. (1965) *Fourth Wave: The Challenge of Leisure,* London: Civic Trust.

Evans, G. (1998) 'Urban leisure: edge city and the new leisure periphery', in Collins, M.F. and Cooper, I.S. (eds) *Leisure Management: Issues and Applications,* Wallingford: CAB International.

Fyson, A. (1998) 'Sports fields to be encouraged, not sold off', *Planning,* 18 December.

Glyptis, S. (1991) *Countryside Recreation,* Harlow: Longman/ILAM.

Hall, M. and Page, S. (1999) *The Geography of Tourism and Recreation,* London: Routledge.

Hewison, R. (1987) *The Heritage Industry,* London: Methuen.

Law, C. (1992) 'Urban tourism and its contribution to economic regeneration', *Urban Studies,* 29, pp. 599–618.

Law, C.M. (1993) *Urban Tourism: Attracting Visitors to Large Cities,* London: Mansell.

Mathieson, A. and Wall, G.(1983) *Tourism: Economic, Physical and Social Impacts,* London: Longman.

Matless, D. (1990) 'Definitions of England, 1928–89. Preservation, modernism and the nature of the nation', *Built Environment,* vol. 16, no. 3.

Patmore, J.A. (1983) *Recreation and Resources: Leisure Patterns and Leisure Places,* Oxford: Blackwell.

Paxman, J. (1998) *The English: A Portrait of a People,* London: Michael Joseph.

Pocock, D. (1992) 'Catherine Cookson country: tourist expectation and experience', *Geography,* vol. 77, pp. 236–44.

Seabrooke, W. and Miles, C.W.N. (1993) *Recreational Land Management,* London: Spon.

Selman, P. (1992) *Environmental Planning,* London: Paul Chapman Publishing Co.

Shaw, G. and Williams, A.M. (1994) *Critical Issues in Tourism: A Geographical Perspective,* Oxford: Blackwell.

Sidaway, R. (1988) *Sport, Recreation and Nature Conservation,* Sports Council/ Countryside Commission, Summary, pp. i–iv, and Introduction.

Strachan, A. and Bowler, I. (1976) 'The development of public parks in the City of Leicester', *East Midland Geographer,* vol. 6, pp. 275–83.

Swarbrooke, J. (2000) 'Tourism, economic development and urban regeneration: a critical evaluation', in Robinson *et al.* (eds) *Reflections on International Tourism: Developments in Urban and Rural Tourism,* Sunderland: Centre for Travel and Tourism.

Travis, A.S. (1990) 'Recreation in the woods today: a United Kingdom review', in Countryside Recreation Research Advisory Group, *People, Trees and Woods,* proceedings of CRRAG conference, pp. 19–36.

Urry, J. (1990) *The Tourist Gaze,* London: Sage.

Williams, R. (1973) *The Country and the City,* London: Chatto & Windus.

Further reading

A number of texts covering the geography of leisure and tourism are useful in the context of this chapter, such as Hall and Page (1999) *The Geography of Tourism and Recreation*; Shaw and Williams (1994) *Critical Issues in Tourism: A Geographical Perspective*; and Williams (1998) *Tourism Geography*, London: Routledge.

Sharpley, R. (1996) *Tourism and Leisure in the Countryside* (2nd edition), Huntingdon: Elm Publications, provides a useful coverage of rural environments while Williams, S. (1995) *Outdoor Recreation and the Urban Environment*, London: Routledge, covers the urban setting.

The text by Mather, A. S. (1986) *Land Use*, Harlow: Longman, provides a detailed analysis of land use issues, while that by Urry (1990) covers useful perspectives on the social construction of place.

Useful websites

www.countryside.gov.uk/
www.disneylandparis.com/

www.nps.gov/
www.english-nature.org.uk/

Chapter 8 ● ● ● ●

The political framework for leisure provision

An understanding of the political framework for leisure provision – essentially those public sector or semi-public sector organisations operating in the leisure field – is important because it provides the context within which all leisure organisations must operate. However, such political frameworks are constantly changing as new governments and/or politicians are elected with new priorities for some or all of the leisure industries. Consequently, leisure policy is a dynamic subject of study, and students can only obtain a completely up-to-the-minute picture through reference to journals and quality news media. Therefore, this chapter can only provide an historical and theoretical starting point from which a contemporary knowledge can be maintained.

The leisure sectors in Britain are characterised, both historically and in the present day, by fragmentation. The sports, arts, tourism, and heritage sectors have developed independently of each other and even today, under the umbrella of the government's Department for Culture, Media and Sport, such fragmentation continues. This is exacerbated by the situation in Wales and Scotland, where the sports, arts, tourism and heritage sectors report not to the Department for Culture, Media and Sport, but to the Welsh Office and Welsh Assembly and Scottish Office and Scottish Parliament respectively. Furthermore, countryside issues, many of which are important to the leisure sectors mentioned above, are the responsibility of the Department for Environment, Food and Rural Affairs (DEFRA). It is within the context of this historical and continuing separation that this chapter attempts to analyse the way in which leisure policy is made.

Objectives

To:

- *describe the broad historical context of the development of leisure policy*

- *examine, in turn, three of the main leisure sectors – sport, tourism, arts – highlighting the key organisations and relationships in these sectors.*

● ● ● ● Historical development of leisure policy

The historical development of policy for leisure is obviously closely linked to the historical development of leisure itself as outlined in Chapter 1. Therefore, in order to avoid repetition, this section will attempt to identify themes in government policy for leisure rather than going into too much detail about specific policy initiatives.

The Industrial Revolution was identified in Chapter 1 as a defining period in the development of leisure, and consequently it is with the advent of the Industrial Revolution in the late eighteenth century that this analysis of the development of leisure policy begins. The period from this time until the mid nineteenth century was characterised by considerable social change, which inevitably caused various tensions. Chief among these were the divisions that were created between the new urban working classes and the middle-class mill and factory owners who employed them. Government policy during this period was essentially non-interventionist, being based on the thinking of the economist Adam Smith, whose book *The Wealth of Nations* (1776) advocated the 'invisible hand' of market forces as the most efficient determinant of production. This was complemented by an almost non-existent social policy that focused on sending the poor to workhouses where conditions were so awful that only the most desperate would be prepared to accept a place. This government approach to economic and social policy meant that the working classes were at the mercy of their employers in terms of the hours of work and working conditions they were forced to accept. The inevitable tensions that resulted between the working and middle classes, and a general fear of civil unrest related to the relatively recent memory of the revolution in France, led to government policy for leisure, in contrast to its general approach at this time, developing in a strongly interventionist manner.

The considerable social change of the time had given rise to fears of instability, particularly among the working classes. Cunningham (1980) describes how many working-class leisure activities – such as folk football, prize fighting and animal sports – were not only cruel and aggressive, but attracted large crowds that were perceived to be a threat to social order. Furthermore, in addition to the fear of social disruption, Thompson (1967) highlights how industrialists saw working-class leisure as incompatible with the development of work discipline, which they felt was essential to industrial production. Much absenteeism and drunkenness was attributed to working-class leisure activities, and consequently such activities needed to be controlled in the interests of profit levels. It was in this climate that both national and local government sought to intervene in the leisure lives of the working classes. Various pieces of legislation were enacted to control large gatherings, limit alcohol consumption, and generally curtail any pursuits that were seen as a threat to social order. Street football was made illegal by the Highways Act of 1835, while the enclosure of common land restricted the playing of folk football. Animal sports, popular with the working classes, were outlawed by the Suppression of Blood Sports Act (1833) – however, middle-class pursuits, such as hunting and shooting, remained – and beer houses were licensed from 1820, thus limiting the times that alcohol could be sold. While some claimed that this legislation was part of a civilising movement, clearly much of it was aimed at maintaining social stability. Such legislation continued until the mid nineteenth century (for example, the banning of betting shops in 1854); however, at this time a more positive approach to working-class leisure was starting to emerge.

The mid nineteenth century marked a positive change in direction in terms of general social policy. The state was beginning to intervene in areas relating to working-class well-being. For example, the Factories Acts of 1847 and 1867, legislated for better working conditions and shorter hours of work, initially for women and children, but later for a wide range of workers. There was also a concern for public health – three Public Health Acts (1848, 1872 and 1875) and the 1866 Sanitation Act seeking to improve health and sanitation in towns and cities – while the Public Baths and Washhouses Act (1846) was mainly concerned with ensuring working-class hygiene rather than promoting swimming. In addition, the foundations of a universal system of education were laid with the 1870 Education Act – which included provision for physical education in the form of military drill.

This new wave of positive interventions was also manifest in leisure policy, where the tide was turning away from regulation and suppression towards state support of 'worthwhile' recreations. Such support mainly took the form of fostering both philanthropic provision among and by the middle classes, and the self-improving activities of the working classes – who, through the embryonic trade union movement, were starting to take greater responsibility for their own lives and well-being. These directions in leisure became known as *rational recreation*, and support for this movement came from a realisation that suppression of working-class recreation was neither possible nor practicable, and that the provision of what the state and the middle classes believed to be worthwhile activities would be a much better civilising strategy (Bailey, 1987). The Church was involved in such provision through promoting the benefits of being a 'Muscular Christian', while the trade union movement contributed through the establishment of Working Men's Clubs – which successfully resisted the attempts of the middle classes to make the clubs teetotal.

The main theme of state activity during the period up to the end of the nineteenth century was one of encouraging appropriate provision by voluntary groups. Setting the tone for the next century, legislation that was enacted was *permissive* in allowing the use of public funds for leisure, but not requiring that they be so used. Examples of such legislation were the Museums Act (1849), the Public Libraries Act (1850), and the Recreation Grounds Act (1852). Greater provision, and increasing time released from work during the second half of the nineteenth century, saw an increase in working-class leisure during this period and, as Chapter 10 describes, the commercial sector was not slow to capitalise on this. However, while the state had shown a more enlightened attitude to the working classes during this time, it was in the early years of the twentieth century that the state showed a real commitment to social reform and welfare.

Leisure policy in the twentieth century

The trade union movement had, by the early twentieth century, organised itself into a fledgling political force that was to become the Labour Party. The Labour Representation Committee supported the new Liberal Government of 1905, which embarked on a range of social reforms that indicated a genuine concern for the welfare of the working classes, and a recognition that society in general, and the state in particular, had a responsibility to ensure a basic standard of living for all its citizens. The Unemployed Workmen's Act (1905) provided the first dole payments, school meals were introduced in 1907, and old age pensions in 1908. Alongside this concern, the state was also beginning to develop leisure policies of its own (rather than simply encouraging others to provide). Open space for recreation was designated as a recognised use of land by the 1909 Town Planning Act, while the establishment of the Forestry Commission in 1917 marked the first governmental body to be given a statutory duty for recreation. Further to this, the voluntarily established Travel Association of Great Britain began to receive public funding (£5,000) in 1929, to promote Britain as a travel destination overseas. In the cultural sector, the British Broadcasting Corporation (BBC) was established in 1926 from the commercial British Broadcasting Company. However, its programming policy at the time was generally elitist, aiming to develop appreciation of culture by the masses, rather than to reflect popular cultural tastes, and as such it was not part of the general social reforms of this time.

The voluntary sector's influence in the leisure area increased in the early twentieth century. For example, the National Trust Act (1907) incorporated what had previously been a purely voluntary body into the loop of state decision making. In addition, other voluntary organisations, such as the National Playing Fields Association and the Central Council for Recreative and Physical Training, were of the size and influence to affect legislation in their respective areas of interest.

However, perhaps most significant in the period up to the Second World War was the Physical Training and Recreation Act (1937), which represented landmark legislation in terms of leisure, as it not only provided (although permissively) for physical recreation, but also allocated £2 million to support such provision. While it is likely that the prime motivation for this Act was related, as was much legislation in later years, to concerns for other areas of policy – in this case high unemployment and worries about the nation's fitness to fight a war – it was also affected by Britain's declining reputation in international sport and reflects the general trend of the time towards state provision in all areas related to social policy (Henry, 2001).

The surprise defeat of Winston Churchill's Conservative Party in the post-war 1945 general election resulted in a Labour Government led by Clement Attlee. Attlee's government had one of the most radical reforming agendas of any government this century, being responsible for the Family Allowances Act (1945), the Distribution of

Industries Act (1945), the National Insurance Act (1946) and, most significantly, the establishment of the National Health Service in 1948. In addition, it had inherited the 1944 Education Act – which extended compulsory schooling – from the wartime coalition government. This post-war administration set the tone for government policy over the next thirty years, with the state intervening to provide for the population's welfare. Such provision became known as the welfare state, and its legacy, traceable back to Attlee's post-war government, is still apparent today. The growth of the welfare state was assisted by the existence during this period of what has become known as a social-democratic consensus among the two major political parties, who both accepted the need for the state to intervene in the sphere of welfare.

Many of the organisations and structures that shape state policy and provision for leisure today were established during this post-war consensus period. However, as mentioned previously, they were not established in any coherent or co-ordinated way, but in a piecemeal manner according to the perceived needs of the individual sectors (i.e. sport, tourism, arts, etc.) and other government policy imperatives of the time.

There was a general consensus among political parties that the arts should be given state support, and therefore the Arts Council succeeded the wartime Committee for Entertainment, Music and the Arts (CEMA) when it was granted its Royal Charter in 1946. The Arts Council was the first leisure organisation to be granted quango (quasi-autonomous, non-government organisation) status, and initially it focused almost entirely on the elitist high arts, thus reflecting the direction of the BBC described above.

Much leisure policy in this period was stimulated as much by external policy concerns as it was by a concern for leisure provision in its own right. Shoard (1980), for example, characterises the National Parks and Access to the Countryside Act (1949) as being directed as much towards conservation and the protection of countryside-based industries as the promotion of countryside recreation. However, the Act did designate nine national parks, which still remain today. A further example is provided by the Wolfenden Report (1960), which advocated the establishment of a Sports Council. The rationale for such an organisation was the emergence of youth subcultures which, it was felt, could be directed away from anti-social tendencies if they were provided with the opportunities to participate in sporting activities (Henry, 2001). Finally, the Development of Tourism Act (1969), which established the British Tourist Authority and the four National Tourist Boards, was concerned almost exclusively with the contribution of tourism to the national economy. The concept of social tourism (the provision of subsidised holidays for the less well off), prevalent in many other European countries, has never played a significant part in UK tourism policy.

However, in the late 1960s and early 1970s, a greater element of welfare thinking crept into state provision for leisure. An Advisory Sports Council was established in 1965 and was later granted quasi-autonomous status by Royal Charter in 1971. The Sports Council reported to the Ministry for Housing and Local Government, which later became the Department of the Environment. The government White Paper from this department, *Sport and Recreation* (1975), identified sport and recreation as 'one of the community's everyday needs' and designated leisure provision as 'part of the general fabric of social services' (DoE, 1975). This clearly indicated that leisure was now considered as a legitimate part of state welfare provision. Such provision was aided and boosted considerably by the reorganisation of local government in the mid 1970s (see Chapter 11), which saw the creation of large local authority leisure departments, providing a huge increase in leisure spending in the community by the local state. Following this theme of community participation, the organisation of state support for the arts was re-assessed during the 1960s. The range of art forms being supported by the Arts Council was widened, decision making was decentralised away from London, and Regional Arts Associations were developed. Further to this, the 1970s saw the Arts Council beginning to fund community arts, and the seeds of a move towards cultural democracy were sown. The 1960s also saw the establishment of the Countryside Commission (1968), with a remit to foster countryside recreation through grant aid to local authorities and other providers. The provision of *country parks* was seen to be of particular importance as they would bring opportunities for countryside recreation to less affluent, geographically dispersed populations, who did not have access to the national parks.

However, the late 1970s saw, by necessity, a squeeze on government spending that was to lay the foundations for the market-oriented policies of the Thatcher administrations of the 1980s. In 1976, as a result of a weak economy and fears about the value of the pound, the British government approached the International Monetary Fund for a loan. This loan was granted on the condition that Britain would cut public expenditure, and consequently financial support for a whole range of areas came under pressure. It might be expected that, in this climate, spending on leisure would be the first area to be cut; however, rather than reduce government support for leisure, the nature of the support changed. Leisure increasing came to be regarded as an instrumental tool that could achieve economic, social and public order policy goals, rather than as part of welfare provision. The 1977 White Paper *A Policy for the Inner Cities* (DoE, 1977), for example, promoted the use of leisure services in deprived areas as a means of reducing expenditure on policing and petty crime. Even the *Sport and Recreation* White Paper alluded to this: 'By reducing boredom and urban frustration, participation in active recreation contributes to the reduction of hooliganism and delinquency among young people' (DoE, 1975, p. 2). In pursuing these instrumental goals, governments would increasingly 'earmark' additional funds given to the leisure quangos. For example, in 1978 the government made a further £1.8 million available, over and above its grant aid, to the Sports Council for schemes that focused on deprived inner-city populations.

This theme is one that continued into the Thatcher years of the 1980s. For example, the Young Report on Tourism, *Pleasure, Leisure and Jobs* (Cabinet Office, 1985), outlined the role the government felt tourism could play in job creation in deprived areas, and switched responsibility for tourism to the Department for Employment. Thus, in a general climate that saw many areas of public service being exposed to market forces and expenditure cuts, spending on leisure had survived intact. It should be emphasised, though, that the survival of this spending in no way reflected the Thatcher government's interest in leisure, or any recognition of its intrinsic value; it was merely being used as a tool to help address the social and economic problems of the time. In fact, as the urban riots and public disorder of the early 1980s faded into the past, the government began to squeeze the funding given to the leisure quangos as it attempted to take more direct control over many areas of policy. Such direct control was reflected in the way the Thatcher government attempted, through, for example, rate-capping, to control the expenditure of what it saw as irresponsible Labour-controlled authorities. During this period both the Arts Council and the Sports Council were being encouraged to raise more private sponsorship (Treasury, 1988, 1990), and were increasingly having to justify their claims for grant aid in terms of the externalities that might accrue, rather than intrinsic value. The general theme of the 1980s was one of centralised government control and the introduction of market forces to public services and this was highlighted by the introduction of compulsory competitive tendering (CCT) in the late 1980s, which attempted to put the management of many local authority services with private sector organisations (see Chapter 11 for further details). During this time, as described above, expenditure on leisure became instrumental, focusing on its contribution to other policy goals. As these contributions became less important towards the end of the decade, spending was squeezed, as the Thatcher administration saw no other use for leisure provision. However, the election of John Major in 1990 as leader of the Conservative Party, and consequently Prime Minister, saw a considerable change in attitude towards the leisure sectors.

Although John Major became Prime Minister in succession to Margaret Thatcher in 1990, he did not win a general election in his own right until 1992. It was following this election that his government's approach to leisure started to develop. Immediately following the election victory, he established a new Department of National Heritage (renamed the Department for Culture, Media and Sport in 1997) that brought together under one roof the leisure sectors of sport, tourism, the arts, heritage and broadcasting – although responsibility for the countryside remained with the Department of the Environment (now the Department for Environment, Food and Rural Affairs). This department gave these sectors, for the first time, a voice at the cabinet table, and the intentions for the department were outlined by its new Minister, David Mellor:

> What we have is a department for our cultural heritage...I plan to give it dynamic leadership. In the long run a society is judged not so much by its economic achievements but by its cultural ones. It is the biggest department of its kind in the world.

However, despite bracketing these leisure sectors together, the department remained fragmented, 'on the familiar Whitehall model, merely an agglomeration of interests' (*The Guardian*, 1992). Nevertheless, with the advent of the National

Lottery (responsibility for which was also located within the Department for National Heritage) and the designation of sports, arts and heritage as three of the good causes, the profile of these leisure sectors was lifted considerably. Furthermore, the rationale for providing for these sectors was clearly identified as being for their own intrinsic value. This was clearly stated by John Major himself in his introduction to *Sport: Raising the Game* (DNH, 1995), the government's sports policy statement:

> I have never believed that the quality of life in Britain should revolve simply around material success. Of equal importance, for most people, is the availability of those things that can enrich and elevate daily life in the worlds of arts, leisure and sport.

Restructures of both the Sports Council and the Arts Council followed which, while perhaps resulting in them being less independent of government, expanded their role and capabilities in providing for sport and the arts, particularly through their role as Lottery fund distributors. Tourism, while receiving less financial support from government, was increasingly being promoted as a key industry. However, in contrast to the other sectors, government saw tourism primarily as a commercial sector concern that could benefit from government support in terms of research, co-ordination and advice. As such, as described later, the government's financial support to the tourism industry continued to be squeezed, as it had been in the pre-Major period.

Many of the leisure policies of the Major years continue today: the UK Sports Institute, the promotion of arts and sports in schools, and the use of Lottery funding are all policies of the Major government that leisure is still benefiting from. However, perhaps a significant feature of the Major years was an apparent change in motivation for the provision of leisure (with the exception of tourism), which appeared to shift from being related to external policy goals to focusing on the intrinsic value of the activities themselves.

The more recent initiatives of Tony Blair's Labour Government, elected in 1997, would, however, appear to indicate that the brief flirtation with intrinsic rationales for provision is at an end. Tourism continues to be promoted for its economic benefits, while both sport and the arts have played a significant part in the Blair government's social policy agenda. This has been made possible as a result of the revised directions regarding the National Lottery in 1998. These directions allowed agencies such as Sport England and the Arts Council to be strategic in their distribution of funds within guidelines laid down by the Department for Culture, Media and Sport. Such guidelines directed Lottery funding, particularly in the sports sector where programmes are now almost exclusively based on the Lottery Sports Fund Strategy (Sport England, 1998), towards initiatives such as social exclusion and the delivery of Best Value (see Chapter 9). As such, the original intention that National Lottery funding would be *additional* to existing funding and would enhance provision in the cultural sector has all but been abandoned, as funding is increasingly directed towards the government's social policy priorities.

However, a significant change for leisure in the decade since John Major became Prime Minister has been the vast increase in the political profile and significance of the leisure sectors. This has been partly a result of the creation of the Department of National Heritage (now Department for Culture, Media and Sport), and partly a result of the personal interest of high-profile politicians – initially John Major and David Mellor, and more recently Chris Smith and Tony Banks – in the leisure area. It certainly marks a change from the Thatcher years, when leisure policy was seen by government as largely insignificant. The implications of this increased profile for leisure is one of the issues covered in the analysis of the sport, tourism and arts policy communities in the rest of this chapter.

The leisure policy universe

A useful concept in examining policy for leisure is that of the policy universe. The leisure policy universe is simply a collective term for the large number of organisations, groups, associations and individuals that share a common interest in the leisure policy area, and attempt to contribute to policy development on a regular basis. The policy universe includes government departments and agencies, voluntary clubs and associations, commercial sector firms, charities, and any other group or individual with an interest in the development of policy for leisure.

The leisure policy universe has never been particularly cohesive, historically being characterised by fragmentation and the separate development of its individual sectors. However, the collective identity of the leisure policy universe was enhanced considerably with the creation of the Department for Culture, Media and Sport (then the Department of National Heritage) in 1992. Yet it is not only the responsibilities of this department that fall within the policy universe as, for example, countryside issues, which are a significant part of leisure policy, are the responsibility of the Department for Environment, Food and Rural Affairs (DEFRA). Within the leisure policy universe it is possible to further identify more specific policy sectors, such as sport, tourism and the arts, which can be referred to as policy communities (Wilks and Wright, 1987). A policy community refers to those groups sharing an interest in a policy sector that interact with each other on a regular basis to maximise the benefits of their relationships with each other. The structure of such policy communities, and consequently the relationships between organisations within them, may vary along a continuum, from a tightly knit policy circle to a larger, loosely structured issue zone (Weed, 2001). The features of this continuum are outlined in Figure 8.1. The first four features – membership, interdependencies, insulation from other communities and resource dependence – will vary along the continuum, while the fifth – dominant member interests – may be governmental, economic or professional at any point on the continuum. This model will now be used as the basis for the following analyses, which highlight the key organisations and relationships in the policy communities for sport, tourism and the arts.

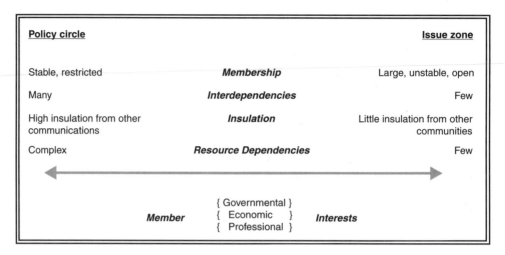

Policy circle		Issue zone
Stable, restricted	**Membership**	Large, unstable, open
Many	**Interdependencies**	Few
High insulation from other communications	**Insulation**	Little insulation from other communities
Complex	**Resource Dependencies**	Few

| **Member** | { Governmental }
{ Economic }
{ Professional } | **Interests** |

Figure 8.1   Features of the policy community continuum

Source: Weed, M.E. (2001) 'Towards a model of cross-sectional policy development in leisure': the case of sport and tourism, *Leisure Studies* (www.tandf.co.uk) vol. 20(2) pp. 125–41 (adapted from Marsh and Rhodes, 1992).

The sports policy community

As Figure 8.1 highlights, policy community membership varies from being fairly stable and restricted to being unstable and open to a wide range of groups. In a tightly formed policy circle, a single government department or agency will usually provide the lead to the community. In the sports policy community the issue of leadership is somewhat complex as the Department for Culture, Media and Sport, UK Sport, and Sport England all have a legitimate claim to the leadership role. As the government department responsible for sport, the Department for Culture, Media and Sport (DCMS) could clearly claim to lead the sports policy community. However, traditionally the British government has delegated policy making in the leisure sectors to semi-independent government agencies with quango status (such as UK Sport, Sport England, the Arts Council for England, and the British Tourist Authority). Although these agencies receive their grant aid directly from the DCMS, which also appoints the chair and members, theoretically they work at arm's length from government (although in recent years their independence has been eroded as government has intervened directly in their work). Consequently, both UK Sport and Sport England could claim to lead the sports policy community. Of course, there is a further tension here with both a UK and an English body – both of which were created in 1997 following the demise of the former Sports Council, which had responsibilities for both Britain and England.

UK Sport is by far the smaller of the two bodies, working mainly on those few issues that have UK-wide significance. It would therefore appear that Sport England, which receives a far greater sum in grant aid from the government, would be the more important body in most areas. (Alongside these bodies there also exists Sport Scotland and the Sports Council for Wales, which operate in their national areas. While these agencies might be expected to provide a lead to Scottish and

Welsh bodies, like UK Sport, they are much smaller bodies than Sport England, both in terms of staffing and government grant aid received.) However, this still leaves unresolved the tension between Sport England and the DCMS. The 1990s have certainly seen Sport England (and its predecessor the Sports Council) lose much of its independence; this was highlighted by the policy statement of the previous Conservative government, *Sport: Raising the Game* (DNH, 1995), which not only laid down policy directions for what was then the Sports Council, but also specified particular initiatives it wanted to see developed (such as the UK Sports Institute). This has meant that the nature of the delegation from the government to Sport England has changed, Sport England has lost much of its independence, but its role within the sports policy community has become more central. The advent of the National Lottery, and Sport England's position as distributer for the Lottery Sports Fund, has seen its funding role expand. Furthermore, unlike some of the other leisure quangos (e.g. the former English Tourist Board – see next section), Sport England is clearly valued and trusted by the DCMS as any sporting initiatives from government are carried out through, rather than bypassing, Sport England. It is rare that Sport England publicly conflicts with the DCMS, and it would therefore seem that the leadership structure for the sports policy community is clear. The Department for Culture, Media and Sport provides a general lead, but it does this through Sport England, which then gives a lead to the community, but generally as an implementor rather than a developer of policy.

Returning to the more general issue of membership, Laumann and Knocke (1987) believe that policy communities have primary and secondary communities. The primary core contains the key actors, who set the rules of the game and determine membership and the main policy directions, while the secondary community contains the groups that, although abiding by the rules of the game, do not have the resources or influence to greatly affect policy. The sports policy community would appear to have a fairly stable primary community, which includes the DCMS, Sport England, Sport Scotland, the Sports Council for Wales, and UK Sport. The secondary community, the membership of which appears to be fairly open, contains a wide range of interest groups, sports organisations and clubs, and local authorities. It might be argued that local authorities, or at least their representative organisations (such as the Local Government Association) form part of the primary community, although empirical evidence (Weed, 1999) suggests they have little input into the development of national policy. It would appear, therefore, that the sports policy community is showing some of the characteristics of a policy circle in this area as, while having a fairly open secondary community, it has a primary community of which membership is fairly stable and restricted.

The sports policy community has generally found it difficult to insulate itself from the interference of other, more powerful policy areas in its work. The use of sport in combating inner-city problems, as described in the previous section, is one example of this. Houlihan (1991) also cites the response to the problem of football hooliganism in the 1980s, where the sports policy community was superseded by the law and order policy community in defining responses to that problem. In this respect the sports policy community has displayed the characteristics of an issue zone, having little insulation from other policy areas. However, it might be assumed that the reasons for this lack of insulation are related to the prime motivation for the provision of sport having been, until relatively recent times, based upon its impacts on other policy areas. In the mid to late 1990s, sports provision has been increasingly justified on its intrinsic value and, as such, there has been less interference from other policy areas, as sport has not impinged on their work. Nevertheless, as sport increasingly becomes an important factor in delivering Best Value (see Chapter 9) and combating social exclusion, it is possible that sports considerations may again become secondary to those of other policy areas.

The level of interdependency in a policy community is often linked to resources. Resources come in a range of forms: most obvious are financial resources, but also important are knowledge, information, legitimacy and the goodwill of other groups (Smith, 1993). A policy circle has many interdependencies, and the relationships between groups are often exchange relationships, while in the more loosely structured issue zone, the relationships become more one-sided. In recent years, Sport England has exchanged (although not necessarily willingly) much of its independence and control over general policy direction for a central role in the distribution of Lottery funds. This has led to the development of a range of resource relationships on which the sports policy community is dependent. In the primary community, the relationship between the government and Sport England (and indeed UK Sport, Sport Scotland and the Sports Council for Wales) is important, as they are dependent on the government's grant aid. This relationship helps ensure that Sport England accepts the lead of the Department for Culture, Media and Sport over general policy direction. However, the government in general does not wish to involve itself with the detail of all aspects of sports policy, and thus Sport England's expertise is required to convert general policy direction into implementable specifics. It is this exchange relationship that ensures these agencies comprise the primary core of the sports policy community. Their relationship with the secondary community is as a result of the dependence of much of that secondary community on Sport England grant aid and Lottery Sports Fund money. The organisations in the secondary community do not have anything to exchange for these resources and, as a result, have to accept the general policy direction and terms and conditions under which they are offered. Again, the debate re-arises about the position of local authorities in the sports policy community. Although they are major providers of sport and recreation provision, and the sports policy community as a whole relies on that provision, they are also answerable to their local community charge payer. Consequently, the members of the primary community know that it is unlikely local authorities would cease to provide sport and recreation services for fear of the backlash from their local population and, as a result, they do not go to any great lengths to involve them in the primary community. Nevertheless, Sport England does realise the importance of local authorities, and particularly local authority-employed sports development officers, in delivering its policies. However, because Sport England (and the former Sports Council) initially grant-aided many local authority sports development posts, and because they provide these officers with much professional support, one Sport England regional officer commented that they might be regarded as 'ex-officio Sport England employees, our Indians on the ground' (quoted in Weed, 2001). This emphasises Houlihan's (1991) assertion that professional groups and connections can be significantly important in defining relationships within policy communities.

In summary, the sports policy community, while perhaps not strong enough to be labelled so, does exhibit some of the characteristics of a policy circle. The membership of its primary community is stable and restricted, although the secondary community is fairly open; there are a number of major interdependencies, both in terms of finance and expertise, that dictate the structure of, and relationships within, the community; and its interests are mainly governmental, supplemented by professional connections. The one factor that prevents the sports policy community becoming a policy circle is its historical lack of insulation from other, more powerful policy areas and thus, at times, its inability to define its own agenda.

The tourism policy community

The tourism policy community shows significant differences in its organisation and structure to the sports policy community. The structure of the community is, to a large extent, dictated by member interests which, due to the significant commercial sector operating in tourism, are mainly economic. This is further complicated by the relationship that has existed between the government and the English Tourist Board, which has served to create instability within the tourism policy community. Although the English Tourist Board was replaced in July 1999 by a new English Tourism Council, it is worth examining the relationship between the English Tourist Board (ETB) and government during the 1990s, as this has had considerable bearing on the tourism policy community.

Following the formation of the Department of National Heritage (now the Department for Culture, Media and Sport) in 1992, the government announced, as part of a pre-public expenditure survey of tourism, a series of radical cuts in the English Tourist Board's funding over four years – from £15.4 million in 1992/3 to £9 million in 1995/96. In the event, funding only dropped to £10 million, but this still represented a reduction of 35 per cent. The effect of these cuts was to leave the ETB with only £2 million to fund its own core functions because the government stipulated that a greater proportion of the ETB's funding should be directed through the Regional Tourist Boards. The Regional Tourist Boards are not semi-government bodies, as the English Tourist Board was; they are partnerships between local authorities in the region, the region's commercial sector, and English Tourist Board funding. They are independent of each other and of the English Tourist Board (and now the English Tourism Council). However, this increased funding did not greatly benefit the Regional Tourist Boards, as it was earmarked for specific initiatives and offered on a competitive bidding basis. In fact, the change in nature of the funding meant that the Regional Tourist Boards actually faced a reduction in the amount of money coming from the English Tourist Board that they could use to fund their core functions – basic staffing, building and equipment costs and, most importantly, strategic development services. This resulted in a slimmed down core operation, which meant the range of projects the Regional Boards could get involved in was reduced, because they did not, and still do not, have the basic core resources required to sustain such projects. Consequently, this increasing propensity for government to cut money to tourist organisations set a context within which self-generation of funds and commercial activity became, and still remain today, increasingly important.

As government cuts its funding to the tourist industry, the increasing commercial influence that results creates a significantly different set of structures of member interests in the tourism policy community. Because Regional Tourist Boards increasingly have to generate a greater proportion of their own funding, they need to develop closer relationships with the commercial sector. This, allied with the government's desire to use tourism as an economic tool, means that the dominant member interests in the tourism policy community are economic. This means that, unlike the sports policy community, there is little governmental influence or control within the tourism policy community and, because of the weak position the English Tourist Board occupied, very little in the way of leadership.

The English Tourist Board appeared to have lost a certain amount of credibility in the eyes of other members of the tourism policy community since the creation of the Department of National Heritage. Not only did the Department of National Heritage cut the English Tourist Board's funding by 35 per cent, it also appeared that it would rather intervene directly itself than use the expertise that the English Tourist Board was set up to advise government with. The last English Tourist Board strategy, *Success Through Partnership* (ETB/DNH, 1997), was a joint publication with the Department of National Heritage, an unprecedented move as far as the leisure quangos are concerned and one that indicated a greater level of government intervention in the work of the English Tourist Board. More recently, the Department for Culture, Media and Sport established, in 1997, a Tourism Advisory Forum, made up of prominent figures from the tourism industry, to advise it on tourism matters – the exact role the English Tourist Board was set up to fulfill in 1969. These interventions appeared to provide clear evidence that the government had little faith in the English Tourist Board. Such suspicions were subsequently confirmed when the English Tourist Board was replaced in July 1999 with a new English Tourism Council. The government describes the role of the English Tourism Council as being a business-to-business organisation, providing research and advice services to the commercial sector. The creation of the English Tourism Council has also resulted in many of the roles of the former English Tourist Board passing to the Regional Tourist Boards, which would appear to strengthen their position within the tourism policy community. However, such relationships are at an early stage and it is not possible to comment on how they will impact on the tourism policy community.

Discussions of the sports policy community resulted in the identification of a primary core of key actors and a wider secondary community. However, it would appear to be more difficult to identify such a division in the tourism policy community. The marginalisation of the now defunct English Tourist Board meant that it was not really possible to regard it as a member of a primary community, and the new English Tourism Council, as a business-to-business organisation, does not really have a wide enough remit or a central enough role to be included in a primary community. It might be expected that the Department for Culture, Media and Sport and its Tourism Forum would form part of a primary community. However, the Forum mainly comprises industry representatives, who are not necessarily interested in setting an agenda across the whole range of issues. Therefore, only the government department remains and, as the Department for Culture, Media and Sport appears to be increasingly emphasising the role of the private sector in the tourism industry, it must be assumed that it does not wish to be involved in a major way. This leads to the conclusion that the tourism policy community shows the characteristics of an issue zone in respect of membership, which is unstable, with groups joining or leaving the community according to the issues being discussed.

The above discussion appears to indicate that the Regional Tourist Boards have a key role within the tourism policy community. In fact, within their regions they are at the centre of a range of interdependencies in the community. They have resource relationships with the government and English Tourism Council, with local government and with the commercial sector. In particular, their increasing need to generate their own funding means that they have developed a complex pattern of resource relationships with the commercial sector. These relationships are supplemented by their strategic services to local authorities – particularly in terms of writing local tourism strategies – which mean they are able to wield subtle influence over local policy direction. Furthermore, they are looked to by the tourism industry within their regions to provide an overall strategic view and co-ordination. This means that, although they are not particularly powerful in being able to influence other members of the tourism policy community directly, they are key players because they retain a more subtle form of influence over policy in their individual regions, as they are the only organisation able to take a strategic overview. However, their independence from the English Tourism Council and from each other has often meant that their activities have not been co-ordinated outside their regions.

Like all policy communities within the leisure policy universe, the tourism policy community is unable to insulate itself from the work of other, more influential policy areas. In fact, as government objectives for tourism are almost exclusively linked to other areas of policy – such as economic and social regeneration, job creation and export earnings – the tourism policy community is almost continually facing the interference of other policy areas in its work. This serves to highlight the privileged position the government holds within the tourism policy community due to its greater resources. The government is not interested in setting an agenda or providing funding in all areas of policy or provision. However, it knows that because the Regional Tourist Boards are relatively underfunded, they will almost certainly bid for or accept any funding that is offered to them. Therefore, it is possible for the government to influence policy direction by offering funding with attached conditions relating to, for example, job creation or regeneration, which it knows the Boards will almost certainly accept. In operating in this way the government is able to retain a 'golden share' in the tourism policy community, which allows it to influence those areas it considers to be important without providing extensive funding to the tourist agencies.·

In summary, in contrast to the sports policy community, it is possible to characterise the tourism policy community as showing many of the characteristics of an issue zone. It has an unstable, open membership with no clear leadership and, perhaps more than any other policy community in the leisure policy universe, it faces continual interference from other policy areas from which it has virtually no insulation. Furthermore, while there is a complex range of relatively small interdependencies and resource relationships at local and regional level, there are no major resource dependencies upon which the policy community is dependent. This is a consequence of the dominant member interests within the tourism policy community being economic – the tourism industry operates, in the main, through market forces, rather than through government funding and subsidy, which means no one organisation or agency is dominant in setting policy because the community is not dependent on any one agency or organisation for funding.

The arts policy community

Since the creation of the Arts Council (of Great Britain) in 1946, the arts policy community has been faced with ongoing tensions between the established or 'high' arts and the community arts movement. Such tensions between community and high arts are significant because they tend to reflect social divisions in wider society. Many supporters of the high arts are from the upper-middle classes and view members of the community arts movement as 'Philistines' who debase the national heritage. Conversely, the community arts movement sees the high arts as class-based with little relevance to the lives of much of the population. While community arts have been used as part of social programmes in deprived communties in an attempt to effect positive social change, it has been argued that the high arts reinforce social divisions by offering social status to participants (Henry, 2001). Although the high arts lobby has traditionally been more powerful in the arts policy sector, the community arts movement has clearly made significant progress in recent years. It is useful, therefore, to examine how the community/high arts debate has affected the membership and structure of the arts policy community.

Unlike the Sports Council and its successor bodies and the tourist organisations, which have both been involved in direct provision activities in the past, the Arts Council and its successor bodies have been solely concerned with the distribution of funding. Traditionally this has been focused on professional artists and fostering excellence although, as discussed later, some recent programmes have changed this focus to a certain extent. The Arts Council has also, unlike (until recently) the sports and tourism bodies, traditionally provided revenue grants for artists, and particularly for institutions such as the Royal Opera House, to help finance their ongoing upkeep and running costs. The rationale for such funding is that the Arts Council works through its grant-aid recipients to promote cultural opportunities. However, there is tension within the arts policy community as to the extent to which such opportunities should be provided for the high arts or for community arts.

It is perhaps helpful to examine how the membership of the arts policy community has changed over the last twenty years or so. At the end of the 1970s, arts policy making was very much dominated by the high arts, and it could be argued that the individuals involved were drawn from an upper-middle-class group comprising Oxford and Cambridge graduates and career civil servants who, as a result of their upbringing, were often patrons of the traditional art forms. The government department responsible was the Office for Arts and Libraries (OAL), which was staffed by civil service professionals who were largely sympathetic towards the demands of the arts lobby in general, and the high arts in particular. The OAL was not generally seen by government as comprising part of its mainstream programme and, as such, it received little attention from politicians and was largely left to its own devices in its formulation of policy and its supervision of the Arts Council. Consequently, given the sympathies of its staff, it could be argued that the OAL was the voice of the arts, particularly high arts, within government, rather than the voice of the government in the arts sector. At the end of the 1970s, therefore, it would be possible to identify a primary arts policy community comprising the Office for Arts and Libraries, the Arts Council, and the various national companies (e.g. Royal National Theatre, Royal Opera House) to which a significant proportion of arts funding went. The secondary community comprised the Regional Arts Boards (to which had been delegated responsibility for community arts in 1979), local authorities, and the rest of the community arts movement. The issue of leadership at this time is difficult to resolve, as it is not possible to identify a lead organisation, but it could be argued that the lead came from an elite group within the arts policy sector that crossed organisational boundaries in the primary community. This elite group led by the consent of the members of the primary policy community, because there were very few differences in the interests of the members of the primary community and, therefore, little debate over decisions.

However, the arts policy community in the present day has changed considerably from that described above. In 1994 the Arts Council of Great Britain was split into the Arts Council for England, the Scottish Arts Council, and the Arts Council for Wales, but it was the establishment of the Department of National

Heritage in 1992 that had the most significant implications for the arts policy community. The formation of the DNH brought the arts closer to the mainstream activities of government, with the Office for Arts and Libraries becoming a section within the newly formed department. This resulted in a greater interest in its activities by politicians and broke up, to a certain extent, the cosy relationship that had existed between the OAL and the primary arts policy community. While the OAL and the arts lobby had always tried to emphasise the culturally improving nature of the arts as a rationale for public sector funding, the DNH, while not eschewing this rationale, was increasingly interested in the contribution of arts to tourism. This changing emphasis has implications for the extent to which the arts policy community can insulate itself from other policy areas. In comparison to the sports and the tourism sectors, the arts policy community has received relatively little interference from other policy areas. However, a focus on the economic potential of the arts results in a greater interest in the arts sector from the tourism policy community, and also from non-leisure communities, such as that for urban policy.

There are clear lines of resource dependency within the arts policy community, with the rest of the community being dependent on the Arts Councils for funding. This has always been the case; however, while such dependencies in the sports policy community result in Sport England holding a relatively powerful position in relation to other members of the community, this has not been the case in the arts area. This is because there have been other interdependencies within the arts policy community that are based on a shared ideology about those arts forms which should be supported. Those sharing this ideology – the elite who have provided the lead to the arts policy community – have, until recently, been able to ensure that the traditional lines of funding continue without any additional conditions being attached to this funding. However, the changes brought about by the Department for Culture, Media and Sport since the election of the Labour government in 1997 have altered the nature of these interdependencies.

The late 1990s saw the DCMS institute a comprehensive spending review of the organisations and activities it funds and one of the results of this review was the replacement of the English Tourist Board by a new English Tourism Council, as described in the previous section. However, there were also wide-ranging implications for the arts. First, there would be a greater delegation of funding to the Regional Arts Boards, where decisions would be made about smaller grants and smaller Lottery awards. In fact, with the accompanying integration of Lottery and traditional grant-aid funding, this meant a doubling in the amount of funding chanelled through Regional Arts Boards. This move was widely welcomed by the community arts movement, which has much closer links with Regional Arts Boards than with the Arts Council for England, and is seen as part of a move to democratise arts funding and policy making. Such a move is further emphasised by the halving of the number of staff employed by the Arts Council for England to 150 full-time equivalents, and the focusing of its role on efficiency and the monitoring of its contracts. These contracts are those with the Regional Arts Boards in relation to its delegated funding, and newly established contracts with the major national companies it has traditionally funded. Such contracts have been established to ensure that the Regional Arts Boards and the national companies are accountable for the funds they receieve, and it could be argued that they are aimed at breaking up the elite group that has traditionally dominated arts policy and funding. In fact, an indication of this intent is given by the spending review document, which states, 'Resources must follow priorities, rather than maintaining historic patterns of funding for their own sake' (DCMS, 1998).

Recent priorities in the arts sector have included elements both of 'democratisation of culture' (the popularisation of high arts forms) and of 'cultural democracy' (the encouragement of popular art). The *New Audiences Programme* falls into the former category and attempts to generate an interest in the traditional high arts among non-participants by attempting to examine and overcome relatively obvious constraints, such as prices and transport, that have been long recognised as barriers in other areas of leisure. Conversely, the *Arts for Everyone* initiatives focus on outreach work within communities – again, a concept long used in other areas of leisure – to involve as many people as possible in art forms that they feel are relevant to their lives. Key elements of the Arts for Everyone initiative have been a focus on education and social exclusion, central parts of the current Labour Government's programme and a further indication – along with the changes of the comprehensive spending review – that the government is now taking a closer interest in arts policy.

In summary, the picture of the arts policy community today is very different to that of twenty years ago. The increased delegation to Regional Arts Boards, and the contracts for funding the national companies mean that it is no longer possible to identify a primary and secondary arts community. While the tensions still exist between community arts and high arts, the recent interventions by the DCMS mean that the high arts lobby is no longer dominant. Consequently, structural barriers and divisions between interests within the arts policy community are less prevalent, but the membership of the community is still relatively stable.

A second consequence of the recent DCMS interventions is that the arts policy community is now less insulated from other policy areas than in the past. The move from intrinsic rationales for provision relating to cultural improvement to economic rationales, and the more recent addition of rationales relating to social policy and social exclusion have seen the arts policy community less able to exclude other policy areas than it was previously able to do so. Interdependencies in the arts policy community are now contractual, and in many cases are based on resources, rather than on the shared ideologies of the professional elite as in the past. Furthermore, while professional member interests are still prevalent within the community, govermental interests are becoming increasingly important.

Traditionally, the arts policy community has demonstrated many of the characteristics of a policy circle. However, the recent interventions by the Department for Culture, Media and Sport may see changes in the structure and operation of the community that result in movements, in some areas, towards the characteristics of an issue zone.

● ● ● ● Conclusions

This chapter reviewed the historical development of leisure policy and gave a contemporary overview of the sport, tourism and arts policy communities. A separate analysis of these three sectors was necessary because, although they are now all administered through the same government department (the Department for Culture, Media and Sport), they have developed almost entirely seperately and independently of each other. This is because they each have very different historical legacies and contemporary problems. However, this is not to say that they are unconnected. For example, both sport and arts contribute to the tourism industry, while all three sectors have been used as part of urban regeneration programmes and, more recently, sport and the arts have been incorporated within the Best Value and social exclusion agendas (see Chapter 9). In fact, the focus of the current Labour Government on the economic rationale for tourism, and the social policy rationale for sport and the arts, seems to indicate an end to the brief flirtation with the intrinsic rationales that John Major's Conservative Government seemed to favour. The fact that the sports policy community is likely to be more comfortable with the social policy agenda than is the arts policy community gives a further example of the different historical legacies that exist within the leisure policy universe, and perhaps an indication that the individual policy communities are likely to continue to develop independently of each other in the future.

Questions

1 Discuss the extent to which the historical development of leisure policy affects present-day policy priorities in leisure.

2 To what extent might leisure be considered a coherent sector in terms of policy development?

3 Evaluate the usefulness of the policy community concept in understanding policy formulation in leisure.

4 Discuss the extent to which policy formulation in leisure is increasingly based on the direct intervention of Ministers and government departments, rather than on the deliberations of the leisure quangos.

5 Choose a leisure sector and discuss the extent to which the advent of the National Lottery has affected policy in that sector.

References

Bailey, P. (1987) *Leisure and Class in Victorian England* (2nd edition), London: Methuen.

Cabinet Office (1985) *Pleasure, Leisure and Jobs*, London: HMSO.

Cunningham, H. (1980) *Leisure in the Industrial Revolution*, London: Croom Helm.

Department for Culture, Media and Sport (1998) *Comprehensive Spending Review*, London: HMSO.

Department of the Environment (1975) *Sport and Recreation*, London: HMSO.

Department of the Environment (1977) *A Policy for the Inner Cities*, London: HMSO.

Department of National Heritage (1995) *Sport: Raising the Game*, London: HMSO.

English Tourist Board/Department of National Heritage (1997) *Tourism: Success Through Partnership*, London: HMSO.

Guardian, The (1992) 'What is he there for?' 12 May, p. 20.

Hall, C.M. and Jenkins, J.M. *Tourism and Public Policy*, London: Routledge.

Henry, I.P. (2001) *The Politics of Leisure Policy* (2nd edition), London: Palgrave.

Houlihan, B.M.J. (1991) *The Government and the Politics of Sport*, London: Routledge.

Hutchinson, R. (1982) *The Politics of the Arts Council*, London: Sinclair-Brown.

Laumann, E.O. and Knocke, D. (1987) *The Organisational State*, Madison: University of Wisconsin Press.

Marsh, D. and Rhodes, R.A.W. (1992) 'Policy communities and issue networks: beyond typology', in Marsh, D. and Rhodes, R.A.W. (eds) *Policy Networks in British Government*, Oxford: Oxford University Press.

Shoard, M. (1980) *The Theft of the Countryside*, Aldershot: Temple Smith.

Smith, M.J. (1993) *Pressure, Power and Policy*, Hemel Hempstead: Harvester Wheatsheaf.

Sport England (1998) *Investing for Our Sporting Future: Sport England Lottery Fund Strategy 1999–2009*, London: Sport England.

Thompson, E.P. (1967) 'Time, work discipline and industrial capitalism', *Past and Present*, vol. 38.

Treasury (1988) *The Goverment's Expenditure Plans 1989/90–1991/2*, London: HMSO.

Treasury (1990) *The Goverment's Expenditure Plans 1991/2–1993/4*, London: HMSO.

Wilks, S. and Wright, M. (eds) (1987) *Comparative Government–Industry Relations*, Oxford: Clarendon Press.

Weed, M.E. (1999) *Consensual Policies for Sport and Tourism in the UK: An Analysis of Organisational Behaviour and Problems* (PhD thesis), Canterbury: University of Kent.

Weed, M.E. (2001) 'Towards a model of cross-sectoral policy development in leisure', *Leisure Studies*, 20(2).

Further reading

A more detailed review of the historical development of leisure policy can be found in Ian Henry's *Politics of Leisure Policy*.

Marsh and Rhodes, in their edited collection *Policy Networks in British Government*, provide a useful overview of the policy community literature.

Barrie Houlihan's *Government and the Politics of Sport* provides a useful, if now somewhat dated, review of the policy community for sport in Britain, while Hall and Jenkins, in *Tourism and Public Policy*, discuss the tourism sector, and Hutchinson discusses, albeit again largely historically, the arts sector in *The Politics of the Arts Council*.

The best sources of up-to-date information on policy priorities are the websites of the organisations concerned.

Useful websites

Central Office of Information (government press releases):
www.nds.coi.gov.uk
Department for Culture, Media and Sport: *www.culture.gov.uk*
UK Sport: *www.uksport.gov.uk*
Sport England: *www.sportengland.org*
Sport Scotland: *www.sportscotland.org.uk*
Sports Council for Wales:
www.sports-council-wales.co.uk
British Tourist Authority corporate website:
www.britishtouristauthority.org.uk

English Tourism Council: (includes links to Regional Tourist Boards)
www.englishtourism.org.uk
Scottish Tourist Board:
www.visitscotland.com
Wales Tourist Board:
www.wtbonline.gov.uk
Arts Council for England:
www.artscouncil.org.uk
Regional Arts Boards: *www.arts.org.uk*
Scottish Arts Council: *www.sac.org.uk*
Arts Council for Wales:
www.ccc-acw.org.uk

Chapter 9 ●●●●

Leisure and local government

As discussed in Chapter 8, the role of government in leisure is constantly evolving and changing. However, local government is perhaps not subject to the dramatic changes in direction that central government policy can take with the election of a new government. It is fair to say that policy changes initiated by central government take some time to filter down to local authorities because such authorities have partial autonomy from central government. That said, local government exists as a result of central government legislation, and its authority and autonomy is granted and delegated by Parliament. Theoretically, it could be removed (as was the case with the Greater London Council and the metropolitan authorities in the mid 1980s – see below).

Wilson and Game (1994) define local government in the United Kingdom as:

> a form of *geographical* and *political decentralisation*, in which...*directly elected councils*...*created by* and *subordinate to parliament*...have *partial autonomy*...to *provide a wide variety of services*...through various *direct* and *indirect means*...*funded in part* through *local taxation*.

It is this ability to raise funds through local taxation (currently the council tax for private citizens, but also taxes on local businesses) to supplement the central government grant that enables local authorities to fund such a wide range of services. As a result, their contribution to the overall picture of leisure provision, in terms of both facilities and services, is considerable.

This chapter will examine in greater detail the role of local authorities in leisure provision, examining the historical context, traditional provision and recent changes.

Objectives

To:

- *briefly outline the origins of local government in the United Kingdom and subsequently examine the evolution of its current structure and organisation*

- *examine the contribution of local government to leisure provision and outline some of the challenges it faces*

- *examine recent developments and new directions in the role of local authorities in leisure provision, including the effects of, first, compulsory competitive tendering and, latterly, Best Value.*

Structure and organisation of local government

The origins of local government

The roots of the current structure of local government can be traced back to Anglo-Saxon times (around the tenth century), when England was not a unified state and most people never travelled outside their immediate settlement. The government of local affairs was based on the *feudal system*, whereby the king would grant land tenure to barons, nobles and bishops, and in turn they would grant authority to local *freemen*. This system of patronage lasted, with some modifications, until the fifteenth century, and the early boundaries of modern local government (for example that of the *shire* counties) date from this time. In most cases local communities would form naturally, with alliances and friendships forming among families based on the exchange of resources required for survival – food, shelter, etc. Generally leaders would emerge, or would otherwise be appointed by the king or the king's representative, to positions such as *shire reeve* (or sheriff) and justice of the peace. Such leaders formed the basis of a limited local authority and were charged with the basic tasks of local government, namely:

- prevention of crime;
- punishment of offenders;
- provision of poor relief and welfare;
- control of nuisance; and
- management of public land.

Later in this period, a range of self-help groups, voluntary organisations and sometimes even commercial organisations became involved to varying extents in the government of local communities. Non-statutory bodies, such as charities, guilds and the Church, all played a part but by the late Middle Ages (around the fifteenth century) their influence had declined. However, by this time three types of authority had emerged and were firmly established. At the most local level there was the parish, based on the church parish, which was further subdivided into vestries (local committees). Above the parish was the shire authority, existing at what would now be recognised as county level. In addition to these two authorities, which were mainly based in rural areas – which meant most of the country at this time – there was the corporate town (borough in England, burgh in Scotland).

These structures survived largely intact until the time of the Industrial Revolution in the early nineteenth century, when it became obvious that reform was necessary.

By the start of the nineteenth century the *urbanisation* of Britain was well under-way (the move of the population from an agrarian existence in the countryside to an urban existence in the new industrial towns is discussed in Chapters 1 and 8). Obviously, systems of local administration based on small church parishes and vestries were not equipped to deal with this very different mode of existence, particularly as urban living brought with it particular kinds of problems. A more anonymous population, based less on family and kinship, led to higher levels of poverty; a more concentrated population also led to higher levels of both disease and crime and the urban environment needed to be serviced by proper systems of sanitation if it was to be prevented from degenerating into general squalor. The answers to such problems lay in the enacting of central government legislation to develop a more efficient system of local government (see Table 9.1). As a result of this legislation, the system of local government at the end of the nineteenth century was *three tier*: first tier – county councils; second tier – district/borough councils; third tier – parish/town councils.

Local government reform in the twentieth century

The early twentieth century saw the 1929 Local Government Act that abolished the Boards of Poor Law Guardians and transferred their powers and responsibilities to local authorities. However, this legislation aside, the structures that were established during the nineteenth century survived largely intact until the 1960s, when local government reform became a key political issue. The process of change began when, in 1960, the Herbert Report (London) recommended a two-tier system of

Table 9.1 Nineteenth-century legislation on local government structures

1834	Poor Law Amendment Act	Established *Boards of Guardians*, which replaced the role of the parish in caring for the poor
1835	Municipal Corporations Act	Created elected municipal councils with a range of powers to administer the major industrial towns
1888	Local Government Act (similar legislation in Scotland in 1889)	Established in England and Wales: 62 elected county councils 61 all-purpose county borough councils
1894	Local Government Act (similar legislation in Scotland in 1900)	Established within county council areas of England and Wales: 535 urban district councils 472 rural district councils 270 non-county borough councils revived parish councils

Table 9.2 Royal Commissions on local government reform

Redcliffe-Maude Commission (England and Wales)

Recommended the establishment of single-tier unitary authorities to:

reduce the number of small authorities
simplify administration
end service fragmentation and facilitate planning

Wheatley Commission (Scotland)

Recommended a similar but larger reduction in the numbers of smaller authorities to the Redcliffe-Maude Commission, *but*:

favoured a two-tier system of regional and district councils

Table 9.3 Local government reform (1972)

Local Government Act, 1972 (effective April 1974, England and Wales)

Abolished county boroughs
Reduced number of counties to 47 (from 58)
Established 333 non-metropolitan district councils (reduced from 1,250)
Established 6 metropolitan counties and 36 metropolitan districts

Local Government (Scotland) Act, 1972 (effective May 1975)

Established 9 regional councils
Establishes 53 district councils
Established 3 unitary island councils
  (these new structures replaced over 400 local authorities)

local government in London, and consequently the London Government Act, 1963 established 32 London boroughs and the Greater London Council. This report and legislation sparked a debate about the number of *tiers* or levels of authority that are required for efficient local government that has still not really been adequately resolved today. Two Royal Commissions were established on local government reform in 1966, both of which reported in 1969 (see Table 9.2).

While both Royal Commissions recommended a reduction in the numbers of small authorities, they did not agree on the number of tiers of local government required. The Wheatley Commission had recommended a two-tier system in Scotland, while the Redcliffe-Maude Report proposed unitary authorities for England and Wales. However, while the recommendations of the Redcliffe-Maude Commission were accepted by the Labour Government in 1969, they were rejected by the incoming Conservative administration in 1970, which preferred a two-tier system of county and borough/district councils. Consequently, the resultant legislation (see Table 9.3) of 1972 established a rationalised two-tier structure in England and Wales and in Scotland, with the aim of permitting more integrated planning and improving service delivery.

The 1972 Acts reflect the underlying rationale of both the Redcliffe-Maude and Wheatley Commissions that larger units of local government could provide large-scale solutions to the large-scale social, economic and environmental problems faced by local authorities. Not only were the authorities themselves larger, but the corporate management philosophy that they embraced resulted in the amalgamation of service areas into larger service departments. Typical examples of such amalgamated departments were social services and leisure services. Consequently, these Acts are often identified as key factors in the development of local authority leisure provision as the new large leisure services departments provided the focus for the expansion of local provision in the following decade, and also assisted greatly in the development of a recognised leisure profession and in establishing leisure provision as a legitimate activity of local government.

The ideological polarisation of the major two political parties in the early 1980s, with the Conservatives following a New Right agenda and the Labour Party adopting a traditional Socialist agenda, which in the eyes of many rendered them virtually unelectable, resulted in the emergence of what Henry (2001) identified as a New Urban Left approach to local left-wing politics. This approach saw local-level Labour politicians, such as Derek Hatton in Liverpool and Ken Livingstone in London, frustrated by the lack of any prospect of a Labour victory in national general elections, using their power base in major urban areas to provide political opposition to the national Conservative Government. Leisure was used as part of this opposition – for example, Bianchini (1987) highlights the Greater London Council's use of cultural events, such as the London Marathon, to promote policies such as the 'Fares Fair' subsidy of public transport and the 'London for Jobs' campaign. However, the Conservative Government retaliated by enacting legislation (the 1985 Local Government Act) to abolish this troublesome tier of local government – the Greater London Council and the metropolitan counties. This struggle serves as a reminder that local government in Britain exists by Act of Parliament, and may be subject to such extreme measures as abolition if it exceeds what central government perceives as being its remit.

Aside from the politically expedient reform of one aspect of local government described above, the debate regarding the number of tiers required for efficient government was laid to rest until various Local Government Acts in 1992 and 1994, which established unitary authorities in Wales and Scotland and a mixture of two-tier and unitary authorities in England (see Table 9.4). This legislation would seem to indicate that the unitary debate has still not been resolved. Consequently, it would be useful to examine some of the aspects of this debate, and their implications for leisure provision.

The Unitary authority debate

One of the criticisms levelled at the larger authorities created in the mid 1970s was that they were unwieldy and unresponsive to local interests and did not allow the levels of local participation recommended in the Skeffington Report of 1969. In fact, critics argued that these authorities created alienation in communities that felt remote, both socially and geographically, from their local administration. Proponents of the unitary system would argue that unified authorities, despite

Table 9.4 Local government reform (1992–98)

Local Government Act 1992 (England, phased-in in stages until April 1998)

Replaced former Boundary Commission with the Local Government Commission for England

Some county councils disappeared, with all their underlying districts becoming new unitary authorities

Other counties retained, but with one or more of their districts becoming independent unitary authorities

New structure comprises:

    35 county councils
    46 English unitary authorities
    36 metropolitan councils
    33 London borough councils
    247 non-metropolitan district councils

Local Government (Wales) Act 1994 (operational April 1996)

Replaced the 8 county and 37 district councils with 22 new unitary authorities

Some boundary alterations, splits, mergers and name changes

Local Government (Scotland) Act 1994

Established 32 unitary councils:

    53 district and 9 regional councils replaced by 29 unitary councils
    3 island councils (unitary) largely unchanged

being large, are more responsive to local needs as it is not possible for them to abdicate responsibility for services, or to blame failings on another tier. Consequently, unitary authorities are more clearly accountable for decisions and for spending. A further argument for the unitary system is that strategic frameworks and planning are better co-ordinated and, in particular, inter-service co-ordination is simplified. This can have positive benefits for liaison between, for example, education and leisure, as the education function has traditionally resided at county level, while leisure services are a borough or district level function. The opening up of school and further education facilities to the local communities for sports, arts and other activities is simplified and is therefore more likely under a unitary system.

However, supporters of a two-tier system would argue that there are inherent democratic benefits in having two levels of authority. A unitary system lacks the checks and balances that prevent the abuse of power – this is a key feature of pluralist administrations. Furthermore, a two-tier system mirrors citizens' commonly perceived identity and affiliation to twin communities – a village, town or neighbourhood, and a county or major city. For example, many people would support their local football team – e.g. Manchester United or Leeds United – but would also support a broader-based county cricket team – e.g. Lancashire or Yorkshire. Similarly, people identify with diverse local communities in London – for example Tottenham and Bromley – but both of these sets of people would also see themselves as Londoners.

Unitary authorities render the formation of partnerships with other organisations (such as those developed under compulsory competitive tendering and Best Value) much simpler and more straightforward, something that is particularly important in the contemporary *neo-pluralistic* approach of the enabling or facilitating authority (see discussions in later sections). A unitary system can also enhance local government's credibility with central government, as they can legitimately claim to speak as the singular voice for the local area. There are also economic arguments of economies of scale associated with unitary authorities, as costs are reduced by the removal of the duplication of core support and administrative services. Flexibility is increased, as authorities have greater freedom to switch resources between competing priorities, which also contributes to the responsiveness of the unitary system.

Critics of the unitary system would, however, point out that the concept of unitarism is a misnomer. There are many examples of smaller unitary authorities that require joint arrangements with neighbouring authorities for major strategic services, such as public transport or parks maintenance. Conversely, larger authorities find that they often have to devolve some services either administratively or geographically.

Most other countries have more than one tier, and it is unclear why Britain should be considered a special case in its apparent need for a unitary system. However, these arguments may become superfluous in the near future, as the current Labour administration has discussed the idea of regional assemblies, providing similar, although perhaps more limited, devolution in England to that which they have already established through the Scottish Parliament and Welsh Assembly. In fact, the establishment of a London mayor and a Greater London Assembly had been talked about as a model for other cities. However, following the election of Ken Livingston as Mayor of London and the associated political problems the government encountered, it may be considered likely that plans for elected mayors in other cities may be on the back burner for the moment. Nevertheless, plans for city mayors and/or regional devolution, if realised, would add another tier to sub-national government that would, inevitably, not only draw power down from Westminster, but also draw power up from local authorities.

Local delivery of leisure policy and provision

The changing ideological rationale for leisure provision

It is useful, before examining the mechanics of local authority leisure provision, to briefly review the changing rationale for leisure provision at local level. Both Henry (2001) and Coalter (1988) have identified four phases, commencing with the early forms of modern local government in the mid nineteenth century. An initial rationale of *welfare pluralism* with several strands of provision including private benefactors, wealthy philanthropists, commercial operators and the voluntary sector working together with local government is identifiable from the mid nineteenth century. This was based on a broad ethos of *social welfarism*, with communities accepting the notion of collective responsibility for provision.

The local government reforms in the 1960s and 70s, however, saw a move towards *corporate welfarism*. As discussed above, large leisure departments and directorates were created that embraced a corporate management philosophy, and attempted to deal with the social problems of the day – rising structural unemployment and the 'leisure shock' that many faced in having too much free time – through direct provision of leisure facilities and services. The 1970s saw an unprecedented expansion in provision of leisure centres, sports halls and swimming pools, funded not by admissions – which were kept low – but by high levels of local authority subsidy. Access to leisure was seen as a right of citizenship and there was a prevailing belief in 'Leisure for All' which, in many cases, was operationalised by positive discrimination – identifying target groups of people who were either low-level participants or non-participants (e.g. women) or who, it was believed, were in need of structured leisure provision as a result of some of the social problems they faced (e.g. the unemployed).

The late 1970s, however, saw Britain hit by economic problems and being forced into taking out a loan with the International Monetary Fund in 1976. One of the conditions of this loan was that there would be substantial cutbacks in all forms of public expenditure. Such a tightening of public expenditure was further emphasised by the election of the 1979 Conservative Government, led by Margaret Thatcher, which hailed the abandonment of Keynesian interventionist policies and the adoption of free market economics, where market forces were seen as the key determinants of demand. This period has been labelled as one of *economic realism*, which saw the introduction of compulsory competitive tendering into local authority services from 1980, and into local leisure provision from 1989. Leisure was no longer seen as a right of citizenship, but as something for which demand should be determined by the market. Local authority provision was seen as a safety net for those who could not afford private sector provision, and some critics (e.g. Ravenscroft, 1993) highlighted the danger of a two-tier system that would emphasise economic divisions in society.

The mid 1990s saw local authorities facing the changes enacted during the Thatcher era. The Conservative Government, led by John Major, was more centrist than its predecessor and such centrist or 'Middle Way' tendencies were continued under the Labour administration led by Tony Blair. In this period the role of local authorities was changing from that of direct providers to facilitators or enablers of provision. Local authorities would be attempting to encourage others to provide and would seek out partnerships with both the private and voluntary sector. This neo-pluralist approach, encouraged by the Best Value legislation (1999) enacted by the Labour Government, was a return to the plurality of leisure providers that existed in the early part of the twentieth century, and several alternative forms of funding local leisure provision emerged (see later discussions).

Local authority service provision

Hollis *et al.* (1992) identified four broad categories of service provision by local authorities. The first of these are *need services*, which are provided for all, without direct charge, because they are seen as a necessary part of provision in a civilised society. Examples of need services would be education and social services. Also provided for all with no direct charge are *protective services*. Protective services are provided to nationally determined standards to ensure security and include policing and the fire service. *Amenity services* are provided to locally determined standards, according to what the local authority assesses or perceives to be the needs of each local community. There is no direct charge for amenity services because it is usually impractical to levy such a direct charge. Examples of amenity services are refuse collection, cleaning and lighting of streets, and parks and public open spaces. Although no direct charge is levied for these three types of service, local residents do, of course, pay for them indirectly through their Council Tax. The final type of service that Hollis *et al.* identify are *facility services*, which are provided for people to draw upon if they so wish. In some cases there is a direct charge (e.g. leisure centres), but in others they are provided free of charge (e.g. libraries). Where a direct charge is levied, it is likely that it has been subsidised and does not, therefore, reflect the true cost of use of the facility. Leisure provision would normally fall under amenity and facility services; however, some need provision will assist the provision of leisure opportunities as, for example, in the opening up of premises provided primarily for educational services to the local community for leisure participation.

There is little legislation that requires local government to be involved in leisure or recreation provision – most legislation relating to leisure is permissive, allowing discretionary provision. Permissive legislation allows local authorities to make provision in certain areas if they so wish. However, statutory legislation stipulates that provision is mandatory, so local authorities are then required to make some provision in that area. In England and Wales, statutory legislation exists in only three leisure-related areas: library services, adult and youth education, and allotments; however, no indications of scale are given – this means that local authorities are free to decide on the extent to which they provide for these areas; all that is required is that some provision is made.

In most areas of leisure, therefore, provision is discretionary and is motivated by social concerns for the welfare of the community, or political objectives regarding the retention of control of the authority by political parties. However, regardless of the nature of legislation as permissive or statutory, local authorities are free to interpret community needs and demands in their own ways. Consequently, the level of provision varies considerably between authorities, dependent on a range of factors such as the controlling political party, historical legacy of provision, or the geographical dispersement of the local population.

More recently, however, some attempts have been made to standardise the way in which local authorities (in England) approach their leisure provision through the 'expectation' that cultural strategies will be produced:

> Although the development of a Local Cultural Strategy is not a statutory duty, the Department expects that all local authorities in England, whether individually or as part of joint or consortium arrangements, will prepare a Local Cultural Strategy for their area within the next three years. (DCMS, 1999, p. 11)

Such strategies are not focused solely on local authority provision, but include the cultural activities of the voluntary and commercial sector and other public sector agencies in the area and should provide 'a vision of how the local area and its culture may develop' (DCMS, 1999, p. 4). The strategies, therefore, identify key partners, but they must also pay heed to the Best Value initiative (see later discussion) and be located within the context of the strategies and plans produced by other agencies and departments at national and local level (Figure 9.1)

A statutory requirement for local authorities to produce leisure strategies has long been lobbied for by organisations such as the Institute of Leisure and Amenities Management (ILAM, 1996) and the Chief Leisure Officers Association (CLOA, 1997) and, although local cultural strategies are not statutory, the 'expectation' of the Department for Culture, Media and Sport is such that the vast majority of local

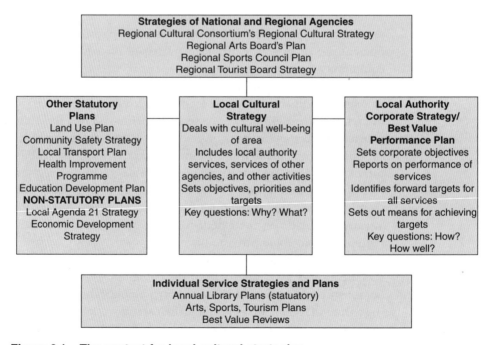

Figure 9.1 The context for local cultural strategies

Source: Adapted from DCMS (1999) *Creating Opportunities*, London: DCMS.

authorities will almost certainly produce such strategies. This is the result of their inextricable link to the Best Value process and that they are cited as acting 'as a lever for gaining funding from external agencies' (DCMS, 1999, p. 5). It is likely, for example, that National Lottery funding applications (see later discussion) will be judged in the light of strategic priorities laid out in local cultural strategies.

Challenges and changes in local authority leisure provision

As the previous discussions show, there have been substantial changes in a number of areas during the last twenty years that have affected local authority leisure provision. However, as described at the start of the chapter, local authorities remain a major provider of leisure opportunities, but they do face many new challenges, including changes in their role and the funding arrangements they can employ. Such challenges and changes may be demographic, socio-political, user-led, legislative, or financially determined.

Obviously demographic changes have major implications for leisure provision as they will determine for whom, when and how leisure provision is made. Demographic changes in recent years have included:

- increase in primary school and decrease in secondary school populations;
- increasing numbers of retired people;
- increasing numbers of working women with restricted free time, but with potential spending power.

Changes such as the increasing numbers of retired people are likely to continue as healthcare improves and people live longer, and also as the number of early retirers increases. Such populations now show higher levels of health awareness and, as such, demand for low-level physical activities is likely to increase. The increase in working women with little free time but increasing spending power means that provision must be made close to the workplace or the home, and that quick and easy access is a priority.

As discussed earlier in this chapter, socio-political changes in recent years have seen a general shift towards market-led provision. With this change has come a recognition that consumer demand is heterogeneous and that provision needs to be targeted at a diverse range of user groups demanding a wider range of facilities and services. This obviously puts pressure on resources and necessitates that local authorities seek out partnerships with providers in both the commercial and voluntary sectors in order to attempt to meet such demands. Such needs have seen many local authorities taking on the role of facilitators or co-ordinators of provision, rather than getting involved directly themselves. Even when partnerships are formed, many local authorities find they have to make tough decisions about priorities, as they find that resources dictate they cannot meet the needs of all consumer groups.

Further pressure is put on local authority providers with the growth in consumerism. Users have increasing expectations of the highest ambience and are more ready to complain when services do not meet their expectations. Expectations are now for a wide variety of choice, a high-quality full and complementary service, and value for money. Increasingly users expect their local authority leisure provision to be comparable with that available in the private sector. Such high expectations have resulted in a number of requirements that could be said to be user-led. Facilities must be constantly upgraded – something long recognised as a problem as many of today's facilities are outdated legacies of the expansion of provision in the 1970s. The National Lottery has helped in some areas (see later discussion), but many facilities are in need of extensive refurbishment or replacement to meet service expectations. The investment required is not only one-off capital expenditure, but also supporting ongoing revenue expenditure on quality staff training, market research, innovative and flexible policies and initiatives that must be responsive to ever-changing demand, and ongoing facility maintenance. Many local authorities find they cannot meet such investment requirements from their own resources alone and must, therefore, search for innovative mechanisms to fund provision. Such changes in funding mechanisms have also been the result, to a varying extent, of a number of legislative changes with implications for provision (see Table 9.5).

Several of the Acts listed in Table 9.5 have been the basis for some significant changes in local authority provision that might be labelled as financially determined changes. The requirement (between 1993 and 1998) to apply the compulsory competitive tendering process to most public sector leisure facilities – only arts centres and educationally linked centres were exempted – has, in many cases, resulted in a greater emphasis in local authority provision on financial objectives at the

Table 9.5   Legislative changes with implications for leisure provision

Local Government Act 1988 (Competition in Sport and Leisure Facilities Order 1989)
Provided the basis for compulsory competitive tendering

Local Government Act 1999 (effective April 2000)
Places a duty on local authorities to provide Best Value services

Education Reform Act 1988
Stipulated that any community leisure element in joint-provision arrangements (see Chapter 12) must now be self-financing

Children Act 1989
Regulations relating to the protection of children had many implications for children's play provision, sports coaching and playschemes

Town and Country Planning Act 1989
Provided the basis for planning gain of leisure facilities (see Chapter 10)

Local Government and Housing Act 1989
New system of controls on the way in which local authorities could invest in capital expenditure

Health and Safety Legislation (various dates from 1974)
Succession of Acts have major implications for public and employee safety and the potential for litigation

expense of social objectives. Even where local authorities won the contract to manage their own facilities (see later section for explanation of process), in order to do so they had to focus on greater efficiency and meeting financial objectives in order to beat commercial competition. While, in some areas, some imaginative alternatives to compulsory competitive tendering (CCT) were implemented – for example, charitable trusts and partnerships with other sectors – in most cases CCT changed significantly the *ethos* of local authority provision to that of more market-led provision.

It might be argued that it was partly in order to refocus local authority provision on to social objectives that the Labour Government introduced the Best Value legislation to replace CCT in 1998. The Best Value concept, alongside some of the other recent developments and new directions in local authority provision, is examined in the next section.

Recent developments and new directions in provision

The previous discussion identified a range of changes and challenges for local authority leisure provision; however, there has been some debate as to whether such changes are challenges for local authorities or threats to the level and quality of provision. Particular concern has been expressed over the maintaining of social priorities and safeguarding the needs of minority and low-income groups. Such concerns spark discussion over the appropriate nature of public sector leisure services: Should it focus resources on the needs of the socially and recreationally disadvantaged? Should it attempt to provide low-cost leisure for all? Or, should it be attempting to rival the provision of the private sector?

Many of the above questions were addressed by Bennington and White (1988), who believed that, with the impending application of CCT to local government leisure services, such provision was 'at a crossroads' and 'under real threat'. Some of the contributory factors identified have already been discussed in this chapter. Problems were seen as being caused as a result of:

● the lack of a firm statutory base for most local leisure provision;
● the lack of a coherent client or consumer lobby, a voice for leisure;
● the abolition of the Greater London Council and the metropolitan counties (seen as leaders in local leisure provision);
● the phasing out of New Town Development Corporations (also seen as particularly imaginative leisure providers);
● commercialisation and the impending contracting out (CCT) of the management of leisure services.

This range of problems prompted responses from local authorities that Henry (1988) saw as ranging between two extremes. One approach, in line with the thinking of the Thatcher-led central government, was the *contract management model*, which was, perhaps, what the CCT legislation was aiming to precipitate. This approach saw local provision being regarded as the provider of last resort, seeking only to provide in those areas where there was no commercial sector provision. This approach, of course, has implications for minority groups or those on low incomes, whose needs are unlikely to be met at prices they find affordable. The alternative approach, from the other end of the political spectrum, was that of *municipal socialism*, which saw local authorities playing a major role in the provision of leisure opportunities. Local authorities would actively intervene in the market in order to counteract commercial providers. Leisure facilities, such as the Crowtree Leisure Centre in Sunderland, would be built by local authorities on a large scale to rival provision by the commercial sector and thus, given the levels of subsidy, price commercial competitors out of the market. In many cases such provision would be used by left-wing councils to gain political capital, to make the case for municipal socialism, as discussed earlier in relation to the Greater London Council and the metropolitan counties. However, given the previous abolition of this tier of local government, the political climate nationally, and the introduction of CCT, it is not surprising that, in the majority of cases, the response of local authorities tended towards the contract management model. This approach led to a number of criticisms of local authority provision in the 1990s from a range of authors.

Price has long been identified as a barrier to participation in leisure, and many previous initiatives by local authorities have been aimed at overcoming such barriers. However, Coalter (1993) questioned whether pricing was becoming more important than priorities in addressing such barriers. He found some evidence that entrance costs were increasing, and that such increases were acting as a barrier to participation. This was not just in the case of non-users, but his research suggested that the participation patterns of committed users were being affected in that they were now using facilities less often.

In addressing price barriers to participation, one of the most widely used strategies had been that of a blanket subsidy, keeping entry costs low for all. However, Ravenscroft (1993) criticised this approach because it created what he labelled two-tier provision. This is because those benefiting from blanket subsidies were not, as was intended, those on low incomes who found prices to be a barrier, but those users who were already regular participants and who, in most cases, could afford to pay higher unsubsidised prices in any case. Hence Ravenscroft identified a group of leisure gainers – largely middle-class, employed, white males – who reaped the benefits of subsidies aimed at attracting low-income and traditional non-participant groups – the leisure losers – to local authority facilities.

The climate of the early 1990s saw many local authorities feeling the financial squeeze of recession, and Taylor and Page (1994) found that in many areas local authority leisure services were 'in crisis'. They found that 75 per cent of local authorities in the United Kingdom suffered leisure budget cuts, and that the average level of such cuts was 10 per cent. There were, however, examples of more extreme cuts in some areas – 14 per cent of local authorities suffered cuts of 20 per cent or more, while for 4 per cent of authorities the cuts were greater than 40 per cent. In addition to such cuts in expenditure on leisure services, Taylor and Page also found substantial cutbacks in capital expenditure (money spent on building new facilities or refurbishing older ones). Inevitably, such cutbacks led to problems for leisure provision, particularly the reduction or elimination of services. The cuts identified above were often directed at those areas of leisure that had the least revenue potential and, in many cases, it is work aimed at stimulating participation among low-income and disadvantaged groups that shows least return in the accounts. It was therefore unsurprising that the Taylor and Page research discovered that over 50 per cent of local authorities suffered a severe reduction or loss in important areas such as community recreation services and sports development services.

Further to the above findings, a report by Craig (1993) on the effects of compulsory competitive tendering on quality found that in addition to reductions or losses in services, the quality of those services remaining was also suffering. A small, but significant, loss of service quality was found in most public sector leisure services, but such losses were particularly noticeable in certain important areas, such as cleanliness and speed of services. Craig identified these problems as being directly linked to cutbacks in staffing, as facilities were being run on the minimum staff that would satisfy Health and Safety regulations. Allied to this lack of quality in service, Taylor and Page (1994) also found that maintenance of facilities was being neglected. Between 25 and 50 per cent of authorities were identified as possessing built facilities and physical amenities that were suffering from neglect of maintenance. In fact, this report confirms the findings of an earlier Audit Commission report (1989) that identified the ageing stock of leisure facilities as being a long-standing problem. The Commission reported on the lack of new capital investment in the public sector (as mentioned above), which was exacerbated by the recessionary financial climate.

It was as a result of these pressures and criticisms that many local authorities – 70 to 80 per cent (Taylor and Page, 1994) – expressed an interest in new or non-standard ways of organising their leisure provision. In the early 1990s, some of these non-standard forms were a way of avoiding the CCT process, but later they were encouraged by the advent of the National Lottery and the replacement of CCT by Best Value legislation.

Contemporary local leisure service provision

An attractive option for non-commercial leisure facilities – which includes the vast majority of local authority owned facilities – has been charitable trust status. This was particularly attractive in the early 1990s to those authorities that wished to avoid the CCT process. There are many financial advantages associated with charitable status, perhaps the most significant being an 80 per cent exemption from Uniform Business Rate, which for many facilities can be a very substantial saving.

Such status can also provide access to otherwise unobtainable external forms of assistance, such as grants for charitable organisations, low-cost or interest-free loans, sponsorship and, of course, goodwill and help-in-kind. In addition, there are tax incentives that encourage charitable donations to the trust by companies. None of these advantages would be available to a standard local authority facility.

An example of such a charitable trust is the London Borough of Greenwich, where the Greenwich Leisure Trust has set up a workers' co-operative to run all the leisure facilities in the borough. An illustration of the scale of advantage offered by charitable trust status is given by the reductions in Greenwich Leisure's costs of £400,000 by savings on Uniform Business Rate alone. However, charitable trust status is not as widespread as it might be due to interventions by the Audit Commission, which has claimed that charitable trusts are permissible for arts and entertainments, but not for sport and recreation. Although this ruling is disputed, it has undoubtedly checked the growth in local authorities organising their leisure provision in this way.

Funding from the National Lottery has, of course, been of considerable assistance to local authorities in providing injections of cash, particularly for building and rebuilding facilities. The legislation providing the basis for the National Lottery was the National Lottery Act 1993. It established five good causes that, between them, would receive 20 per cent of the revenue generated by the National Lottery. The funds were distributed by the Charities Commission (Charities Fund), the Arts Councils (Arts Fund), the Sports Councils (Sports Fund), the Heritage Lottery Fund (Heritage Fund), and the Millennium Commission (Millennium Fund). The Labour Government added a New Opportunities Fund to these five in 1998. The estimated turnover of the National Lottery over the licence period 1994 to 2001 was just over £36 billion, while the estimated amount available to sport and leisure by the end of 2000 (drawn from a number of funds) was £220 million.

The government initially emphasised that all funding from the National Lottery would be additional to existing grants and funding. National Lottery distributers were instructed to focus on capital expenditure on facilities at national, regional and local level that would not otherwise be provided. However, since the first funds were distributed in 1994, this principle has gradually been eroded, and now little attempt is made to defend the additionality principle. In fact, the advent of the New Opportunities Fund in 1998, along with revised directions from the government allowing distributing agencies to be strategic in the distribution of funds rather than simply having to be reactive to bidders, has meant that Lottery funds are now used in a range of areas that were not originally envisaged, including revenue funding (see discussions under Best Value).

A further aim of the National Lottery was to encourage partnerships between the public, private and voluntary sectors, as Lottery Awards have a requirement that a percentage of the costs of a project must be found by the bidding organisation and its partners. In the sport and leisure area this is usually around 35 per cent of the cost of the project. However, it is not just in relation to National Lottery projects that partnerships are emerging; partnership arrangements are becoming increasingly common across the range of local authority leisure services.

The financial pressures described in earlier sections have driven local authority leisure providers increasingly to seek joint arrangements with partner organisations for the provision of leisure services. Some, such as those with educational establishments, have been around for some time, while others are relatively new; partners may include:

- commercial property developers and construction companies (particularly through planning gain);
- commercial owner-operators (health clubs, squash clubs, retail and hospitality);
- other public sector providers (educational and NHS establishments);
- CCT operators (either commercial or in-house);
- voluntary sector organisations.

Partnerships with property developers are usually centred around a planning agreement where a local authority will grant planning permission for a housing development in return for the property developer agreeing to make some leisure or recreational provision for the new community they will be creating – often referred to as planning gain. Private health clubs may enter into an agreement with the local authority whereby they open up their facilities to all local residents in return for a subsidy from the local authority. Such an arrangement exists in the London Borough of Barnet, where all squash provision is delivered through private sector operators. Joint arrangements for provision with educational establishments – whereby facilities are opened up to local residents outside school/college hours – are discussed in greater detail in Chapter 12, while CCT and voluntary sector partnerships are discussed in the next section.

There are three broad categories of partnership arrangements that local authorities may enter into. First, there are partnerships that are designed to provide capital investment in new or refurbished facilities. Such partnerships often represent a one-off investment by the partner agency and many planning gain partnerships take this form. Second, management partnerships that were established under compulsory competitive tendering assisted with revenue funding, and often also made some provision for limited capital funding – such partnerships are now being replaced by the Best Value approach (see discussions below). Finally, there are a range of partnerships that focus almost exclusively on revenue support. These may take the form of local sponsorship, marketing partnerships, GP referral schemes or grant aid for sports development.

Partnerships are, and will continue to be, a key part of contemporary local authority leisure provision. Public–private partnerships were a key element of the CCT process, and partnerships including all sectors are a feature of the new Best Value legislation. It is therefore useful to examine briefly the CCT process and the recent transition to the Best Value approach.

The abolition of CCT and the transition to Best Value

The process of CCT involved the compulsory opening up of the management of local authority owned leisure facilities to a tendering process in which commercial organisations could bid for the contract to manage the facilities. However, local authorities were also allowed to bid for their own contracts and, as a result, many formed direct services organisations (DSOs) for this purpose. Compulsory competitive tendering necessitated the splitting of local authority leisure services into client side (which would award and supervise the contract) and contractor side (the DSO, which would bid for the contract and, if successful, manage the facilities). The CCT process meant that contractors, even local authority DSOs, had to operate in a manner that emphasised commercial goals, financial objectives and economies, as the legislation required that the contract be awarded to the lowest bidder, subject to there being no reservations about quality. In practice, the great majority of contracts were won by in-house DSOs; however, their operation had become very commercial in orientation, as this was almost a necessity to win contracts. The result of CCT, therefore, was to commercialise much of the delivery of local authority leisure services, even where the contract had been won in-house.

Prior to the 1997 general election, the Labour Party gave a manifesto pledge to discontinue compulsory competitive tendering in its present form. This stance was in response to a wide range of criticisms of the CCT process, some of which were discussed earlier. The shortcomings that were cited included:

● neglect of service quality;
● uneven/uncertain efficiency gains;
● inflexibility to vary contracts in practice;
● employee demoralisation and resultant high staff turnover;
● antagonism as a result of its compulsory nature.

Compulsory competitive tendering has now been replaced by a duty of Best Value, with the aim to continually improve the quality and cost of local services delivered to local people. The proposals for Best Value were set out in the 1999 DETR White Paper *Modernising Local Government: In Touch with Local People*. In contrast to CCT, Best Value is less prescriptive, is voluntary rather than compulsory, and is not just about economy and efficiency, but also about effectiveness and quality. In addition, unlike CCT, Best Value encompasses all local authority services. A key element of Best Value is that it should be more responsive to customer need. The White Paper sees it as focusing on the need to fundamentally change the ways local authorities communicate with local people, structure and organise themselves, and procure and deliver services; it describes how:

> A modern council – or authority – which puts people first will seek to provide services which bear comparison with the best…Continuous improvements in both the quality and cost of services will therefore be the hallmark of a modern council and the test of Best Value. (DETR, 1999)

In addition, the Local Government Bill, published in 1998, defines Best Value as follows:

> A Best Value authority must make arrangements to secure continuous improvement in the way in which its functions are exercised, having regard to a combination of economy, efficiency and effectiveness.

The duty of Best Value comprises the four Cs, a requirement to: challenge (to prove worth of services), consult (to establish support), compare (with examples of best practice and nationally set performance targets), and compete (to continually improve service delivery). The ways in which local authorities will address the four Cs must be set out in Best Value Performance Plans (which all local authorities were required to produce by 31 March 2000) that will be subject to fundamental Best Value Reviews over a five-year cycle. This presents both a challenge and an opportunity for local leisure services, as not only do local authorities have a duty to show that they are providing Best Value in their delivery of leisure services, but leisure services directorates also have the opportunity to show that leisure-related initiatives can contribute to the delivery of Best Value across the broader local authority policy agenda, including health, education, social exclusion, community safety, community regeneration, the economy and the environment. An examination of the context for local cultural strategies (see Figure 9.1) shows the range of policy areas that leisure might contribute to. Much work has been done by the Local Government Association in conjunction with Sport England (Sport England/LGA, 1999a) to demonstrate that leisure can make a difference to people's lives and to the communities in which they live. A case study of such a 'cross-cutting agenda' is the Pathways 2000 Project implemented by Bolton Metropolitan Council (Box 9.1).

Best Value also seeks to encourage a 'multi-agency' approach to the delivery of leisure services, rather than the commercially-led approach of compulsory

Box 9.1

The Pathways 2000 Project (Bolton Metropolitan Council)

The Pathways 2000 project aims to address issues of community safety and youth crime and is a key part of Bolton Metropolitan Borough Council's strategic objective to promote safe, healthy communities. The project is aimed at diverting young people aged 8–24 years away from criminal activities and thus contribute to community safety.

An outreach/response team aimed to develop a multi-agency approach, including the provision of information and counselling services for young people and their parents, the development of drama/arts/music workshops and playschemes, and opportunities for vocational training for young people in youth work, community development and sports.

In addition, young people have been involved in the consultation process, with a panel of 116 young people highlighting the need for community facilities of which the local community can feel ownership. A result of this has been the conversion of disused play areas into modern 'recreation zones' catering for a wide range of formal and informal activities.

This project provides an excellent example of the contribution leisure services can make to wider aspects of individual and community life, demonstrating how leisure can provide the Best Value in tackling youth crime and developing communities.

Source: Adapted from Sport England (1999) *Best Value Through Sport: Case studies*, London: Sport England.

Box 9.2

Tamworth Borough Council – a multi-agency approach

In its Best Value Review of leisure services, Tamworth Borough Council took a conscious decision to develop a cross-departmental and multi-agency approach. A strong corporate direction emphasised the importance of a mixed economy, multi-sector approach to the future delivery of council services.

Leisure services was identified as one of a number of services where weaknesses existed and, within an imperative to reduce the overall budget, customer panels (including residents, local interest groups, the police, the health authority and social services) were invited to comment on the priorities for such services and the agencies that might best be involved in addressing them.

Council officers used (and continue to use) the panels as sounding boards for ideas which resulted, in the leisure services area, in the implementation of a mixed-economy approach to the provision of facility-based services. Consequently, the voluntary sector, on behalf of the community, now manages a bowls centre and athletics venue; five dual-use agreements have been established between the council and local schools; the commercial sector, under a range of partnership and lease agreements, operate a range of other facilities, including a traditional leisure centre; and a golf course is operated by an in-house DSO. This approach highlights the flexibility of the Best Value system, and demonstrates how local authorities have the freedom to be innovative in the provision of services and that a universal approach is not appropriate for all facilities.

Source: Adapted from Sport England (1999) *Best Value Through Sport: Case studies*, London: Sport England.

competitive tendering. The case of Tamworth Borough Council provides a useful illustration of both an internal cross-departmental and a multi-agency approach (Box 9.2).

Numerous other cases could be provided to illustrate the range of issues associated with the Best Value process. However, the key element is that, in contrast to compulsory competitive tendering, the process of Best Value is left to local interpretation, albeit within a general framework set nationally. This allows local authorities to refine the process to take into account particular local circumstances, problems and policy priorities, and thus be innovative in providing a range of leisure services appropriate to the particular needs of local residents, through a range of means. The other side of this coin, however, is that, given the nature of leisure services as a discretionary area, such local interpretation may, in some instances, encourage the marginalisation of leisure as a non-essential service. As such, the challenge for local authority leisure services is to demonstrate, as with the Bolton example, that leisure can play a key part in enhancing quality of life, and that Best Value in a range of related policy areas can be provided through leisure-based initiatives. It is arguable that this is a challenge that local leisure service provision has always faced.

● ● ● ● Conclusions

Changing roles and concepts

Henry and Bramham identified in 1990 a hegemonic shift in local authority leisure services, from a social democratic consensus, where leisure opportunities are seen as a right of citizenship, to a more mixed economy approach, where the role of the state is reduced to one of regulation and safety net provision. However, it is possible to identify, from the mid to late 1990s, a further shift that emphasises the role of local authorities in developing partnerships with both the private and voluntary sectors to facilitate provision. Furthermore, this facilitation role has recently been made clearer by the 'expectation' that local cultural strategies will be produced, which identify priorities and key partners in local authority provision. As such, the role of the local authority in leisure provision may now be described as that of an active enabler or influencer in developing provision among a range of partners – now through the Best Value process – rather than as a direct provider as in the past.

In addition to the changing role described above, it is increasingly evident that leisure is now seen as having a contribution to make to a range of related areas at local level – some of these are new, others are revisitations of past uses of leisure. However, it is likely that the new millennium will see local leisure playing a key role in areas as diverse as social exclusion, community development, urban and economic (re)generation, lifelong-learning and education.

Questions

1 To what extent does the way that local authorities are organised affect the delivery of leisure services?

2 How far does the nature of local leisure provision as a largely discretionary service affect the extent of provision for leisure by local authorities?

3 Discuss the impact that the 'expectation that all local authorities will prepare a Local Cultural Strategy' might have on the way in which local leisure provision is delivered.

4 Analyse the long-term effects of the now abolished compulsory competitive tendering process on local leisure provision.

5 To what extent does the Best Value legislation provide new challenges for local authorities in delivering leisure services?

References

Audit Commission (1989) *Sport for Whom? Clarifying the Local Authority Role in Sport and Recreation*, London: HMSO.

Bennington, J. and White, J. (eds) (1988) *The Future of Leisure Services*, Harlow: Longman.

Bianchini, F. (1987) 'GLC – RIP: cultural policies in London 1981–1986', *New Formations*, no.1, Spring.

Chief Leisure Officers Association (1997) *The introduction of a statutory local leisure plan for all United Kingdom local authorities – National Consultation Paper*, London: CLOA.

Coalter, F. (1993) 'Sports participation: price or priorities', *Leisure Studies*, 12(3), pp. 171–82.

Coalter, F. (1988) *Recreational Welfare: The Rationale for Public Sector Leisure Policy*, Aldershot: Avebury.

Craig, S. (1993) *Has CCT Led to Better Quality Services?* Reading: ILAM.

Department of the Environment, Transport and the Regions (1999) *Modernising Local Government, In Touch with Local People* (CM 4014), London: HMSO.

Department for Culture, Media and Sport (1999) *Local Cultural Strategies – Draft Guidance for Local Authorities in England*, London: DCMS.

Henry, I.P. (2001) *The Politics of Leisure Policy* (2nd edition), London: Palgrave.

Henry, I.P. (1988) 'Alternative futures for the public leisure services', in Bennington, J. and White, J. (eds) *The Future of Leisure Services*, Harlow: Longman.

Henry, I.P. and Bramham, P. (1990) 'Leisure, politics and the local state', in Botterill, D. and Tomlinson, A. (eds) *Leisure Policy, Ideology, and Practice*, Brighton: Leisure Studies Association.

Hollis, G., Ham, G. and Ambler, M. (eds) (1992) *The Future Role and Structure of Local Government*, Harlow: Longman.

House of Commons (1998) *The Local Government Bill*, London: HMSO.

Institute of Leisure and Amenities Management (1996) *Local Leisure Plans: Policy Position Statement – Consultation Paper*, London: ILAM.

Ravenscroft, N. (1993) 'Public leisure provision and the good citizen', *Leisure Studies*, 12(1), pp. 33–44.

Sport England/Local Government Association (1999a) *Delivering Best Value Through Sport*, London: Sport England.

Sport England/Local Government Association (1999b) *Best Value Through Sport: Case Studies*, London: Sport England.

Taylor, P. and Page, K. (1994) *The Financing of Local Authority Sport and Recreation: A Service Under Threat?* Sheffield: Institute of Sport and Recreation Management.

Wilson, D. and Game, C. (1994) *Local Government in the United Kingdom*, Basingstoke: Macmillan.

Further reading

The texts by Henry, *The Politics of Leisure Policy*, and Coalter, *Recreational Welfare: The Rationale for Public Sector Leisure Policy*, provide a useful background to the history and rationale for local authority leisure provision.

Some of the challenges faced by local authorities outlined in this chapter are outlined in greater detail in the listed sources by the Audit Commission, Bennington and White, Craig, Hollis *et al.*, Ravenscroft, and Taylor and Page. However, as time passes these texts become increasingly out of date, particularly since the advent of the Best Value legislation. An up-to-date appreciation of current issues should be maintained by reference to quality news media and the leisure press, perhaps particularly *Leisure Management* magazine, *Leisure Opportunities*, and *The Leisure Manager*.

The range of literature from the Local Government Association and Sport England provides useful information on the challenges of the Best Value process that is relevant not just to sport, but also to a range of other local authority leisure services.

Current developments and proposed legislation can be found on the government's local government website (www.local-regions.dltr.gov.uk), which also provides links to the websites of individual local authorities.

Chapter 10 ● ● ● ●

Commercial sector leisure

While this and other chapters (8 and 9 on the public sectors and 11 on the voluntary sector) discuss the various sectors involved in leisure provision, it is important to recognise that the lines of demarcation between the sectors are becoming increasingly blurred. Throughout the twentieth century and, in fact, before that, leisure has always been provided through a *mixed economy*, with each of the sectors playing a significant part. Yet, as Britain moves into the twenty-first century, it is becoming increasingly difficult to identify where the provision of one sector ends and another begins.

However, it is important to understand that the commercial sector is fundamentally different from the voluntary and public sectors in one significant respect. The objectives of commercial sector provision are related to the extent to which such provision can be profitable. Conversely, both the public and voluntary sectors generally incorporate some elements of public service, community well-being or self-help as part of their objectives. Consequently, while partnerships are important, the very different motivations of commercial sector providers are an important factor in understanding their behaviour and separating such behaviour from that of the other sectors.

Objectives

To:

- *examine the role and structure of the commercial sector in leisure provision, including its historical context, and the differences between the commercial sector and the voluntary and public sectors*

- *outline the range of provision of the commercial sector, identifying the nature and size of the leisure market in a range of different areas.*

A key element in analysing the commercial sector is an understanding of the debates surrounding the definition of leisure (see Chapter 2), as what some individuals regard as leisure (e.g. decorating or mowing the lawn), others would regard as a chore. This obviously has implications for an analysis of the extent of commercial sector provision. However, generally, analyses tend to be inclusive rather than exclusive, and so include activities such as decorating and gardening as part of commercial leisure provision.

The role of the commercial sector in leisure

The influence of the commercial sector pervades all areas of leisure provision. The most obvious area where the commercial sector is involved is in the direct provision of facilities, such as health clubs and cinemas. However, the commercial sector is involved on a much wider scale than an analysis of its direct provision activities would suggest: the commercial sector may provide equipment or clothing, supply ancillary services or provide advice. Take as an example a traditional public sector leisure centre that is managed by a public sector DSO (direct services organisation – for further details see Chapter 9). The staff uniforms in this public sector facility are most likely to be provided by a private sector concern, as is most of the equipment in the swimming pool, gymnasium and sports hall. In addition, it is likely that the catering provision is supplied by an outside contractor, which may be as straightforward as one or two vending machines, or a fully staffed cafeteria. Finally, private sector accountants, surveyors and consultants are likely to be employed at various times to offer further advice to the management team (see Box 10.1)

A later section will deal with the wide range of areas in which the commercial sector is involved; however, it is important to understand at an early stage the extensive nature of the commercial sector's influence. In fact, the wider commercial culture has had an important influence on leisure provision as a whole through the increasing commercialisation of the other sectors. The voluntary sector has become more commercial and businesslike in recent years – it has begun to employ staff, rather than rely on volunteers, and has had to negotiate with private sector firms and submit professional business plans in order to obtain Lottery and other funding (a useful illustration of this is the Polo Farm Sports Club case study in Chapter 11). The public sector has also had to take an increasingly commercial attitude to provision, particularly as a result of legislative changes at local level during the Thatcher years of the 1980s, which emphasised the contracting out of services and the need to be self-sufficient. This meant that the public sector had to be able to compete with private sector contractors in order to retain functions in-house (see Chapter 9 for an extended discussion of this). However, despite the recent influence the commercial sector has exerted over other sectors of provision, the commercial sector in leisure has itself evolved in the light of developments in the voluntary and public sectors.

Box 10.1

The role of consultants

The role of consultants in leisure provision can be wide ranging. Consultants may undertake feasibility studies, advise on appropriate financing and corporate structures, and on long-term stability and viability.

Consultants may be involved in offering advice on small projects, such as the addition of an all-weather pitch to a new facility, or on larger-scale projects, such as the development of a new facility on derelict land.

Consultants vary in size, from the large general management consultants, such as KPMG Peat Marwick or Touche Ross, to smaller *leisure specialist* consultants, such as Knight Kavanagh Page or Strategic Leisure.

Renata Drinkwater of KPMG Peat Marwick says: 'It is vital that consultants are equipped not only to understand the leisure issues, but also to offer credible financial, tax, property, project development and other relevant expertise, particularly where there's a complex partnership or joint venture at stake.'

Peter Mann of Strategic Leisure says: 'Consultants have to identify the value which can be generated from a leisure development, along with the associated risk and then promote the opportunity in a professional and targeted way.'

Source: Adapted from *Leisure Management*, July 1994.

The historical context for commercial sector leisure

An historical perspective on commercial sector leisure provision is important because it facilitates an understanding of the 'philosophical legacy' or conventional wisdom concerning the appropriate divisions between the public, commercial and voluntary sectors (Coalter, 1988). Such divisions have been questioned and, to a certain extent, overturned in recent times as a result of the Thatcherite emphasis on competition in all sectors and the subsequent emphasis on cross-sectoral partnerships that influences much leisure provision today.

Perhaps surprisingly, the rational recreation movement of the mid nineteenth century (see Chapter 1) is a useful starting point for an historical analysis of the commercial sector in leisure. Much of the work of the rational recreation movement was repressive and regulatory (Henry, 2001) and it resulted in the suppression of many small-scale 'commercial' leisure provision operations – such as bear baiting and cock fighting – many of which were focused on betting. Although the public sector was involved in promoting rational recreation – through regulatory legislation, such as that mentioned above, and through enabling legislation (see Chapter 9) that allowed local authorities to provide 'appropriate' forms of leisure, such as museums, libraries and baths – much of the actual provision depended on private philanthropy, as local authorities were reluctant to spend income from local taxation on recreation provision. Coalter (1988) highlights the limits of public sector provision at the end of the nineteenth century and states that, despite the political rhetoric, the public sector was reluctant to become directly involved in provision. Central government set the limits of behaviour and morality through regulatory legislation and licensing, but local government rarely exercised its permissive powers of provision and so much was dependent on voluntary sector effort, which was, by its very nature, also limited. It was from this situation that the seeds of commercial sector leisure provision were sown.

Coalter (1990) attributes the relative failure of the rational recreation movement to the fact that the reluctant public sector and limited voluntary sector had to compete with the many new 'entertainments' provided by the commercial sector. The public house continued, of course, to be important, but to this was added a whole new range of leisure opportunities, such as professional football, excursion trips (facilitated by the railways), piers and seaside resorts and the music hall. In fact, there had been large-scale investment in music halls in the latter half of the nineteenth century. This was accompanied by increases in both free time and disposable income, which increased the demand for commercially provided leisure. Furthermore, these new commercial organisations were becoming more acceptable to authority because, as Cunningham (1980) suggests, their large size and almost public sector nature meant they were less threateningly privatised and were open to regulation, licence and control by government. Consequently, at the turn of the century, the mixed economy of leisure, in which the commercial sector played a significant role, was starting to develop.

As detailed in Chapter 8, the public sector began to take a more active role in leisure in the early twentieth century, with the enacting of much new legislation encouraging and facilitating leisure provision. Perhaps surprisingly, although the inter-war period saw economic depression and high unemployment, commercial sector provision continued to grow during this period as the masses sought solace in the 'feel-good' properties of mass spectator sports, such as professional football, and technological developments allowed the development of cinema, which Jones (1986) argues was the main leisure institution of the 1930s. Cinema was supplemented by the 'wireless', which provided further commercial opportunities, but the establishment of the British Broadcasting Corporation in 1927 meant that much radio output was centrally controlled and essentially conservative, seeking to improve the cultural tastes of the masses (see Chapter 8).

However, by the end of the 1930s a strong commercial sector had developed within a mixed economy of provision, which included a more active public sector and a now often highly organised voluntary sector (see Chapter 11). At this time it was possible to identify two categories of commercial leisure firm. First there were those that provided leisure services, such as cinema, travel and attractions; second, there were leisure commodity firms supplying, for example, books, radios, and sports equipment.

The post-war period saw both an expansion and a decline in leisure provision by the commercial sector as a major growth took place in home-based leisure at the expense of more traditional out-of-home activities. As the economy became stronger in the 1960s, real wages rose and working hours decreased as unemployment fell. This led to the creation of a new mass consumer market for leisure opportunities (Coalter, 1990). A contribution was made to increased leisure time by the advent of some goods that have a dual function. An example of such a good would be a washing machine which, while clearly not a leisure good in its own right, facilitates leisure by creating more free time. Further technological developments resulted in the creation of new in-home leisure activities and the television, video recorder and, later, computers and home gaming machines contributed to the increase in leisure in the home. However, some forms of out-of-home leisure did expand. Greater wealth and expanding social aspirations – often created by the wider view of the world given by television – led to a 700 per cent increase in the number of holidays taken abroad (Open University, 1981). Investment in the travel industry increased to cater for such tastes, and the increase in car ownership contributed significantly to the popularity of the leisure day trip.

The late 1970s and the 1980s saw a decline in many traditional industries, which made the emerging service sector an attractive investment. Furthermore, a significant part of this service sector was involved in leisure provision of some kind and, consequently, commercial sector investment in leisure increased significantly during this period. The attractiveness of these leisure areas for investment resulted in increasing levels of market concentration that still continue today, with many leisure markets being dominated by a relatively small number of large firms.

The purpose and nature of commercial leisure organisations

A major feature of the commercial sector has been high levels of market concentration, and it has also been characterised by large conglomerates that are highly diversified in their leisure interests, with some exhibiting elements of vertical or horizontal integration in some areas. Vertical integration is the expansion of a business into other areas of the chain of supply – for example, many tour operators also own travel agencies, airlines and hotels, thus controlling all areas of the supply chain and consequently reducing commercial risk. Horizontal integration is the ownership of similar businesses in related sectors – for example, the Apollo Leisure Group owns both theatres and cinemas. The reasoning behind such strategies is that expansion into related areas carries less risk than moving into areas in which the company has little relevant expertise. However, while traditionally many of the large leisure firms are widely diversified, recent years have seen the break up, or scaling down, of many leisure conglomerates. Many operators are now focused on individual markets; for example, the bookmaker William Hill has separated from Brent Walker, Gala Bingo Clubs have been sold by Bass, and Odeon Cinemas have been bought out from the Rank group. It is perhaps useful at this stage to briefly review some of the major changes that have taken place in recent years.

Two of the firms that have recently rationalised their interests are former brewers that have sold their brewing interests. Bass PLC sold its brewing concerns to

Interbrew at the beginning of 2000 in order to concentrate on its hotels, pubs and restaurants. Bass also formerly owned interests in bingo, bookmaking and amusements, but sold these between 1997 and 1999. Its main brands now are O'Neill's Irish themed bars, All Bar One wine bars, Harvester restaurants, InterContinental Hotels and Holiday Inns. The other former brewer is Whitbread plc, which is now a broadly based leisure retailer, owning pubs, restaurants, off-licences and hotels, and the UK's largest sports club chain, David Lloyd Leisure (see Boxes 10.4 and 10.7).

Until May 1999 the Hilton Group was called Ladbroke plc and had operated in a range of leisure-related retailing, property and tourism areas. However, the disposal by Ladbroke of what it regarded as non-core activities in the 1990s enabled the company to invest in the Hilton Hotel brand, and to adopt the company name for the group. The Hilton Group plc now operates in hotels and health clubs under the Hilton brand, and in gambling under Ladbrokes Bookmakers and Vernon's Pools. It sold its casino division, inherited from the purchase of the Stakis hotel chain, to Gala in 2001.

Until 2000, the Granada Group plc was the one UK-based leisure firm that still had a widely diversified portfolio, although, like many others, it had sold off several of its interests. Granada's activities in 2000 included media (ITV franchises, satellite and digital television), electrical retailing (television rental and sales), catering (Little Chef, Wheelers of St James and contract catering), and hotels (among others, Forte and Travelodge), the last two of these coming together in its ownership of motorway and other roadside service stations. However, the hotel and catering divisions were sold to Compass Group Holdings in 2000, and consequently Granada is now almost entirely a media company. Other interests that Granada had previously divested itself of included cinema, tenpin bowling and bingo halls.

Despite the rationalisation programmes of these big leisure firms, market concentration has not been reduced in many leisure areas (as the later discussion of areas of commercial provision will show), and consequently the supply of a whole range of leisure opportunities and activities is still provided by only a limited number of companies. However, what has happened is that such firms have reconstructed their interests so that they are no longer widely diversified in a range of largely unrelated areas, but are either vertically or horizontally integrated with interests in related or very similar sectors.

However, the extent to which such high levels of market concentration and integration are healthy for the leisure consumer has been questioned by Clarke and Critcher (1985). The purpose of commercial organisations is likely to be related to increasing the ratio of revenue to expenses (i.e. profit) through providing for popular public or market demands; it is unlikely that the enhancement of human or environmental well-being will be a primary objective, as it often may be in the public or voluntary sector. Regulation of the commercial sector should take place through the market, where a large number of competing firms ensure that prices do not become artificially high, that standards are maintained, and that potential consumer choice is wide. However, critics such as Clarke and Critcher (1985) would argue that the control of leisure markets by a small number of large firms

Table 10.1   Differences between public and commercial sector leisure provision

Public sector	Commercial sector
Social goals	Commercial goals
Concessions	Buyer/seller relationship
Inclusiveness	Exclusiveness
Basic levels of service/comfort	High levels of service/comfort

threatens both the principle of regulation by the market and the range of choices available to the consumer.

Differences between commercial and public sector provision

Before moving on to examine the various areas of commercial sector provision it is useful to make some comment on the differences that exist between provision in the commercial and public sectors. There are many examples of areas where both the commercial and public sector provide the same leisure forms, for example, swimming pools, leisure/health clubs and theatres/concert venues. There are, however, important differences in the nature of such provision. Provision by the public sector is generally aimed at providing a basic level of facilities for the local community, while commercial sector provision is profit oriented. Levels of service are likely to differ, and prices in public sector facilities are likely to be lower, as they are often subsidised, and in many cases will offer concessions for groups such as pensioners, the unemployed and students (Table 10.1).

In the current climate, where leisure provision is provided for by a mixed economy, the duplication of commercial sector provision by the public sector might be questioned as a waste of resources. However, because it has different goals to those of the commercial sector the public sector can justify making provision for leisure in some areas. Generally, the public sector would limit itself to providing for those areas that the commercial sector would not provide for but, in addition, in some areas the public sector provides for those user groups that cannot afford commercial sector prices. Consequently, public sector leisure centres, swimming pools and venues attract a different type of user to commercial sector facilities and are seen as public service facilities, subsidised and available to all.

● ● ● ● Areas of commercial sector provision

Perhaps one of the hardest tasks in examining areas of commercial sector leisure provision is to decide on a way of classifying such eclectic provision that is not too cumbersome or over-lengthy. Keynote Market Information, in their report on the UK leisure and recreation market (Keynote, 2001a), identify ten areas of provision, while Torkildsen (1999) separates home-based leisure and leisure outside the home, but then goes on to identify twelve sub-areas in the latter category. Other analyses of the commercial sector in leisure do not identify areas of provision but talk generally about the sector as a whole. Neither of these approaches is particularly useful – the first is too cumbersome and the second too generic.

The following analysis uses five categories of commercial sector provision adapted from those identified by Torkildsen in a conference presentation in 1984. This approach allows a useful analysis of the commercial sector without being too unwieldy. It also facilitates the identification of those providers that are active in a number of sectors – a key characteristic of the commercial sector in leisure. The areas identified are:

(a)   Recreation in and around the home
(b)   Social recreation
(c)   Entertainment and the arts
(d)   Sport and physical recreation
(e)   Tourism, holidays and informal recreation

(a) Recreation in and around the home

This area is perhaps the largest and most varied of an already eclectic commercial sector as a whole. It ranges from largely sedentary activities, such as reading and watching television, to fairly active pursuits, such as gardening and home exercise. Its providers include equipment manufacturers and suppliers, DIY stores, garden centres, and newspaper and book publishers. Furthermore, it is increasingly difficult to comment on the fortunes of the home-based leisure sector as a whole, as some areas (e.g. computer gaming) are experiencing more rapid growth than others.

The newspaper market, for example, is facing a period of declining circulations. The Audit Bureau of Circulation (2000) shows that in the period 1998–99 the market as a whole fell by over 1 per cent, while eight daily papers saw a decline in their circulations. Within the newspaper market it is possible to identify different types of product: the more populist tabloid titles, such as the *Sun* and the *Mirror*, mid-market tabloids, such as the *Daily Mail* and the *Express*, and the quality broadsheet papers such as the *Times* and the *Daily Telegraph*. Each of these sectors have employed different strategies to attempt to increase readership, with the lower end of the market often offering promotions, such as cheap holidays and flights, while the upper end of the market has used initiatives, such as free copies at hotels and discounts on pre-paid subscriptions. Such strategies are reflective of the readership that the respective newspapers are attempting to attract. Newspapers are an interesting area to examine because while many are read at home – particularly on a Sunday – many others are read on the train or at work. In fact, the Sunday papers are one of the hardest hit sectors in terms of declining readership, and this has been attributed to less leisure time being allocated to newspaper reading at home at weekends. In fact, the overall decline in newspaper circulations may be attributed to the growth in popularity of other areas of news media, such as television, local radio (which has enjoyed a recent resurgence) and, increasingly, the Internet.

In contrast to newspaper circulations, book sales have been on the increase in recent years; however, much of this was due to the market for education titles and so, like newspapers, this area does not really fall into the leisure around the home area. Nevertheless, sales of paperback books are increasing, suggesting an increase in home reading. Such an increase is likely to be further encouraged by the growth in Internet book sales, which make buying easy and cheap and facilitate such buying through another key area of home-based leisure, home-computing. Furthermore, many of the providers of home-reading materials are part of larger conglomerates that are involved in the provision of Internet services and other media sectors (see Box 10.2).

Home viewing, perhaps the most popular of home-based leisure activities, has experienced major changes in recent years as a result of the introduction of digital technology and non-terrestrial channels. Currently, the provision of digital television changes only the technology, not the programming, as the majority of channels available on digital TV are also available elsewhere through satellite, cable or terrestrial television. However, as the traditional analogue signal is due to be turned off within the next decade or so, provision of digital television is set to grow. This growth will be aided by further new technology that allows people to access the Internet through digital television.

Provision for home viewing is not, however, limited to broadcasters. Programme makers, companies providing equipment and consumables such as video cassettes, and companies renting equipment and consumables are all part of this market sector. Therefore, examples of key players would be BSkyB, and Carlton Communications (broadcasters and programme makers), and Sony, Panasonic and Hitachi (suppliers of equipment and consumables), while Granada, which is active in each of these sectors, is also involved in the rental market.

Box 10.2

News Corporation and Bertelsmann

News Corporation

Rupert Murdoch's News Corporation is one of the largest publishing and media groups in the world, and its interests in the UK include the *Times* and the *Sun* newspapers, magazines, and the publishing company HarperCollins, which recently sold its academic publishing divisions to concentrate on consumer titles. Rupert Murdoch is also owner of the BSkyB group, which operates satellite and digital broadcasting services.

Bertelsmann

The German company Bertelsmann has various media and publishing operations and is the owner of Random House, the world's largest English language trade book publisher. Imprints include Crown Publishing Group and Hutchinson. Bertelsmann also owns Gruner and Jahr, an international publisher of around 80 magazines and ten newspapers and it has a 41% stake in the Internet bookselling operation run by Barnes and Noble.

Other examples of new technology affecting the home viewing sector are the DVD (digital video disc) and, yet again, the Internet. DVD is expected to do for the video cassette what compact discs did for the audio cassette, whilst there are the seeds of provision in Internet broadcasting that extends choice and allows viewers to decide which cameras they view action through. The highly popular Channel 4 series *Big Brother* was broadcast over the Internet 24 hours a day during its 9-week runs in 2000 and 2001.

Many of the organisations involved in provision for home viewing are also involved in the home listening market. As above, the market includes equipment, consumables and broadcasters, and it is widely recognised as one of the strongest leisure markets, with 80 per cent of BMRB International's target group index respondents (BMRB, 2000) rating this as a popular evening's entertainment. Sales of consumables (i.e. CDs, audio cassettes, etc.) are particularly strong, with an increase of 10.2 per cent during 1995–98 (BPI, 1999). Commercial radio is now putting increased pressure on the BBC's radio services, with its combined audience now being larger than the BBC's combined radio audience (RAJAR, 2000). This has led to the BBC, despite being a public service broadcaster, putting a much greater emphasis on its commercial activities (Box 10.3), for which it has received some criticism.

Developments in technology have contributed to the development of a range of electronic games and video games, which are increasingly displacing the more traditional board games, jigsaws and construction toys (e.g. Meccano) in this broad market sector, particularly among children. The three dominant companies in the 'electronic' sector are all Japanese – Nintendo, Sega and Sony – with Sony also being a key player in other areas of the home entertainment market. While the large manufacturers of traditional board games and toys have suffered a little, some, such as Scrabble and Lego, have developed computer software packages that mirror their traditional product. However, as the main purchasing group for board games is adults aged 25 to 44, the technological trends in the sales of children's toys and games are not as much in evidence. It should be noted that, as in many other leisure

Box 10.3

The British Broadcasting Corporation

The British Broadcasting Corporation (BBC) is still the leading broadcaster in the UK, with two public service television channels, cable and digital news and entertainment channels, an online news, information and features service, five national and a network of local radio stations, and publishing and world broadcasting interests. Its website is now one of the most visited in the country and its commercial subsidiary, BBC Worldwide, has three international television channels while also selling, marketing and licensing pre-recorded and blank videos and audio cassettes, books, magazines, clothing and a vast array of other merchandise associated with its programmes. Despite this increased emphasis on commercial activity, 90% of the BBC's funding still comes from the licence fee.

areas, while the main players in this market are relatively large multi-nationals, the vast majority of companies are small businesses producing specialist products or serving particular sectors (ONS, 2000a).

At the more active end of the 'recreation in and around the home' sector are activities such as home exercise, DIY and gardening. Television programmes such as *Changing Rooms* and *Ground Force* have stimulated interest in home and gardening improvement, while home fitness videos, fronted by prominent television personalities, have contributed to the market for home exercise. In spite of this, the home exercise market is traditionally static, and many equipment purchases – for example, exercise bikes, weights and dumbells – take place through the second-hand market.

While there are obviously numerous manufacturers of DIY equipment, the nature of DIY retailers has changed considerably in recent years. The DIY superstore (e.g. B&Q and Homebase) has to a large extent displaced the independent hardware store. Furthermore, both B&Q and Homebase are increasingly positioning themselves as 'home lifestyle stores', selling both DIY and gardening equipment and supplies, as well as plants and other horticultural products. There is, however, still a significant niche for specialist garden centres and, while there are some national chains (e.g. Wyvale and Country Gardens), most are small, family-owned nurseries and growers operating in local areas.

(b) Social recreation

Social recreation is an area that tends to be neglected in analyses of leisure activities, which often focus on more formal forms of leisure. However, with the exception of home-based activities, it is the most popular form of leisure, with 75 per cent of all target group index respondents visiting public houses, which make up only one element of social recreation (BMRB, 2000). In fact, social recreation encompasses visits to public houses, wine bars, restaurants and establishments such as cinemas and tenpin bowling alleys.

The nature of the British public house has been changing in recent years, with a division between the traditional 'local', which largely generates income from drinks, and a range of other establishments such as café bars, themed pubs and family pubs, which depend on food sales to supplement their drinks income. In fact, it was estimated that in 2000 food sales accounted for 17 per cent of total pub sales (Keynote, 2001b). The general trend has been the growth of 'branded' pubs, such as Murphy's, JD Wetherspoon, and Brewers Fayre, at the expense of the smaller, tenanted, community pub, many of which have been facing economic problems. Murphy's, an Irish themed pub, is a good example of a branded chain, often located in town centres, where the evening customers are largely young people. However, as licensing laws have relaxed and longer opening hours have been allowed, the pub can open to serve morning coffee, lunches and drinks after work. Other chains operate in a similar way but with different brands – All Bar One is a café bar/wine bar that operates similarly but is designed to attract more women. Many such chains are often built in converted buildings previously used as post offices, banks and cinemas. The use of converted buildings has also been a feature of the trend towards 'retro' pubs, where there is little background noise and no music, led by the JD Wetherspoon chain, which at the end of 2001 had 540 outlets throughout the UK. Initially the focus for this chain was on creating an atmosphere suited to the quiet enjoyment of drink and conversation, with catering kept to a discreet minimum. However, the popularity of the cheap food served in Wetherspoon pubs has led to a greater focus on this element of their operation. A key growth area has been the family pub/restaurant, exemplified by the Brewers Fayre chain, which includes children's play areas and is aimed at young families (Box 10.4). The trend toward increased pub usage, but on a less regular basis, is something that is, perhaps, a feature of consumers making use of the themed outlet rather than regular visits to the 'local'.

The restaurant market is one of the most buoyant sectors in the commercial leisure sector, with a central trend being the increase in the number of brands and expansion by major players such as Whitbread. Such expansion means that independent operators have to compete through catering to particular market niches, such as Indian or Chinese food, or providing excellent levels of service that become known by personal recommendation in local areas, thus generating much repeat

Box 10.4

Whitbread plc (social recreation)

Whitbread has over 3,000 restaurants, public houses and fast food outlets, and has brands in more 'social recreation' categories than any other operator. Since the sale of its brewing interests in 2000, its operations have been divided into three divisions: inns, pub partnerships and restaurants.

The inns division includes the highly successful Brewers Fayre brand, which has over 400 outlets, with around a third of these including 'Charlie Chalk' children's play areas. Interestingly, while the Brewers Fayre chain is in the inns division, over 55% of sales come from food. Other brands include Hogshead, Wayside Inns, Family Inns and Pitchers. The pub partnerships division comprises mainly leased, non-branded, 'traditional' local pubs, of which there are over 1,700 outlets.

The restaurants division included a number of brands that could be classified as either pubs or restaurants, the prime example being the Beefeater chain (of which there are over 250 outlets). Falling more clearly into the restaurant sector, albeit at the lower end of the market, are TGI Fridays and Pizza Hut (which are operated through a licensing agreement with the brand owners, Tricon Restaurants International). In the informal dining sector, expansion is planned of brands such as Café Rouge, Mama Amalfi and Bella Pasta, along with further growth of the Pizza Hut chain.

In addition, the Whitbread group owns a number of hotel chains, and consequently 40% of Beefeater outlets and one quarter of Brewers Fayre Inns are sited alongside its Travel Inn Hotels. Whitbread also has an interest in the fitness sector as it owns David Lloyd Leisure Clubs (see Box 10.7).

business. However, around half of all sales in this sector are generated by fast food outlets, such as McDonald's, Burger King and KFC, but because these outlets cater largely for convenience eating rather than 'social' eating, they will not be examined in any detail here.

There has been a growth in what might be characterised as 'premium' pizza and pasta chains, such as Pizza Express and Ask Pizza Pasta, which appear to have benefited from customers seeking a slightly more upmarket eating experience than that offered by the standard pub-restaurant chains. The downside of this has been the demise of brands such as Pizzaland. Other themed restaurants experiencing expansion are Garfunkels and Caffé Uno.

Restaurant visits are increasingly popular, both during the day and in the evening, with around half of adults being regular daytime visitors and 60 per cent of adults using restaurants regularly in the evening (BMRB, 2000). Furthermore, young people, particularly couples without children, eat out in even larger numbers, 75 per cent of 25 to 34-year-olds doing so on a regular basis. For many, eating out is an important leisure activity in its own right; however, the location of branded outlets in 'leisure park' developments – often on the edge of town and providing convenient access and parking – including multiplex cinemas, leisure centres and, in some cases, nightclubs, has contributed to the increased numbers in this younger age group.

The growth of the multiplex cinema, following a decline in cinema visits in the early to mid 1980s largely attributed to the arrival of the pre-recorded video, has undoubtedly led the expansion of the 'leisure park' concept and is a major element of commercial sector leisure. Cinemas situated on such complexes offer ease of access, a broad range of films and a number of peripheral activities, such as movie stores, cafés and gaming areas. In fact, figures from the Cinema Advertising Association (1999) show that in 1998, for the first time, the number of screens on multiplex sites outnumbered those in all other locations. The developing 'package' surrounding cinema and films is fuelled by the promotion and 'hype' that surrounds major film releases and, consequently, cinema operators also derive significant revenues from advertising. Furthermore, the contribution of cinema-going to leisure experiences is somewhat broader than mere visits to the cinema, as films are a major topic of conversation in other social recreation contexts. There are over 500 cinema sites throughout the UK, mostly run by major chains such as Odeon/ABC (which are now owned by the same parent company and are largely town centre cinemas), UCI, Warner Village and UGC (formerly Virgin).

Most cinema operators are planning periods of expansion and, while such expansion will undoubtedly be concentrated on the multiplex concept, the life of the out-of-town 'leisure park' may be limited. This is due to a change in planning legislation which, focusing on urban regeneration priorities, now favours town centre projects. Developers may still gain permission for out-of-town sites, but they must first demonstrate that they have attempted to site the development within a town. However, this does not mean the end of the multiplex cinema, as there are an increasing number of examples of town centre 'leisure park' developments (Box 10.5).

Tenpin bowling has experienced mixed fortunes in the UK, with some sites experiencing lack of demand and closing after a very short time. In fact, the volatile nature of this market in some geographical areas led the Granada Group to sell its bowling interests. Nevertheless, there are four main players in the UK, each with multiple sites, namely AMF, Bowlplex, Hollywood Bowl and MegaBowl. MegaBowl has recently combined with SuperBowl to create a chain of 58 outlets throughout the UK, while the US-owned AMF Bowling Incorporated has 37 UK sites. There are almost no independent tenpin bowling operators, although David Lloyds Leisure does include a Lanes brand at a few of its health club sites.

(c) Entertainment and the arts

This sector overlaps considerably with other elements of commercial leisure. Much entertainment takes place in pub venues, with background music, karaoke, quiz nights, discos, live bands, pool, televised sport and gaming machines being part of the product mix in pubs. Furthermore, cinema and tenpin bowling (see above) might also be regarded as part of the entertainment sector. In addition, many elements of the arts, such as museums and heritage attractions, are either run or owned by the public or voluntary sector, or are subsidised to a very significant extent by the public sector. Consequently, the discussions in this section focus on theatres and entertainment venues.

Commercial sector theatre is focused on productions in the West End, which are dependent on populist themes (e.g. musicals), overlaps with other media (e.g. *The Lion King* – a production replicating the Disney film), semi-theatrical productions (e.g. pantomimes) and the patronage of foreign tourists. The lack of

---

Box 10.5

Southbury Corner, Enfield

Southbury Corner is an 'urban' leisure park that became possible when Enfield Football Club sold the lease on its ground to developers Laing in 1999, and additional land was bought from the adjacent Kingsmead School. Some new housing was built on the site, but the main part of the development is the 'leisure park'.

The site includes fairly generous car parking space, given its location, a UGC multiplex cinema, which is visible from the A10 (a main arterial road into the centre of London), a Pizza Hut and Old Orleans restaurant and, currently under development, an eight-lane short-course swimming pool, financed by the local authority. In addition, the arrival of this development has been the catalyst for the redecoration and interior development of the Southbury Pub, situated next to the site. The development is a prime example of the types of partnerships that government is trying to promote between the public and commercial sectors.

tourist theatregoers outside London means many provincial theatres struggle to be profitable. Ownership of the numerous West End theatres is concentrated in the hands of only a few firms. However, perhaps unlike other areas of commercial leisure, such concentration has been a relatively recent development. As a result of acquisitions and mergers in the early months of 2000, the three big players are now Cameron Mackintosh, Really Useful Theatres and the Ambassador Theatre Group. Both Cameron Mackintosh and the Really Useful Group also finance productions, and are thus vertically integrated within this sector (Box 10.6). Beyond the West End, it is difficult to distinguish commercial operators, as many provincial productions are heavily subsidised. The one major operator outside the West End is the Apollo Leisure Group, recently acquired by the American company SFX Entertainments, which has a diverse portfolio including cinema, largely provincial theatres, bingo halls and two arenas. However, with the exception of Apollo, many of the almost 30,000 companies whose business is 'live theatrical presentation' (Business Monitor, 2000) are very small, in some cases single-person, production companies rather than theatre owners. In fact, almost three-quarters of these have a turnover of less than £100,000, whilst only 2 per cent turn over more than £1 million.

Entertainment venues can range from a relatively small 'concert room' in a working men's club, through venues such as Sheffield Arena and the National Indoor Arena in Birmingham, to sports stadia such as Wembley (which is now out of action and its future is the subject of continuing debate as Sport England and the government struggle to make a decision on the location of a national stadium). The larger venues are usually multi-purpose and in many cases have some public sector subsidy (both Sheffield and the National Indoor Arena were subsidised, while Wembley's redevelopment is being partly financed by funding from the National Lottery). Other venues, such as Earls Court Olympia and the G-Mex Centre in

---

Box 10.6

The Really Useful Group

Founded and controlled by Britain's most famous theatrical 'impresario', Lord Andrew Lloyd Webber, the Really Useful Group was originally a production company based on his musicals. For a short while it was a public company quoted on the London Stock Market, but Lloyd Webber brought it back into private ownership and bought out the 30% share that had been taken by the entertainment company Polygram.

In recent years the group has developed publishing, music and media divisions and has taken out long leases or bought many West End theatres. This activity expanded in January 2000 with the purchase of Stoll Moss Theatres Ltd from the Australian Heytesbury Group. A separate 'Really Useful Theatres' company has been established, with backing from NatWest Equity Partners, to manage the theatres and leases. In addition to the theatres and leases, Really Useful Theatres has also established a ticket distribution division.

Manchester, concentrate largely on exhibitions (e.g. The Ideal Home Exhibition). The commercial operation is usually handled by the promoters, often relatively small firms with no assets because they hire venues, which co-ordinate the venue, the event, marketing and ticket sales.

(d) Sport and physical recreation

The sport and recreation sector is huge and diverse, but in terms of the commercial sector it comprises: facilities (health clubs, gyms, private leisure centres and some individual sports clubs, such as golf and tennis); products (equipment, clothing and footwear); retailing (sports shops and outlets); passive interests (various forms of media and sports spectating); and, often neglected, sponsorship.

Participation in the sports market is shifting away from traditional sports and towards fitness activities, where the focus is on keeping fit for its own sake. Such activities require less regularised commitment and can be organised and reorganised around other work and family commitments as, unlike many sports, they are essentially individual activities. It is likely that the trend for fitness activities, rather than traditional competitive sport, is set to continue to rise in the future. Such a trend is good news for the private sector, which has traditionally been the market leader in such fitness activities.

Facility provision can be categorised into three sectors. First, the private sector health/leisure club or gym; second, public sector leisure centres and associated facilities, such as floodlit pitches, which in some cases are managed by private sector firms; and finally, single sport clubs (e.g. golf and tennis) that may originally have been part of the voluntary sector but are now run for a profit. As each of these has some commercial element they will be examined in turn.

Health clubs have evolved from what were once essentially one-room gyms primarily offering free-weights and weight-training machines to become much larger centres with a usual minimum of a gym with weight-training and cardiovascular facilities, a small pool and a sauna/jacuzzi suite. While there is still a small market for the traditional urban gym, it is the health centre concept that has seen considerable growth, with spending on private health clubs doubling between 1995 and 2000 (Keynote, 2001c). In many cases, similar facilities to those offered by private health clubs can be found in public sector leisure centres, but the sophisticated equipment and exclusive atmosphere of the private club is something that attracts many affluent professionals in the ABC1 categories. A poll conducted by Gallup in 1999 reported 14 per cent of adult respondents claimed they were 'active members' of a health club; however, this figure clearly includes many casual, and perhaps aspirant, users because it is a much higher figure than that reported by other sources. BMRB (2000) report that membership of health clubs extends to 3.5 per cent of the population, of which 2.2 per cent are regular users. As with many other sectors, the key players are the large groups that control branded chains, although there are a large number of independents – over 75 per cent of sites are operated by single-site independents or are part of very small chains (fewer than five sites) (Keynote, 2001c). The first big player in this market was David Lloyd Leisure, now owned by Whitbread (Box 10.7), but other operators, such as Fitness First, Holmes Place and Esporta (formerly First Leisure), are also significant. In addition, there are those companies that operate clubs for 'or as part of' hotel chains (such as the Hilton Group and De Vere) or as corporate facilities (such as Tweedpark).

The compulsory competitive tendering (CCT) legislation, which compelled local authorities to invite commercial sector tenders for the management of their sports facilities, brought a new dimension to commercial involvement in the sports area. While this legislation has now been replaced by a new system of Best Value, the new framework still provides for commercial sector management of public sector facilities, although there is no requirement to involve the commercial sector. In the CCT process, the vast majority of management contracts were won by local authority in-house teams, although at the beginning of 2001 there were over 200 centres managed by private companies dating back to this process (see Chapter 9 for a fuller discussion of these issues). While many commercial management companies are single-contract operators, a significant number of multi-site companies developed to exploit the opportunities offered by the CCT legislation. The largest of these, Kunick PLC operating under Relaxion, has recently bought Circa Leisure and now controls 50 contracts at 177 facilities. Kunick's Leisure Connection subsidiary now houses these two brands and, in September 2000, was appointed fitness contractor for the National Sports Centres owned by Sport England.

Single-sport clubs (or those limited to a small number of sports) may often have a voluntary sector history, or it may be difficult to draw the line between voluntary and private sector involvement (see the discussion of the Polo Farm Sports Club in Chapter 11 for an example from the voluntary side of this divide). Traditionally, such clubs have developed for sports that the public sector is not willing to support, as they are perceived as elitist or, because the sports are preferred by affluent groups, they lend themselves to being organised around membership fees. Golf is perhaps the most obvious example of such a sport and continued growth means there are now over 6,600 clubs in the UK compared to 5,000 ten years ago

---

Box 10.7

Whitbread plc (health and fitness)

In addition to its interests in social recreation (see Box 10.3), in 1995 Whitbread diversified into health and fitness by acquiring David Lloyd Leisure. These clubs, built up by the former tennis professional whose name they bear, average a membership of 4,000 for each of the 43 sites. They are usually large establishments offering at least a dozen tennis courts (both indoor and outdoor), swimming pools, squash courts, fitness rooms, and health, beauty and catering facilities. Whitbread followed this acquisition by adding the eight Curzon clubs, which are smaller than David Lloyd and branded as sophisticated urban clubs, and the six Racquets and Healthtrack clubs, which were considered a direct competitor and were re-branded as David Lloyd, to its health and leisure portfolio. Whitbread also has 60 clubs in its Swallow Hotels, which were all re-branded as Marriot during 2001.

(Keynote, 2001c). Invariably such clubs are single-site concerns and there is much of the 'self-help' of the voluntary sector about many of their operations. Another example of such clubs are those for tennis which, although publicly provided for in parks, attract members who prefer the better facilities, tuition and social circle offered by the private sector.

The suppliers of sports clothing and equipment and sports retailers have benefited from the growth in sportswear as general leisure- or fashion-wear and, although this look appears to be less popular than in the past, many suppliers and retailers are trying to cater for both the fashion-conscious and the serious sportsperson. Equipment suppliers have suffered a little from the trend (identified earlier) away from sports that require equipment, towards activities geared towards keeping fit for its own sake, such as jogging or the use of health clubs. In this sector many suppliers are small specialists that manufacture only certain types of equipment for a single sport, an example being Duncan Fearnley, a specialist supplier of cricket bats. There are a few large multi-sport companies, such as Slazenger and Dunlop, but generally the market is fragmented among sports.

Of course, the supply of sportswear is a global industry, with production often controversially located in the Far East, where labour costs are minimal, and dominated by three worldwide brands, Nike, Reebok and Adidas. Other brands are more specialised or indigenous to particular countries – in the UK examples of such companies would be Hi-Tec and Umbro. All these companies, but particularly the multi-nationals whose names have become a fashion statement in themselves, attempt to provide fashionwear alongside more practical sportswear for the serious participant.

Similar to the multi-national suppliers, sports retailers also find themselves treading a line between supplying sportswear and fashion clothing. In addition, many general clothing stores, such as Burtons and Marks & Spencer, supply sportswear, while catalogue and mail order suppliers, such as Freemans and Argos, and department stores, such as John Lewis, supply both sports clothing and equipment. In the specialist sports sector, as in many other areas, the trend has been towards consolidation and the domination of the market by nationwide brands, such as JJB Sports and JD Sports, that have expanded by acquiring competitors and buying up independents, although the latter still retain a significant 28 per cent share of the market (Keynote, 2000a).

Sports spectating is dominated by football, with over 12 per cent of the population spectating at football matches in 1999 (BMRB, 2000). However, the market is fragmented, as each sport has its own social climate and attendance conventions. While football spectators are apt to attend every other week throughout the season, many horse racing attendees will be occasional or only annual visitors to special meetings. The commercial beneficiaries of sports spectating are fragmented and largely single-operation concerns, such as football clubs, horse racing venues, speedway/greyhound stadia or athletics stadia, and some of these will be owned by the public sector. However, sports spectating and the broader interest it creates generates commercial revenues through a whole range of media and publishing interests. Commercial television benefits considerably from sports coverage and, although large sums of money are paid for the television rights to the most popular sports, such coverage has been used to sell, initially, satellite dishes and, latterly, digital television technology. Sports coverage has also become important in selling national newspapers and many now produce separate sports supplements. The National Readership Survey (2000) reveals that just over half of men usually read the sports pages. In addition, there are now a vast array of sports magazines, although the signs are that this market has reached saturation point in some areas. While most titles focus on single sports some, such as *Total Sport*, provide general coverage. In some sports, such as football and rugby, magazines are targeted at spectators, but many titles exist – e.g. *Runners World* and *Swimming Times* – that are aimed at participants. Publishers of such magazines often own more than one title, but generally the market is fragmented and overlaps with the overall market for magazines.

Sponsorship is often neglected in an analysis of the commercial sector in sport, and this is perhaps because it involves many non-sporting organisations. Consequently, it is not possible to identify a 'sector' of sports sponsors as they are drawn from a wide range of non-sporting areas, each with different objectives. However, it is possible to give an official figure for the sum of sports sponsorship in 1997 from Sportscan of £322 million. Such sponsorship may be of teams (e.g. Guardian Direct sponsors the British Davis Cup Tennis Team), of clubs (e.g. Newcastle United is sponsored by Newcastle Brown Ale), of individuals (e.g. Nike sponsors Michael Jordan), of events (e.g. Flora London Marathon), of leagues or championships (AXA Sponsored FA Cup), of stadia (e.g. Bolton FC's Reebok Stadium), of televised events (e.g. Volkswagen sponsors Channel 4 sports broadcasts), of programmes (e.g. Frosties sponsors the Amateur Swimming Association's learn-to-swim programme) or of boards and hoardings within grounds and arenas. There are also numerous very small deals at local level where clubs or individuals will be given free clothing or equipment by local businesses.

(e) Tourism, holidays and informal recreation

Of the areas of commercial leisure discussed here, tourism is perhaps the most obviously commercial, almost in its entirety. With the exception of a few publicly owned attractions and resources, the vast majority of operators in the tourism and informal recreation area are commercial concerns. Some, such as airlines, operate internationally; others operate internationally but largely to cater for travellers from the UK, such as many tour operators and travel agents; some are entirely domestic concerns, many of whom are very small operators, for example, cafés and ice cream vendors. As with many other areas of leisure, the picture is not only of a number of big players, but also of an industry that is, as a whole, considerably fragmented with many small concerns. While the tourism industry in the UK accounts for more than 5 per cent of Gross Domestic Product, it is made up of more than

120,000 businesses. This includes many in what can be termed the informal recreation area, by which is meant such things as day trips to the countryside, to urban or rural parks and to the coast.

Most overseas holidays from the UK are catered for by travel agents and tour operators, who account for around 60 per cent of the outbound market. The rest comprises what might be termed independent travel, which is booked directly by the traveller. The increase in Internet facilities for direct bookings is causing this sector to grow and it is likely to eat further into the market share of the travel agent/tour operator. However, the convenience offered by travel agents/tour operators means that they are likely to retain a considerable market share into the forseeable future. The desire for such convenience is evidenced by the fact that over 80 per cent of the holidays sold by travel agents are air inclusive tours, more commonly known as package holidays (ONS, 2000b). Many areas of the travel agent/tour operators' business are characterised by price wars, discounts and last-minute reductions, as the nature of the sector is such that it is better to sell a holiday at a rock-bottom price than to leave hotel rooms and aeroplane seats empty. Yet, despite this, there are high levels of market concentration and vertical integration, with the top four tour operators collectively holding a 90 per cent market share and the top five travel agents holding a share of over 65 per cent. Furthermore, each of the top four tour operators – Thomson (Box 10.8), Airtours, First Choice, and Thomas Cook – own travel agencies and airlines, while Airtours also operates cruise ships and hotels.

The airline sector might usefully be segmented into long-haul and non-budget, charter and budget airlines. British Airways, the largest in terms of turnover, and Virgin Atlantic are both largely oriented towards long-haul business, while British

---

Box 10.8

Thomson Travel Group plc

Now owned by the German group Preussag, Thomson Travel Group is one of the largest integrated tour operators in the world, although until 1996 it was entirely UK based. It has been the UK market leader for 25 years and has three main activities: tour operating (Thomson Holidays), charter airline (Britannia) and travel retailing (Lunn Poly). Furthermore, it was also involved in cottage-letting until 2001, when it sold its Holiday Cottages Group.

Thomson's strategy has been to maintain market leadership through acquisitions and organic growth, a strategy that aims to take advantage of vertical integration – in 1998, 47% of tours sold by Lunn Poly were Thomson Travel Group products. During 1999, Thomson added to its group through the purchase of three regional travel agents – Callers-Pegasus, Sibbald Travel and Travel House. Thomson packages are largely sold under the Thomson, Skytours and Portland brands, although recent acquisitions have added, among others, Crystal Holidays, Jetsave and Tropical Places, each retaining their own identity, to the Thomson stable.

Midland and KLM are more focused on short-haul flights. Key operators for charter flights, those which carry only passengers on package holidays, are Britannia, Monarch and Caledonian. Generally speaking, airlines focus on either chartered or scheduled flights, with very few operating in both areas. The recent growth of budget airlines, such as Ryanair and easyJet, has captured a growing share of the intra-European market and, while there is debate about the potential size of this market, further growth seems likely. Furthermore, budget airlines, and easyJet in particular, are seeking to make use of the Internet, offering discounts for bookings made online.

One of the key factors driving UK demand for holidays is that many people now take multiple holidays, and it is this rather than market penetration that supports, particularly, the UK domestic market. Holidays taken in the UK tend to be short breaks, usually long weekends, and many are taken with a particular activity, event, or pasttime in mind. As such, key factors in the domestic market are hotels, attractions, events/activities and camping/caravanning and holiday camps. While there are a vast, almost incalcuable, number of independent hotels, guest houses and bed and breakfast establishments, competition in the UK hotel industry has intensified with the development of a number of UK groups with a focus almost entirely on hotels. Many of these companies are former widely diversified conglomerates that have been disposing of other interests (see earlier discussion). The relevant groups are Holiday Inn (Bass plc), Marriot and Travel Inn (Whitbread plc) and Hilton (Hilton Group plc, formerly Ladbroke).

While the hotel market has seen an increase in major group presence, visitor attractions are seeing a widespread withdrawal of large firms and many attractions are being bought out by management teams or single-site operators. There are still one or two big players – such as the Tussauds Group, which owns Alton Towers, Chessington World of Adventures, Thorpe Park, Warwick Castle, Madame Tussauds, the London Planetarium and Rock Circus – but the sector is now widely fragmented. Of course, many attractions are owned or managed by the public sector, particularly those which are free to use and largely part of the informal recreation sector, such as country parks and heritage attractions. However, many heritage attractions, such as Stonehenge, now charge a fee for close access, and there has been some debate regarding the extent to which charges can be made for access to the countryside.

While much domestic short-break tourism and informal day-tripping recreation focuses on events or activities, the market is almost impossible to categorise as the product is so diverse. An event may often be something from another area of leisure, such as a sports match, a theatre visit or even a craft fair or car boot sale, while activities may be canoeing, walking, painting or shopping. However, regardless of the nature of such events/activities, there is little in the way of a collective sector, and so analysis of them is almost impossible.

Camping and caravanning might be regarded both as leisure activities in their own right and a mode of holiday-taking. Commercial operations might be divided into two broad sectors, both of which are fairly fragmented. Equipment sales, including caravans and camping equipment, were valued at over £950 million in 1999, although there is also a thriving second-hand market, while park and site operations generated an estimated income of £2.4 billion (Keynote, 2000b). Many of these campsites are now much more than the traditional field with a toilet and, in fact, many offer facilities – such as a clubhouse, swimming pool, shop, bar and other sport and leisure facilities – that would be found on the traditional holiday camp. In fact, the British holiday camp, while less popular than in its heyday, still generates a significant amount of trade and some companies, such as Haven Holidays, offer camping alongside the traditional chalet accommodation at many of their sites. While some holiday camp operators, such as Warners, have repackaged themselves as leisure resorts and upgraded some sites to country house hotels, others, such as Butlins, still aim for the traditional working-class family and offer themed weeks or weekends throughout the year, focused on relatively well-known entertainers, sports tuition or health and beauty activities.

Conclusions

The pervasive influence of the commercial sector

The discussions in this chapter show that the influence of the commercial sector reaches, to varying extents, into all areas of leisure. It is involved in formal partnerships with the public sector for the management and promotion of facilities, and supplies equipment, clothing and services to both the voluntary and commercial sectors. While many large commercial firms are no longer as widely diversified as they have previously been, in many areas of leisure, supply or ownership is concentrated in the hands of a limited number of large chains or brands. However, in a great many areas there are also almost incalculable numbers of small independent companies, many of which are single-person operations serving particular geographical or market niches. In a few sectors – e.g. sports clothing and media – companies such as Nike and Rupert Murdoch's News Corporation operate on a global scale and enjoy, with one or two competitors, near worldwide market dominance.

Because the singular aim of the commercial sector is to be profitable, the extent of its operations depends on the profitability of the area in which it is operating. Consequently, while in the arts commercial activity outside London's West End is limited or is highly subsidised by public sector grants, in the more profitable tourism sector almost all provision is by the commercial sector. However, it is likely that future development of the commercial sector in many areas of leisure, particularly those where it has a low market share, will be through partnership, rather than competition, with the public and voluntary sectors.

Questions

1 Evaluate the ways in which the commercial sector differs from the public and voluntary sectors in its approach to, and motivations for, leisure provision.

2 Providing examples, outline the extent of market concentration in areas of commercial sector leisure and the ways in which this might affect the 'leisure product' offered to consumers.

3 How does horizontal and vertical integration differ from general diversification? What are the advantages of such integration for commercial leisure providers?

4 Analyse the reasons for the varying levels of commercial sector involvement in different areas of leisure provision.

5 Discuss, using examples, the trends in the evolution and development of the large leisure firms in recent years.

References

Audit Bureau of Circulation (2000) *ABC Review*, Berkhamstead: ABC Ltd.

BMRB International Ltd (2000) *Target Group Index*, London: BMRB.

British Phonographic Industry Ltd (1999) *BPI Statistical Handbook*, London: BPI.

Business Monitor (2000) *Multinational Telecommunications Companies 2000*, London: Business Monitor International Ltd.

Clarke, J. and Critcher, C. (1985) *The Devil Makes Work: Leisure in Capitalist Britain*, London: Macmillan.

Cinema Advertising Association (1999) *CAVIAR – Cinema and Video Industry Audience Research*, London: CAA.

Coalter, F. (1988) *Recreational Welfare: The Rationale for Public Sector Investment in Leisure*, London: Avebury/Gower.

Coalter, F. (1990) 'Leisure: the historical background to the development of the commercial, voluntary and public sectors of the leisure industries', in Henry, I.P. (ed.) *Management and Planning in the Leisure Industries*, London: Macmillan.

Cunningham, H. (1980) *Leisure in the Industrial Revolution*, London: Croom Helm.

Henry, I.P. (2001) *The Politics of Leisure Policy*, London: Macmillan.

Jones, G.S. (1986) *Workers at Play*, London: Routledge.

Keynote Market Research (2000a) *Market Report: Sports Clothing and Footwear*, London: Keynote Ltd.

Keynote Market Research (2000b) *Market Report: Camping and Caravanning*, London: Keynote Ltd.

Keynote Market Research (2001a) *Market Review: UK Leisure and Recreation*, London: Keynote Ltd.

Keynote Market Research (2001b) *Market Report: Public Houses*, London: Keynote Ltd.

Keynote Market Research (2001c) *Market Review: UK Sports Market*, London: Keynote Ltd.

National Readership Surveys Ltd (2000) *The UK National Readership Survey* (Volume I), London: NRS Ltd.

Office for National Statistics (2000a) *The UK Service Sector*, London: HMSO.

Office for National Statistics (2000b) *International Passenger Survey*, London: HMSO.

Open University (1981) *Popular Culture and Everyday Life*, U203 Popular Culture: Block 3, Units 1 and 11, Milton Keynes: Open University Press.

Radio Joint Audience Research (RAJAR) (2000) *The Radio Audience*, London: RAJAR.

Seward, K. (1994) 'Getting expert advice', *Leisure Management*, July.

Torkildsen, G. (1999) *Leisure and Recreation Management* (4th edition), London: Spon.

Torkildsen, G. (1984) 'Commercial involvement in recreation: a study of provision in the private sector', in Howell, M. and Brehaut, J.R. (eds) *Proceedings of the VII Commonwealth and International Conference: Volume 4 – Recreation*, Brisbane: University of Queensland.

Further reading

The chapter by Coalter in Henry's edited collection, *Management and Planning in the Leisure Industries*, provides a good background to the development of the commercial sector within a mixed economy approach.

Clarke and Critcher, in *The Devil Makes Work: Leisure in Capitalist Britain*, are more critical of the role of the commercial sector in leisure.

The range of reports by Keynote, some of which have been referred to in this chapter, are updated every two or three years and will continue to provide contemporary information on the fortunes and trends in the range of areas of commercial leisure. Other sources, such as Mintel, provide similar market information. The activities, mergers and acquisitions of the large leisure firms are usually reported in the financial pages of quality news media and in the monthly leisure press: *Leisure Management*, *Leisure Opportunities* and *The Leisure Manager*.

Chapter 11 ● ● ● ●

Leisure and the voluntary sector

Voluntary groups play an important role in most of our lives, with the vast majority of people belonging to at least one such organisation. They range from small local interest groups with a handful of members, such as recreational clubs, parent–teacher associations and tenants associations, to large national organisations, such as political parties, trade unions and environmental groups such as the National Trust; they involve virtually any conceivable activity and interest; and they help provide resources and facilities and other benefits that would otherwise not occur. They are particularly important in the area of leisure, with voluntary organisations playing a major role alongside the commercial and public sectors in providing resources and facilities.

Objectives

To:

- *identify the range and size of the voluntary sector*
- *trace the historical growth and development of the voluntary sector*
- *examine the different roles of voluntary organisations in leisure provision*
- *explore the links between the voluntary sector and the public and private sectors*
- *assess the importance of volunteerism as leisure.*

● ● ● ● The nature of voluntary organisations

The voluntary sector is located between the commercial and public sectors and essentially exists due to the failure of the other two (see sections below). The principal objective of voluntary groups is to maximise benefits for their members, although many groups will also provide collective goods and benefits (to a wider population) and, as a result, will at times appear similar to the public sector. Some groups may even claim the provision of collective goods as their principal *raison d'être*. Nevertheless, the voluntary sector differs from the public sector in that voluntary groups *may* aim to exclude the general public and reserve the benefits for their own members. In fact, this social exclusivity aspect may also be seen as a further benefit. For example, sports clubs may only allow their members to use their facilities, or possibly have priority access, and nature conservation groups may allow only their members access to their nature reserves. The voluntary sector also differs from the public sector in that it cannot raise tax revenues. Voluntary organisations may receive tax exemptions as charities or through covenants but this will be at the discretion of government and outside their control.

Similarly, there are a number of features that differentiate voluntary organisations from commercial ones. Unlike commercial operators, voluntary groups do not aim to maximise profits for their owners or shareholders. They may seek to make profits, or at least break even, but whatever profit is received is used to further the aims of the organisation and improve the benefits of members. Voluntary organisations do receive income and may also be involved in trading – groups such as the National Trust and RSPB have multi-million-pound trading operations and at times might well look very similar to a commercial organisation. But, overall, the sources of income are different. Commercial organisations receive their income exclusively from selling their goods and/or services, whereas voluntary organisations receive their income from a variety of different sources – e.g. membership subscriptions, grants, legacies and fund-raising appeals, as well as, in some cases, the sale of goods and services.

Within the leisure field it is estimated that there are over 200 national voluntary organisations and there are a great many more that operate at the local level. Such groups cover all aspects of leisure and Torkildsen (1999) provides a useful list that illustrates this variety together with a classification (Table 11.1). Some of these groups have leisure as their central concern but even those that at first sight do not appear to be involved with leisure *per se* will still relate to leisure in some respects, either through their lobbying activities, their social activities or simply due to the fact that their members, through volunteerism, are enjoying some form of leisure activity (see section on volunteerism as a leisure pursuit, below). The more obvious leisure voluntary organisations cover a variety of leisure forms and operate at many different scales. At the national level a number of key groups exist that have played, and continue to play, a key role in the development of leisure. The largest of all is the National Trust, with 2.9 million members, and the Royal Society for the Protection of Birds has over 1 million members.

Table 11.1   Range of voluntary organisations

Community organizations	Community associations, community councils
Community action groups	National Council for Voluntary Organisations, Inner-City Unit, Inter-Action Trust Limited, Gingerbread
Children's groups	Pre-School Playgroups Association, Toy Library Association
Youth organizations	Scout Association, Girl Guide's Association, National Council for YMCAs, National Association of Youth Clubs
Women's organizations	National Federation of Women's Institutes, National Union of Townswomen's Guilds, Mother's Union, Women's Voluntary Service (WVS)
Men's groups	Working men's clubs, servicemen's clubs
Old people's groups	Darby and Joan Clubs, Senior Citizens
Disabled groups	Gardens for the Disabled, Disabled Drivers' Motor Club
Adventure organizations	Outward Bound Trust, Duke of Edinburgh's Award, National Caving Association
Outdoor activity organizations and touring groups	Camping Club of Great Britain and Ireland, Youth Hostels Association, Central Council of British Naturism, Ramblers' Association, British Caravanners' Club
Sport and physical recreation organizations	Keep Fit Association, British Octopush Association, Skating Association of Great Britain, Cycle Speedway Council, GB Wheelchair Basketball League
'Cultural' and entertainment organizations	British Theatre Association, Museums Association, English Folk Dance and Song Society, British Federation of Music Festivals
Educational organizations	National Institute of Adult Education, Workers' Educational Association, National Listening Library
Hobbies and interest groups	National Association of Flower Arranging Societies, Citizens Band Association, Antique Collectors Club, Handicrafts Advisory Association for the Disabled, British Beer Mat Collectors' Society
Animals and pet groups	Pony Club, Cats Protection League
Environmental, conservation, heritage groups	National Trust, Friends of the Earth, Royal Society for the Protection of Birds, Keep Britain Tidy Group, Save the Village Pond Campaign, Rare Breed Society
Consumer groups	Consumers' Association, Campaign for Real Ale (CAMRA)
Counselling organizations	British Association for Counselling, Citizens Advice Bureaux, Alcoholics Anonymous, Marriage Guidance Councils, Samaritans Incorporated
Philanthropic groups	Rotary International in Great Britain and Ireland, Inner Wheel, Variety Club of Great Britain, Golddiggers
Paramedical organizations	British Red Cross Society, St John Ambulance Brigade
Uniform groups	Voluntary reserves, Territorial Army, Sea and Army Cadets, Air Training Corps
Religious groups	Methodist Church Division of Social Responsibility, Church Army, Church of England Children's Society
Political groups	Political parties, trade unions

Source: Torkildsen, G. (1999) *Leisure and Recreation Management*, 4th Edn., Table 10.1, pp. 287–8, London: E & FN Spon (Routledge).

While some of the largest individual groups are clearly associated with particular forms of countryside recreation, voluntary organisations have also been essential in the development and provision of other leisure forms. For example, sports clubs and associations have been the means by which millions of people participate in leisure pursuits (Torkildsen, 1999). According to recent estimates, almost two-thirds of the adult population of Britain participates in some form of sport or physical activity (ONS, 1996), which involves many different activities and many more individual organisations. Some sports can boast national memberships of well over a million (for example, football, billiards/snooker and golf) but this is usually organised through small local clubs. Football has over 46,000 clubs, producing a combined membership of over 1.6 million, whereas billiards/snooker has 1.5 million members in 4,500 clubs. Overall it is estimated that there are about 150,000 sports clubs involving various different sport and recreational activities. *The General Household Survey* (ONS, 1996) found that 67 per cent of those who played bowls belonged to clubs, as did 47 per cent of golfers and 34 per cent of soccer players, although the numbers were relatively low for certain sports (2 per cent for cyclists and 4 per cent for tenpin bowlers).

The origins of voluntary groups

The voluntary leisure sector can claim a long history. According to Torkildsen (1999), an early example of such activity involved the eighteenth-century coffee houses for 'gentlemen of leisure' which, although in theory open to all, often developed into clubs with restricted memberships. This is a useful example of groups of individuals with similar interests getting together to provide for their own 'collective' wants and this pattern has occurred repeatedly throughout the nineteenth and twentieth centuries in many different forms of leisure. For example, it has been estimated that in mid nineteenth-century Britain there were about 100,000 separate field clubs and natural history societies catering for the middle-class Victorian interest in wildlife. These clubs organised lectures and trips to the countryside and provided an important leisure outlet for substantial numbers of people. Similarly, in the latter part of the century, religious organisations such as Sunday Schools promoted educational day trips and sports, and mutual improvement societies and working men's clubs provided additional leisure opportunities for the working classes.

Although it is not difficult to see how like-minded people might organise themselves in this way, a number of more formal, theoretical explanations have been provided to explain the growth of the voluntary sector. Henry (1993), for example, suggests that it is 'a product of the dissolution of the "organic" ties of rural agrarian society' which people had clearly left behind when moving to the growing industrial towns. Whereas in the traditional rural communities many of the social and individual benefits that people enjoyed could have been generated by informal links, in the new urban societies more formal frameworks were required (Tomlinson, 1979).

Another explanation is rooted in economics. Voluntary groups exist as a result of both the commercial and public sectors failing to provide the necessary resources that people demand. According to Gratton and Taylor (1985), government does not compensate for all private sector failings and it is this situation that leads to the formation of voluntary organisations. Government may lack adequate information on consumer demands and also is unlikely to possess the resources to provide for the myriad leisure pursuits that the commercial sector fails to provide for. Even mass participation sports, such as football, athletics or golf, have adult participation rates of less than 4 per cent and the participation rates for the vast majority of leisure activities are extremely small. Clearly tax payers are not going to be prepared to provide for a vast array of minority interests and government cannot take political risks with such expenditure unless it can demonstrate other public benefits (such as health).

The growth, persistence and continual expansion of voluntary groups is also due to a number of key attitudes and values that have had an enduring influence on many aspects of British social life during the last couple of centuries – those of philanthropy, amateurism and self-improvement. Many of the organisations referred to above were aided in their establishment and development by key individuals and organisations that felt a need to help provide for others' needs. Religious establishments are an obvious example of this and, although it could be argued that such organisations may have ulterior motives, for example giving support to state aims in helping to establish various forms of 'rational recreation' (Henry, 1993) (see Chapter 1), many recreational voluntary groups would not have existed were it not for this help.

A further illustration of philanthropy, can be seen in the fact that not all voluntary organisations operate necessarily to provide leisure opportunities for those who are directly involved in their operation. For example, many of those who run sports clubs do not participate in the sports themselves, although they may have done so in the past when they were younger, and many other people become involved in voluntary groups because they believe they can contribute in some way to the benefit of others (see also the section on volunteerism, below). In addition, a number of groups exist that have been described as *principle* groups in that they uphold certain values and campaign on behalf of broader interests within society (Lowe and Goyder, 1983). Throughout the nineteenth and twentieth centuries many groups have emerged to campaign to protect key resources from damage or destruction, for example: Commons, Open Spaces and Footpaths Preservation Society (established in 1865), Royal Society for the Protection of Birds (1889 – Royal in 1904), the National Trust (1895), the Council for the Preservation of Rural England (1926) and Friends of the Lake District (1930). Others have campaigned to establish particular resources – for example, National Playing Fields Association (1925) and Standing Committee on National Parks (1935).

Throughout the development of many areas of leisure there has been a strong belief in the importance of the amateur ethic. This has been particularly prominent in the development of sport, where character building and the ideals of fair play, working for others and participation have been highlighted as being more important than winning. And it is easy to see how such ideals fit comfortably with the altruistic ideals of volunteerism. An important part of the history of sport has involved a struggle between those who wanted to retain the amateur ethos, for a variety of reasons, and those who supported professional and commercial forms (Cross, 1990; Horne *et al.*, 1999). Nevertheless, despite the widespread development of commercial and professional sport, primarily as spectator entertainment, the bulk of actual participation is still amateur in nature and organised round the voluntary club or organisation. However, there are other aspects of the amateur ideal that are inextricably linked with the concept of voluntary groups. The very definition of an amateur is someone who possesses a deep interest in something, and the freedom that voluntary groups provide for people to pursue such interests is clearly important.

Another key value that has played a significant part in the development of voluntary organisations, one of the so-called Victorian values promoted more recently by Thatcherism, is that of 'self-improvement'. This was a value promoted in the nineteenth century by the ruling classes and other sections of the so-called 'establishment', such as the Church. Encouraging the establishment of self-help and mutual aid societies, which would provide opportunities for adult education and healthier forms of leisure, was very much in keeping with this ideal and could be seen in the many forms of 'rational recreation' that developed at this time. In the latter part of the nineteenth and early twentieth century a variety of leisure organisations emerged that embraced this philosophy, such as the Cyclists Touring Club and National Cyclists' Union, along with many sports clubs. In addition, holiday organisations, such as the Workers' Travel Association, the Holiday Fellowship and the Co-operative Holidays Association, attracted large memberships by the 1930s and the Youth Hostels Association membership grew from 6,400 in 1930 to 79,800 by 1938 (Henry, 1993). Other organisations that were prominent in the early part of the twentieth century and are also clearly linked to the self-improvement ideal include those that provided opportunities for women and girls. According to Henry (1993), 'Women's Institutes offered a wide range of cultural and social activities', and he cites other groups that grew significantly at this time such as the Women's League of Health and Beauty (166,000 members in 1939), the Young Women's Christian Association (27,000 members in 1934) and the Girl Guides (47,000 members in 1934).

The role of voluntary groups

From the preceding discussion it is clear that voluntary organisations fulfil a number of important roles and it is the intention of this section to examine these in more detail. Such roles include: the provision of leisure resources, both private and collective; the engagement of voluntary labour; campaigning and lobbying; organising and regulating leisure activities; providing useful links with government and the public sector; and providing various social and psychological benefits.

Provision of leisure resources

One of the principal contributions of the voluntary sector is that it provides specific resources that would otherwise not exist. Many voluntary organisations possess physical resources ranging from a club hut or small sports facility to large areas of land such as that owned by the National Trust or RSPB. The National Trust is in fact a major landowner, possessing over 1 per cent of the total land area of Britain. Some areas of leisure are particularly dependent on the provision of the voluntary sector, especially countryside recreation and sport. In addition to the land holdings of the National Trust, various other groups also own and/or manage substantial swathes of land, as can be seen in Table 11.2. Although some of this land is only accessible to the members of the respective organisations, some is open to non-members also. For example, large areas of countryside owned by the National Trust afford access to the wider public, sometimes involving a charge but not always. The area of Kinder Scout in the Derbyshire Peak District, which witnessed the mass trespass in the early 1930s, is now owned by the Trust and provides free public access, as does Mam Tor in the same vicinity. Similarly, while some RSPB reserves do not allow any access, the vast majority allow access to their members and to the general public for a fee, and some afford free access. For example, the Titchwell reserve on the north Norfolk coast, which receives nearly 100,000 visitors per year, over half being non-members, does not charge (due to a public right of way running through the reserve), although a charge is made for the use of the car park.

The collective benefits that many of these national voluntary organisations provide extend beyond that of simple access to their properties. These organisations play a substantial part in protecting and managing important landscape resources that form an important backdrop for a great many countryside recreations (for a detailed account of this work see Dwyer and Hodge, 1996). The National Trust, for example, owns about 10 per cent of all land in the national parks, over 30 per cent in the Lake District. In some places, where its land is farmed by tenant farmers, it may require such farmers, as part of the tenancy agreement, to farm in ways that preserve the traditional landscape (e.g. Bransdale in the North Yorks Moors). Consequently, were it not for this body, the appearance of the landscape in many of these regions might be very different.

Table 11.2   Area of land owned or managed by selected countryside voluntary organisations

	Area of land holding (ha.)
National Trust	248,000
RSPB	97,000
County Nature Conservation Trusts	74,000
Woodland Trust	17,500

Many sports clubs also possess their own facilities, which they will have acquired through the income they receive from membership subscriptions and, in some cases, government grant aid, which in recent times will also include Lottery funding. Although in some cases facilities such as golf courses, tennis courts and cricket and hockey pitches are provided by commercial enterprises and local authorities (many municipal golf courses exist in Scotland, for example), many such resources are provided by voluntary clubs (see Polo Farm case study). The facilities are provided in the first instance for the members, although non-members may also be able to hire them. Where sports clubs are relatively small, although they may not be able to own their own facilities, they may instead be able to hire resources and premises.

The engagement of voluntary labour

In addition to owning land and water resources for various forms of leisure, voluntary organisations also play a crucial role in their management. This may take a number of forms. As was explained in Chapter 7, such resources require regular attention simply to maintain their existing characteristics and in some situations it may be necessary to create completely new environments or facilities. Large organisations, such as the National Trust or RSPB, will possess enough financial resources to employ people to undertake management tasks, but many others will be entirely dependent on volunteers. One of the great benefits of the voluntary sector is that it provides a means whereby voluntary labour can be assembled for a wide array of tasks including practical site management activities such as scrub clearance, tree planting or fence repairing. In fact the British Trust for Conservation Volunteers exists solely for this purpose and different county groups undertake management work for both the public sector and other voluntary organisations. Other tasks undertaken by volunteers may involve various types of office work, fund-raising activities (e.g. rattling a tin outside supermarkets) or delivering newsletters. Furthermore, many sports clubs will engage the services of their members to referee/umpire matches, act as stewards and marshals, organise fixtures and bookings, provide refreshments and launder the kit. In addition to the many people who are happy to undertake such tasks, it is also invariably the case in some voluntary organisations that the membership will contain various professionals – e.g. solicitors, accountants, graphic artists, journalists and planners – who may be prevailed upon at certain times to volunteer their expertise and thus save the organisation considerable expense.

A number of studies have attempted to estimate the importance of the volunteer input in sport. A report by Gratton *et al.* (1997) has suggested that there are 1.5 million volunteers in United Kingdom sport with an estimated annual value of over £1.5 billion, whereas another study by Gratton and Kokolakakis (1997) claims much higher estimates, with over 5 million volunteers providing nearly £6 billion of value to the sector. The LIRC figures are based on the volunteers investing an average of 2.5 hours per week for 48 weeks of the year (125 hours per year) and the total equates with what would otherwise be provided by 108,000 full-time employees. According to Torkildsen (1999, p. 294):

> Volunteers are the lifeblood for the organization and running of minor and major events. For example, the European Swimming Championships held in Sheffield in 1993 involved 700 volunteers working an average of 8 hours a day for up to 17 days – a total commitment of approximately 95,000 hours.

In addition to the importance of volunteers for sport and countryside recreation, their importance to the arts also should not be underestimated. There are thousands of art clubs and societies that are run by volunteers. According to Torkildsen (1999, p. 295), 'volunteers are a substantial support network for active and passive participation in "cultural" pursuits such as arts, crafts and heritage'. He refers to the fact that local libraries use volunteers to deliver library materials to the house-bound and that 25,000 volunteers work in museums and art galleries across the country. Museums and art galleries often rely on volunteers to act as guides and many small tourist attractions, such as heritage centres, are also run entirely on a voluntary basis.

Organising and regulating leisure activities

Voluntary groups also play a significant role in helping to organise and regulate certain leisure activities, especially in the area of sports. In many sports it is voluntary clubs or associations that are responsible for rules and codes of practice. Virtually all national governing bodies for sport are organised on a voluntary basis and, while there are some notable exceptions in sports that have a large financial turnover, bodies such as the Amateur Rowing Association, the Amateur Swimming Association and the Badminton Association of England, while in some cases being incorporated as limited companies or as registered charities, are run and organised as voluntary organisations. These bodies are responsible for the organisation of their respective sports, and most have structures and committees staffed almost entirely by volunteers at regional level. In addition to drawing up codes of conduct and ensuring the implementation of the laws of the sport, governing bodies are also responsible for training and education programmes for coaches and teachers, and for the training of officials.

The organisation of fixtures and leagues usually falls within the role of voluntary organisations. At the national level, again, this will be the remit of the governing bodies, but at the local level specific voluntary organisations exist, in the true self-help spirit, to run and organise entirely recreational leagues in such sports as five-a-side or pub football, table tennis and badminton. In such cases these leagues will often be organised by a single secretary and, in many cases, for such people the involvement with, and administration of, the league may be their main leisure activity (see section on volunteerism, below).

Campaigning and lobbying

As mentioned in the earlier section, some voluntary organisations play a significant role in campaigning for various leisure resources and benefits. Some bodies, such as the National Trust and RSPB would see this as one aspect of their work but, for other organisations, this is regarded as the primary role. The Commons Preservation Society, for example, provides a useful example in this respect in that it was established in 1865 to campaign for the protection of common lands and open spaces which were rapidly disappearing as a result of the profits to be gained from urban development and speculative building. Various lords of the manor were attempting to enclose commons and extinguish the rights of commoners and the Society fought in the courts to protect these rights and also, on occasions, took direct action in defence of their stand (see Cunningham, 1975, for a detailed description of this). Its most famous, and successful, action involved the campaign to secure Epping Forest, a traditional pleasure resort for East Enders but other notable successes included the eventual safeguarding of Berkhampsted and Plumstead Commons. Furthermore, the Society also played a part in the establishment of the National Trust (see case study below).

As outlined in the previous section, many other organisations have played a prominent role in campaigning and lobbying for different forms of leisure. Many have been involved with protecting wildlife and landscape resources, while others have been more concerned about providing new facilities or ensuring that particular standards are met – for example, the National Playing Fields Association, the Central Council of Physical Recreation and the Royal Society of the Arts.

At times individual groups come together to campaign for a larger objective of mutual interest and one of the best examples of this involved the campaign for national parks. This arose in the 1930s and involved two very different types of group coming together. On the one hand, there were those groups concerned with landscape and wildlife protection, such as the National Trust, RSPB, Council for the Preservation of Rural England and Friends of the Lake District and, on the other, groups such as the Ramblers Association, the Youth Hostels Association and the Cyclists Touring Club, which were keen to see greater access opportunities for urban people. Although all these organisations wanted national parks, the two groupings differed somewhat in terms of how they perceived such places; in fact, the protectionist bodies did not want to see too much access. Nevertheless, they both felt that by coming together and campaigning on a broader front they would be more likely to achieve their overall mutual aim. In 1936 the Joint Standing Committee for National Parks was formed to represent all the various groups involved and co-ordinate and develop the campaign, which it did very successfully. In many ways the campaign achieved its purpose with the 1949 National Parks and Access to the Countryside Act and subsequent establishment of the national parks in the 1950s. However, although national parks were established, they were effectively preservationist designations and did not really do much to fulfil the aspirations of the access groups (for a full discussion of this see Dower, 1977, and McEwen and McEwen, 1987).

Despite the fact that, at times, voluntary organisations campaign for public goods and many are viewed as playing a major role in providing leisure for a far wider public, this role does need to be qualified. As certain writers have pointed out (Mennell, 1979, and Limb, 1986), the organised voluntary sector is unrepresentative. Virtually all leisure activities are minority activities and thus it is minority interests that are being pursued. In addition, those who join the principal campaigning organisations are primarily middle class and already enjoy significant leisure advantages. The lobbying activities of voluntary organisations inevitably promote the sectional interests of their members and, if those less privileged members of society do gain leisure advantage from this, it is largely fortuitous. It is just as likely that their leisure interests may be disadvantaged by such lobbying, as illustrated by the national park example where the more powerful interests of the preservationists effectively prevented national park areas being developed for more popular, gregarious forms of leisure.

Government

In certain circumstances governments are very happy to see the involvement of voluntary groups, simply because they save the government from the responsibility of having to provide. Governments have often encouraged the voluntary movement for this very reason and this was as valid in the nineteenth century as it has been in the twentieth century. As has been demonstrated, not only do voluntary organisations provide many physical resources and facilities that otherwise government might feel obliged to provide, they also tap into this extremely large resource of voluntary labour. While voluntary organisations might be able to persuade their members to give up their free time to undertake various tasks, it is not difficult to imagine what success government might achieve if it tried to do this. While not all groups are considered to be helpful, especially if they are pressure groups that are often at odds with government policy, many groups are regarded as 'helpful' (see Lowe and Goyder, 1983), and most associated with leisure would fall into that category. For example, in its publication *Sport, Raising the Game* (DNH, 1995) government stressed how the mobilisation of competent volunteers provides scope for enhancing the support given to coaching and sports development. In this respect, government is very happy to encourage volunteerism and voluntary groups and will in fact provide help. This may be achieved in a number of ways: providing funding through grants; providing tax incentives, and involving groups in policy making.

In relation to funding, this may involve various mechanisms. The simplest is by direct grant aid and some voluntary organisations operate almost as an arm of government, as a result of their links with the respective grant-aiding quango. One of the principal roles of bodies such as the Arts Council, Sport England and the Countryside Agency (which incorporates what was previously the Countryside Commission) is to channel government funding to various voluntary leisure groups. For example, in 1999/2000 the Arts Council for England awarded grants totalling over £182 million and the Lottery Sports Fund (now called Sport England Lottery

Fund) has distributed over a £1 billion to capital projects, many involving voluntary organisations in a four-year period up to 2001 (see Chapter 8 for further details relating to lottery funding).

In fact, in the area of wildlife conservation the voluntary sector is responsible for such a large proportion of the overall conservation effort, and possesses such a high reputation for doing a good job, that in the late 1980s the government was actually considering transferring its own involvement (the work of the then Nature Conservancy Council) to the voluntary organisations and providing the necessary funding for all nature conservation to be undertaken by this sector. Although this ultimately did not happen – instead a reorganisation of government effort took place – it does provide testimony to the substantial work that the voluntary sector can do and government recognition of this fact.

Apart from funding, voluntary groups also benefit financially from government links as a result of tax incentives. One of the principal ways in which this operates within the leisure sector is through charities. Organisations can be deemed a charity if they are seen to be working for the public benefit through the relief of poverty, the advancement of education, the advancement of religion, or other purposes beneficial to the community. Leisure generally falls into this last category and is covered by the Recreational Charities Act 1958 where certain leisure groups may be seen to be operating 'in the interests of social welfare'. Torkildsen (1999) lists the many advantages, and some disadvantages, from obtaining charitable status but foremost among these are the financial ones. Charities can benefit in the context of their own tax as they are exempt from stamp duty, inheritance tax, development land tax, national insurance surcharge, certain trading profits and certain aspects of VAT, and they are eligible for rate relief. They can also benefit from the tax paid by their supporters by means of covenanted donations and subscriptions. Once again, a full list of all these benefits is provided by Torkildsen (1999).

Apart from providing resources and labour that government might otherwise feel obliged to provide, voluntary organisations also fulfil a number of other useful roles for government. Although under certain circumstances governments may feel uncomfortable as a result of lobbying, it is generally recognised that lobby and pressure groups are an important part of the democratic, pluralist political system. They are a safety valve and means of actually controlling and organising protest, they are a convenient means of linking government with the wider population and they are a useful source of advice. Were voluntary groups not to exist, campaigning would be likely to be far more volatile, disorganised and unpredictable, with consequences for social order. While this may not be a major problem in relation to most leisure issues, this is certainly true of other walks of life and leisure is not entirely immune from radical protest. In the past the access issue has produced violent protest and, more recently, the campaign to retain fox hunting has also highlighted the potential for major public demonstration. While the existence of a recognised pressure group may not guarantee total immunity from such protest, as has been shown by the Countryside March in 1999, the actual impact of protest may be lessened as street protest is more likely to be marshalled and organised. Furthermore, people may be less likely to take to the streets because they know someone is able to speak to government on their behalf and thus a potentially explosive situation can be diffused.

A final advantage that government obtains from the voluntary sector is information and expertise. Voluntary organisations are useful channels through which government can keep in touch with public opinion on particular issues. As voluntary groups exist to further the benefits of their members, the executive members of such groups are going to be very knowledgeable about their particular area of leisure and the needs and wants of the membership. By maintaining contacts with such people, possibly by appointing them as advisers or inviting them to join key committees, government can keep abreast of what certain groups within society are demanding and respond accordingly.

The relationship between the voluntary sector and other sectors

Voluntary organisations may operate independently, in concert with other voluntary groups (particularly in relation to joint campaigns and lobbying) and also in partnership with the private and public sectors. In fact, partnership and co-operative schemes between the various sectors are becoming increasingly common in the provision of leisure facilities and services. The link with the public sector has already been explained to some extent in the paragraphs above. However, there are also some specific partnerships in which voluntary organisations are involved in more formal arrangements with government, especially local government, and the private sector.

A number of reasons can be offered to explain the current enthusiasm for this trend. The need under successive governments to control public spending has clearly reduced the level of public funding available for leisure at a time when people are demanding greater leisure opportunities, and partnerships are thus seen as a way of spreading the financing of projects more widely. In the last couple of decades support for the free market has grown and the idea that the public sector should automatically compensate for the failings of the commercial sector has been challenged (see Chapter 6). In addition, it has also been suggested that local authorities did not always provide for people's leisure requirements anyway. The study on *Leisure Provision and People's Needs* (Dower *et al.*, 1981), for example, argued that 'a better matching of people's leisure needs would be provided by an approach to provision based on community involvement rather than on one which continued to rely on a traditional "standards" approach used by most local authorities' (Harrison, 1991). More recently, the new Labour Government has stressed the importance of the civil society and the need for citizens to become more involved with their local communities. At the end of the millennium volunteerism and partnerships came to be seen as very 'politically correct' and such involvement could thus help to establish an organisation's legitimacy and demonstrate or improve its reputation, image or prestige.

Although partnerships have proliferated in recent times, some partnership schemes have a longer history. Urban fringe management projects were first developed as long ago as 1972 with a pilot scheme in the Bolin Valley in the southern urban fringe of Manchester. The essential feature of such schemes involved bringing together different interest groups, such as farmers and landowners, conservation and access groups, the local authority and various national public agencies, to reconcile conflicting claims. Initiated by the Countryside Commission, by the mid 1980s there were 25 schemes operating in various parts of Britain with the aim of encouraging positive use of urban fringe land, eliminating dereliction and making fuller provision for recreation (Glyptis, 1991). In relation to the latter, the projects sought to increase facilities for informal recreation and public access and deal also with problems of illegal access to private land. As Glyptis (1991) points out, work to increase recreation provision 'focused on creating bridleways, re-using derelict land, developing circular walks, and providing small scale facilities for informal recreation, especially near the urban edge'. Most of the schemes involve a large number of small individual projects, many of which utilise the efforts of local groups and conservation volunteers working with other sectors to a mutually agreed and co-ordinated management plan (see Elson, 1986).

The rural–urban fringe is an area which has seen additional partnership initiatives including the Groundwork schemes and the more recent community forest developments (see Chapter 7). The success of Operation Groundwork in the St Helens–Knowsley area of the north west in the early 1980s led to the establishment of Groundwork Trusts in other parts of Britain. The principal aim of such bodies was to improve the physical environment of hitherto derelict and degraded areas of the urban fringe and extend recreational opportunities. The trusts were constituted as limited companies with charitable status and involved representatives from local authorities, local businesses and voluntary groups with environmental and recreation interests. Although the trusts obtained initial government funding on a 'pump-priming' basis, essentially for clearing derelict land, a principal objective was that such bodies would eventually secure private funds and sponsorship and become self-financing. However, this target was eventually recognised as being unrealistic and thus government grant aid has continued for longer than was originally anticipated.

More recently the community forest developments have involved similar partnership arrangements with county and district councils, Countryside and Forestry Commissions, local farmers, landowners and other businesses, together with the voluntary sector in terms of conservation and recreation bodies and various residents' and community groups. In the planning exercise involving the Marston Vale Community Forest, for example, 14 separate voluntary organisations were acknowledged as providing information and materials (Marston Vale Community Forest, 1995).

Many towns and cities, especially where tourism is important to the urban economy, have also developed partnership initiatives to manage the urban centre.

They bring together the various groups that have a direct interest in the appearance, management and economic prosperity of such areas. One such scheme is the Canterbury City Centre Partnership (or City Centre Initiative as it was originally called when first established in 1994), which involves representatives from public sector bodies such as the city council and county council, the local university and university college, representatives from local businesses, and also representatives from voluntary organisations, such as the Dean and Chapter of Canterbury Cathedral and residents' groups. Tourism attracts over 2 million visitors a year to the city and, while it is a major contributor to the local economy, employing about 4,000 people directly, it does produce significant impacts for the local community in the form of overcrowding and congestion, especially at peak times of the year. The partnership has, among other things, discussed various ways in which tourism can be managed more effectively and this has produced a number of modest initiatives, such as better signage, establishing and publicising alternative attractions, better marketing of the benefits of tourism to local residents, the introduction of a booking system for coaches, and the employment of 'city shepherds' (guides) who can welcome tourists as they arrive at the coach park and direct them along certain routes. Perhaps more importantly, however, the partnership is an opportunity for the different interest groups to discuss issues together, with the possibility of improved mutual understanding.

While partnerships have clearly been embraced and encouraged by policy makers to the point where it would appear almost irreverent to criticise them, there are some cautionary aspects that need to be highlighted. Partnerships may not always serve the best interests of all the members. In an ideal world all partners should have equal power and influence but, of course, this is rarely achieved in practice. As a result, it is the most powerful partners that gain most from such arrangements, often using the partnership to strengthen the legitimacy of their actions. Another weakness of partnerships involves their level of representation with the likelihood that certain groups are left out. Even those partnerships that purport to involve local communities may tend to be dominated by middle-class representatives. For example, the study by Limb (1986) of various community initiatives in open space provision in the London Borough of Hillingdon suggested that formidable barriers existed that prevented lower socio-economic groups from participating in these forms of community involvement. These involved poor knowledge of the lines of communication, the reliance of the local authority on recognised groups, which tended to represent middle-class interests, a reluctance by local authority officers to talk to ad hoc groups, and a general lack of the necessary 'professional' skills to get involved in such activity.

● ● ● ● Volunteerism as a leisure pursuit

While most of this chapter has been concerned with the way in which volunteers help provide a wide variety of leisure pursuits, it is also important to realise that volunteering itself may be seen by some as a leisure activity. The majority of members of voluntary organisations no doubt join such groups in order to enjoy the more explicit benefits that membership provides, such as improved access to leisure resources, or because they strongly support the aims of the organisation if its work is primarily concerned with lobbying. However, many people actually become involved in the work of the organisation as active volunteers. And, although there may be a certain amount of genuine altruism involved, it is also possible to identify other motives. The various physical, social and psychological benefits that are often claimed for leisure pursuits can be equally valid for volunteerism.

For some, becoming involved with a voluntary organisation provides a social circle, and this is especially important for certain people, such as the elderly or retired, who, as a result of their situation, may have reduced social networks. Such work may also provide the retired with a continued sense of worth and, given that they obviously have more time to devote to voluntary work, a useful system of reciprocity is established. Much of this social benefit is informal but many voluntary groups also hold social events, especially if they are also linked to fund raising. Some organisations clearly recognise the importance of the social factor in retaining their active members and specifically organise part of their work on a local group basis with the opportunity for regular meetings. For example, the RSPB and some county nature conservation trusts have a well-developed system of local groups. Furthermore, groups like the National Trust (2002) and British Trust for Conservation Volunteers (2002) organise working holidays for volunteers (Turner, Miller and Gilbert, 2001).

While some members are actively involved in more mundane tasks, and might thus be described as 'foot soldiers', others take on leadership roles. In some instances the positions are self-selecting, with people transferring the skills they exercise in their working lives to the operations of the voluntary organisation. However, voluntary organisations also provide opportunities for others who would otherwise never have such chances to undertake, one might even say play, management roles. In this way they may fulfil certain ambitions and goals and they may obtain satisfaction from their endeavours, as well as prestige and social position, and even feelings of elation from the exercise of power.

Case study

Two contrasting leisure organisations

The final section of this chapter examines two very contrasting case studies to illustrate some of the issues discussed above, as well as certain aspects of their organisation and resource. The case studies include a large national organisation, the National Trust, and a local sports club in the city of Canterbury.

The National Trust

The National Trust for Places of Historic Interest or Natural Beauty is the largest voluntary organisation in Europe. With a membership of 2.9 million and an annual income of £166 million it dwarfs all other voluntary bodies. It was established in 1895 partly as a result of the

▶

Case study continued

campaigning of three key individuals: Miss Octavia Hill, a social worker famous for her pioneering work on housing reform; Sir Robert Hunter, a solicitor who had been a leading light in the Commons Preservation Society; and Canon Hardwicke Rawnsley who lived in and loved the Lake District. Although the Commons Preservation Society had achieved much success, it was essentially a campaigning organisation and was not legally consti-tuted such that it could own land itself. The National Trust, however, was set up as a public company not trading for profit, with powers to acquire land and property. In 1907 its position was further enhanced when an Act of Parliament provided the Trust with a mandate to promote 'the permanent preservation for the benefit of the nation of lands and tenements (including buildings) of beauty or historic interest'. This Act also gave the Trust its unique power to declare its properties 'inalienable', which means that they can never be sold or mortgaged without the approval of the Charity Commission. Furthermore, subsequent legislation in 1946 gave the Trust further powers of appeal if a public authority proposed to take its inalienable land by the use of compulsory purchase.

The Trust began with 100 members and during its early history membership growth was somewhat modest. It was not until 1926 that membership exceeded 1,000 and thereafter membership grew at a steady rate, reaching over 10,000 in 1946 and 100,000 in 1961. It was in the last quarter of the twentieth century, however, that the Trust experienced its most spectacular growth, with member-ship exceeding 1 million in 1980 and 2 million by 1990. The Trust's first property was a gift of 4.5 acres of cliff land in North Wales; its second, the purchase of – for a mere £10 – the fourteenth-century timber-framed Clergy House at Alfriston, East Sussex (National Trust, 1997). Since then, with help from legacies, gifts and public subscription, it has acquired a wide range of properties and today it protects and opens to the public 630 sites which include: 165 historic houses, 19 castles, 48 industrial monuments and mills, 49 churches and chapels, 9 prehistoric and Roman properties, 12 farm buildings, 114 other historic buildings, 160 gardens and 74 landscape/deer parks. It also protects some 272,000 hectares of countryside and 570 miles of coastline (National Trust, 1997). The National Trust is the UK's largest private landowner.

One of the advantages of the Trust is that further legis-lation has made it easier for it to acquire properties. Under the Trust's Country Houses Scheme, dating back to a Parliamentary Act of 1937, a house, with or without its contents, may be presented to the Trust with a financial endowment to maintain it in perpetuity. In return, the donor and his/her family may go on living in the house, subject to public access and measures to retain the essential character of the property. Until the 1960s the Trust acquired virtually any heritage property that it was offered. However, around this time it began to be more selective and established a specific acquisitions policy (Tunbridge, 1981). Although the Trust might be able to acquire properties free of charge, this did not necessarily mean there was no financial burden, as not all properties came with financial endowments to provide for their main-tenance. As a result, the Trust decided that it would need to target its resources on those properties that it deemed to be most important. Part of this thinking involved the Enterprise Neptune Scheme in 1965, when the Trust embarked on a campaign to acquire and protect the most attractive stretches of the British coastline. It already protected 187 miles but its own survey of 1962–63 had concluded that one-third of the coastline of England and Wales was 'of outstanding natural beauty and worthy of permanent preservation'. Enterprise Neptune enabled £25 million to be raised and, through this, some 570 miles of unspoilt coastline is now protected from development and permanently available to the public.

The Trust came into being, like many voluntary organ-isations, because a small group of people believed that a problem existed which neither the private nor public sectors were willing or able to address. In fact, in this particular case, the problem, resulting from unchecked industrial and urban development, was actually being caused by the private sector. The Trust is thus a classic example of a *principle* organisation (see p. 239) involving both leisure and environmental concerns. In the late nineteenth century the idea that government should adopt an interventionist policy to protect landscape and other heritage resources was not part of prevailing political thought. However, government was certainly keen, almost from the start, to support the National Trust in its work and throughout the Trust's history government has seen it as a particularly important and helpful body. While the Trust clearly benefits from its charitable status and from other tax benefits that government allows, it has in addition managed to acquire a substantial amount of financial and other resources to protect what many would regard as 'national treasures'. Figure 11.1 illustrates the

▶

Case study continued

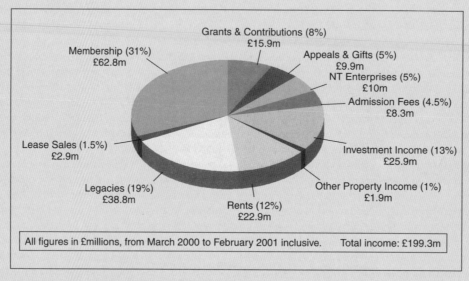

Membership (31%)
£62.8m

Grants & Contributions (8%)
£15.9m

Appeals & Gifts (5%)
£9.9m

NT Enterprises (5%)
£10m

Admission Fees (4.5%)
£8.3m

Investment Income (13%)
£25.9m

Lease Sales (1.5%)
£2.9m

Other Property Income (1%)
£1.9m

Legacies (19%)
£38.8m

Rents (12%)
£22.9m

All figures in £millions, from March 2000 to February 2001 inclusive.   Total income: £199.3m

Figure 11.1   Sources of National Trust income, 2000/1

Source: National Trust (2001), *The National Trust: Trust Facts*, www.nationaltrust.org.uk/learning, London: National Trust.

various forms of income that the Trust is able to attract and, if such an organisation did not exist, government would no doubt have to find such finance from the taxpayer. Furthermore, the Trust also relies on the support of over 35,000 volunteers.

As might be expected from its size, the Trust requires a large organisation to run its operations. In addition to the volunteers, it also employs 4,000 staff and the day-to-day administration is organised through a head office and 11 regional offices covering England, Wales and Northern Ireland. Policy is determined by the Trust's council, half of whose 52 members are nominated by institutions such as the British Museum, the Ramblers Association and the Royal Horticultural Society, and half elected by Trust members at their annual general meeting (National Trust, 1997). The full organisational structure of the Trust's committees and its head office operations are illustrated in Figures 11.2 and 11.3 respectively and the size and complexity of its work is clearly highlighted. This is further reflected in Figure 11.4, which shows the various areas of expenditure.

The overall significance of the National Trust for leisure is enormous and its operations provide opportu-

nities for a great many different forms of leisure. Many forms of countryside recreation are in some way catered for by the Trust, either in terms of specific sites or as a result of the large areas of rural landscape that it protects. It played a prominent role in the campaign for national parks and also in the 'Countryside in 1970' conferences and their subsequent influence on the 1968 Countryside Act. It has also been instrumental in developing rural tourism, not just through its rural attractions and scenery, but also through its accommodation and hospitality operations. The Trust has a wide variety of holiday cottages and also over 2,500 staff are employed in its catering operations during the peak season. Finally, given the nature of some of its properties, the Trust also makes a significant contribution to the arts.

Polo Farm sports club

Polo Farm is a leading private sports club situated just outside Canterbury in south-east England and is home to Canterbury Men's and Ladies' Hockey Clubs, Canterbury Lawn Tennis Club, Canterbury Cricket Club and Chartham Hatch Croquet Club. Although not the smallest of voluntary organisations, and therefore not

Case study continued

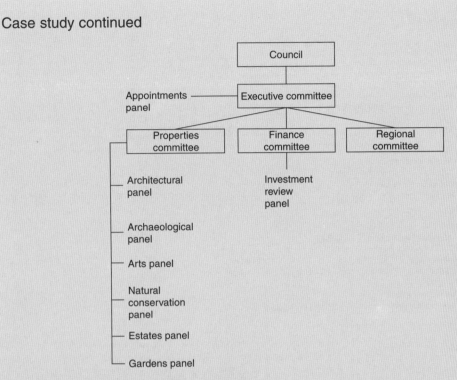

Figure 11.2   National Trust committee structure

Source: National Trust (1997), *The National Trust Education: Notes for students*, London: National Trust.

Note: The National Trust committee has since restructured.

representing the ultimate contrast to the National Trust, it is nevertheless a useful case study as it illustrates voluntary effort providing for a different form of leisure at the local level.

The club was established in 1980 at its current location, although the individual sports clubs are of much older foundation. The Men's Hockey Club, for example, which will form the principal focus of this case study, was formed in 1901 and for the first forty years or so of its existence did not have a pitch of its own and had to use various locations around Canterbury, with no pavilion or clubhouse. The modern Club re-formed after the Second World War, with fourteen members present. Funds were raised through monthly dances held in local hotels, together with club suppers, and the Falstaff Hotel was used as the Club's headquarters, although there was still no changing room available. In 1952 the Club leased a pitch from Canterbury City Council on land reclaimed from an old rubbish tip, but the playing surface was

poor due to ground settlement. Eventually a Nissen hut was purchased in the early 50s for changing accommodation, but for years the playing surface remained poor and required frequent levelling. Gradually the playing strength of the Club improved and finances increased so that by 1960 four or five sides were playing on a regular basis. In the early 60s the Club made a move towards improving the pavilion facilities with a building extension, which included social facilities and a bar. The pitches, however, remained in a very poor condition with frequent cancellations; nevertheless, by the mid 60s Canterbury was one of the top four or five clubs in East Kent, with several players getting county representation. The future remained uncertain because the playing field had been obtained on a twenty-one-year lease and there was little security of tenure beyond that date. Consequently, in the early 70s the Club began looking for alternative locations and eventually Polo Farm was purchased with the aid of a Sports Council grant,

▶

Case study continued

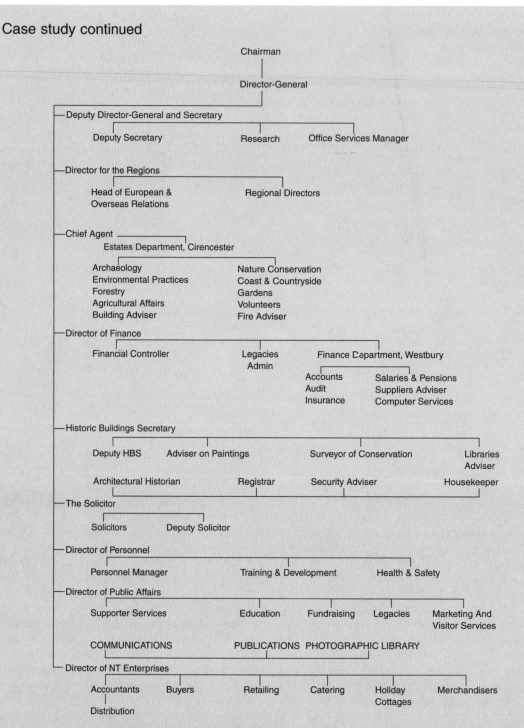

Figure 11.3 National Trust Head Office organisation

Source: National Trust (1997), *The National Trust Education: Notes for students*, London: National Trust.

Note: The National Trust Head Office has since restructured.

►

Case study continued

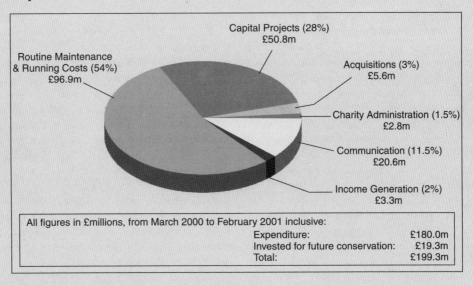

Routine Maintenance & Running Costs (54%) £96.9m

Capital Projects (28%) £50.8m

Acquisitions (3%) £5.6m

Charity Administration (1.5%) £2.8m

Communication (11.5%) £20.6m

Income Generation (2%) £3.3m

All figures in £millions, from March 2000 to February 2001 inclusive:

Expenditure:	£180.0m
Invested for future conservation:	£19.3m
Total:	£199.3m

Figure 11.4   National Trust expenditure, 2000/1

Source: National Trust (2001), *The National : Trust Facts*, www.nationaltrust.org.uk/learning, London: National Trust.

together with substantial loans from players and an intensive period of fund-raising.

Since moving to Polo Farm in 1980, substantial improvements and expansion have occurred. The first year at Polo saw the beginning of mini-hockey for ten- to fourteen-year-olds, with more than fifty youngsters attending, as well as the first Easter Festival, which continues today. In 1986 Polo Farm became only the second club in the country to own its own artificial pitch, a facility costing £160,000, and this enabled the Club to host county games as well as the Hockey Association semi-finals. During this time the First XI had been growing in strength and moving up the Kent leagues into the regional leagues and eventually into the national league. In 1992 the artificial surface was improved and a second artificial pitch was added at a total cost of £290,000. The First XI was now becoming one of the strongest clubs in the country, finishing top of the Premier League in 1998, and throughout the 90s a flourishing youth section was developed. In 1999 the Club's facilities were further improved with the opening of a water-based hockey pitch, complete with a powerful modern floodlighting system, at a cost of approximately £500,000, a sum raised through Lottery money

together with help from sponsorship and playing membership.

Like most voluntary organisations, the Club was formed by a small group of individuals to enable their particular interest to be pursued but has expanded to embrace wider aims. Not only does the Club provide sporting opportunities involving state of the art facilities for an expanded membership (in 2001 the men's hockey section had approximately 200 members), but it also makes its playing fields available to schools at a discounted rate and provides coaching. Five quality coaches are employed with the help of limited sponsorship and the youth coaching programme has clearly contributed to the success of school and club youth sides in area and national competition. In addition, its success has also allowed wider recreational benefits in the form of various social facilities and the development of a spectator sport, as playing in the national league has meant that its games attract a significant spectator element. Furthermore, its elite players, especially its former ones, are able to provide coaching, leadership and umpire resources and thus the Club provides an additional role, allowing what is entirely an amateur sport to prosper.

▶

Case study continued

As might be expected, funding comes from a variety of sources including membership subscriptions and match fees of playing members, sponsorship, fund-raising events and fees charged for coaching and use of facilities by non-members. In more recent times, however, as with many other voluntary groups, the Club has been able to obtain government funding, and especially that from the Lottery. It was a Sports Council grant that enabled the original purchase of Polo Farm itself and, more recently, Lottery funding has enabled the various facility improvements to take place, with more planned for the future. As mentioned earlier in the chapter, central government is keen to support those voluntary organisations that undertake roles which comply with its own aims. The National Trust was a good example of such an organisation and so are many sports clubs. Polo Farm, with its cricket and tennis as well as hockey facilities, and its commitment to sports development in the locality, is clearly contributing to the achievement of the government's sports strategy to widen participation and thus must be viewed as an obvious candidate for Lottery funding (see Chapter 8).

Another key issue affecting various voluntary organisations that is clearly illustrated by Polo Farm concerns the problems of coping with growth. Those voluntary groups and clubs that remain small can operate entirely on voluntary effort but organisations that expand beyond a certain size, especially those which embrace wider, possibly philanthropic, concerns, may find relying on voluntary effort alone becomes a struggle and paid staff may need to be employed. In 2001 Polo Farm Sports Club decided that it had reached this position and appointed a manager, to be part-time in the first instance.

The transitional period through which voluntary groups pass as they make this change can be problematical and fraught with tensions. For some members, the idea of becoming more professional and operating in a more businesslike way conflicts with the notion of volunteerism and may challenge the original idea of a members' club. For others, however, the volume of work involved in looking after members' needs, managing budgets and facilities, and the increasingly onerous paperwork associated with Lottery and other funding bids, makes the appointment of full-time staff inevitable. The proposed change at Polo Farm clearly involved much discussion on this issue, with members concerned that they would still retain control and that voluntary effort would remain important. In this regard, a full audit of club tasks was made to determine what would be undertaken by the manager and what should still be done by the members.

Unlike the National Trust, which operates almost as a semi-public agency pursuing broad aims of national significance, Polo Farm still remains essentially a local club, relying primarily on voluntary effort and with its principal aim being that of pursuing the interests of its members. In this way it provides sporting opportunities for several hundred people who might otherwise not be able to pursue their interest. But it is clear that Polo Farm does not merely provide for its own members, important though this is. In recent times its role has expanded to provide facilities to a wider population, as well as helping the broader development of its various sports, and it has plans to extend this still further with a bid to the English Hockey Association to establish a Regional Hockey Academy and, possibly in the longer term, similar academies for its other sports.

● ● ● ● Conclusions

This chapter has examined the nature and role of the voluntary sector and has shown how a great variety of voluntary organisations have developed to play a substantial role in the provision of leisure opportunities. Some organisations, especially in the areas of sport and countryside recreation, play a crucial role in the provision and management of facilities and other physical resources; some fulfil important roles in the organisation of particular pursuits and some play an important role in lobbying for funding and other needs, especially from government. While most, if not all, groups exist to provide benefits for their own members, some organisations play a much wider role in the provision of leisure opportunities for the public at large, and it is for this reason that many are encouraged and supported by government. The voluntary sector should not, therefore, be viewed in isolation, as it often works in partnership with the other sectors.

Questions

1 Define 'voluntary group' and show how the voluntary sector differs from the public and commercial sectors in leisure provision.

2 Examine the reasons for the origins and expansion of voluntary leisure organisations.

3 Discuss the different roles that voluntary leisure organisations fulfil.

4 To what extent are voluntary leisure organisations regarded as helpful and unhelpful by the public sector?

5 How far do you agree that volunteering can be a leisure pursuit in itself?

References

British Trust for Conservation Volunteers (2002) *Conservation Holidays: Your Chance to Change the World*, Wallingford: BTCV.

Cross, G. (1990) *A Social History of Leisure Since 1600*, State College, PA: Venture Publishing.

Cunningham, H. (1975) *Leisure in the Industrial Revolution, c. 1780–1880*, London: Croom Helm.

Department of National Heritage (1995) *Sport: Raising the Game*, London: HMSO.

Dower, M. (1977) 'The promise – for whom have we aimed to provide, and how was it to be achieved?' *Countryside for All?* CRRAG conference proceedings, Cheltenham: Countryside Commission.

Dower, M., Rapoport, R., Strelitz, Z. and Kew, S. (1981) *Leisure Provision and People's Needs: Stage II Report*, London: Dartington Amenity Research Trust/Institute for Family and Environmental Research.

Dwyer, J. and Hodge, I. (1996) *Countryside in Trust: Land Management by Conservation, Amenity and Recreation Organisations*, Chichester: Wiley.

Elson, M. (1986) *Green Belts: Conflict Mediation in the Urban Fringe*, London: Heinemann.

General Household Survey (1996)

Glyptis, S. (1991) *Countryside Recreation*, Harlow: Longman/ILAM.

Gratton, C. and Taylor, P. (1985) *Sport and Recreation: An Economic Analysis*, London: Spon.

Gratton, C. and Kokolakakis, T. (1997) 'Show of hands', *Leisure Management*, October, supplement, p. 11.

Gratton, C., Nichols, G., Shiblis, R. and Taylor, P. (1997) *Valuing Volunteers in UK Sport*, London: Sports Council (cited in Torkildsen, 1999).

Harrison, C. (1991) *Countryside Recreation in a Changing Society*, London: TMS Partnership.

Henry, I. (1993) *The Politics of Leisure Policy*, London: Macmillan.

Horne, J., Tomlinson, A. and Whannel, G. (1999) *Understanding Sport: An Introduction to the Sociological and Cultural Analysis of Sport*, London: Spon.

Limb, M. (1986) 'Community involvement in leisure provision', in Coalter, F. (ed.) *The*

Politics of Leisure, Brighton: Leisure Studies Association.

Lowe, P. and Goyder, J. (1983) *Environmental Groups in Politics*, London: George Allen and Unwin.

MacEwen, M. and MacEwen, A. (1987) *Greenprints for the Countryside? The Story of Britain's National Parks*, London: George Allen and Unwin.

Marston Vale Community Forest (1995) *Forest Plan*, MVCF.

Mennell, S. (1979) 'Theoretical considerations on cultural needs', *Sociology*, vol. 13, no. 2.

National Trust (1997) *The National Trust Education: Notes for Students*, London: National Trust.

National Trust (2002) *Working Holidays: 35th Anniversary*, Cirencester: Centurion.

Tomlinson, A. (1979) *Leisure and the Role of Clubs and Voluntary Groups*, Sports Council/SSRC.

Torkildsen, G. (1999) *Leisure and Recreation Management*, London: Spon.

Tunbridge, J.E. (1981) 'Conservation trusts as geographic agents: their impact upon landscape, townscape and land use', Transactions of the Institute of British Geographers, NS vol. 6, no.1, pp. 104–125.

Turner, R., Miller, G. and Gilbert, D. (2001) 'The role of UK charities and the tourism industry', *Tourism Management*, 22, pp. 463–72.

Further reading

A comprehensive and detailed coverage of the voluntary sector in the leisure field can be found in Torkildsen's *Leisure and Recreation Management*.

A more theoretical perspective can be found in Gratton and Taylor's *Sport and Recreation: An Economic Analysis* and Henry's *The Politics of Leisure Policy*.

A comprehensive account of the voluntary sector as a whole is provided by C. Pharoah and M. Smerdon's (1998) edited collection *Dimensions of the Voluntary Sector: Key Facts, Figures and Trends*, West Malling: Charities Aid Foundation.

Useful websites

www.charitynet.org
www.nationaltrust.co.uk
www.rspb.org.uk/

Chapter 12 ● ● ● ●

Education and leisure

Previous chapters in Part Two of this book have examined varies aspects and structures that affect provision for leisure. One final aspect that plays a major role in influencing provision is education. Education and leisure are undeniably and unavoidably intertwined. This at times is an uneasy marriage, formed through the interplay of different yet interlinked factors, which results in partnerships and services of different types.

Objectives

To:

- *examine the concept of education for leisure*

- *analyse education as a leisure form*

- *assess the opportunities for education through leisure*

- *explore dual use and joint provision schemes.*

●●●● Education for leisure

Education for leisure is not a modern phenomenon. Philosophers such as Aristotle, Plato and Socrates identified it as an essential part of an individual's education. However, as leisure has increasingly become a more integral and important part of modern living, the importance of being equipped to make wise use of our leisure time has been increasingly recognised. In the same way that we need vocational skills development to be effective during work time, leisure skills development is necessary for the effective use of our leisure time.

Peterson and Gunn (1984, cited in Graefe and Parker, 1987, p. 57) defined leisure education as 'a broad category of services that focus on the development and acquisition of various leisure related skills, attitudes and knowledge'. At the heart of the leisure education process is the development of relevant skills and knowledge that allow individuals to meet the needs of society and self through their effective use of leisure. Skilled leisure participants have better prospects for self-fulfilment and social integration through their use of leisure. Effective leisure education can facilitate quality of life improvements for the individual, for the local community and for society as a whole. Mundy and Odum (1976, cited in Graefe and Parker, 1987, p. 57) recognise this when they define leisure education as 'a total development process through which individuals develop an understanding of self, leisure and the relationship of leisure to their own lifestyles and the fabric of society'.

Effective leisure education needs to incorporate the development of a number of different elements:

(i) *A knowledge of specific games/craft skills.* This is perhaps the most obvious aspect of leisure education and facilitates basic participation in key leisure activities. Instruction, for instance, on the bowling action used in cricket or the mixing of basic colours in painting.

(ii) *A knowledge of leisure opportunities.* Access to leisure is intrinsically linked to education. Knowledge of a leisure opportunity is a key factor in participation. Put at its simplest, a total ignorance of the existence of a particular leisure activity ensures you will never participate in that activity.

(iii) *A knowledge of leisure boundaries.* A recognition of the effects of individual leisure lifestyles on the community within which leisure is pursued results in an individual being able to make an informed choice as to the social acceptability and appropriate context for specific leisure behaviours. This does not necessarily mean that an individual will automatically choose to allow some form of social control to be exercised upon their leisure lifestyle, but it does mean that they are aware of the consequences of the choices they make. An individual may still choose to use recreational drugs but will be aware that a consequence of this may be finding themselves charged with an illegal act.

(iv) *A knowledge of leisure cultures.* It is important that leisure education not only deals with an awareness of leisure opportunities but also addresses the subculture that forms an integral part of participation in specific leisure activities. It is essential that the education process provides information on the behavioural norms of the group pursuing a specific form of leisure. This allows more immediate access to a leisure activity through an ability to recognise and adapt to the relevant group subculture involved. The cultural norms, for example, of those groups participating in polo, golf, darts and football are very different.

The importance of a knowledge of the cultural norms for leisure participation is not confined to the sporting arena. A lack of appropriate education can prove a barrier to participation in many leisure spheres including the arts. A recent discussion with a close friend, who is now retired from teaching, highlighted the extent to which subcultures can restrict participation. As part of the teaching programme in a Cambridge secondary school, a theatre trip was proposed as the culmination of a term's work for one of the year groups. Groans and general dissent from the pupils greeted this suggestion. Surprised at the reaction that was provoked, the teaching staff enquired further.

When asked about their reluctance, the pupils responded by saying that 'the theatre wasn't for the likes of them and they knew they wouldn't enjoy it'. Further probing established that, in the main, those who were not happy with the theatre trip had never actually visited a theatre. After much discussion it was established that the pupils' reluctance stemmed from a fear that arose from their lack of knowledge of the required protocol for participation in this leisure form. Pupils were concerned about being made to look foolish because they were unsure how to dress and how to behave at the theatre. Following more in-depth discussion about the expectations in terms of dress code and behaviour, most pupils were persuaded to give the theatre visit a try. This first visit was so successful that it progressed into a termly event and a long-standing school tradition, not forgetting the education process prior to visits taking place.

The education for leisure process, regardless of the context in which it occurs, needs to take an holistic approach and incorporate all of the above elements in order to facilitate maximum fulfilment from participation. This process of education for leisure must place the basic skills required for the various forms of leisure in a wider lifestyle context. It needs to equip individuals with an ability to recognise the potential benefits to quality of life available through leisure participation, and also place them in a position to access their desired leisure pursuits and incorporate these into their own lifestyles.

Approaches to education for leisure

The way in which such knowledge and skills are acquired and the implementation of an integrated and comprehensive system of education have largely been neglected in the UK. The two key formal institutional contexts for such education are the schools system and leisure services. There can, however, also be no doubt that other institutions make a significant input, including the family and the commercial (see Chapter 10) and voluntary sectors (see Chapter 11).

There are two key approaches to education for leisure – curriculum and systems approaches. The first contemporary curriculum model of leisure education was developed in Florida, with the support of the State Department of Education (Mundy, 1975 cited in Graefe and Parker, 1987, p. 58). This model is known as the Scope and Sequence of Leisure Education and was based on a sequence of 107 objectives set within the following six categories:

1 Self-awareness
2 Leisure awareness
3 Attitudes
4 Decision making
5 Social interaction
6 Leisure activity skills.

In recognition of the life-long learning process necessary for leisure, these learning objectives cover pre-kindergarten to retirement. While incorporating the period an individual spends in formal education, it did not confine itself to this period.

In addition to such curriculum-based models, the Systems Model of Education has been developed, which identifies five major components at the core of programme design. These are:

1 Leisure awareness
2 Self-awareness
3 Decision making
4 Leisure skills
5 Social interaction.

This model is implemented by dividing each of these components into smaller sections, each of which have input, process and output statements (Mundy, 1976 cited in Graefe and Parker, 1987, p. 58).

Mundy (1976) developed upon the above approaches, combining them to produce a step-by-step guide that provides 'an objective, the focus or content of the objective, and the specific learning experience, activities and work sheets'. In practice most of the practical implementation of education for leisure within the education system or leisure services actually takes this approach and incorporates both curriculum and systems approaches.

The family

The life-long process of education for leisure usually starts with the family. Family background can prove both restrictive and advantageous. The leisure lifestyles of family members, both nuclear and extended, can be highly influential, as can those of individuals found within the family's social network. The family and its social network can provide ready access to a range of leisure pursuits and the required knowledge for effective participation. On the other hand, this network may be somewhat isolated from a whole range of other activities. The level of participation, the time for participation and the resources available to family members form the basis for the leisure education, particularly of its pre-school members, and can have a lasting impact on the leisure lifestyles of family members.

In addition, family background influences the type of formal education an individual receives. Not only does family background determine the type of school attended, but also the attitude of the child to school. This will either limit or facilitate the education process. Material resources available to the family may also affect the possibility of leisure education through participation in extra-curricular activities or the further development of skills acquired in school through membership of a leisure club. (See Chapter 4 for further details on the family and leisure lifestyles.)

The education system

Formal education systems make an important contribution to leisure education and 'while largely concerned with the world of work and necessity, have increasingly begun to pay attention to leisure and its uses' (Godbey, 1994, p. 256). Their contribution to leisure education is not simply curricula or extra-curricula based. This sector may provide the context for both intentional and unintentional links between leisure and education (Sessoms and Henderson, 1994).

Education within the formal system can have latent effects that are leisure based, particularly in relation to the use of space and free time. Compulsory education can provide leisure space and direct access to leisure companions, as exemplified by the groups of girls and boys often found smoking in school toilets or cloakrooms and/or discussing pop music, pop stars and potential partners during break-times (McCabe, 1981, cited in OU, 1984, p. 7) Some pupils will also engineer and manipulate the formal time in a way that becomes leisure based – 'having a laugh at the back of class with mates'. Such unintentional links may mean that school simply provides a place or a focus for leisure; a place for meeting friends and talking about common interests.

The formal education sector is, nevertheless, an important place for the more formal teaching of key leisure skills. Most schools teach a range of subjects that may be considered vocational but may equally be regarded by an individual, either at the time and/or in the future, as leisure. This is particularly obvious in subjects like home economics, music, physical education and some of the craft subjects. The extent to which both the vocational and leisure aspects of education are present will be dependent on the attitude of the individual and the teaching style adopted.

Schools and colleges, for obvious reasons, tend to concentrate on specific skills relating to the core curriculum and to be curriculum centred as opposed to lifestyle focused. Activities, therefore, often ignore the essential social and culture knowledge required if someone is to progress to use arts, crafts and sports skills outside the formal education system. This is particularly clear where there is a tradition of subjects like crafts, physical education and home economics being regarded as subjects of primary importance for the pupils of lower academic ability. This often places the emphasis within these subjects on education for the workplace, as opposed to a more holistic approach that encompasses a broader education based on self-fulfillment in work and leisure.

The broad education potential of subjects like physical education (see Parry, 1988) and music may also be limited by an approach that is focused on a few exceptional athletes and musicians and on competition performance or examination targets. A tendency for staff to concentrate on levels of performance and achievement, rather than enjoyment of participation, can lead to a perception that certain activities are meant for pursuit by a talented few rather than for the more widespread enjoyment by all those interested in taking part. It is precisely such an approach that often results in the alienation of pupils from certain leisure activities and leads to avoidance of them as adults. Perceptions of leisure activities are developed or reinforced by a school's approach and commitment to them.

Competition for, and allocation of, resources between departments such as music, performing arts and physical education can reinforce an internally perceived hierarchy within the institution, and more widely within society. This can lead to pupil perceptions of what are the 'better/higher' leisure forms. The approach of the formal sector needs to be carefully balanced and needs to address obvious pitfalls that can affect the participation of pupils not just while they are within the formal system, but also once they are outside it.

The effects of pupils failing examinations in areas that may form part of their leisure lifestyles can further complicate the lack of an holistic approach to certain subjects. This has become increasingly possible with recent moves to formalise and examine a wider range of arts, crafts and physical education. This may have aided in the development of the leisure profession and further recognition of the importance of leisure, but there is a need for vigilance and caution around the potential problems that may arise in relation to an individual's leisure lifestyle and leisure education. To fail an examination in an area that incorporates activities which are currently or may in the future be pursued as leisure can mean that this activity is given up or never explored in a non-academic context. Human nature means that we have a tendency to avoid areas where we are likely to experience negative feedback. The negative feedback, therefore, of examination failure may mean that certain activities are avoided thereafter.

There is a need for a balanced approach to the work ethic, the leisure ethic and the quality of life issues within compulsory education. This is not easy to achieve and is profoundly affected by the political environment of the day. Governments have, for instance, during times of increased youth unemployment moved to a stronger emphasis on education for leisure within the curriculum and a less strong emphasis on purely vocational skills. This was particularly evident in the late 1980s and early 1990s. This period saw an attempt by government to cement society by replacing the work ethic with a leisure ethic, especially through the provision of leisure courses for the long-term unemployed, as well as a change in focus in the formal education curriculum. This has more recently been reversed as the unemployment situation has improved and there has been an increasing emphasis on education standards relating to vocational objectives. The creation of the Department of Education and Employment (now the Department of Education and Skills) from the previously separate departments signified this change in emphasis.

Current government emphasis on basic literacy and numeracy skills, and core-curricular targets, seems to leave little room for issues such as leisure education. There is little direct evidence of attention to the broader curriculum within the current environment of material and human resource limitations – a context that tends to draw the system towards core vocational rather than wider life skills. The education system today clearly recognises the potential benefits of studying leisure and recreation-based subjects, as indicated in recent decades by its increasing support with specialist staff. The place of such subjects and the balance of the overall curriculum are far less clearly supportive of a more holistic lifestyle approach to education. It is indeed difficult to ascertain whether the schools system and/or government views the broader leisure education process as an area of responsibility to be recognised, at least in part, as its own. Such an approach and lack of clarity may again lead to criticisms such as those of Jenkins and Sherman prior to the 1980s focus on leisure education:

> our education system has singly failed to provide people with enough knowledge to make their own choices concerning leisure activities. It has seen its function in a totally different light. But in the same way that the higher levels of education widen people's job options, leisure should be one main factor in both the primary and secondary systems. Education, both conventional and life-long, will have a great part to play in the future, but there will have to be a re-appraisal of its overall role. (Jenkins and Sherman, 1979, p. 12, cited in OU study unit, 1984, p. 21)

Such a reappraisal should be avoided as a reactive technique applied in a climate, for example, of rising unemployment or health problems that may result in a focus on leisure education during specific periods. A more proactive and holistic quality-of-life and long-term view that incorporates such considerations alongside equipping individuals with the ability to achieve greater self-fulfillment, social integration and healthier, more balanced lifestyles is needed.

Such an approach requires attention to the wider educational context and environment as well as the curriculum and its delivery. As identified by Godbey (1994, p. 262), a balanced curriculum needs to be supported by a system that recognises the individual's need for play within the learning process, that is, the development of a leisure ethic alongside a work ethic. This means providing times that are unstructured and in which pupils exercise the choice and self-discipline that facilitates relaxation, play and fun and hence re-creation from work. School design, common areas and timetables often do not reflect the recognition of the need for a work hard, play hard philosophy.

The postmodernist would call for a system that goes one step further than Godbey and moves away from a leisure and work ethic balance to an approach that strives towards 'leisure as a state of existence'. This would mean moving from a system where there is an emphasis on compulsion and discipline to one of intrigue, self-discipline and an enjoyment of the learning process itself. This is not excluded from Godbey's system but is ultimately dependent on the attitude of the individual. To facilitate this, however, there needs to be room for a more creative and less regimented approach to education than many feel is currently allowed for.

Achieving a balanced approach that incorporates effective leisure education is not only an issue for compulsory education. While higher education may provide time for, and exposure to, a wider range of leisure skills and environments, there are questions to be asked of the system in relation to a broader intellectual development. Does the system encourage intellectual growth and a freedom of exploration that allows individuals to engage with the world as a whole rather than simply with the world of work? A university education must surely strive to educate in a way that does more than simply prepare individuals for the world of work; it should prepare them to ask the bigger questions in relation to what is worthwhile and important, having met their basic material needs. In recent years, however, many higher education courses have moved away from what may be regarded as a more traditional academic approach based on educating the whole person to a more vocational training-centred approach.

Nevertheless, despite any criticisms that may be made of the formal education sector it is clear that it makes an important contribution to the leisure education process. There are clear correlations between leisure lifestyle and levels of education. Individuals who remain within formal education for longer tend to participate in a wider range of leisure activities and activity types that differ from those of the early leaver. The higher an individual's level of education, the greater the tendency for that individual to be involved in a wider range of leisure pursuits. Those who have taken higher education courses are 'more likely to participate in most forms of outdoor recreation, sports, high culture, tourism, continuing education, reading and volunteer activities' (Godbey, 1994, p. 272). This is in part linked to the tendency to have more disposable income for leisure due to higher paid employment, but it is also linked with greater education for leisure through access to a wider range of opportunities, leisure companions and environments.

Leisure providers

While education for leisure may be recognised as a necessary part of compulsory education, the development of leisure lifestyles is the primary aim of the recreation and leisure sector. This sector, therefore, has an inevitable interest and input into the leisure education process. A vast amount of resources are provided for leisure and recreation in the UK through the combined efforts of the public, private and voluntary sectors (see Chapters 9–11 for further details). This incorporates a massive range of facilities including national parks, urban parks, lakes, rivers, sports and arts facilities, libraries, museums, city farms, theme parks, theatres, pubs, clubs, casinos, children's play areas and adult education. While different providers may have different motives for provision – from public recreation and social provision through to a pure profit motive – all are dependent on the participation of their target audiences for success. All are, therefore, dependent upon that audience being or at least feeling they are sufficiently informed/educated to participate or to seek information that will facilitate participation. Education for leisure is an essential investment for all providers if they are to maximise profit, whether this is an investment in the social balance sheet of a community or essential pump-priming for a healthy end-of-year balance sheet. Simply providing a facility will not ensure its use.

There are increasing attempts to provide more effective leisure information systems that assist individuals in identifying leisure opportunities, including an increasing range of leisure guides, telephone hotlines and even Internet sites. The tourist industry now provides lectures to support visits to some sites, and as part of certain cruise packages, in order to enhance the visitor experience. Taster sessions in the sports and adult education arenas have also gone some way to providing a wider range of skills training to facilitate access and increased participation in both sport and the arts. In some areas, for instance in weight-training and weightlifting, the provision of introductory sessions and courses has been promoted by a need to avoid litigation and protect participants from injury. However, there is still little available in terms of cultural information required for access to the clubs and societies within the different leisure areas.

Provision within this sector for leisure education occurs within a policy framework and network that is no more comprehensive than is the case in the education sector. It is therefore not surprising that, when we then move to look at the co-operation between these two sectors, successful projects are not as numerous as logic might lead us to expect. Such links and co-operation are particularly important when we are dealing with young people, especially school leavers. This group is one of the key targets for local authority Sports Development projects because of the dramatic decrease in sports participation when individuals leave compulsory education. It is important that a bridge is provided between provision within the school through the curricular and extra-curricular activities and out-of-school and post-school provision. Links between schooling and other forms of provision need to be more effectively built if the needs of young people are to be met. Opportunities to raise the level of awareness of young people, to encourage sports participation and an active lifestyle that allows self-fulfillment need to be sought by both sectors. One of the most effective ways of providing such links is through dual use and joint provision schemes, which involve partnerships between the leisure and education sectors (see below p. 272). These links are not only relevant in sports provision but also across the whole range of leisure activities.

An holistic approach

Mundy and Odum (1979, cited in Godbey, 1994, pp. 258–9) provide a clear outline of what leisure education encompasses; i.e. leisure education is:

● A total movement to enable an individual to enhance the quality of his or her life in leisure.

- A process to enable the individual to identify and clarify his or her own leisure values and goals.
- An approach to enable an individual to enhance the quality of his or her life during leisure.
- Deciding for oneself what place leisure has in [one's] life.
- Coming to know oneself in relation to leisure.
- A lifelong, continuous process encompassing pre-kindergarten through retirement years.
- Relating to one's needs, values and capabilities of leisure experiences.
- Increasing the individual's options for satisfying quality experiences in leisure.
- A process whereby the individual determines his or her own leisure behaviour and evaluates the long- and short-range outcomes of his or her behaviour in relation to his or her goals.
- A movement in which the multiplicity of disciplines and service systems have a role and responsibility.

If all of these elements are to be addressed, leisure education needs to be placed more firmly within a comprehensive policy framework that recognises all the key players within this education process. Resourcing and support need to be provided in a form that facilitates a co-operative and complementary approach and allows all parties to participate fully.

This means that leisure education taking place within formal education must go beyond simply being regarded as yet another subject to be taught in the form of a curriculum course or a series of courses. It also means moving beyond an approach that simply uses leisure examples in core subjects or relates all core subjects to leisure. Leisure education needs to be about much more than this. In addition, a more holistic and creative approach within formal education needs to be supported by a stronger relationship between education specialists and leisure providers at all levels. Education for leisure, as identified by Brightbill (1960, cited in Godbey, 1994, p. 257), is not about fulfilling a curriculum requirement or about regimenting leisure and ensuring the use of facilities such as libraries, parks and sports centres.

At its most effective, leisure education is about equipping an individual to actively participate in their own leisure education and the modelling of a personal leisure lifestyle throughout the life cycle. Due to changes in leisure values with maturity, no one party can possibly be expected to equip an individual with the skills and attitudes that will serve them throughout the whole life cycle. An individual's needs change with physical, social and emotional development. A capacity and confidence to explore and to be creative therefore needs to be developed that allows effective adaptation of the leisure lifestyle alongside life cycle changes.

Equipping people to use their leisure time in a positive and self-fulfilling manner throughout the whole life cycle can, however, only be achieved through a collaborative and comprehensive education system that develops an individual's resourcefulness in developing their own interests and leisure lifestyle. Education for leisure is therefore about a complementary education through home and family, the formal education sector, leisure providers and the community.

Education as leisure

As well as contributing both intentionally and unintentionally to the development of an effective leisure lifestyle, education may itself be a form of leisure. Indeed education has historically been regarded as a key pursuit of the 'leisure' classes and an important leisure activity (see Chapter 1 for a discussion on rational recreation). Haywood *et al.* (1995, p. 81) view 'education' as a leisure activity when it is pursued without an element of compulsion. Evening and day classes that are pursued out of free choice are highlighted as leisure experiences.

Sports and arts and crafts classes that are taught as part of compulsory education are seen as falling outside this definition of leisure because of the absence of freedom of choice for the student participant. The reality of this situation is, however, more complex than it might first appear. While certain activities may be a compulsory part of the curriculum, given a free choice some students may still decide to participate in these activities. The student participant may regard such activities as leisure whether or not they are compulsory. The definition of a leisure activity in this instance is, however, being determined by the student using different parameters from those above. The activity is regarded as leisure because of their attitude to it and the pleasure they derive from it, not because there is no element of compulsion involved (see Chapter 2 for further discussion of leisure definitions).

Regardless of which approach we take, what is common to both is the fact that the reasons behind participant involvement are relevant to whether or not an educational activity is regarded as leisure. Participation in adult education classes, a core area of education as leisure, therefore needs to be explored from a motivational perspective. Adult education classes provide an opportunity to learn new skills or improve on existing skills with the support of an expert in the field. This self-improvement may be undertaken for reasons that are leisure related, vocational or both.

A class may be attended out of mere curiosity for the subject, out of a desire to develop or further develop skills for the pleasure gained from a particular activity or for work-related personal development motives linked to a career change or gaining promotion. Some participants are motivated to attend such courses by the potential for social interaction and the broadening of their social network. The social gatherings and much needed stimulation linked with adult education classes are often a very important part of their attraction and, from the participant's perspective, the reason they regard their attendance as a leisure activity. For many participants their interest in these classes will be more about the process of attending and the presence of classmates than the education process itself. The classes provide an opportunity for getting out and meeting people with similar interests and will often lead to additional social activities arising – for example, a visit to the pub with classmates after the class has finished. Different individuals on the same course may participate for different reasons and regard their participation as a leisure activity for different reasons. There is often enough flexibility in many of the activities, because of the absence of the element of compulsion, to accommodate a wide variety of personal needs and wants.

Classes that at first sight may appear vocational may be taken as leisure-related studies. Someone who enjoys creative writing as a leisure pursuit may take a typing/computer course in order to improve their keyboard skills and enhance their enjoyment of the creative writing process. Others may take examination-based foreign language courses in order to improve a forthcoming foreign holiday and may simply take the examination as a spin-off, a pass mark being regarded simply as an added bonus. Others may simply take the classes and not bother with the examination. More formal OU and part-time degree courses, not just evening and day classes, may also be pursued primarily for leisure. Indeed, there are a significant number of retired people, especially with increased early retirement, who pursue full-time degree/education courses for leisure.

Haywood *et al.* (1995, p. 83) identify adult education classes as a particularly attractive and acceptable form of leisure for women, a perception supported by enrolment statistics for such course (Table 12.1).

Evening classes offer an opportunity for 'escape' or time out in an environment that is safe, public and stimulating. They may also be more affordable and perhaps more acceptable than some of the more consumer-based activities such as nightclubs. Such classes take place in a specific time slot, which can make childcare easier to arrange and may be regarded as self-improving, making it more acceptable for a partner to take over domestic responsibilities in such circumstances.

There is an increasingly extensive range of options for participation in education and leisure for both men and women – including sports, cultural studies, arts and crafts, as well as more formal academic subjects – which may or may not be linked to qualifications and examinations. In November 1998, 1.1 million adults enrolled onto adult education classes. Seven out of ten of those who chose to enroll in England chose courses that did not lead to formal qualifications (www.statistics.gov.uk, Department for Education and Skills, National Assembly for Wales, *Social Trends Dataset*, November 1998). Hence, it is clear from these figures that adult education forms an important area of partnership and provision between education and leisure.

Table 12.1 Gender and participation rates in adult education courses

	Course type (000)			
	Academic	*Vocational*	*Other*	*Total*
Male	20.3	57.3	220.6	298.2
Female	47.6	160.3	638.6	846.5

Note: 'Other' includes basic education and general courses, that is, languages, physical education/sport/fitness, practical craft/skills, role education, and other education.

Source: www.statistics.gov.uk and adapted from Department for Education and Skills, National Assembly for Wales, *Social Trends Dataset*, November 1998, as stated by the Department for Education and Skills.

Education through leisure

Leisure activities have a great deal of potential for naturally incorporating learning and the reality is that most forms of leisure involve some form of learning. Early childhood play especially has great potential for naturally incorporating learning, but this potential continues throughout our lifespan:

> Children who have the opportunity for challenging forms of play develop differently from those who receive little stimulation. People who use leisure to engage in challenging experiences develop intellectually in ways in which those who use leisure merely to relax do not. (Godbey, 1994, p. 254)

The way we use our leisure time, therefore, can have an impact on the extent to which we achieve our intellectual potential.

Leisure activities have an important capacity for social education. Sport has been seen as having a role to play in character development and moral education. Sports are often used to teach children about competition and the application of agreed rules. Education in both these areas is important in order to be successful in civil society. It is essential, therefore, that we recognise the role of leisure in such areas and ensure that leisure activities are presented in such a way as to develop preferable traits. We need to ensure, for example, that the presentation of an activity, especially to children, does not encourage excessive valuing of competition or children to be rule-bound. Education through leisure needs to be carefully considered and developed with caution. A well-balanced exposure to a wide range of different leisure pursuits requiring different physical, intellectual and social skills can aid in effective character and social development through the course of an individual's lifetime (see Chapter 2 for further information on play).

Godbey, (1994, pp. 255–6) suggests that not only should learning be carefully incorporated into leisure activities but that the use of leisure time must include an opportunity to learn, to acquire skills and for personal development in order to be particularly pleasurable. He sees there to be mounting evidence that to seek pleasure through entertainment in the absence of an opportunity for learning, skill acquisition and personal growth is actually not very pleasurable. Therefore, if we accept pleasure as an essential part of the definition of leisure then leisure is, by its nature, an educational process.

Csikszentmihalyi (1990, cited in Godbey, 1994, p. 256) seems to be in agreement with Godbey when he states that:

> To fill free time with activities that require concentration, that increase skills, that lead to a development of self, is not the same as killing time by watching television or taking recreational drugs . . . the former leads to growth, while the latter merely serves to keep the mind from unraveling.

While it cannot be denied that much pleasure can be obtained through participation in leisure that incorporates education and personal development, this approach may be seen as denying the re-creative nature of leisure. The important use of leisure for recuperation and relaxation, especially when used in opposition to work that is highly structured and goal directed, seems to be missing from the above approach. It is important to recognise the potential of leisure as an educative process and tool and the pleasure derived from this, but it is also important to recognise that the value of leisure for the individual may lie in other benefits gained from its use.

Educational tourism

Tourist attractions in an environment of increased competition have become increasingly aware of their potential educational value. The educational aspect of a visit to many attractions has been used in promotions to add value, especially for the family and educational visits markets. This is particularly evident in examining the publicity materials of historic buildings, museums, art galleries, zoos, wildlife parks and countryside recreation sites. Education packs and on-site demonstrations and talks are now available for schools, families and individuals at many sites. These include games, quizzes and fact sheets aimed at enhancing both the leisure and educational experiences, alongside more contemporary interpretative techniques that use technology to encourage hands-on experience through interactive exhibits and actors to bring to life historic periods and artifacts (Bloch, 1997).

Magna Science Adventure Centre
The UK's first Science Adventure Centre, opened in South Yorkshire in 2001, is a visitor attraction that markets itself as having all the advantages of a traditional museum combined with the entertainment usually associated with a theme park. It is marketed as an attraction that provides an opportunity for all ages to learn through play. Based in a former steel mill, Magna explores the theme of steel and the four elements of earth, air, fire and water. This attraction is based on involving visitors in a range of interactive challenges. The centre's exhibits provide opportunities such as making a mini-arc furnace, watching a blacksmith at work, taking the controls of an electromagnetic crane, firing a water canon and using water to power a hydrogen rocket. Visitors can also experience a virtual coal mine, operate a JCB, use airwaves to make music and travel through time to learn about the formation of Earth's rocks.

●●●● Dual use and joint provision

The concepts of dual use and joint provision are key approaches to provision and management, that potentially form a mutually beneficial practical relationship between education and leisure.

> Dual Use is the use of leisure facilities by the general public as well as by the particular group for whom the facilities were primarily provided. (Veal *et al.*, 1990, p. 5)

> Joint Provision is where two agencies combine to provide facilities for shared use from the beginning... (Veal *et al.*, 1990, p. 5)

Although dual use facilities have been provided by the armed forces, churches and employers, giving the general public access to facilities provided primarily for their employees, schools and colleges are the premises most often used as dual use. This is also the case with joint provision projects, which most often involve collaboration between a local education authority and the local authority leisure services department. Certainly some of the most successful dual use and joint provision projects have occurred when education authorities have embraced the idea of community access to school sites for recreation.

This collaboration between education and leisure is not a new idea. There is a long history in rural communities of school halls being used by the local community. Henry Morris, while education officer for Cambridgeshire, more formally piloted the idea as the 'village college' in the 1920s. The 'village college' provided education for both adults and children and a centre for leisure for both. A similar idea was also pursued in Leicester in the 1950s through the community school. This was primarily focused on secondary education provision that was widened to provide an education facility for the whole community.

The 1960s then saw the real flurry of activity in this type of provision. This was due to a need for more schools to be built, combined with an increased awareness of the benefits of a joint provision approach and the relative prosperity that allowed for such a building programme. Increased activity continued into the 1970s, supported by government documents in particular emphasising the economic advantages of this approach. These included:

1964 – Department of Education and Science with Ministry of Housing (*Provision of Facilities for Sport*: Joint Circular 11/64: 49/64).
1966 – Ministry of Housing and Local Government Circular 31/66 (*Public Expenditure: Miscellaneous Schemes*).
1970 – Department of Education and Science (*The Chance to Share*: Circular 2/70).
1975 – Department of the Environment White Paper (*Sport and Recreation*).

(Badmin *et al.*, 1988, pp. 46–9; Tancred, 1992, pp. 120–4.)

More recent government documents have also recognised and highlighted the benefits of dual use and joint provision. The 2001 DFES White Paper, *Schools – Achieving Success*, states:

Many schools already recognise the benefits for them and their communities of providing additional services to their pupils, pupils' families and the wider community. Most schools already provide some before and after-school study support; some provide space for sports and arts activities, community group and Internet access, others work closely with other public bodies to provide integrated services such as health services, childcare or adult education. (Section 8.16)

This document also carries statements of support and commitment to such schemes through changes in legislation and attention to appropriate building design:

We shall legislate to make sure that there are no barriers to schools developing these innovative approaches. We will establish pilots to test out such 'extended schools' and generate examples of good practice. And where schools have already demonstrated the advantages of this approach we will help them develop further to become Centres of Excellence, celebrate their achievements. (Section 8.16)

Deregulatory proposals – Removing current restrictions on the usage of schools for non-education purposes. (Section 8.5)

We are also working to make sure that school buildings meet the needs of the future. Schools must be a focus for learning for the whole community, accessible to all, with modern and attractive learning facilities for families and people of all ages…We want to design and create school buildings suitable for a transformed and diversified education service. (Section 8.24)

Advantages and disadvantages

Interest in and support for dual use and joint provision projects from a political and management perspective stem from the range of potential benefits from such collaborative provision. These include:

1 Integrated approaches to education and leisure

Such projects provide an opportunity to involve family, school and the wider community in education for leisure. They provide a facility in which the family and the local community can be involved in bridging the gap between school activities and club membership through the use of one key community facility for both. This can, however, have the disadvantage of pupils who have a bad school experience also avoiding the community leisure facilities because of memories linked to that facility.

2 Cost efficiency

The use of one building means less capital spending and shared running costs, which makes more effective use of key resources. The combination of funds from mainstream education, adult education, youth and community projects, as well as the income earned from user fees, can provide a greater range of, and higher-quality, facilities for all parties. This helps to ensure quality leisure and education experiences that provide for a wider range of needs and wants for the whole community. Where the building supports a school and a local community leisure facility this also leads to more effective overall use of the site. School buildings are utilised for less than 40 per cent of their viable time and are utilised at concentrated periods during restricted daytime hours. These hours are not peak leisure time hours. School use is limited in the peak leisure hours of evenings, weekends and holidays.

3 Security

The extended use of dual use/joint provision buildings means that they are left unattended for shorter periods of time, which can prevent some vandalism. There is also some evidence that there is a general decline in anti-social behaviour with such projects. This is because, by their nature, these facilities can provide a key focus for the local community and a stronger sense of ownership.

4 Demand

As the demand for leisure facilities continues to increase, dual use provision is a way of satisfying demand at limited cost to local authorities, especially in rural areas. Also supply-led latent demand can be stimulated by convenient local provision. Increased participation may occur for pupils, staff and their families because of ease of access to facilities.

It is surprising, given the above stated advantages, especially the cost efficiency savings that are highlighted as key advantages in a wide range of research studies and government reports on dual use and joint provision, that such projects are not more numerous. This is in part due to the difficulties of overcoming a range of philosophical and practical management problems, as follows:

i Professional philosophies

There is a need in dual use and joint provision for a strong sense of co-operation and commitment from both education and leisure specialists. This at times means overcoming philosophical differences, especially where there is a commitment by school staff to children being educated in an environment that is free from adult pressures. A strong and more comprehensive government framework that takes an integrated approach to education for leisure and incorporates the benefits of education through leisure would aid such co-operation, especially if such principles were to be incorporated into teacher education and the education and training programmes for the leisure profession.

ii Operational management

If dual use and joint provision schemes are to be effective there are a range of key practical issues that need to be addressed:

(a) Financial arrangements must be worked out in detail, answering basic questions such as who pays for equipment replacement and maintenance.

(b) Clear communication structures must be in place which include agreed complementary administration procedures. For example, who takes facility bookings and how are inappropriate enquiries directed away from or redirected from people such as school secretaries?

(c) Staffing rotas and line management must be clear. How are caretaking and cleaning duties arranged and when do they take place, given the heavy use of the site?

(d) Time allocation for facility use must be clearly prioritised and used to separate user groups where necessary.

(e) Security arrangements must ensure that children are kept safe, especially where there is public access and deliveries during the school day, through the use of a separate entrance and visitors' logs.

(f) Staffing levels, salaries and appointments must be carefully managed, especially where there may be overlapping areas of expertise between physical education and leisure services staff. Resentment can arise where salaries are viewed as not comparable and expertise is not equally respected.

These are all potential problem areas but can be overcome by effective planning, communication and management.

iii Site design and location

Especially in dual use facilities where the original building was only built for one user, usually as an education facility, there is a need for careful consultation, flexibility and compromise in adapting the original site. Primary schools will have basic problems such as toilet and shower sizes and secondary schools are usually located on the outskirts of key centres of population and transport problems need to be overcome.

Dual use and joint provision projects provide the potential for very effective integrated approaches to the potentially beneficial relationships between education and leisure where strong co-operative management and planning teams are supported in pursuing these goals (Badmin *et al.*, 1988, pp. 50–69; Tancred, 1992, pp. 124–31).

● ● ● ● Conclusions

Education and leisure may be linked by intentional, unintentional, formal and informal means. Where education is viewed as an holistic process that extends beyond formal institutions and involves the life-long acquisitions of skills and knowledge, there is a profound impact of education upon leisure and leisure upon education. Many of our interests are developed through learning and incorporate learning.

Family, education establishments, leisure providers and the wider community all have important roles to play in facilitating these leisure–education links and in preparing and supporting individuals in the effective use of education and leisure to enhance their quality of life.

The leisure lifestyle and the experience of education–leisure links, such as education through leisure and education as leisure, are, however, highly individualistic and very dependent upon individual perceptions and experience of the activities and processes involved. The benefits of holistic and complementary approaches that develop the leisure–education links will, however, only be fully appreciated by the individual and society when they are supported by a comprehensive policy framework and targeted resources which, in turn, facilitate an integrated and comprehensive approach and the full involvement of all parties.

Questions

1　To what extent does our education determine our leisure participation?

2　Is the pursuit of 'education as a leisure activity' a contradiction?

3　What are the advantages and disadvantages of dual use and joint provision?

4　What do we mean by 'education for leisure' and what might it entail?

5　Who is involved in 'education for leisure' and what is their involvement?

References

Badmin, P., Coombs, M., and Rayner, G. (1988) *Leisure Operational Management, Vol. 1: Facilities*, Harlow: Longman.

Bloch, S. (1997), 'Future for Museums', *Insights*, London: British Tourist Authority/English Tourist Board.

DFES (2001) White Paper: *Schools – Achieving Success*, 5 September 2001, London: HMSO.

Graefe, A. and Parker, S. (eds) (1987) *Recreation and Leisure: An Introductory Handbook*, State College, PA: Venture Publishing.

Godbey, G. (1994) *Leisure in your Life: An Exploration* (4th edition), State College, PA: Venture Publishing.

Haywood, L., Kew, F., Bramham, P., Spink, J., Capenerhurst, J. and Henry, I. (1995) *Understanding Leisure* (2nd edition), Cheltenham: Stanley Thornes.

Open University (1984) Block Seven, 'Education for What?' Unit 31, Education, *The Family and Leisure*, Milton Keynes: The Open University.

Parry, J. (1988) 'Value Judgements', *Sport and Leisure*, March–April.

Sessoms, H.D. and Henderson, K.A. (1994) *Introduction to Leisure Services* (7th edition), State College, PA: Venture Publishing.

Tancred, B. and Tancred, G. (1992) *Leisure Management*, London: Hodder & Stoughton.

Veal, A.J. with James, R.D. and Pearce, M.P. (1990) *Joint Provision and Dual Use of Leisure Facilities*, CELTS Papers in Leisure and Tourism Studies, London: PNL Press.

Further reading

Badmin, P., Coombs, M., and Rayner, G. (1988) *Leisure Operational Management*, provides a clear and concise section outlining the core issues for dual use and joint provision.

Corbin, H.D. and Tait, W.J. (1973) *Education for Leisure*, New Jersey: Prentice Hall, provides a broader discussion of aspects of education for leisure.

Field, J. (2000) *Lifelong Learning: Education Across the Lifespan*, Reading: ILAM, is a comprehensive and contemporary text that analyses life-long learning including the education and leisure partnership.

ILAM (1995) *Working Effectively with Schools/Links to Clubs – Factsheet*, Reading: ILAM, provides practical guidelines for a compulsory education and leisure partnership project.

Siedentop, D. (ed.) (1994) *Sports Education: Quality PE Through Positive Sport Experience*, Leeds: Human Kinetics, explores the broader contribution of sports education and its effective implementations.

Torkildsen, G. (1999) *Leisure and Recreation Management* (4th edition), London: Spon, examines the facts of the education and training of the leisure profession.

Useful websites

Department for Education and Skills website including departmental White Papers: www.dfes.gov.uk/index.htm

Government website containing all White Papers: www.gov.za/whitepaper/

Magna Science Adventure Centre site: www.magnatrust.org.uk

Government statistics: www.statistics.gov.uk

Chapter 13 ● ● ● ●

Leisure and the future

Any text on leisure, and especially one written at the beginning of the twenty-first century, requires a postscript. In recent decades leisure has undergone profound change and there is no reason to suppose that such change has ended. Thus it is useful at this stage to speculate on what the future may hold. Forecasting is, of course, fraught with dangers in that no one can foretell the future with absolute certainty. Who, for example, at the beginning of 2001 would have predicted the foot and mouth epidemic and its resulting effects on tourism in the UK or, even more importantly for leisure as a whole, the terrorist attack on the twin towers of the World Trade Center in New York? In fact, at the time of writing, the full economic and political consequences of the events of 11 September are still unclear. Its substantial consequences for tourism were immediate and its psychological impact on reducing people's desire to enjoy themselves has also been documented. But how long such effects will last and what the longer-term consequences on the economy and people's ability to purchase leisure will be are clearly unknown. Despite such problems, however, leisure forecasting is a pursuit that is well established and a variety of organisations regularly publish forecasts on leisure futures (see, for example, the reports from the Henley Centre, Mintel and Leisure Industries Research Centre). Although outwardly concerned with statistics and often linked to market intelligence, such reports inevitably take account of both economic change and the broader trends associated with leisure. It is these more fundamental aspects that constitute the principal concern of this chapter.

Objectives

To:
- *examine changing work regimes and leisure time*
- *explore the development of leisure forms*

- *assess the increasing commercialisation and commodification of leisure*
- *consider potential changes in the framework for leisure provision.*

● ● ● ● Changing work regimes and leisure time

The last few decades have witnessed a number of significant changes in work regimes. Apart from some marginal reductions in the working week and increases in holiday entitlement, with their obvious consequences for leisure, there are also more fundamental changes associated with the decline of manufacturing and the growth of the service sector. Such economic restructuring has meant that many people can no longer assume secure jobs for life and may have to contemplate the prospect of changing jobs and possibly having to retrain at various points in their working lives. Furthermore, the restructured economy, including the growth of the service sector, demands a more flexible workforce with the consequence that increasingly workers are on temporary short-term contracts and many are low paid and de-skilled. The new demands of the economy, together with the demands of a population that is increasingly leisure oriented, are ones that are clearly going to continue to exert their effects into the future; in fact, some would argue that their full significance is only just beginning.

Of particular relevance in the context of leisure is the way in which such changes have led to the restructuring of work time itself. In the 1970s the key development was flexitime, with people no longer having to work set hours per day but instead being able to begin or finish work at various different times as long as they worked so many hours per week. Similarly, holiday time, as it increased, became equally flexible, allowing people to take weeks or individual days off work as they wished up to an agreed maximum. The new trend in work regimes, and one that is likely to become even more significant in the future, is the emergence of what some people refer to as the '24-hour society', in which businesses and services operate continually round the clock. In some cases this becomes the '24–7 society', where business never stops. In the first instance this has been driven by the demands of certain industries that are able to operate in this fashion. Those that rely heavily on computer technology have led the way, as computers do not need to rest and, if you have invested heavily in such technology, why have it lying idle for a significant part of the 24-hour cycle? After all, a 'traditional' 8-hour working day would mean that the machine was idle for two-thirds of the time! New industries have also meant that new work times emerge to accommodate new requirements. One of the fastest growing areas of employment in the UK at the beginning of the twenty-first century involves call centres but, certainly at present, most people that such companies need to contact are unlikely to be at home during the normal daytime hours and, thus, many call centres will operate primarily in the evenings and at weekends; their employees therefore working at times when others are not.

This increase in shift work and people working what, in the past, would have been regarded as unsocial hours has led to similar changes in many service industries. Once increasing numbers of people start working different hours then they may wish to – may be forced to – purchase services at 'irregular' times. If previously shopping was undertaken on the way back from work at 5 or 6 p.m. but work now finishes at 10 p.m. or 6 a.m. then there may be a demand to shop at these times. However, of more fundamental importance on the nature of such patterns has been the growth of female employment and changing family roles. In the past, when most families were reliant on one breadwinner, it was usually the role of married women to do the shopping, which could be under-taken during the usual working day. With increasing numbers of families now having both members at work, this becomes more problematical and thus other times become more convenient for shopping. As has been witnessed in recent times, shops, especially supermarkets, have both lengthened their opening hours in the evening and, with the relaxation of Sunday trading laws, opened on Sundays. In fact, some stores are now open 24 hours a day. Once some shops begin to extend their opening hours, others will necessarily follow, as well as a myriad other industries linked to servicing shoppers, such as banks, transport services, petrol stations, fast food outlets and so forth; and the number of people working 'irregular' hours grows inexorably. Furthermore, if people are now working at times when previously they might have been pursuing leisure, they will pursue their leisure at other times and, if this requires the provision of a leisure service, those who supply that service will also have to work at different times.

It is very clear, therefore, how the organisation of the working day and week is being dramatically transformed, with substantial consequences for leisure and, once such a process of change begins, the very reasons for maintaining the original highly structured day and week must inevitably be questioned. If substantial numbers of people are able to work in different ways, what is to stop others doing the same? Such change would appear to be unstoppable. This is not to say that such a process of change will engulf everyone, even the majority, as many indus-tries and services will still utilise the traditional patterns. Most people are still going to sleep during the hours of darkness and work during daylight. Nevertheless, significant change is clearly occurring and the old certainties are disappearing. Even such established structures as the school day may well not last for ever as ideas are voiced as to whether school should begin earlier in the morn-ing and finish at lunchtime, thus 'freeing' the afternoon for extra-curricular activ-ities, homework clubs and/or possibly leisure. Certainly, plans are being discussed to change the school year with the possible introduction of five terms, separated by shorter holidays, with significant implications for tourism. Colleges of further education now run classes all year round, only being closed for bank holidays and, while talk of running fast-track degree courses over two years by abandoning the long vacations has now subsided, there is no guarantee that such ideas will not return to the agenda in the future.

Much of the above discussion is linked to a question which has been debated in the leisure literature for several decades and that is whether people are gaining more or less leisure time. The general view has been that since the mid nineteenth century people have acquired increasing amounts of leisure and that gradually society has inched towards a state whereby leisure has become ever more important. In the 1970s, for example, some pundits were proclaiming that we were on the verge of achieving the *leisure society*, where leisure would replace work as the central motivating force in people's lives, and various parts of this book have suggested the increasing importance of leisure. Yet not all would agree with this view. As long ago as 1970 Linder introduced the concept of the 'harried leisure class', referring to various groups of middle-class professional people who worked exceptionally long hours and there is every indication that over the last few decades their situation has not improved and, if anything, has deteriorated. The computer age, which was supposed to free people from work and create more time for leisure, has seemingly produced the exact opposite. Rather than reduce the volume of work, the computer has produced new tasks. One clear example of this is the amount of 'paperwork', actual or electronic, that computers are helping to produce. Before computers materialised there would simply not have been enough secretaries to produce a tiny fraction of the paperwork that is now demanded. In fact, many professional people now add secretarial duties to their other roles as they do these themselves on their desktop computer, on their PC at home or on their laptop travelling to and from the office. Thus, for some, even the brief respite of reading the newspaper or novel while travelling on the train has been replaced by work. Much of the recent grievance by groups such as teachers and doctors concerns the excessive paperwork that the current culture of accountability demands and yet this would not be possible were it not for the computer.

Another key aspect of this new technology's impact on leisure concerns the ever increasing speed at which computers operate and the corresponding effects on the pace of work. Computers and modern communications mean that the world of business never stops. Offices may complete deals with other offices anywhere in the world at any time of the day or night, and contact with the office may be continually maintained through facsimile machines, e-mails and mobile phones. The speed with which contact can now be made brings additional demands, as those generating the contact demand ever faster replies which simply adds to the workload. There are few signs that such processes will slow down; in fact there is every likelihood that such changes will increase further. A recent report by Mintel (1999) found that 51 per cent of adults claimed to have less leisure time than 5 years earlier, while 44 per cent said they had more money to spend on leisure. Consequently, for key groups within society, increased leisure is illusory and the 'harried leisure class', or 'time poor, money rich' as they are now frequently called, is possibly growing (although whether 'money rich' is an entirely accurate description of some sections of this harried class may be questionable).

The development of leisure forms

It is clear from the various statistics outlined in Chapters 3 and 6 that participation in many leisure forms is continuing to grow, with a number of existing activities having displayed substantial growth in the 1990s, and there is every indication that these trends will continue for the foreseeable future.

According to Mintel (1999), gambling, health and fitness and cinema attendance have experienced some of the highest growth, with expenditure on gambling and health and fitness having increased by 77 per cent between 1994 and 1999. Both the Lottery and various forms of deregulation have had a major influence on the growth of gambling, while changing attitudes to health and image, together with substantial capital investment in facilities, have been key factors in the growth of the health and fitness market. Similar investment in the provision of multiplex cinemas, with their modern, more spacious facilities and their ability to provide for a greater variety of audiences, has meant that the growing popularity of cinema-going shows no sign of abating. Other forms that have displayed growth have included eating out and foreign holidays.

Apart from the increasing numbers of people with less time but more money, other factors that are likely to influence leisure in the future, certainly in the next decade or so, include the growing influence of women, a greater acceptance of the needs of families, the ageing population, the growth in the number of students and specific changes in the age structure of the population (Mintel, 1999). The increase in working women is not only providing more disposable income for leisure but also making women more independent, whether they are single or married. As a result, those forms of leisure that are more female oriented are likely to become more important, a trend that has already been demonstrated in the emergence of women-only health and fitness clubs. More provision for the needs of families has already taken place in relation to pubs with dining facilities and play areas, the growth of fast food outlets in towns and cities enabling family days out, the increasing provision of crèches at leisure centres – especially important for single-parent families – and the use of interpretative facilities and related initiatives at visitor attractions aimed at a younger audience.

The growth in the number of full-time students is expected to continue to expand as government is clearly committed to such growth and, ideally, would like to see as many as 50 per cent of all school leavers eventually experiencing some form of higher education. This is likely to affect those forms of leisure that rely heavily on younger people, such as cinemas, pubs and bars and nightclubs, but will also include other leisure forms oriented around universities and colleges. As outlined earlier, continuing in full-time education enables various sports and other activities to be pursued through the various clubs and societies to be found in such institutions and thus this sort of activity will inevitably increase with additional student numbers. The other influence of students is that they are less well off during their student years than they would otherwise have been if they had gone straight into the workforce on leaving school. Consequently, those forms of leisure that are most likely to be sought by students are those that offer value for money (Mintel, 1999).

The numbers of people over 50 will increase, partly as a result of higher numbers of people entering that age band and also because people are living longer. While there are different groups within this age range, it is expected that there will be an increasing number of people with increased disposable income who will be seeking to spend it on leisure. Already a significant segment of the holiday trade is seen to cater for this 'grey market', with companies such as Saga having developed specifically on its strength, and it is likely that demand for this type of holiday will continue to grow, as will the demand for other leisure activities catering for the elderly.

In addition to the growth or decline in the popularity of existing forms of leisure, a number of more fundamental trends in the nature of leisure activities may be emerging. Martin and Mason (1998), in their analysis of future leisure and work patterns over the next quarter century, suggest two possible contrasting scenarios. One, which they refer to as 'conventional success', suggests that patterns will follow the trends of the last couple of decades, with well-maintained economic growth and little reduction in working time. The other, 'transformed growth', involves a future where good economic growth continues but where significant rethinking of lifestyle priorities takes place involving a new emphasis on the quality of life and the related contribution of leisure time. Although it is impossible to say which of these directions will be followed, Martin and Mason suggest that 'transformed growth' is the more likely. In such a future individuals may well spend less time on travel and more in the local neighbourhood, and it is suggested that 'more constructive and satisfying activities (learning, sport and exercise, community work) will be stimulated' (Martin and Mason, 1999, p. 12). Some of these potential developments have clear parallels with the rational recreation of Victorian times, the demand for more creative learning, self-improvement, sport and exercise being obvious examples.

The nature of home-centred leisure is also likely to develop new forms as computer technologies allow ever more leisure experiences and virtual realities to be brought into the home. To date, one of the motives for visiting events and performances is to experience the atmosphere, but the ever improving quality of virtual realities may provide such experiences in the home. Furthermore, the communications revolution, involving video phones, will enable people to communicate more effectively with their friends without leaving the home. In fact, the idea that such developments could produce a nation of 'couch potatoes' is seen by some as a worrying development!

The other key scenario that some have suggested is one that involves responses to the money rich, time poor situation. Here the objective is to make the most of the limited time available and, thus, one possibility is that people will participate in individual activities for shorter periods of time and also pursue packages of leisure activities where various different activities are undertaken in the one place in the same time that might previously have been devoted to a single activity. As suggested in a recent *Sunday Times* article, '2010 a Leisure Odyssey' (28 November 1999):

> Instead of going to the gym for a couple of hours, people will have 20 minutes on the running machine, 10 minutes surfing in an internet café, see a film and have a meal – all within the same leisure centre.

In addition, people may also flit between different hobbies and leisure activities, possibly trying five or six a year but none in any depth. Problems with leisure time will make it less easy to devote substantial chunks of time to a particular hobby and thus the level of interest will remain superficial, a state influenced also by the fast pace of modern lifestyles and the constant search for new experiences.

Shortage of time may also mean that 'short break' holidays, currently the fastest growing segment in tourism, will become even more numerous, not simply because people have less leisure time but also because they need to escape from the home environment in order to escape any contact with work. In addition to the growth of short breaks, another aspect of tourism that is likely to grow is the so-called *new tourism*, with people seeking different tourist experiences away from the mass tourist centres. Trekking in the Himalayas, whale-watching off the Californian coast, exploring coral reefs or studying the wildlife of Antarctica are some of the more exotic examples, but cottage holidays in rural Britain or *gîtes* in France are more accessible and affordable examples. The key issue is that tourism embraces the idea of sustainability being sympathetic to the physical environment and local communities.

While much of this discussion has suggested the future will involve more neighbourhood- and home-based leisure, the continual search for excitement and new experiences may also encourage the growth of more active pursuits further afield. Some forms of new tourism would be obvious examples of such a trend but adventure tourism and extreme sports are other forms that are clearly growing.

Increasing commercialisation and commodification of leisure

The growing commercialisation of leisure has been well documented in various parts of this book and recent trends would suggest that this is likely to continue in the years ahead. The continued growth in disposable incomes has meant that more money has been available for leisure and various businesses have not been slow to exploit this situation, a fact clearly illustrated in the household expenditure figures where leisure spending is now the single most important item. Some forecasts suggest that in the next decade up to 50 per cent of household expenditure may be devoted to leisure (Mintel, 1999).

If the various developments discussed above prove to be correct then it is inevitable that leisure will become ever more commercialised as businesses respond to the money rich, time poor situation. People will clearly be prepared to spend additional money to utilise their leisure time more efficiently. Thus, as mentioned above, leisure industries are going to provide new leisure complexes, or 'megaplexes', to cater for those who want several leisure experiences in the one location. These are becoming possible with major commercial operators within the leisure industry employing increased horizontal integration. Already such entertainment centres are occurring, involving the more traditional areas of leisure with a multiplex cinema, tenpin bowling, shopping, fast food outlets, a pub and a nightclub all on the same site and, in the area of tourism, a hotel together with pub, restaurant, sports centre and shopping.

Another possible response to the money rich, time poor situation is that companies will be undertaking more of the chores that hitherto people have done themselves in order that more time can be freed for leisure. According to Oliver Laschese-Beer, accounts manager of Time Energy Network (a new company that organises dinner parties, holidays and household chores for the rich), many middle-class people will have shed their guilt about employing a butler for an evening dinner party and will be contracting out everything from cooking to chequebook management (quoted in the *Sunday Times*, 28 November 1999).

Another key area that commercialism will exploit is the continual demand from consumers for new leisure experiences: new toys to play with, new places to visit and new forms of entertainment and excitement. In the mid 1980s some people were referring to their children as the 'fast-forward generation', the analogy of the video recorder being used to illustrate the idea that they would be rapidly moving on to the next exciting experience. Nearly two decades later, however, the pace of life has increased still further, so the analogy of the DVD might now be more appropriate. The onward development of computer and communications technologies will no doubt continue to exacerbate this craving for instant entertainment, but it will also supply the demand, and leisure will become an even more important market for the computer industry. New places will be packaged and commodified for visitors and existing destinations will be repackaged, especially where visitor numbers have declined and new attractions are needed to lure visitors back.

●●●● Potential changes in the framework for leisure provision

As previously outlined, it is likely that the future will bring increased opportunities for the commercial sector. Similarly, the voluntary sector is also likely to expand as increasing emphasis is placed on community involvement and partnerships. Not only is the 'transformed growth' scenario suggested by Martin and Mason (1999) likely to stimulate greater community involvement, but government is also seeking to involve and empower local people through its community-based regeneration policies. While change in the commercial and voluntary sectors has been, and is likely to remain, incremental, the state sector has the opportunity to produce more radical change and this, of course, has occurred in the recent past with the introduction of compulsory competitive tendering and Best Value (see Chapter 9). Best Value, along with community-based regeneration, is of course part of a new social policy agenda that is likely to have a significant impact on leisure development in the first decade of the twenty-first century. Other key aspects of this policy include those relating to quality of life within a sustainable development philosophy and social inclusion.

According to Martin and Mason (1999) there are three key areas on which local authorities should focus in the future. First, there is the role of ensuring that facilities and services needed by the local population are made available. Martin and Mason (p. 12) envisage new 'local neighbourhood leisure centres' combining new communications technologies to bring relays of events and performances, and other virtual leisure experiences, to the local area, as well as facilities for learning, health and community activities alongside the more obvious sports, entertainments and catering. Second, they suggest local authorities should develop stronger co-operative relationships with other providers and, third, that they should play a major role in promoting leisure to individuals and other organisations as a major opportunity for improving the quality of life and easing social problems

Much of this is clearly consistent with emerging government policy. The emphasis on local and neighbourhood facilities, together with increased promotion, is part of the social policy agenda outlined above, and especially social inclusion. For example, the local cultural strategy policy aims at giving local people the chance to get the most out of life by exploiting cultural and recreational opportunities on their doorstep. As the Secretary of State at the Department of Media, Culture and Sport (DCMS) outlined in launching the related *Creating Opportunities* guide in December 2000:

> Cultural services play a crucial role in our society. They can also help tackle social
> exclusion, contributing to regeneration, promoting safer communities, encouraging
> healthier lifestyles as well as providing opportunities for voluntary and
> community activity and stimulating lifelong learning.

Other policies promote similar aims. For example, the government strategy for sport, *A Sporting Future for All* (DCMS, 2000), emphasises widening access and highlights the importance of co-ordinating sport between schools and local clubs and organisations, while the Neighbourhood Renewal Action Plan (DCMS, 2001) includes references to the contribution of arts and sports to neighbourhood renewal. Even the government's tourism strategy, *Tomorrow's Tourism* (DCMS, 1999), has references to social inclusion.

Government has clearly recognised the importance of leisure and, while it may see leisure as a means of achieving a variety of social goals, it also recognises its intrinsic importance to people. While there is no suggestion that government itself will reverse the decision of the 1980s to retreat from the direct management of leisure facilities, there is every indication that it will continue to fund, direct and encourage various forms of leisure, and especially provide help for those groups that are increasingly excluded from leisure as it becomes more commercialised. Much of this involvement, however, will be directed at encouraging others to undertake this work and the voluntary sector and various partnerships will play an ever increasing role in delivering its objectives.

● ● ● ● Conclusions

This chapter has attempted to suggest some possible developments for leisure in the foreseeable future and has inevitably indulged in a certain amount of speculation. Speculation can be a useful exercise which, apart from being intellectually stimulating, can also produce creative solutions to planning and management. Although speculative, the various suggestions have not simply been plucked out of the air but have been based on existing trends and a detailed knowledge of leisure and the various factors that influence it. In fact, all the chapters in this text are, hopefully, able to contribute to such an understanding. However, a better understanding of leisure and its likely future development should not be seen as an end in itself but something that should enable better planning and improved future leisure provision. It is hoped that this text as a whole may be able to make some small contribution to this endeavour.

Questions

(You may also wish to refer to earlier chapters in the text.)

1 Discuss the likely consequences for leisure of the '24-hour society'.

2 Provide examples of 'time poor, money rich' groups within society and suggest how their leisure might be influenced by their occupational circumstances.

3 What new forms of leisure might develop in the future and what will influence such developments?

4 In what ways and for what reasons is leisure likely to become more commercialised in the future?

5 Examine the likely future role of central and local government in leisure provision.

References

DCMS (1999) *Tomorrow's Tourism*, London: HMSO.

DCMS (2000) *A Sporting Future for All*, London: HMSO.

DCMS (2001) *A New Commitment to Neighbourhood Renewal: National Strategy Action Plan*, London: HMSO.

Linder, S. (1970) *The Harried Leisure Class*, New York: Columbia University Press.

Martin, B. and Mason, S. (1998) *Transforming the Future: Rethinking Free Time and Work*, Sudbury: Leisure Consultants.

Martin, B. and Mason, S. (1999) 'Change of a quarter', *The Leisure Manager*, January.

Mintel (1999) *The Leisure Business: The Future*, 07/09/99, BMRB/Mintel

Index

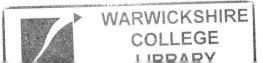